THE AMERICAN POET

Weedpatch Gazette
For 2000

Samuel D. G. Heath, Ph. D.

iUniverse, Inc.
New York Bloomington

The American Poet
Weedpatch Gazette For 2000

iUniverse books may be ordered through booksellers or by contacting:

iUniverse
1663 Liberty Drive
Bloomington, IN 47403
www.iuniverse.com
1-800-Authors (1-800-288-4677)

ISBN: 978-1-4401-4783-8 (sc)
ISBN: 978-1-4401-4816-3 (ebook)

Printed in the United States of America

iUniverse rev. date: 05/18/2009

CONTENTS

CHAPTER ONE   1

CHAPTER TWO   29

CHAPTER THREE   54

CHAPTER FOUR   79

CHAPTER FIVE   93

CHAPTER SIX   115

CHAPTER SEVEN   157

CHAPTER EIGHT   191

CHAPTER NINE   239

CHAPTER TEN   288

ABOUT THE AUTHOR   325

CHAPTER ONE

Welcome to TAP for the new millennium. Here we are in spite of Y2K bugs, kooks, and prophecies of gloom and doom.

In the spirit of this beginning of the next thousand years, TAP will continue in the humorous vein of bringing joy and laughter into people's lives together with the mild sprinkling of serious commentary for which its author (most humble me) is known and ~~reviled~~ revered.

And with that judicious remark concerning serious commentary in a minor key, you just have to admire the chutzpah of any company that is marketing an anti-flatulence pill named *Beano*; but with everything from odor-eaters, toilet paper, condoms, tampons, to you-name-it being advertised I still don't understand the Viagra ads being couched in such a polite euphemism as erectile dysfunction? Since Madison Avenue, following the lead of Hollywood, seems to have lost all sense of civilized propriety and decorum, why doesn't Bob Dole just come right out and say: Hey guys, havin' trouble gettin' it up? (But then one can well imagine Elizabeth's reaction to this). Much to my immense relief my own personal plumbing appears to be Y2K compliant.

XMAS
DON'T FEEL SORRY FOR ME

Don't feel sorry for me during this holiday season. Though I am cold and alone with only the cat for company, I'll be just fine. I will bring in a fresh pinecone, just as I did last Xmas, and put some pine needles and a candy cane on it for decoration during this festive time of year. I will candy-stripe the cat's tail and dye her ears red and her paws green so she won't feel left out.

I will celebrate Xmas Eve with a small handful of peanuts together with a fine dinner of Stovetop Stuffing Mix topped off with a nice refreshing glass of cool water and a Hostess cupcake. I'm toying with the idea of even putting a candle on the cupcake this year. Heck, it's Christmas Eve; why not go all out? The heat of the candle would be most welcome in any event.

But Xmas is the time to think of others, to celebrate the spirit of the season by giving to others. With this most noble of sentiments, I've made a gift list for my friends and acquaintances that I believe really represents this charitable holiday spirit.

I will give one acquaintance, an Episcopal Priest, a book entitled: Accepted Techniques of Self-flagellation, Nun-beating, and Pope-abusing. Being such a close friend he will also receive one of my favorite pics, that of Janet Reno in drag, for inspiration... or maybe the alternate, one of Hillary.

My friend Junky Jerry will receive a new bottle of black Shinola for his hair. He's always running out.

An acquaintance known affectionately as Jabba the Hut because of his resemblance to a modestly sized Sperm whale or an enormous, white slug, will receive my favorite recipe for stuffed chocolate fudge with maple syrup and meringue topping. Yummers.

My friend Slugger will get gift certificates for the local prostitutes that frequent her bar. This is only fitting since the girls will be giving gift certificates and some truly amazing pictures to their patrons. And remembering that hallowed phrase: It is more blessed to give than to receive, also remember: It's the thought, not the gift.

Another close friend will receive an updated arrest record suitable for framing together with a Get out of jail free card. It won't really get him out of jail free but, again, it's the thought, not the gift.

Being a compassionate man and especially mindful of the needy in foreign countries at this time of the year, my philanthropy will extend to the impoverished in Mexico. I will send a supply of Michelin sandals to replace the Firestone Radials that are commonly worn since they have been recalled and may suffer blowouts causing injury as the Border Patrol pursues illegal aliens. This will have the dual benefit of lessening the chances of resulting lawsuits by said illegals against Firestone for said injuries.

Since it is the Xmas season, even politicians should be remembered. Ralph Nader will get a copy of the picture of Ronald Reagan as he vetoed the bill that would have prevented homosexuals from teaching in classrooms. John Wayne is standing at Reagan's side. Al Gore and Hillary will get copies as well.

Joseph Lieberman will receive a copy of my study determining that the Dome of the Rock is actually built on the site of an ancient Hebrew brothel.

Jesse Jackson and Al Sharpton will get copies of *White Men Can't Jump* together with my study that shows African-Americans are low-achieving academically because too many live in taxpayer subsidized housing and play basketball.

Chairman Arafat will get a copy of my study proving that wine and sand are a holy blessing of Allah and oil is unholy.

The last millennium did not end triumphantly for me. Not a single soul sent me the lyrics for the Dooky Bird Song or The Mush Rushed Down My Father's Vest.

Another failure was my being unable to discover the physics involved with chipped cups and glasses. Like any well-mannered circle, a cup or glass has a 360-degree circumference. A chip may occupy only 5 degrees on the lip of this circumference. Yet, if I pick up such a cup or glass and take a drink from it, I will invariably encounter that tiny area as though the other 355 degrees didn't exist. One of the enemas of life.

I also failed to make many converts to dried marshmallows. If you place an open bag of marshmallows in your refrigerator for a couple of months, they will dry satisfactorily to the point that when you bite one it will crack like a walnut. Just the cracking sound alone makes it interesting.

And while it seems I did my best in the old millennium to alienate virtually every group in religion, politics and education, someone recently pointed out that I had not paid sufficient attention to left-handed mulatto touch typists. I sincerely apologize to those in this group for the unintended slight though I did contribute substantially to my favorite charity TSFTPOCTL-HMTT (The Society for the Prevention of Cruelty to Left-Handed Mulatto Touch Typists).

But I took what comfort I could in the minor triumphs. I remain capable of changing my mind and willing to accept facts that jar with some of my beliefs, and I have managed to retain my sense of humor and poetic/romantic sensibilities as well as my skill at a pool table in Slugger's Saloon.

Every religious leader you can name still refuses to respond to the amendment for the protection of children (a not so minor triumph), and in spite of my bachelorhood none of my culinary efforts such as the squirrel and raccoon stew with dumplings and turnips resulted in food poisoning. I managed to sew a button on one of my sweaters and I didn't join an outlaw motorcycle gang, commune or Buddhist fraternity, avoided spotting any UFOs and was not abducted by space aliens. Exercising rare fortitude and forbearance, I neither killed Clinton nor had sex with Monica (not wanting to waste a perfectly good cigar) nor propose to Janet Reno, and I didn't beat a single nun nor abuse the pope. And not really being into self-abuse I never watched any sports, game shows or a single episode of Seinfeld, Jerry Springer, Rosie, Judge Judy or Saturday Night Live.

Displaying rare courage and good taste, PBS did an entire broadcast honoring *Doo Wop* and to the consternation of many who had flattered me by prophesying my becoming a dumpster-diving wino living on Union Avenue in Bakersfield, I surprised everyone by remaining sober and alive in spite of those who seriously wanted to do me great bodily injury and I outlasted some who had actually seen a *Red Ryder* and *Little Beaver* film and remembered *Maggie and Jiggs*.

3

And I did learn a few things during my stint in the old millennium. For example: Never trust someone who claims to be an expert in computers and doesn't keep the cover removed from his own or doesn't still have an old 286 with fourteen-inch monochrome monitor and nine-pin dot matrix printer.

Weedpatch University has every reason to look forward to the beginning of this new millennium with unbridled enthusiasm. While the media ignored the part of the university in the confrontation with the World Trade Organization in Seattle, it was WU and frogs that made the difference. Had the Disney Frog been there you can rest assured the university and frogs would have received their due attention. But lacking the token Disney Frog, his contract disallowing civil disobedience, the smug media kept silent. Just another blatant act of discrimination against WU and our little green friends solely on the basis of their color and dietary habits! Unconscionable!

Not surprisingly, and quite appropriately, Time Magazine named Albert Einstein *Man of the Century*. Einstein incorporated the best of the genius of science tempered by poetic humanitarianism and his mathematics gave us the fundamental tools to understand the mechanical basis of the universe. Though, as with Newton, he knew and acknowledged he stood on the shoulders of giants in order to see so far.

Now that this beginning of the new millennium promises the mapping of the human genome, of computers which will emulate brain function and so much more, I am encouraged that the great art, music and literature of the past millennium, having met the only true criteria of greatness, TIME, remain the standard for the new. The trash and pretenders pass away and Rembrandt and Monet, the great operas, Tolstoy and Melville remain.

And as we begin the greatest odyssey of human exploration into the most significant *terra incognita* The Frontier of the Mind, I take comfort in the fact that it remains unlikely science will supplant what no computer will ever be able to emulate, the soul and spirit of creativity, the so very human elements of love and self-sacrifice that separate us from any dictates of science and technology and keep them servant to their master, the human being.

But it will obviously take great wisdom to maintain this servant/master status. And since k+w=p remains true, it is that wisdom we must attain if we are to capitalize on our science and technology to the benefit of humanity. Einstein would be the first to agree with this.

A most sober, even somber, question at this point: Of the some six billion of us who now live to see a new millennium ushered in, how many are actually the beneficiaries of the science and technology that promise so much to the betterment of life (provided we become wise)? And how many are still willing in this new millennium to murder for the sake of race, culture or political ideology, to murder in the name of God, some possessing the nuclear capability of carrying out some jihad of monstrous, Armageddon proportions?

It may be this question that led me to consider the following:

A little history lesson to start the new millennium. Both John Henry (Doc) Holliday, despite the film Tombstone, and James Wesley Hardin are described by historians as having been psychopathological homicidal maniacs. Other than this minor flaw in their otherwise sterling characters, they were probably ok guys, the kind a nice girl would like to take home to meet the folks (as an aside, there are many who think even homicidal maniacs need love and understanding. But these are the same people who think the child molester can be rehabilitated).

It is still debated whether it was James Butler (Wild Bill) Hickok or Hardin who initiated the Walk Down, the quaint Western custom of seeing who could draw and kill the other guy first in a face-off. Hardin is said to have been the originator of this romantic duel during a train robbery though Hickok was known to have performed this civilized act of Western chivalry as well.

Alleged human John Hardin was, quite appropriately, shot dead in a saloon (as was Hickok). But it was said of him at the time by witnesses that apart from being dead, he was in remarkably good physical condition.

Having been among the first to own one of the remanufactured Colt Single Action Army six-shooters, such things as the histories of the old gun-fighters (and homicidal maniacs in general) have always held an interest for me. And as a certified gunsmith and tool and die maker, I love to puncture the myths of the ignorant. The new Colts varied from the originals in only two ways. The screws were fine thread and the metallurgy was greatly superior. Dry-firing was a no-no with the old guns but greatly improved steel-making and heat-treating techniques made it perfectly acceptable with the new guns.

But ignorant people will still tell you it is harmful to the guns. There are still people who will come to blows over the relative merits of hanging the toilet paper one way or the other or how someone squeezes toothpaste tubes. Like the poor, such people will always be with us.

Our little fast draw club had a qualified instructor, which prevented me from following in the path of those who were popularizing the sport by shooting themselves in the foot when the activity came into vogue and *Shane* and *Gunsmoke* were taking Americans back to their genteel roots of homicidal activities involving gunplay and the nostalgic odor of burned gunpowder as per the romantic West.

I suppose my life-long affinity with guns and explosives has something to do with my taking on professional religionists, politicians, and the universities;

though I am not altogether sure of the connection since I have not as yet resorted to becoming a mad bomber. Just mad.

But as to those who seriously want me out of the way permanently, many are in the camps of religion, politics, and the universities. Peaceable, mild-mannered, shy around women and self-effacing as I am (did someone mention Clark Kent?), maybe it has to do with some of the things I have said and written? For example, I recently sent the following letter to a number of politicians:

When it comes to our children, there should not be any politically sectarian boundaries. And whether you agree with my proposed amendment for the protection of children or not, I know you will agree that our children are suffering from a failed system of public education.

It was in another life it seems that I sat with California State Senator Ed Davis in his office in Sacramento. We had established a warm correspondence when he was LAPD Chief of Police and I was a fledgling freshman teacher at David Starr Jordan in the Watts district of South Central Los Angeles.

By the time of this meeting, I was no longer the naive young man who thought the problems in education would be relatively easy to fix. The travesty of the sixties in education such as *Innovative Designs In Learning*, which cast out the things that had worked and instituted the things that made no sense whatsoever, had done their dirty work. Children were going to pay the price of the adult abrogation of responsibility for their education.

The sacred cows remain the same, the universities that produced a failed system of public education which were untouchable then and are equally untouchable today in spite of the damning indictment of them through research and writing like that of Professor Reginald G. Damerell and so many others including myself.

I focused on Accountability in Education in my own Ph.D. dissertation only to discover it was such a hot button no publisher would touch it. Only one Ed. publisher at the time was honest enough to tell me that the material in my dissertation was such an indictment of the schools he didn't dare publish it!

I discovered that the school systems from the universities on down are so rife with corruption and such cronyism and nepotism as to be inbred to the point of impotence. Then I discovered that legislators were dedicated to asking the very people who created the problems in education for answers to the very problems they had created! Insane on the face of it!

And while I would never accuse the educational hierarchy of the purposeful destruction of public education, I do say they could not have better designed a system for failure had they done so intentionally!

I found that schools are not held fiscally accountable because of such creative bookkeeping it is impossible to audit them and the money is embezzled at will in the amount of countless hundreds of millions of dollars every year throughout California alone. The fox that guards the henhouse, the State Department of Education, has its reasons for not wanting this publicized, not the least of these being the public outcry it would cause together with the potential loss of so much federal funding.

I discovered first hand how tenure was abused to the point that the worst teachers who wouldn't have been allowed to continue to work a week in the private sector were guaranteed jobs for life in education, especially in the universities, and children and college students paid the price for such incompetence and lack of accountability throughout the entire system of public education.

I was at ground zero when Special Education began to be the cash cow for schools, a blank check no one questioned as empire building at its very worst became the norm in the public schools. Had I not personally witnessed what I have in this system alone, I don't think anyone could fictionalize the enormous boondoggle of this single education bureaucracy!

I began to try to tell parents and legislators like Ed Davis and Gary Hart, governors like Pete Wilson, that the problems for children in education were not as bad as they thought, they were far, far worse!

I saw our classrooms being filled with teachers, products of the universities, who could not spell or do arithmetic and no one dared say anything about it! Why not? Because virtually every leader throughout society is a university graduate and would never criticize the institutions on which their own academic credibility and future success were based!

And teachers such as me with industry backgrounds knew the Ivory Tower mind-set was incapable of preparing children for real life. And most teachers who witnessed the terrible destruction of education would not speak out for fear of losing their jobs or becoming pariahs.

It has become the stock in trade of politicians to talk about educational reform. But politics being the trade of generalities does not deal with specifics and politicians always evade answering in specifics because they do not have any specifics when it comes to educational reform (or a host of other problems)! But no one knows better than I the enormity of the problems in education and the enormity of what will be required to fix them.

But as long as our children are defrauded of an education because politicians refuse to deal with the specifics, or even worse, have no idea of what the specifics are, I will continue to be a voice raised against the tragedy of ignorance that has invaded America and become the legacy of so-called educators and their crony political quislings passed on to our children.

Governor Gray Davis saw fit to thank me personally and pass my critique of *To Kill A Mockingbird* on to State Senator Gary Hart, the head of California's Education Committee. Senator Hart sent me a personal *Thank You* note.

Politicians have always been very gracious in thanking me for my concerns about our children and their education. But not a single one has ever followed through by doing the hard things my own research and experience proves need to be done. One school board president who tried to institute just a couple of the needed reforms I had suggested lost in the next election because of this.

In spite of my cautionary words, he didn't believe the furor this would cause among teachers who actively campaigned (illegally of course) against him in their very classrooms, even sending home with their pupils flyers produced in the school audio/visual department and taking out ads in the local paper against this man's re-election.

Of course, things were made pretty hot for me as well. I was betraying my kind and biting the hand that fed me.

It is easy to do the trend-forecast of where the present concerns about the latest enormously expensive and tragic boondoggle of education, that of Special Education, will lead. Nowhere. Once the noise dies down, it will be back to business as usual. The educational hierarchy from the universities on down depends on this.

Oh yes, audits there will be. A few arrests may even be made for blatant offenses and thefts that cannot be hidden no matter the creative book- and record-keeping. The lawsuits will proliferate and taxpayers will foot the bill as usual while the guilty in the schools from the universities on down will wring their hands and refuse to accept any responsibility.

But as in the case of the I.R.S. and California's Social Services, particularly Child Protective Services, the enormity of the task will make any meaningful audits virtually impossible. The educational hierarchy knows and depends on this to, as one principal told me, do their own dirty laundry and not expose it to the public.

His refreshing, albeit self-serving, candor reminded me of that of a Downey Chief of Police who told me in an interview: We're not here to help people; we're here to slam the door on them!

Like expressed concern about child abuse, the problems in the Evil Empire of Special Education will sell papers and make for News at Eleven and political rhetoric for a while. And then, quietly fade away until someone sees a way of making headlines and political hay of it once more.

Harper Lee addressed the failure of the schools in Thirties' Alabama. I witnessed it as a teacher in Sixties' California. And not just during my tenure in the war zones of the ghetto of Watts and the barrio of East San Jose, but places like lily-white Castro Valley and throughout Stanislaus County; and, of course, my home county of Kern, the target of Edward Humes' Pulitzer-winning book.

It was in my home County of Kern that a group of high school seniors applauded me for telling them: Any real education you get here will be because you earnestly desire and work for it, not because this school is really prepared and dedicated to giving you an education.

These seniors knew the truth of what I was telling them. Their applause was for my being the only adult school authority to make to them such a bald and honest confession of the failure of the school system to provide them the opportunity for an education, to have in fact defrauded them of an education.

The applause caught the attention of teachers and administrators. When they discovered the reason for it, I was not invited back. But I knew that would be the result. I have always been known as a high roller on behalf of the kids against the system. It is one reason I have worked in so many different school systems in spite of reaching tenure in two of them.

Tragically for our children and young people, my words to that group of seniors would apply with equal truth in schools across America. And while young people like the class of seniors mentioned know the truth, and will applaud me for telling it like it is; it doesn't win me any friends among adult authorities who should be my friends for my honesty.

The enormous fraud of Special Education has succeeded because those outside the system have no idea of what it is really all about. To understand how this is possible, you must understand that the field of education as a whole has its own manufactured language, a foreign language if you will, that admits of no outsiders learning it.

There is an incredible amount of paranoia in both Social Services and the schools. While working in Child Protective Services, I'll never forget my visits to the schools. Because of my experience in Special Ed. I knew the language and what to ask for concerning things like Individual Education Plans (IEPs). There was an absolute look of horror on one principal's face when he realized I was knowledgeable of such things. He was used to being able to dance around other CPS personnel who didn't know what questions to ask.

But CPS workers seldom visit the schools and don't know the system. And the schools rely on this kind of ignorance on the part of Social Services and the general public as well as parents and politicians. It is this kind of ignorance that enables the schools to continue to perpetrate this enormously successful con game of Special Education.

The con would not be so successful if parents and politicians were knowledgeable enough to ask the hard questions and demand answers. But they aren't. And I'm often in the position of asking myself: Does anybody really care?

But ignorance can be a real killer. When Robert Duvall made the picture *The Apostle*, I pointed out the weakness of the film was in his having never been raised a true believer in the charismatic religion. As a result, he simply was not believable in the role. He didn't really know the language and manners of the charismatic Christian.

But this did not prevent his being able to fool those like Siskel and Ebert who gave the film two thumbs up. Thus displaying their own ignorance of charismatic Christianity.

Even the genius of Sinclair Lewis in *Elmer Gantry* could not succeed in fooling those born and raised as true believers. And while the lessons in both Duvall's film and Lewis' novel are universal and as such well worthwhile, the believability in their works falls short because of the lack of real experience.

It is this lack of real experience that dooms the efforts of parents and politicians who would genuinely like to make a contribution to reform in education.

Such people are unaware that unlike true academic subjects, education is itself lacking any empirical body of knowledge and has borrowed wholesale from legitimate disciplines in an attempt to legitimize itself. The resulting language of education is to be compared with a corrupt kind of pidgin, a virtual gobbledygook best compared with meaningless psycho-babble and its own kind of fraternal understandings available only to members of the club.

The system of Special Ed. particularly is a Byzantine labyrinthine monstrosity of nonsense within a larger system of nonsense. The language of Special Ed. is representative of the whole *Alice in Wonderland* field of education that reflects the language of the *Jabberwocky*. But unlike that delightful children's piece, the nonsensical words and phrases of Special Ed. make the pretense of sensibility.

In no other field of education is this smoke screen of pretended expertise of knowing what you are talking about when you do not through an invention of the imagination as evident as in Special Ed.

If things are ever going to take a turn for the better in education, they will only do so when political leaders take on the responsibility for confronting this enormous fraud and call it what it is: An Enormous Fraud!

The entire system of education must be called to account and held accountable. But it will take leaders of rare courage and a genuine concern for the welfare of America's children to bring this to pass. If I did not believe there were a few leaders of whom this is true, I would not have burdened them with my concerns.

It was known in 1954 that the bottom 15 per cent of college graduates were going into the field of education and nothing was done to correct this. Those responsible in the universities did nothing to change this and encourage the best and brightest to enter our classrooms. Today, we live with the result of this failure of the universities to act and be responsible; not to mention the failure of the political leadership which should have known and done better.

I expect better of those who have a genuine concern for children than I do of the amoral and literally silly - to use the most charitable word - leadership in the universities which gave us this failed system of public education and has even helped to perpetuate the enormously expensive and counter-productive continuing fraud of Special Education.

Only leaders who are genuinely concerned for the future of America, our children, are going to be able to confront this tragedy for our children and our nation and change things for the better. But elected leaders choose this political vocation and are elected for this very purpose.

I keep a motto posted by my desk that reads: I Don't Want To Know! Every Christmas season I don't want to know about that scholar Hislop's *The Two Babylon's*, which goes into such detail about the pagan origins of the Christmas tree. I don't want to know about the pagan origins of celebrating the winter solstice as the choice of December 25 in the second quarter of the 4th century for celebrating Christmas. I greatly prefer knowing about that bishop of Myra whose love for children developed into the character of Santa Claus who truly represents the spirit of Christmas, the spirit of love and giving centered on children, devoid of any religious prejudices.

With so many things like the ingredients in hot dogs and sausage, it isn't that I want to know; it is too often a case that I need to know. And this need to know has led me in paths I would far rather have never set foot on. After all, I'm a sensitive man who would much rather go along to get along. I bleed when I'm cut and would far rather make friends than enemies.

But let's face it folks, some like Socrates and myself seem doomed to ask the hard questions that others comfortably leave alone. That *Hound of Heaven* keeps dogging my heels and seems to force me to ask these questions. For example, like most normal people I simply do not want to know about the torture and murder of children, I do not want to know of their suffering throughout the world. But I need to know.

I have pointed out many times how naive it is to think some men great philosophers, including Jesus, who never married and had children, let alone believed or considered women as of equal value to themselves, have anything of great value to contribute about the real issues of life. Kind of like the marriage counselors who never married and the experts in child psychology who never had children; or, the university professors and school counselors who never had to punch a clock in the real world.

But then look at how many trust those like unmarried Jesus (and the Pope) or polygamous Mohammed, Joseph Smith and Brigham Young to have been such great philosophers and teachers; and as to women being of equal value to themselves- Laughable if not so tragic in the consequences; consequences not the least of which being the barbaric practice of circumcision of both boys and girls. What's wrong with this picture? Are people really that dumb? When it comes to religion, the answer has to be a resounding YES!

And women seem to want to continue to lead the parade in such dumbness! But one must realize that men have subjected women to literally thousands of years of indoctrination, an indoctrination of being told they are stupid and unable to meet men on an equal basis of intelligence.

Further, the mechanism of religion that teaches women are inferior to men, that women are unclean and unworthy, a sin by definition as per Harper Lee's caustic but accurate of religion in general statement, has taken its toll on women. As a result, women react by trying to expiate their sinful unworthiness through the act of contrition of letting men including Jesus, Muhammad, the Pope, Brigham Young and Jerry Falwell, et al continue to dominate their thinking in this regard. It is as though women feel they deserve to have men beat up on them physically, emotionally, and intellectually. And few inventions of men have been so successful in brainwashing, controlling, and dominating women as that of religion.

As a result of such intransigent foolishness on the part of women in allowing this, I am constrained to begin the new millennium by repeating something from the end of the last millennium's issue of TAP December 1999:

My friend and soul brother Henry Thoreau wrote: Every man is the Lord of a realm beside which the earthly empire of the Czar is but a petty state, a hummock left by the ice.

Henry addressed an issue close to my own heart and mind, and that mind is the empire of which he speaks, an empire largely ignored by most.

Of course, in keeping with the history of the human race, Henry uses the word *man* rather than *person*, which would include women. And history does not allow of women being in possession of such an empire of the mind, which accounts for their being excluded by men from the King of all disciplines, the world of philosophy, which accounts the world of the mind.

I have some very rewarding conversations with my beautiful daughter Karen. She has been witness to many of the changes of my mind in regard to many things, not the least of these being religious views I once held and taught my own children.

The most difficult task I've ever had was in letting my children know that some of the things I had taught them were wrong and due to my own prejudices.

But my children have been marvelous in forgiving me and have been willing to let me explain the causes of my changes of mind in respect to these things.

Our most recent conversation had to do with this frontier of the mind. Karen knows that as a woman she has been limited in many respects and she appreciates what I am trying to do to bring justice and fairness to women, she understands this distinction of equal rights as compared to equal value.

But as I explain to Karen, if I had not had daughters like her and her sister Diana, as a man I would have cared less about these things. It was her and her sister who taught me to care about such things.

Because Karen is exceptionally intelligent as well as beautiful, I feel very keenly the need to get women such as her to understand the vital necessity of addressing the issue of equal value by their taking the initiative for exploring this frontier of the mind which is the purview of philosophy, the discipline from which women have always been excluded by men.

Karen is quick to pick up on points of a discussion and carry them to further areas. One of especial interest to both of us is brain function.

In science we are confronting the fact that computers that will be able to emulate actual brain function are in our very near future. This, together with accomplished facts of genetic engineering, is forcing changes and choices that will require great wisdom to handle appropriately.

Microprocessors are being wired into the optic nerve to give sight to the blind. Some will be small enough to course through our veins and give instant feedback about health conditions.

I can't help but be reminded of that classic old Sci-Fi flick of 1956 *Forbidden Planet*. You may recall that the machines which were guided by the minds of the Krell, machines which were designed to relieve the Krell of all work so they would be able to dedicate themselves to pure thought and philosophy, did not take into account the *Monster of the Id*, the totally and mindlessly selfish primitive beast that lurks in our hearts.

But as long as women are excluded by men as being of lesser value, as long as women are excluded from the very philosophies which will dictate the decisions made by men, there is no hope of wisdom prevailing and overcoming the monster either in the sciences or governments and the Beast will continue to prevail to our own destruction.

I often ask myself: Are we up against terminal and invincible ignorance and prejudice in this respect? Or will women eventually get their act together and do as I have said they must before they will ever be accepted by men as of equal value by forming their own philosophy?

The following is something every woman should take very seriously:

BODFISH PHILOSOPHICAL SOCIETY

The philosophical works of men throughout history have provided the foundation of all societies and their governments. It was the works of men like Hume, Locke, Montesquieu, and Rousseau that provided the Founding Fathers of America the ideas that culminated in Alexis de Tocqueville calling our nation the greatest experiment in Democracy in all of history.

The Founding Fathers themselves, in turn, left an unsurpassed legacy of philosophical writings to future generations of Americans.

But if one turns to the earliest origins of philosophy, there is an entire half of humanity missing and ignored in what is called The Great Conversation.

This Great Conversation is well represented by a set of books entitled The Great Books of the Western World. This set of books, 54 volumes, is supposed to set forth the best of philosophical thought and writings throughout history. But one searches in vain to find a single woman represented!

One is reasonably led to ask: Weren't there wise women, women of a philosophical bent of mind, as well as men during these past thousands of years? There must have been. Then why were they ignored?

There are many reasons for this; some quite legitimate given the facts of our earliest beginnings as a species.

But few people consider that it wasn't until this century that women even began to have a legitimate voice of any kind in philosophy. Still, in spite of all the efforts on the part of women to be heard, that voice is a very small one and remains virtually ignored by men.

Yet it should have been evident in the far, distant past that humanity could never solve the intransigent problems confronting all societies while excluding the voice of an entire half of humanity from the decision-making processes of societies and governments.

Unbelievably, this has been the case throughout history! I say unbelievably because such a thing is insane on the face of it! And as a result of men excluding women in the decision-making processes, by men denying women an equal voice, the history of the world has been one of unremitting hatreds, prejudices, war, and violence of every description.

This exclusion of women can best be stated in terms of men having never accepted women as of equal value to them. The result has been a history of resentment on the part of women, of competition and combativeness rather than fostering and encouraging what should be the compatibility of differences.

The hardness of men and the softness of women should be melded in order to produce an alloy of toughness that is neither too hard nor too soft. But this can only be accomplished once the compatibility of differences, rather than competition and combativeness, is the norm, and the equal value of women to men is accomplished fact.

A large part of the work of the Bodfish Philosophical Society must be directed to the goal of educating men to the need of accepting and welcoming women as of equal value to themselves.

But this begins with educating women to the facts of the history of their exclusion as of equal value, as well as the facts of our contemporary world in this respect.

Once women truly understand these things, their efforts can be directed toward a solution, for it is well said that defining the problem is half of the solution.

Throughout all of history, men have depended on women being their own worst enemies. And this has proven to be the case. The failure of women to recognize and act on the problem has enabled unscrupulous men to continue in their exclusive dominance to the continuing conditions of war and violence.

But if women are to find their own voice in national and world affairs, if they are to represent themselves as equal in value to the wisdom of men, they must begin with a well-reasoned, comprehensive, cogent and intelligible philosophy of their own.

Then the melding of the two halves of humankind in a full partnership, that of both men and women, can be accomplished and world peace can become a reasonable goal.

It would seem obviously insane that we can expect peace in the world when men have always excluded women, half of the human race, from attempts at world peace. But this is, in fact, the case.

It will take women of exceptional intelligence and sensitivity, women of determination and perseverance together with a willingness to commit themselves to change things and develop their own philosophy. Men, of course, are counting on this never happening.

But it must be recognized that men have a vested interest in not allowing women an equal voice in decision-making. They see this as a threat to their dominance over women, a dominance which has kept the world in conflict throughout all of history and is still on going with no end in sight.

Granted, a situation that has existed throughout history, and still exists, is not going to be easy to change. But if the world is ever to know peace and be a safe place for children, such a change is absolutely essential.

I had given a copy of the above to a lovely woman sitting next to me at the bar. Instead of taking it home with her as I suggested, she started reading it immediately. At a couple of points as she read, she exclaimed: This is right on!

Then she reached the end, saw my name and gave a gasp! You mean you wrote this? A man actually wrote this? I thought it was a woman!

Well, as you can easily imagine, that touched off quite a conversation during which several of the other patrons at the bar got involved. But my point is why hadn't a woman written what I did? Why should a man be doing what women should be doing for themselves? And not just for themselves, but for the sake of all humanity?

Then, perhaps it is the responsibility of a man to point this out to women? Ironic? No; simple justice, perhaps, even the fulfilling of my responsibility as a man.

I will state unequivocally that as a man the only real joy and happiness I have experienced in my own life, the motivation to write, sing and make music of the softer and gentler things, the things of real beauty and romance, the things of eternal value, have come to me from women and children.

When Thoreau wrote, for example, that as the spider in a garret, he could be happy in a prison as long as he had his thoughts to sustain him, he was wrong. HDT, as Soren Kierkegaard and so many others, placed too much emphasis on the meditative, contemplative aspect of intellectualism. And, lacking that all-important dimension of a complete life experience, wife and children, such men were blind to the joy and happiness, the understanding and compassion these bring to a man.

As a writer and poet, I know, as these men would freely admit, that Truth can only be found through the experiences of life, not academic disciplines and empirical facts alone.

As philosophers both of these men, and so many like them, failed miserably in many of their attempts at addressing the real issues of life, the things of eternal value. They never were able to present the full picture of life and living.

These worthy thinkers would never say they knew what it was like to be pregnant or give birth. Only a man-fool would do so. But there has never been any deficiency of numbers in this genre.

It is in the philosophies of such men, philosophies that fail so miserably to account for the real basis of strife in humanity, that they too often fall into the camp of those fools that would tell us they know, as men, what it feels like to give birth.

Ladies of the world, your fight is against incomplete philosophies of men that fail to consider or cannot understand you as the other half of the human equation!

Now I would be the last to decry the poetic glorification of God's most beautiful, if often inconvenient, Creation. The stars, a sunrise or sunset, the trees and grass washed and scented by a recent rain, the enchantment of a wild, native trout stream, the grandeur of the Tetons and Rockies, so much to excite the artistic exultation of the artist and poet!

But even Thoreau admitted: What is Nature to me if I have no one with whom to share it? He spoke better than he knew.

The greatest intrigue and mystery of a man's life should be that other half of humanity, a woman. In contemplation of that compatibility of differences I mention so often, I find whole worlds to explore.

A woman at her best is all the intrigue and excitement the best of pioneers and explorers could wish for. I never tire of talking with these mysterious creatures, of learning the differences in their thought processes from my own as a man.

But in most cases, the great thinkers of civilization have done solos when the music required a duet with a woman. My hope in addressing this problem is to get men and women together in making real music.

The purest poetry is rightly defined as an actual recounting of life, of real lives of ordinary people. A part of the poetry of real life is the literature of a culture.

As television and videos began to supplant books, I witnessed the decline of literature and the consequent loss to our young people of virtue and romantic ideals and a plunge into illiteracy and ignorance of our heritage. This, together with the widening gap between haves and have-nots, has cheated our children of the American Dream.

As a teacher with many years of experience, I realized the truth of Robert M. Hutchins' warning that the failure to propagate the heritage of Western Civilization through the great literature of the past would lead to the situation we face today.

Hutchins, Editor-in-Chief for The Great Books of the Western World, made the valid point in 1951 that unless the ideas expressed in the best of our literature of the past was taught to our children, the results would be catastrophic! He was right.

Another point of Hutchins is one I take to heart in my own writing. This has to do with the failure of our schools to blend science and the arts, which has led to over-specialization. Dante's *Divine Comedy* and Newton's *Principia* should be studied together.

But I have to wonder, if Hutchins was alive today and I confronted him with the fact that not a single woman was allowed a contribution to that 54 volume set of books (thought a sop to women is provided in the edition of

1990) purporting to represent the best of human wisdom, would he would be ashamed? I hope he would be.

You will find that I intrude mathematics in my writing. Far from being out of place, it is essential to real learning to bridge the gap between the hard sciences and the arts and social sciences.

This need has resulted in my sprinkling anecdotes throughout my writings, stories that relate to the reality of life. But it is a truism that the difference between reality and fiction is that fiction has to make sense. And while the phrase of Henry James that *life is mostly a splendid waste* rings often true, I contend life needn't be.

A butterfly is a thing of beauty. But part of the charm of the butterfly is its seeming erratic flight. Far from being erratic, that butterfly knows exactly what it is doing.

While I would never make such an outrageous claim of always knowing exactly what I am doing, my writing often takes on the flight pattern of the butterfly, combining diverse elements like poetry and mathematics. But this is in the tradition of poetry and philosophy, of those writers of the past who saw life as multi-dimensional rather than a narrow specific.

The reader will find the essentials of love, music and laughter incorporated in most of my writing. The solutions to the problems of humanity must include these elements. And as with the reality of life itself, these things have a seemingly erratic flight path.

My books *The Missing Half of Humanity: Women!*, and the companion volume *The Missing Half of Philosophy: Women!*, incorporate many diverse elements to make a point; the point being that women have been excluded from the philosophies of men, philosophies that have determined the destiny of nations. By excluding an entire one-half of the human race, the history of humankind has been a history of conflict without resolution.

Much as I admire the great thinkers and writers of the past, much as they need to be studied, I have come to accept the fact that the exclusion of women in The Great Conversation, as Hutchins called it, has resulted in much harm to humanity.

The Missing Half books are not intended to be definitive. They are intended to call attention to the problem and seek a forum where women will be listened to by men; a most uncommon thing. One point alone, a point made by me, a man, should be of great interest to women: There can be no hope of world peace and harmony unless the problem of the historical conflict between men and women is resolved!

As proof of the point, there are several women in positions of power such as columnists and politicians who have asked to be placed on my email list.

The following was a recent communication I shared with these women; and shows the very diversity of the subject:

Miss Cathy, do you have a headache? No. Well let me give you one. What do you think about Mr. and Mrs. God? (It is at times like these that I desperately need to be able to turn to that significant other and say: Sweetheart, what do you think about this? But failing such a one in my life so it would be her headache, I chose to pick on Cathy).

Philosophy must be divorced from theology!

Without dispute religion, with its resulting dogmatic theologies, has been one of the most successful inventions of men to maintain their dominance over women. And it is imperative that women understand this and confront it before they can devise a meaningful philosophy of their own which must begin with the ultimate statement of fact: Men and Women are of equal value! But what about a New Theology that considers Mr. and Mrs. God?

Samuel and Samantha Heath- But just the name Heath does not specify gender. Does the name God (Elohim) specify gender? No. The Adam of the Bible does not specify gender either. God (Elohim, plural and not gender specific) says in Genesis: Let US make man (the Adam, again plural) in OUR image.

If there is any credence to the story in Genesis, the US and OUR in the beginning may well have been a Mr. and Mrs. God. It seems reasonable that God (the plural US and OUR) may well have created male and female in their image. Thus the pattern of man and wife, of equal value, having children would be anticipated by such a union of the creator(s) of humankind; far more reasonable than any Trinitarian nonsense.

That US appears in the casting out of Adam and Eve but the later narrative of the Bible, except for the confounding of language where that US appears for the last time, has been totally masculinized.

The origin of the story of Creation and the Garden as given in the Bible cannot possibly be determined. But if it has any basis in fact whatsoever, how did it happen that what begins with that US comes to be a Masculine God Only in the rest of the Bible?

A father and mother are necessary to life. Why should it have been any different in the original Creation? The early chapters of Genesis lend themselves to the view of a Father and Mother God in the act of the original creation.

We do not know if further material on this theme was lost or destroyed. But we do know there are some very important differences, conflicts and contradictions, in the Creation story in the first chapters of Genesis that at least indicate this to be the case. The question is a nagging one of why the US was retained in those very first chapters and discounted throughout the rest of the Bible (keeping in mind that chapters of the Bible were of a much later invention and the original books were not divided into either verses or chapters)?

If the He of He created them male and female is understood as generic of the plural, just as we use it in English, as it should be since the He had decided to make the Adam in Our image and after Our likeness, it makes it all the more plausible that a Father and Mother God were involved.

The use of the words *Man* and *Mankind* as with *He* is generic of both genders and has a history; and that history is one of male dominance, as in both philosophy and theology, to the exclusion of considering women as of equal value to men. The Biblical history of male dominance is clear. But there is a fracture, if you will, in the retention of the US in the beginning of Genesis. Inexplicable as this is, there it is nevertheless.

But it is logical to assume that the Biblical story of the creation of humanity had a history long before it was given in a written narrative, writing itself being of comparatively very recent invention and very, very far removed from the actual events cited. And much is ignored or not cited.

In fact, it is known that early hominids, long before Homo sapiens appeared, buried their dead with ceremony indicating a belief in an afterlife. What did they worship and how was it that they had such a belief? Did the oral history of creation retain the story of a Father and Mother God and did this oral tradition find its way into the early account of the US in Genesis?

The attempt by theologians to force an explanation for the use of US and OUR in Genesis by use of the imperial WE or supposed trinity fails miserably on the basis of the historical origin philologically as well as within the context of the use of the plural terms in Genesis.

One of the most intractable problems, even a fatal flaw, of a simplistic view of evolution has been the lack of fossil evidence for the demarcation between sexes. When and how did life become male and female, particularly in the higher vertebrate life forms?

Given the theory of evolution, such fossil evidence should be enormously abundant. But it doesn't exist. And while I have no fault to find concerning certain facts of evolution, this missing fossil link alone gives some credence to a special creation of some kind by God.

But since true philosophy has to be divorced from myths and legends and deal with pragmatic facts, it has always been impossible to arrive at a true philosophy when all such attempts are contaminated by beliefs rather than facts. Further, it is my contention that no true philosophy can be had that excludes a full half of humanity: Women.

It is the position of the Bodfish Philosophical Society that conflict has been the history of the human race because women have never been accepted as of equal value to men. Because of this, women have been denied access to philosophy and the result has been the continued failure of women to have a legitimate voice in the decision-making processes of men thereby having no legitimate voice in world affairs.

That women must form a philosophy of their own is absolutely essential to gaining such a voice. But a large part of doing this must consider the argument presented in Mr. and Mrs. God.

Therefore, a New Theology that I have advocated for years should be evaluated on the basis that men have controlled both philosophy and theology for the whole of human history; the result being the continued domination of women by men and the exclusion of women from these two most essential things in world affairs.

That both men and women must find a way to honor the compatibility of differences in such a way as to value one another equally is an absolute essential of world peace.

It is my further contention that this must begin by women presenting men a philosophy of their own which will harmonize with the need of men for such a thing. If both are done correctly devoid of competition and combativeness, the philosophies of both men and women should meld forming a perfect union and thereby making world peace achievable.

Women cannot accomplish the purpose by getting in men's faces. And it isn't women are equal to men, it isn't women are of equal value to men, it is men and women are of equal value period!

Women cannot make their point, let alone win the battle, by getting confrontational with men. Their philosophy must speak for them through logic and empirical facts. Men of good character will then have no choice but to respond in like manner. Once this is accomplished, real dialogue about the actual issues can be enjoined.

There are too many women who believe they must get in the faces of men, that they must make demands and make up in volume and ferocity what they lack in logic and proper, civilized behavior in addressing the facts.

Most certainly women have every right to be angry and frustrated. But when did a temper tantrum ever gain the right end and make a reasoned and logical point?

Ok ladies, I call attention to Hutchins believing women were not worthy to be represented in that 54 volume set of The Great Books of the Western World. But did God decide they weren't worthy to be represented by contributing to the 66 books of the Bible? Or the Koran? Did God believe women couldn't think or write? If women think they honor God by not questioning something so blatantly anti-woman, they are indeed their own worst enemies!

No, concerning God I do not believe She is black. But would it be fair to ask in the light of my comments concerning Mr. and Mrs. God and the intellectual blindness of women: Does Mr. God beat His wife?

But then, as I pointed out earlier, the way women continue to permit men to dominate and control them through religion you might think women would excuse Mr. God for doing so, probably telling themselves that Mrs. God deserved it and undoubtedly had it coming.

Jesus didn't marry or have children. Muhammad preached polygamy. Yet women are willing to credit these men with knowing what is best for them and children, and will even often submit with orgasmic fervor to the religious teachings of both.

But in trying to explain this to women I often feel like I am treating them to an exhaustive explanation of how to overhaul the carburetor of their car.

As with my point concerning Special Education, having the actual experience and knowing the language are vital to understanding the problem and dealing with it knowledgeably.

It may really tick the French and Chinese off that English is the universal language. But that doesn't change the fact. And those not bound to ignorant prejudice, those who truly want to learn and be successfully involved, will accept the fact and learn the language.

A lesson of history is the fact that war with Japan was caused by the misunderstanding of a single word. And the dropping of the atomic bombs on Japan would not have happened had it not been for the misunderstanding of a single word.

From these examples alone it should be clear that exact communication and understanding are of vital necessity in many issues of literally life and death consequence.

Had I not been raised and trained in both fundamentalist and Catholic Christianity, I would never have known the thinking and the language. Had I not been trained in the systems of education and Social Services, I wouldn't know the thinking and the language. Had I not taken my doctorate in human behavior, I wouldn't understand the language, the psychobabble, of systems like those of psychology, education, and Social Services.

But as to religion, no amount of reasoned logic or facts would have convinced me of the errors I believed unless I was willing to submit to logic and facts.

My many years of refusing to yield to logic and facts respecting religion have proved invaluable in at least one respect: I understand the thinking of such people; and so with those in education and Social Services. At least I understand the thinking of the people in these systems. And when it comes to understanding the need to believe, whether in religion, education or Social Services, Fox Mulder has nothing on me.

***

Like many of you, I was looking forward to the Christmas holiday. My children were doing well and were all healthy. What more can any parent ask?

But late in the evening three days before Christmas I got a phone call from Sophie. A young girl we know, Sara, had slipped in her bathtub, struck her head and died.

Sara had struggled with life, she had to fight a battle with drugs, and she was unmarried with a little boy to care for. But her life was turning around for the better. She had her own place, was going to college and had just bought a washer and dryer.

Now you have to understand the import of such a thing as a washer and dryer in the life of someone like Sara. It was, as Sophie pointed out, like owning a new Cadillac to most other people, something of tremendous significance.

One slip in a tub and it all ended for Sara.

Stalin pointed out that the murder of a single individual was a crime, the murder of millions a statistic. As the greatest mass-murderer in all of history, Stalin knew what he was talking about.

While the death of Sara was a tragic accident not a crime, it was significant only to those who knew her. And the little boy she left behind. But as Sophie and I talked about it, we realized that Sara's death really put things in perspective. As Sophie said, she thought to herself looking at Sara in her casket that she was too pretty to bury.

And Sara was a beautiful young woman. But the holiday season was no respecter of such accidents or the feelings of those like her little boy for whom Christmas will always have other than the usual significance. Just as July Fourth, the anniversary of my daughter Diana's death will always have special significance.

Shortly after Sara's death, I was watching the local news and learned of a family that had died in an auto accident on Highway 5 between Fresno and Bakersfield. The roadway was littered with Christmas presents; and the bodies of two little girls.

It seems the father was trying to eat while driving had crossed the median and struck another vehicle head-on. Father, mother, two little girls, and the innocent driver of the other vehicle all died.

Well, all we can do is shake our heads over such things and wish they didn't happen. But they do. And it is a part of life. And it is a part that touches all of us at one time or another.

A couple of months ago, another friend of mine lost her husband. I knew him well. He was a good man, a good husband and father. He went off the road in the canyon and was killed. No one knows what made him veer off the road. Accidents happen.

But we can rightly curse the father for whom feeding his face while driving resulted in the deaths of his wife, his two little girls, and an innocent young man who was simply in the wrong place at the wrong time. Just as we can curse those who are so absolutely selfish and self-centered that the lives of others are of no consequence in comparison to their inexcusable and utterly selfish choice to drink and drive. There are accidents and then there are accidents.

A Christmas funeral does indeed put things in perspective. But Santa remains Santa and those of us who remain try to keep things in perspective. People like my daughter Diana and those like Sara would want it so. The children remain and need the survivors to keep things in proper perspective.

And maybe, I keep telling myself, the amendment will yet accomplish the purpose of making children the priority they must become for humanity to have a future, maybe people will eventually gain the proper perspective of the future because of the amendment. Women like Sara believed this. At twenty-three she died believing this.

***

Well, this is the first issue of TAP for the year 2000. And I know people are going to haggle over whether it should be written 2,000. But we'll wait and see who wins.

Some things will not change, at least not in the beginning of this new millennium. Those in the universities and government will continue to lie to us and we will continue to expect those in the universities and government to lie to us. The only real difference will continue to be the extreme naiveté of those in the universities. I don't believe Clinton, lawyers or politicians (predominantly lawyers) are going to gain in credibility.

I have a friend, Steve, whose skin is slowly peeling away as a result of exposure to Agent Orange (that stuff with dioxin used in Viet Nam that the government said didn't exist. The dioxin that is). It was all in Steve's head until he started literally losing his skin. He won't last much longer and he will be the first to tell you he will meet death as a kind friend.

Then there is the Depleted Uranium armor piercing cannon rounds used in the Gulf War. 60 Minutes did a good job on this story. Those in the field weren't told that the resulting uranium dust was not good to breathe. Good for cleaning the sinuses, in fact.

Well, for centuries tobacco was supposed to be good for us, and it wasn't that long ago that doctors recommended their favorite brands of cigarettes and it was the patriotic thing to do to send them to our fighting boys overseas.

And while the economic importance of tobacco to the early colonies cannot be overemphasized, even to the retention of slavery in spite of the warning of those like Franklin and Jefferson, maybe we would have made it without either tobacco or slavery.

Ignorance of facts can be a real killer, but it is no match for bureaucrats trying to save their hides or the economic bottom line. Or fanatics willing to torture and murder millions in the name of God, race, or political ideologies.

Come to think of it, the beginning of this new millennium seems to be carrying much of the baggage of the old. In fact we seem to be smarter but no wiser. And as long as k+w=p remains true, and it will continue to remain true, we will become wise or perish since the warning of Michio Kaku and others remains true as well.

But wanting to finish this first issue of TAP for the year 2000 on a positive note, I decided to try to get into an attitude of gratitude. And I do have much to be grateful for. I still have my hair and teeth and remain slim and can still shoot a respectable game of pool. I spoiled the expectation of some by not becoming a dumpster-diving wino and remained alive to the surprise of some others. And as noted in the beginning, my plumbing is still in good working order.

My children are well and I have good friends who have not forsaken me in spite of my Mad Hatter status and often-outrageous sense of humor. The sun still rises to shine through the corner windows onto my desk where I write in the morning hours (though my dumb cat, in spite of every effort to train her, still leaves streaks when she does the windows). The quail and critters still occupy this small part of my world and I still have an infestation of peacocks. They scare the cat. And have you ever heard a peacock really go off?

My computer has not crashed in almost two weeks; a record preventing me from buying that elephant gun or harpoon if I have to visit my exceptionally porcine psycho friend and computer wizard again.

Junky Jerry, otherwise known as The Mouth, an old acquaintance that owns a local antique store, hasn't come by for coffee for nearly three weeks. A real blessing; but you would have to know Jerry to really understand the comment and what a real blessing this is. And like my fat computer wacko friend, he is as free with his compliments about me as I am about him. That's what friends are for we remind each other as we freely trade insults; keeps us on our toes and our rapier wits sharp.

In a gentler vein, Thoreau remains my faithful companion and To Kill A Mockingbird continues to inspire me to try harder. Kind people continue to come into my life reminding me that there are more of such people than those who wish me ill.

I can still be in a wilderness environment not far away from where I live when I need to clean out my head and get things back in perspective. My hope of eventually winding up in the middle of Death Valley to finish out my years remains alive though a few critics might not consider this a desirable location.

But the enchanting wide open and mind-expanding, seeming limitless vistas of the desert, like that of the ocean or staring into the heavens, the tremendously varied colors at different times of the day and seasons, always beckon to me. I could never stand fences in spite of the line *Good fences make good neighbors.* Better no neighbors who need fences to make them good neighbors. Like Thoreau, I still seek out that special rock or tree; I still visit the old mining claim and commune with my loved ones now gone on ahead of me, waiting to welcome me.

The magic and enchantment of childhood remain alive in me. I still love the flight of butterflies and the call of quail. I can still think of actually holding a rainbow in my hands. And as long as I have these things, I know I'll be able to continue to carry on the fight for children. And finish my novel someday, even if I have to do it from Death Valley.

But until then, I'll continue to do my best to honor my commitments to all you good civilized folks and try to be worthy of your trust in me. And that optimistic part of me that the child nourishes and keeps alive will continue to chase the occasional butterfly and find beauty and enchantment in God's glorious creation.

Books As Monuments

It may be that the best of philosophical thinking comes with age. If so, and I believe this to be the case, it isn't any wonder that such thinking depended not only on a developing science, but longevity as well. To be a philosopher, there is the need to experience life and carry out actions requiring much time. The needed study, and reflection on what is studied, by itself requires many years. In such a case, we would not expect to find much in the way of excellent philosophical thought among races, particularly ancient ones like that of the Egyptians, that suffered high infant mortality rates and died in their thirties as adults. Nor would we expect to find developed philosophies among cultures without a pronounced and developed science. These factors alone would account for the very slow development of any truly well reasoned philosophical thought in time past, particularly the flaw of omitting women from philosophy.

It is quite probable and understandable that ancient peoples lacking in science and facing death at an early age would be caught up in mythologies and religions concentrating on life after death... the Egyptians epitomizing this in their religious beliefs and concentration on preparations for the hereafter. It would help explain why even Neandertal buried their dead with ceremony.

It would take a science that could promote longevity and stimulate the resulting intellectual brain activity for brain function to increase at the rate it did in the nineteenth and twentieth centuries, most especially the latter.

An enigma presents itself in regard to Cro-Magnon that developed a mastery of art (cave paintings in France) that did not appear again until the fifteenth century A.D. Now why was this not developed in some of the great civilizations of Egypt and Greece? Renowned for work in stone, these great civilizations lacked the Cro-Magnon mastery of painting; very puzzling.

It would seem Cro-Magnon had the brain capacity, measuring larger than modern Homo sapiens, to engage in artistic expression, but lacking the intellectual stimulation of a developed science could not carry this further.

Perhaps the short lifespan of ancient cultures leading to a preoccupation with thoughts of death and hope of something better in an afterlife led to working in stone and the building of monoliths, this material having a sense of permanence, rather than more perishable materials.

It has generally required "patrons" to encourage and subsidize the arts. And many have pointed out the necessity of a leisure class in order for the arts to flourish. But once there were means and incentive separated from religious strictures to encourage scientific discovery and exploration, this aided considerably in stimulating intellectual activity that, in turn, appears to have encouraged a wider exploration and experimentation with various art forms, particularly in literature.

With the modern advent of film, there was a quantum leap of artistic experimentation, the exponential impact of which may have been more profound on intellectual stimulation than is generally recognized.

In its way, film provided a media of monumental importance, much like the invention of movable type together with a suitable written language that made the mass production of books and newspapers possible. It was the increasing availability of books, more than any other factor, which gave the impetus to widespread reading and writing, the dissemination of information, so crucial to the kind of intellectual stimulation that would usher in an age of scientific enlightenment and invention.

The "monuments" of humanity began to be books, rather than stones. The printed word would have an impact of far greater significance and lasting value than any number of pyramids or other stone artifacts. Some may think the pyramids speak of immortality, but nothing speaks more eloquently, nor bears a truer mark of what may be called the immortality of divinity in humankind comparable to the stars better than Shakespeare; and Samuel Clemens who was born and departed with Halley's Comet.

But a difficulty for this monument of the highest achievement of Emerson's "Man Thinking," the written word, has arisen with the advent of television. While films of the past involved going to a theater, TV brought films to the living room, encouraging a sedentary lifestyle and the reading of books was increasingly losing out to a media that did not require the skills and mental activity leading to intellectual stimulation as that of reading.

And books generally, but certainly not always, have some intellectual or artistic merit in order to be successful. It seems TV is not held to this standard. Most importantly, TV as a passive medium does not require the active participation of the mind, of the imagination, that books do… and lacking such, does not provide the kind of stimulation that is so conducive to intellectual brain growth and function.

CHAPTER TWO

Like most of you, I will miss Peanuts. Charles Schultz has retired but he became as much a part of our lives as Apple pie. I miss Clayton Moore, The Lone Ranger, as he joins Roy Rogers. But we need our humorists like Schultz at least as much as we do our heroes, if not more.

I generally get enough exercise just pushing my luck and this issue of TAP will be no exception. One reason being my insisting that women who seek equality with men lack ambition (just kidding, ladies).

Seriously folks, the new millennium has not yet discarded much of the baggage of the old, and we still face the fact that as in ages past if you make something idiot-proof, someone will make a better idiot. And while genetic engineering shows astounding promise for the future, I keep thinking we have enough youth, how about a Fountain of Smart?

And I just know the thinking of many of you in 2000 is still: So many stupid people...So few comets.

Well, the real plus to starting the new millennium is hearing that regular, healthy sex is a preventive for colds and flu. I'm proud to say that scientists at Weedpatch University had begun the research into this phenomenon with volunteer frogs and made quite a contribution to the CDC's findings.

But then men had a pretty good fix on this all along. Our libidos are tuned to good health and that is why God designed men's brains to think like we do about sex, ladies. Now you know our motives are pure and for your benefit as well as ours. So the next time...

I awakened the morning of January 1, 2000 to the welcome of the cat scratching at the door demanding to be fed. The sun was coming up as usual and the quail were calling to each other. A fat gray tree squirrel was chittering in the old pine next to the cottage and various birds twittering in the oaks.

Shortly after getting up I was back on station in this corner of the house, the sun now beaming through my corner windows onto the desk where I write. I'm always grateful for being able to greet Aurora in such a fashion and delight in it ever as much as my soul brother Thoreau did.

And, like many of you folks, I begin by mulling over the prospects of this New Year. Will it be a better year than last? Will it be a better century, a better millennium?

Some really ponderous thoughts intrude on me at such times, some of curiously similar and equally serious significance such as will I shave today, fix breakfast this morning, do the laundry later, or get married this year?

But Y2K certainly was a disappointment to professional grouches and prophets of doom. We have heard it debated endlessly: Was it worth all the expense of preparation?

We will never know. The enormous complexity of modern computers, including the humble home pc, precluded even the experts knowing exactly what would happen when Y2K's clock turned over. One of the problems is that virtually no computer is the work of a single individual. And no one knows exactly how one software program will react to others at all times and under all circumstances. For example, does your defrag or reg.clean recognize all the possibilities with your upgrades of Windows 98, NT, or 2000?

Having a background in fundamentalist Christianity, being born and raised into it and eventually becoming a minister myself, I thoroughly understood the thinking and motives of the professional religionists such as TV evangelists, and (ex) friend Gary North with his radio show, newsletters and books, who were trading on the normal fears of people concerning Y2K. Such prophets of doom like North (and Hal Lindsey of *The Late Great Planet Earth* infamy) make millions off the gullible who think these people speak for God. And since all these people seem to believe God (or Mr. and Mrs. God) can't think or speak for Himself, they let the inventions of men through religion do His thinking and speaking for Him by these charlatans.

I watched a fellow being interviewed who had spent $25,000 dollars stockpiling food and water, a generator and large propane tank and other survival items. He did this because his own pastor, like Gary North, had told his congregation to prepare for the Armageddon of the Great Y2K Disaster!

Now I happen to be among those eternal optimists with a positive attitude who usually subscribe to: It IS as bad as you think and they ARE out to get you, I do draw the line in some instances. Y2K was one of these.

Well, I had already told people who asked me that in my opinion it wasn't something to lose any sleep over, that January 1, 2000 was only going to be another day. Happily for all of us this proved to be the case.

But in retrospect, much of the concern being generated was rooted more in the ignorance and superstitions of people and hype by the media than any real knowledge of computers.

I have no fault to find with those who took prudent precautions. I do find fault with those like Gary North and Hal Lindsey who make their money purporting to speak for God and trading on the fears of people.

Historically, we can go all the way back to Jonathan Edwards and his well-known sermon *Sinners in the Hands of an Angry God* to see the precedent of those like North and Lindsey. And if TV had been around at the time of Edwards you can bet he would have wound up making a bundle off his preaching. But he has to settle for paving the way for the Billy Sundays, Swaggarts, Bakers, Copelands, Schullers, Kennedys, Norths and Lindseys, professional religionists who would rather preach and trade on the fears and gullibility of the saints than earn an honest living.

Well, it can be said: Who are you to cast stones! having once believed in a lot of this nonsense myself. In my defense I can say that I never bought into the charismatic trash and hysteria of the glossalalia, etc. that shames God Himself, and I never preached Jesus is coming today (or tomorrow, etc.), though I still get a chuckle out of the remark by Jerry Falwell that if God does not destroy San Francisco, He owes an apology to Sodom and Gomorrah. But then, to believe this you would have to believe in the Biblical story and I do not.

But I like to believe that I had a streak of honesty, thanks to loving people who had instilled that in me, which prevented my trying to take advantage of the fears and gullibility of those who want to believe in the nonsense of religion, nonsense like believing the Bible being the very word of God, something I was raised to believe and later preached myself.

But the emphasis of childhood was still that kind of honesty that prevented my using the Bible to justify holy lying and stealing in the name of God.

I like to believe it was God who finally took me to the woodshed and cleaned my clock about my own errors and prejudices concerning Him, the Bible and religion, and taught me to separate what I believed from what I knew; a most difficult procedure. Especially in the case of someone like myself who was so firmly rooted and grounded in those errors and prejudices taught me not only as a child, but by professional religionists who formed me in their mold to stand in a pulpit.

Still, like divorce or the death of your child, such learning and experience, which corrected the thinking of a hard case like me, cannot come in a softer fashion. And it proves invaluable in understanding and compassion for others though I would not wish the process on anyone.

And it was an extraordinarily painful process I went through in giving up so many of my beliefs, beliefs taught me by loving and caring people. It was as though I was betraying these people who loved me and meant me no harm.

But I finally had to accept the logic that any Jew or Moslem who teaches his children to hate those who don't believe his way loves his children just as much as any Christian who teaches that everyone is going to hell who doesn't believe in Jesus and the Bible.

Children of all races and cultures may play well together with no hint of discrimination based on differences of race, religion or politics if left to

31

themselves because it takes adults to teach children to be prejudiced on the basis of race, religion and politics. There is, of course, a natural bent in children to discriminate on the basis of personalities, size, and a number of other quite human distinctives.

But it is adult responsibility to be the elder overseers of children, to be the wise counselors in teaching children to be fair in their interactions with others and accepting of those who are different from them, and to avoid prejudicial characteristics and opinions regarding things that fall into the categories of prejudice and bigotry.

The teaching of such errors and ignorant prejudices, which I was taught as a child, does not mean the parent, or other loved ones, hates or intends harm to the child. But such things do create prejudices and hatreds in the hearts and minds of children throughout the world as the song *Carefully Taught* from *South Pacific* so well spells out.

There is a scene in an old movie where the elderly, retired Indian tracker and scout says, "I hunted the Apache until I learned better."

And the task of those like me who have learned better is to do better for the sake of all those children who are being taught to hate others simply because they are different from themselves. And this is the most difficult of all gospels to preach effectively.

And the two things that make this gospel so difficult to preach effectively are two facts that militate against it. This consists of two things that world history proves have never been accepted by men and have prevented our attaining wisdom and kept the history of the world one of conflict, violence and warfare: Women are of equal value to men and children must become the priority of all humanity.

To accomplish the task of women being accepted as of equal value to men, I began to devote much of my writing to educating those who recognize the necessity of this. As to the children, I realized that the proposed amendment was the way to accomplish the beginning of the process. I qualify the amendment as a beginning because it is the first step in a long process. And because it is something never before done in the history of the world, I had no illusions it was going to be either easy or swift. I knew it would generate much controversy and meet with a great deal of resistance, even animosity. But most change does. Particularly change of such monumental magnitude! The Luddites are always with us.

Habit, ritual and routine are generally comfortable and very human characteristics; and generally useful and utilitarian, like brushing ones' teeth. But as a result of the comfort of habit, ritual and routine, we do tend to get set in our ways and do not readily accept changes from these things. We are indeed creatures of habit.

Of course some habits, rituals and routines must be changed from time to time; either by choice or by force of circumstances.

But seldom are the agents for profound and monumental social changes very welcome by societies. Socrates, Jesus, Galileo, Luther, and Gandhi are prime examples.

The Luddites of England toward the end of 1811 were determined on the destruction of technology that they felt threatened their existence. Novels like Charlotte Bronte's *Shirley* and *Ben o' Bills* by D.F.E. Sykes give us real insights into the Luddite thinking.

To avoid falling into hurtful Luddite thinking myself, I first had to accept that America had the responsibility and duty to lead the way in men accepting women as of equal value, and in making children the priority of our nation. And these changes had to come through the political process. But there were going to have to be some monumental changes in the typical Luddite thinking of the great majority of men concerning women and children in this process.

I came to accept the amendment as a logical first step in accomplishing these two goals since it would be women, predominantly, who would recognize the necessity of the amendment and support it. Which is natural enough since it is girls who are the in the great majority of molested children and the history of humankind is men as predators and women and little girls as prey. And while even men join the chorus of saying the law should take more notice of the victims of crime than the criminals, men turn a blind eye to the victims of molestation who are primarily little girls.

But women need to get their minds focused on another necessity; that of being accepted as of equal value to men in order to be effective in the political arena and their voices heard.

Over the years, I have established a network of communication with powerful people in politics. Since I make it a point, quite sensibly, to never ask anything for myself nor abuse my access to them, my credibility with these people is as a consequence quite high.

As a result, nearly two years ago I was able to suggest to Governor George W. Bush that he choose Elizabeth Dole as his running mate. I knew the Governor would be running for President and that it was very likely it would be him versus Al Gore in the next election.

Whatever the final outcome as to candidates, my thinking was that Al Gore should choose Hillary Clinton as his running mate. The historical timing was in place. For the first time in America's history there were two women who had such name recognition and political credentials, together with the necessary things in place historically, that they would be accepted by the general public for the office of Vice President.

But as I write, it seems Hillary has her eyes on the Presidency rather than settling for VP; Hence her run for the Senate. I can't credit Mrs. Clinton with any altruism; I don't believe her motives are pure but rather a way to get even with her husband for his disgracing her. And I can't help believing a woman with Mrs. Clinton's intelligence and political savvy really says to herself *I know I can do a hell of a lot better job than that SOB!* In this sense, I believe Hillary thinks she can show her husband up and has an ego and ambition equal to his.

But her run for the Senate leaves the Republican Party having the opportunity of making this historical first step of choosing a woman as a running mate for the Presidency and presenting the possibility of a woman in the White House as Vice President.

While Governor Bush in his reply to me acknowledged her worthiness and the benefits and contributions of Elizabeth Dole to the Republican Party, he did not commit himself by saying he would choose her as his running mate. And I fully understood his not doing so. Such a thing, and even before he announced his own candidacy, would not have been prudent. And I credit Governor Bush with being a prudent man.

But now that the media is paying attention to this possibility, it seems my assessment was correct. The timing is right and it is absolutely imperative that a woman joins the political system in our highest office as a prelude to women having a real voice in the political process and helping them to achieve being accepted as of equal value to men.

Throughout my writing and speaking of this, I have tried to make the point that it isn't about equal rights; it is about equal value, a far different thing than equal rights.

But to make the distinction, I knew women would have to make their voices heard in the one area where they have never been accepted: Philosophy.

As I keep repeating, because it must continue to be repeated, philosophy guides the course of history and nations. And as long as men only are allowed in this King of all disciplines, so long will we fail to attain wisdom by excluding an entire half of humanity, women, from philosophy which leads to the decision-making processes and the decisions guiding world affairs.

Women got the vote in 1920 with the 19th Amendment. But slavery had been abolished by the 13th Amendment in 1865 though the slavery of women was not a consideration in spite of Article 14 that clearly states the equal protection of law so ably presented by Thurgood Marshall that legally ended segregation. On May 17th of 1954 in the case of Brown v. Board of Education of Topeka, Kansas the Supreme Court finally held that separate educational facilities are inherently unequal and therefore unconstitutional. The 14th Amendment, the NAACP and Thurgood Marshall had done their job. As for women finally being able to own property and getting the franchise, and as shameful as the long delay was, better late than never they say.

It may legitimately be argued that segregation of the schools may have been necessary for a time after the Civil War. There may even be made an argument in favor of some Jim Crow laws considering the time frame.

But denying women the franchise and denying them the rights to hold or inherit property, denying them the right to serve on juries, virtually medieval, Dark Ages laws so prevalent well into the 20th century, how legitimately argue or attempt to justify these?

In discussing this with others, the point is well established that it has only been within the last couple of centuries that women have made any progress at all in education, science, art, and literature. And my point is that it has only been within the last couple of centuries that it has been realistically possible for them to do so. Particularly within this past century, thanks to men who have denied women access to philosophy and dominated them through the inventions of religion.

But few seem to consider that due to these two factors any real rights for women are relatively recent, and very recent. So I argue that since women have always been excluded from philosophy, the King of all studies and the discipline that guides the course of history and nations, it isn't surprising that they have only recently made any progress at all when it comes to the rights men have always demanded for themselves and denied to women.

But the question of equal rights begs the question of equal value, something that women and non-white minorities still face. For example, when Negroes marched in Memphis, the men carried signs proclaiming *I Am A Man!* And not even Martin Luther King, Jr. addressed the issue of the equal value of women. Nor have Jesse Jackson, Alan Keyes or any other high profile Negro leaders (Louis Farrakhan? As a good Moslem when hell freezes over!).

When I tell women that they must take the initiative in forming a philosophy of their own in order to achieve being accepted as of equal value with men, it is with the full knowledge that women have a very long history of being treated with injustice, and indoctrination to the idea of actually being inferior to men, to overcome in doing so. It is going to be a difficult task for women. But it is an absolutely essential one if humanity is ever to gain wisdom and know peace!

The last century saw world-changing things without any historical precedent in the past thousands of years. Before 1900, people believed they could reasonably forecast conditions of the coming century based on centuries past. It didn't happen that way. Just the progress in travel and communications alone would outstrip any ability to forecast. Not to mention nuclear energy that stands alone.

If only differences could be overcome by the common goal of peace. But if we succeed through the amendment in making children the focus of attention and the priority they should be, there is hope of this happening.

But one of the things we confront in this new millennium is the continuing ignorant and hateful prejudice that led to the hijacking of that Indian airliner. And lead to countries like India and Pakistan developing nuclear arsenals like those of China and Israel. Will Hollywood or the homosexual activist organization People For The American Way get the bomb?

At the same time we are developing technology for colonizing other planets and even diverting large meteorites from striking the earth and mining asteroids, how far have we come in civilized behavior as we enter this new era, an era that still too often confronts Sherman's dictum that the crueler the war, the quicker it is over? And when you confront the fact that virtually half of those in a world of over six billion people have never so much as received a phone call?

In the face of such things, I am asking people to consider a New Way, a New Path never before tried in the history of the world! No easy task; neither for me nor for those of whom I am making this request.

Well, the persecution of Galileo continues and for some the world is still flat and Columbus is going to sail off the edge into oblivion or hell. Better than the world some would create through the virtual culture of Hollywood? Or one where God continues to be used as an excuse for good people not accepting their responsibility to confront and do battle with evil with equal determination to win?

Those who consider themselves civilized, informed, intelligent, and unprejudiced have their work cut out for them in this new millennium (disregarding the fact that it is not technically a new millennium yet and half the world or more has a different calendar but forced to conform to the Gregorian for the sake of practicality. But, as with English realistically being the world language, it isn't a point many would try to make much of, apart from prejudice, in a general and practical context).

Another intransigent problem as old as the history of the human species: If you can't make it socially, be contrary. Dress and act outrageously. Like any adult who never grew up: Pay Attention To Me!

Well, fortunately most of us do achieve adult status and learn to mix it up in the social milieu of our respective cultures. But there are always those like Junky Jerry or Tammy Faye Baker.

Outrageous behavior, dress, and things like body-piercing are not just the purview of children and young people as devices to get attention, which brought the darling and walking billboard of the cosmetics industry, Tammy Faye, to mind.

In retrospect, her partner in crime in fleecing the flock, Jim Baker, can now say since his release from prison that as he studies the Bible, Jesus didn't have anything good to say about wealth. Baker hasn't commented on sex since his release.

Well, I know the Bible far better than Baker ever did or is ever likely to and I caught on to this very early. About wealth, that is.

Still, Baker preached that wealth and prosperity gospel he just knew Jesus and God approved and made a large fortune from it before Jessica Hahn went public. She got hers from Playboy (kind of like the warm and fuzzy Cinderella story of Monica L.). In this case, it seems honesty pays after the fact since Jessica knew Jim and Tammy Faye were scamming the public. But Tammy Faye didn't serve any time in spite of the air-conditioned doghouse and, like *The Old Dope Peddler* (and Jimmy Swaggart, et al), still does well by doing good.

My following comments must be taken in the context of the prerogatives of age, and the liberty friends and family have to pick on one another. Like my wacko computer nerd friends I have mentioned. One just ran up a $400.00 phone bill one month with phone sex. He didn't know how much it was costing him. But then his focus wasn't on expenses. To make matters worse, he is on a limited disability (bipolar) income and now has to make installment payments to keep from being disconnected. Then he wouldn't even be able to spend his days and nights looking at the free porn on the net.

But it isn't just the prerogative of friends to pick on one another; it is the God-given right of parents to pick on their children (says so right in the parent handbook the hospital gives you when the child is born). Especially when you have a grown son who still acts like he knows more than his dad about things that only age and experience will teach; if at all. One of these days I just know he is going to give me a bumper sticker reading: Your kid may be an honors student but you're still an idiot.

Just kidding; my eldest son and I may disagree about a lot of things, especially the Amendment, but he would never be disrespectful to me. He really does have gracious manners and is always civil to people, especially to me.

Keeping in mind that criticism among friends and family does not mean they love each other any the less. They just fight and argue a lot. And I am mindful of the need to be nice to your kids; they will be choosing your nursing home.

For example son Daniel is an intelligent, handsome, and well-read young man, a real chip off the old block (couldn't resist that one. It's too true). And there are few better mechanics than Daniel, something else we have in common.

But while we share much in common and generally enjoy each other's company and discussions, while we genuinely love each other as father and son, when it comes to the Amendment we couldn't be further apart. And it is a real bone of contention between us.

Daniel lives in Torrance which means that when I visit him I get to drive through the LAX traffic where the bumper stickers *Cover Me, I'm Changing Lanes, Pardon My Driving, I'm Reloading* and *Forget About World Peace, Visualize Using Your Turn Signal* have real significance. The LA traffic always calls to mind the need for a TV channel dedicated to the coverage of high-speed chases only.

But it isn't just the LA traffic that brings out the grouch in me. For my part, there are few things that make me so grouchy as frozen pipes and a clogged septic line in winter here at home to make me so. And being perfectly human in most ways, I reserve to myself the God-given right to take out my grouchiness on friends and family just like any of you.

But in my defense I still freely admit of my own ignorance and I remain my best source of humor when it comes to doing stupid things like trying to put my broom in the refrigerator and trying to teach my cat to do the windows (which makes me, at times, look at her and think So many cats, so few recipes).

And I have always been quick to point out that I do not know how any one man in just one lifetime could have made as many mistakes as I have. Of course if you never try you'll never fail or make mistakes.

The Luddites are still with us and very much alive and well. I was reminded of this while talking to my friend Junky Jerry, the antique dealer also known locally as The Mouth.

Jerry got this name for not only being extremely loud, but wrong loud. And while we have known each other for years and love each other as friends, warts and all, no one in the Valley wants to get within earshot of Jerry, a major factor in his lack of success in dealing with customers. They don't stay long if the subjects of religion, politics or the weather should arise. To aggravate matters further, he is growing quite deaf but his ego, his vanity (like dying his hair as many older men and women do) won't allow of his wearing a hearing aid.

But he's a good-hearted man and I'm more than willing to discount a lot of the foibles of people on this basis alone. We need all the good-hearted people in our lives that we can find. And when the chips are down, both Jerry and Daniel can be counted on. In a real emergency, we are there for one another. And that's the way it should be. My own love and friendship are never contingent on people agreeing with me, especially my children.

But when it comes to computers, for example, Jerry and my eldest son find common ground. They're a'gin 'em. But then my having so many credentials and degrees, including a Ph.D., mean nothing compared to the intelligence and wisdom of people like Jerry and Daniel.

There are multiplied millions of such people and they are, sadly it seems, a majority. And since I am human, I have made mistakes. And this justifies their criticism of me. Just ask them, they will tell you so.

In regard to the Luddites: No man having drunk old wine straightaway desires new, for he says the old is better. Luddite thinking; and Jerry and Daniel exemplify this attitude when it comes to computers.

While Confucius made the point of old vs. new long before Jesus, the Western world, so very illiterate and ignorant of the Eastern writers and philosophers as Thoreau often pointed out, more easily recognizes quotations from the Bible than other more ancient writings. So, I quote the Bible often, a book I know at least as well as any Seminary professor (and far better than most of them, let alone people like Jim Baker).

Not that this ever keeps people like my son Daniel and Jerry, together with a host of others, believing they know it and understand it better than I do in spite of the fact that they know little or nothing of Hebrew, Greek, or the actual history of the Bible and the church. But when it comes to the prejudices of beliefs, no amount of learning or scholarship is a match for such. On that I am a most unfortunate expert from my own life in the churches.

Well, computers rule. And there is nothing anyone can do about it. And both Jerry and Daniel are free in their criticism of me for trying to point this out to them and for my being computer literate and trying to get them involved for their own sakes.

Yesterday Jerry, together with an acquaintance, an Episcopal priest, and I were having coffee together. The conversation was about the new millennium and Jerry very loudly, as usual, made the outrageous statement so typical of ignorance, and proud of its ignorance, that there was nothing considered new today that he couldn't read in a 1940 edition of Life magazine.

Now it is typical of such ignorance since time immemorial to decry anything of which you are ignorant, the Luddite and Old Wine syndrome. From such people come the experts about virtually everything you can name whether it's the experts on child-rearing who never had children, the experts about marriage who never married, the experts about education who were never teachers, the experts in philosophy who never studied the subject in the disciplined academic environment, the experts about cars who could never overhaul an engine, to ... the list of such experts is seemingly infinite.

Jerry treated the priest and me to his opinion concerning computers; this in spite of the fact that he wouldn't know the difference between a computer and an Etch-A-Sketch and wouldn't even know how to turn one on, let alone use it. And while it remains true that we are all ignorant, just about different things, people like Jerry not only loudly declaim on their ignorance, they seem actually proud of it.

And no one will ever convince Jerry that just because virtually every antique dealer who is prospering is on line while he languishes (and complains constantly and bitterly about it) evidences a need for his doing so. The Buggy Whip syndrome as well as that of the Old Wine and Luddite firmly entrenched in his mind.

Being very paranoid about the consequences of the new millennium, Jerry was screaming at his normal decibel level that sterilizes frogs a hundred yards distant, that only those who had been smart enough to bury gold, silver, diamonds and rubies in their backyard were going to survive (the same doctrine of Gary North, et al). You just have to love this guy.

By matching his screaming (you must do this to get him to shut up at all), I managed to get in the following point:

When I worked in the shops, I met many Germans who had come to the U.S. after the war. And the father of one of my closest friends had virtually escaped with his life from Hitler's Germany.

One of these German acquaintances had lived in Berlin and told the story that after WWI he had taken a bag of jewelry to the country to exchange it for food for his family.

But the farmer looked at the jewelry and told the man: I have plenty of gold and diamonds, what do you have of real value to exchange for my beans?

Another confronted the hatred of Germans by others after WWII with this story.

When you have been watching your children starve and someone like Hitler manages to put meat and potatoes on your table, what would you do?

Well, if I had the wisdom of Jerry and Daniel I wouldn't be, as Daniel put it so belittling of me: Riding this hobbyhorse of the amendment for children.

And in the beginning of Nazism, as so many of these Germans I knew put it, they thought Hitler's ideas were simply his hobbyhorse. They might as well have called Communism the hobbyhorse of Karl Marx and Stalin, hobbyhorses for which wars were fought and multiplied millions of innocent people died. Kind of like my invitation to certain people through my Memorial Wall Of Shame with the names of all the murdered children. Just a hobbyhorse (but Jerry, Daniel, and so many like them in this respect, in spite of my being a well-qualified philosopher in my own right, are quick to tell me they know Socrates better than I do).

This comes with the territory of mixing it up with real people, including friends and family, rather than the cloistered walls of academia. And in spite of the criticisms of ignorant and prejudiced people, I would far rather this than go into some kind of hermitage that would cheat me of the realities of life and people, both the good and the bad.

Still, facing people who in their ignorance simply want to criticize and argue or engage in sophistries while not knowing what they are talking about, well, I just don't have time for this. Especially for those who are given to sophistries, that by their very nature choose to ignore facts and logic, just for the sake of trying to make themselves appear intellectual. For the true intellectual, this grates horribly on the nerves. And this reminds me of something a great old country music picker told me once. He had a title for a song: "I've Just Got One Nerve Left And You're Gettin' On It!" I encouraged him to pursue the song but he died not long after this.

Well, such things often remind me of what Sam Clemens said of the young man who would tell people he was a poet. The trouble, Clemens said, was that the young man couldn't convince anyone else of this.

And in spite of my not wanting to become a monk or hermit, there are times when thoughts of Death Valley become particularly seductive; particularly when I have to deal with sophistries which are far more the resort of the uneducated than of those in academia. And, of course, men like this will always know what it is like to have a baby.

While no one is a greater advocate of reading books than I am (after all, I write books), such reading will never take the place of studying a subject in the disciplined environment of a university. It takes the spirited debate among peers, led of experts in the subject, to obtain real education in academic subjects. And none of my well-justified criticisms of the universities take away from this fact of education.

But as a result of not secluding and insulating myself, of not retreating to places like the Halls of Ivy, I'm used to those like Jerry and Daniel deriding and belittling my efforts in this respect of my battle for the children. They find company with multiplied millions of others of the same opinion that surely proves I'm wrong of course; or, more charitably, simply riding a hobbyhorse as Daniel calls it. A prophet remains without honor to his own friends and family in many cases (my daughter Karen being a wonderful exception in my life in this respect).

Not being without sin in my own life regarding Luddite thinking, and surely to be criticized for casting stones, particularly by son Daniel, I admit that there is much Old Wine thinking left in my own mind. But I have done my best to repent of past mistakes and prejudices and learn from them. A man can do no more than this.

For example, while I have no illusions about the hardships of life on the old mining claim without any power or indoor plumbing, while other kids dreamed of bicycles and I dreamed of a power saw (never got one), I would go back to such a life in a heartbeat if I could and escape the marvels of our technocracy.

But in spite of my poetic/romantic bent of mind, I have a thoroughgoing streak of empirical pragmatism about me. I can just as easily work with hammer and saw, lathe and mill, as my mind (accounting for dual majors: Litt/ Vo.Ed). And maintain an equal appreciation of the value of both mechanical and philosophical expertise. I take justifiable pride in learning new skills with a computer ever as much as I took pride in my ability with hammer and saw, lathe and mill, building a house or overhauling an engine, and writing.

And for someone like myself with the mechanical skills, there are many ways to apply these in working with computers. For example I have three computers and six printers. One of these printers is an eight-year old HP DeskJet 500 that still operates flawlessly because I can do the mechanical work on it. As a full time writer, this old printer has had over 30,000 draft copies put through it. Only when the work is finished do I put the final copies through my laser printer.

But in addition to servicing this printer, I also re-fill my ink cartridges, a considerable savings for someone who writes full-time and prints so many drafts.

In spite of my two online computers, I do all my writing on a nearly ten-year-old 386 with only eight megs of ram. But the only programs in this old computer are DOS, QA3 (the most writer-friendly program ever designed for writers), and Xtree Gold utility. As a result, I have one of the best and fastest glorified word processors you could possibly wish.

But just try to tell people who are nuts about computers that such a system is ideal for a writer. They don't understand, not being writers, that all you want is a fast, simple, word processing system without all the bells and whistles; and especially not any Windows, etc. programs.

Computers, printers and copiers are still as much mechanical as electronic and program devices. And my mechanical skills, together with my old 386 and 500 DeskJet, enable me to keep writing with a minimum of downtime.

Unfortunately, while many have the mechanical skills, the discipline of the mind and critical, logical thinking too often flounders on the rocks of strongly held opinion and prejudice. And in spite of my comments about the Luddites, there are Luddites in the computer field as well which means computers are, sadly, coming of age in respect to prejudices.

Too many display such abysmal ignorant opinion and prejudice when they tell me in the best of sour grapes tradition: I may not have a Ph.D. but I'm just as smart as you! But the same men (and they are generally men) so typical of a Junky Jerry will tell you they know what it's like to be pregnant and give birth. The troubling thing about this is the fact that at the same time they will deny this vehemently, you don't have to listen to them say much to determine that they actually believe this.

You may notice of such people, who very well may be intelligent and read books, that lacking the academic discipline of formal education they often mispronounce words they have come across in their reading. Or have heard equally pretentious people mispronounce.

Now I am not one of those academic nitpickers about such things. And I know language is not static but changes with usage. But I have corrected some on occasion in the hope that they wished to know the correct pronunciation only to have them resent it. This indicates a lack of academic self-discipline and a willfulness that is antithetical to real educational achievement. And this is the crux of America's failure in education and fall into decline as a literate nation. Academic excellence is no longer considered by the general population as something of real value.

If someone tells you it doesn't matter whether you pronounce words correctly, it doesn't matter if you know how to punctuate correctly or use proper syntax and grammar, what does this tell you about such a person?

As a qualified academic and an expert in human behavior (things that mean little to many of those lacking in formal, higher education), I can point out that these things I have mentioned speak volumes about such persons. And they generally fall into the category of those with low self-esteem and other attendant problems grow from this. Such as outrageous dress and behavior which is often rooted in low self-esteem and a childish attempt to draw attention from others to the individual.

But such people are not nearly as interested in true academia or the discipline of the pursuit of real knowledge as they are in trying to prove to others that they are intelligent and have read some books: I may not have a Ph.D. but I'm just as smart as you are! The unwillingness to accept correction and learn from others speaks for itself about such people.

I've often said: Pity the poor disciple whose master has nothing further to learn himself.

It is well said that a mind is a horrible thing to waste. But a good mind is not, in itself, enough. For example critical thinking is not a gift of birth; it is a learned skill. There are very few of the stature of a Newton or Einstein. And even these men benefited from higher education in the sharpening of their own minds in critical thinking which both men credited to their formal education.

And while true intellectualism is marked by language more than any other single factor, I meet too many sophists thinking themselves intellectuals who deny this. And, as a result, condemn themselves.

Because of my reputation and writings, I receive much unwanted material from those considering themselves intellectuals. It is true that I, along with others, am vitally concerned about the decline of intellectualism in America. The intellectual is the bane, and the first target due to the danger they pose to them, of tyrants and despots.

But a great breadth of reading and academic studies in many diverse fields marks true intellectualism. And too many fancy themselves intellectuals and philosophers who lack the essential academic background; and far too many, like Gary North, write very poor books. More than simply reading and studying, the ideas generated and mastered from legitimate studies and reading result in the expression of such by writing. It is in written expression, more than any other, that true intellectualism proves itself and evolves ideas of originality upon which others may build. This is the basis of both Newton's and Einstein's observation that they had stood on the shoulders of others in order to see so far. And in this, they gave expression to another real mark of true intellectualism: A distinct lack of selfish, self-centered, self-serving ego or vanity.

Philosophy as a formal discipline is lost to the sophists. The reason being that philosophy as a formal discipline requires a broad foundation academically.

A good example is found in mathematics. The multiplication tables are the foundation of all mathematics from the simplest arithmetic to the most esoteric physics. The discipline of learning the times tables is absolutely essential to further learning in the field of mathematics.

Now, consider the individual who tries to present himself as a teacher of calculus who never learned his times tables. This is, essentially, the person who tries to convince others of his philosophical expertise who never studied the subject in an academic environment, but presumes he knows more about it than one who is academically qualified. And we meet such pretenders all the time. Our public schools are filled with such teachers.

A friend and I correct each other, even in things like the mispronunciation of words. We are close enough to admit to each other that neither of us is perfect in language usage. But as educated men, we are keenly aware of the need and importance of speaking and using language correctly in grammar and syntax; and especially in correct pronunciation. The lesson of the vital importance of correct speech in *My Fair Lady* is not lost on those like my friend and me.

And since we respect each other, neither of us takes offense at correcting the other. On the contrary, as well-educated men we are grateful for being corrected. Far better between friends than to make a speech before other well-educated people or talk to some Harvard, Yale, or Princeton graduate holding high political office and pronounce potable with a short o, oblique with a long i, or quasi with short a, and i long e.

While it remains generally true that what you have is not as important as what you do with what you have, an attitude of being proud of one's ignorance and attempting to excuse it is in reality nothing in which to take any pride. If a person is sincere, he or she will make every attempt to seek out instruction and make improvement.

And as I watch my little five year old granddaughter Ashley move a mouse and click, drag-and-drop like an expert to perform certain computer operations, there is enough of real intelligence and the scientist in me to know the future when I see it. It is at that point I find myself in opposition to those like Jerry and Daniel, though I love them dearly, who are in this respect of the Luddite and Old Wine persuasion.

The possibility of extraterrestrial life is in the realm of speculation because it admits of no empirical proof as yet (apart from those who say the proof of intelligent life elsewhere in the universe is that it leaves us alone). But people like Jerry and far too many others throughout the world will loudly proclaim that angels and space aliens surround us. To him this is fact, not speculation.

I not only enjoy conversation with those who are academically and intellectually qualified to speculate philosophically on the basis of probability, the great frontier of the mind is explored in such a fashion ever as much as it is through the science of mapping the brain itself.

For example, philosophically, is God a generic term? It is academically. If Mr. and Mrs. God is a better probability than just God, philosophical debate on the basis of probability is both rewarding and quite legitimate.

But just try getting into a discussion of this subject with those lacking the necessary and essential foundation in the subject of philosophy as a formal discipline. In the good old days of the Old Time Religion of murdering Canaanites and offering blood sacrifices to the Deity, or in more recent times of threatening Galileo and selling indulgences, I would be burned at the stake for even suggesting such speculation and discussing it.

Even today in our modern world, there are millions who would willingly hang or burn me for doing so. The more charitable would (and do) settle for cursing me and calling me names, consigning me to hell and the outer reaches beyond redemption. This hurts because I'm really such a nice guy. Apart from being a raving heretic.

Well, with a heavy sigh I have to accept this as fact: Most people believe in things like religion and UFOs as facts that have no empirical basis in facts. And while I know all the Bible passages concerning faith, I rather lean to James: Show me your faith without works and I'll prove my faith by my works.

Still, some of these things such as the possibility of life on other planets are grounds of reasonable speculation. The problem is keeping such things in the realm of reasonable speculation rather than treated as fact due to prejudice.

Philosophically it is argued whether modern humanity with its great brain-to-size-and-weight ratio and the capability to think, imagine and create has an advantage if this brainpower enables us to destroy ourselves.

Humankind with its modern anatomy has only been around for about 125,000 years. Homo sapiens with the sudden and totally inexplicable introduction of art and music, hallmarks of beginning civilization, for only about 12,500 years; but is longevity a predictor of success for the future of our species? Hardly; no more so than it is a predictor for the continuing success of a marriage or the attainment of wisdom. And there is always the unexpected, which caused the extinction of the dinosaurs (for what ever reason).

And there is always the unexpected, which changes the course of human history. Who would have thought some nut's fascination with a woman (no, this is not about Clinton and I won't dignify the nut in this case by even giving his name, I'll leave that to the history books where it properly belongs), Jodi Foster, would nearly cause the death of President Reagan? Who could guess the historical impact if Reagan had died? The possibilities are seemingly limitless in that world of What If?

But if life itself is unique to our planet, if we are unique in the universe as a species, if we are to be the midwives of life in other parts of the universe, will we outlive our propensity for self-destruction? Or will we, as some like Michio Kaku speculates, destroy ourselves in a nuclear holocaust? These are legitimate questions.

Obviously if we are to be midwives to life in other parts of the universe, we must first survive life here on our own planet. And lacking the wisdom part of the equation k+w=p, the prognosis is not good at present.

A well-qualified biologist argues that life had only a billion-to-one chance here on this planet. An equally well-qualified physicist turns the statement around to life may be a billion-to-one shot, but the fact is that it did occur here on the only planet with which we are so familiar so why not elsewhere? It is in such speculations that probability plays an essential role in true academic, philosophical inquiry.

Do fairies (or the religiously correct equivalent: angels) exist in spite of the fact that we haven't seen them? It would seem a fair question unless you accept some fundamentals of science that would preclude, or at least militate, against such a probability.

In sum, there are areas of legitimate speculation based on probability, but if probability shows a less than one-tenth of one per cent chance of something, you know how to place your bet.

Unhappily, even tragically for the human race, the laws of probability have little effect on those whose minds are given to ignorant prejudice and fanaticism; or on buying lottery tickets.

And when it comes to organized ignorant prejudice and fanaticism, whether of religion, race or politics, we don't have to go beyond our own shores to find these in abundance; or, as Thoreau pointed out, to find the organized tyranny of evil in our own government while castigating the governments of others.

A friend came by recently and we were discussing this very point but he had never read *On The Duty Of Civil Disobedience*, the handbook of Gandhi; my point being that of Hutchins, the editor of The Great Books of the Western World. To quote from the last issue of TAP:

As a teacher of many years experience, I realized the truth of Robert M. Hutchins' warning that the failure to propagate the heritage of Western Civilization through the great literature of the past would lead to the situation we face today.

Hutchins, Editor-in-Chief for The Great Books of the Western World, made the valid point in 1951 that unless the ideas expressed in the best of our literature of the past was taught to our children, the results would be catastrophic! He was right.

Another point of Hutchins is one I take to heart in my own writing. This has to do with the failure of our schools to blend science and the arts that has led to over-specialization. Dante's Divine Comedy and Newton's Principia should be studied together.

But then I have to mention the failure of Hutchins in the following: I have to wonder if Hutchins was alive today and I confronted him with the fact that not a single woman was allowed a contribution to that 54-volume set of books purporting to represent the best of human wisdom, whether he would be ashamed? I hope he would be (end quote).

During the politicking and debating going on right now, the statement was recently made by one candidate: If criminals deserve free lawyers, don't children deserve free doctors? Now the candidate did not use the word free, meaning paid for by taxpayers. But he is a politician and that is exactly what he meant.

Well, it can be debated why, if criminals deserve free lawyers, don't their victims? Our justice system seems concerned far too many times with anything but justice, covering its backside and catering to criminals while the victims of crime continue to pay and pay.

As to doctors for children? Of course they deserve doctors. But consider the following story when even doctors, after saving a child, were helpless in the face of an agency with far more power than the AMA.

On January 4th, 60 Minutes II featured the story of a murdered child, Terrell Peterson, in Georgia; and murdered because of the thoroughgoing ineptitude and lack of any real concern for children on the part of Social Services, and especially CPS (Child Protective Services). The case of this murdered little boy, literally starved and tortured to death, was well-hidden, as is usual with Social Services, by the cloak of confidentiality, the resort of the scoundrels in such agencies, including the schools, staffed by people who lie continually and act without conscience.

They say doctors bury their mistakes. They have nothing on those in Social Services who have an even better system of covering themselves by law.

The cause of this little boy's death, in fact, would, like countless others, have gone unknown and unreported had it not been for someone with a conscience anonymously delivering the full case records to an attorney who, being a good man, took up the fight against Social Services without recompense to himself. All jokes aside, too often deserved, as Charles Lamb said: Even lawyers, I suppose, were once children.

The child's foster mother is the one who is being tried now for capital murder in the little boy's death. But his torture was well known long before he died. Skin had been removed from his thighs and grafted to his feet because this foster parent had literally burned the flesh off his feet for complaining about her at his school.

But in spite of the report with all the details from the hospital and teacher involved, Social Services did nothing and completely ignored this case. They actually, in the words of the attorney, handed down a death sentence for the little boy.

I am skipping many specifics of this case for an astounding and absolutely shameful and disgraceful to all Americans reason. Like so many horror stories of molested, tortured and murdered children, it is too common.

One of the reasons for this blanket indictment of Americans is the fact that no psychopath has ever been rehabilitated. And the child abuser, most especially the child molester, is a psychopath by whatever definition you may supply.

But child abuse, and most especially child molestation, is of such slight concern to Americans generally that the psychopaths, like the murderer of this little boy, are allowed wide access to children without consequences commensurate with their crimes; that is until the little victims of such predators, such monsters, are so horribly abused, or murdered, that society can no longer turn a blind eye to them.

And Georgia is not unique in this respect. California, particularly my home county of Kern made so prominent internationally by Edward Hume's Pulitzer-winning book *Mean Justice*, and neighboring L.A. and Tulare counties, is just as bad as anything you will find in Georgia.

When 60 Minutes interviewed the head of Social Services, she admitted of no wrongdoing on the part of the agency. In spite of actual records from the courts and doctors, the teacher and other eyewitnesses, this woman admitted that no punitive action had been taken against any of the parties involved. In fact, the caseworker and her supervisor still held their positions with the agency. And this, from my own actual experience working in the schools and CPS, is usually the result. Even in cases of murder and outright falsifying of records.

People may wonder why I include the following as justification for the Amendment. The case of this little victim in Georgia is the reason:

It (the Amendment) will also dramatically impact Child Protective Services, forcing that agency to act in a far more humane, responsible and professional manner. There is no doubt in my mind, having worked in this agency myself, that with the power of such law as this amendment, CPS will have to do a better job of identifying, establishing factual case evidence and removing the predators of children from society...

In its way, the system of Social Services is no different than that of the schools that cannot rid themselves of bad teachers and administrators. I was called to appear at a state credential termination hearing in my capacity as an expert witness in such cases against a teacher who was growing marijuana and supplying his students. The school board could not fire this teacher and he not only kept his teaching credential, but also remained in the classroom in spite of his having been arrested, tried and convicted in court. But convicted on a plea to a misdemeanor, rather than the felony of which he was guilty.

Now the lawyers and the judge knew this teacher could be terminated and lose his credential on the basis of a felony conviction. In order to keep this from happening, the judge knowingly allowed the plea to a misdemeanor. The corruption of young people by flagrant violation of law, the betrayal of his position of trust as a teacher, was not a consideration to this judge.

49

Those who know me know I would be among the first to vote for the legalization of marijuana. Why legal alcohol and tobacco and discriminate against a less harmful drug like marijuana? And because of the insanity of law, creating an entire criminal class of otherwise law-abiding citizens, clogging our courts, jails, and prisons through such insanity of law?

But the case of the teacher was not about marijuana. It was about children entrusted to this man's care, children and parents whose trust he had betrayed as a teacher.

You fire a bad school administrator the same way you do a bad Social Services administrator, practitioner or a doctor; you give them a glowing letter of recommendation on the condition that they find some other place to work. And the cloak of confidentiality protects these scoundrels.

I have preached this sermon too many times for too many years. And it still goes unheeded. I have preached it to governors and senators to no effect. So why do I keep preaching?

Recently, I got a lovely letter from a dear lady who told me: Keep on doing what you are doing and don't give up.

My response was that I couldn't give up if I wanted to. I have lived too long and I know too much; the Hound of Heaven keeps dogging my heels, the nightmares continue and the children keep dying. And only a mad man like Boo Radley, The Mad Hatter as my friends call me, would be able to keep on. It is madness, but it takes such madness to confront the greater madness of a society that acts as though it hates children through its indifference to them: We've bought you all the toys. Now go play and leave us alone!

The voters in Palmdale, California recently elected a man, one Kevin Carney, who had been a deputy sheriff for L.A. County, to the city council in spite of his having been arrested as a child molester. But he wasn't convicted. This former deputy sheriff, and still city councilman, has been arrested again on eighteen counts of child molestation, one of four of his little victims only six years old. He is currently in jail and his bail set at two million dollars.

My point? Child molestation, in spite of its being the greatest of crimes against humanity and against the most helpless and innocent of victims, children, is of such little consequence to the majority of Americans that a child molester can be elected to political office.

Oh, but he wasn't convicted of the crime when he was elected.

Convicted at the time or not, the fact that he had been arrested and tried on the charge carried no weight with those who elected him. And, I have to ask myself; does this new arrest with an undoubted conviction this time mean anything to these same people who elected this man? I don't think so. They might well vote for him again. Such is the lack of conscience on the part of Americans in our nation today.

Why this lack of conscience about such a brutal and heinous offense against children? The answer to that question is profoundly complex and is one of the reasons I keep preaching the same sermons, it is why I write so voluminously about it, it is why I believe the Amendment to be our only salvation and redemption as a nation.

I keep preaching that the most fundamental and basic of all human rights is the right of a child to a lawfully protected and innocent childhood, a right that belongs with our noble Bill of Rights. But society does not want to hear this sermon.

I started my Memorial Wall of Shame with the names of the murdered children to bring attention to these little ones who never received justice. And if we can have memorials to those who gave their lives, the last full measure of devotion for our liberty and freedom, why shouldn't there be such a memorial for these little ones for whom our honorable dead gave their lives, have such a memorial themselves?

While as Lord Charnwood pointed out in his biography of Lincoln we Americans are quick to take up an apt phrase, why hasn't the phrase "It Shouldn't Hurt To Be A Child!" caught on?

Far from being mere jingoism, such a phrase is not one Americans want to acknowledge. And, admittedly, I don't want to be reminded constantly of the abuse and torture, the murder of children. No normal person does.

But there remains the need to know, the need to be reminded until there is no more abuse, torture and murder of children! And as Thoreau so well said: It may not be our individual and personal duty to solve the problem of evil, but it is every person's duty to not lend themselves to the very injustices against which they cry.

In Thoreau's case, as with Confucius and Socrates, if the government has become so tyrannically inept and corrupt as to not recognize its own evil, it is the citizen's duty to confront it and call attention to such evil. There should never be an attempt at a moment's truce between vice and virtue, no attempt to accommodate evil, since evil represented in its most malevolent and monstrous worst in the child molester, knows no bounds of civilized law and behavior.

And as I keep preaching, since it is not God's responsibility to confront and overcome evil, but ours, why do people continue to lend themselves to injustice by not taking action against the evil with an equal determination to win? Are Ruby Ridge and Waco to continue and the Janet Renos to continue to rule? Are the most heinous of monsters in any society calling itself civilized, the child molesters, to continue to be tolerated, and when caught and convicted get only a slap on the wrist, or be convicted and rehabilitated only to be released to prey on further little victims of society's callous indifference?

Minnesota has started a program where unwanted newborn infants can be taken to any hospital and accepted without any questions. This has started a real controversy about what to do with unwanted babies.

Perhaps those in Minnesota are right in what they are doing. At least it is better than abortion and finding dead babies in dumpsters.

The plight of young girls without resources, without hope of a future and left by callous so-called men to care for the results of their own lust and selfishness, is an indictment of a failed society in regard to children and young people. But in nothing is this failure so evident as it is in the failure to recognize child molestation for the monstrous thing it is in fact!

One of the first attempts to make child abuse a matter of real social concern was the case of Mary Ellen Wilson in 1874. Mary was a horribly abused little girl. But at this time in history, there were few social agencies available to undertake the cause of children like Mary.

The case of Mary Ellen Wilson recently caught the attention of Eric Shelman and Stephen Lazoritz, M.D. and they wrote a book about it entitled *Out of the Darkness*. I met the authors at a book signing and congratulated them on their contribution to raising the awareness of child abuse and its dark history in our nation.

I received an email from Kimbra Martin, a beautiful woman who had come across the web site for the Amendment and got in touch with me.

She has written a book entitled *Snapshots* available through Authorlink Press that is her story of child abuse. She thanked me for doing this work for children and invited me to review her book at http://homepages. go.com/~kimbramartin/ and I invite all of you to look it up. You will be glad you did. The book will stir your soul and conscience.

The reviews for the book are excellent and I am grateful that she wanted mine as well. But Kimbra did not write the book for applause of her gifts as a writer.

The shameful tragedy of America is that Kimbra's story is, as with that of the little victim in Georgia, so common. The bill for America's dirty secret of child abuse and unconcern for the welfare of children, of society's callous and shameful indifference to the subject of child molestation and the welfare of children in general is, as Atticus Finch pointed out concerning America's shameful history of racial prejudice, coming due. The violence in our schools is the proof of this.

And I keep asking others and myself the following question: Why should children any longer be denied the Constitutional rights adults take for granted? Yet nothing in the Constitution is specifically addressed to the needs of children. It thus leaves vulnerable the most helpless of America's citizens and denies them the most basic and fundamental of all human rights, the right to a lawfully protected and innocent childhood.

And I ask: Will this be the year the Amendment comes to national attention by those who know better, by those who ought to be doing better because they do know better?

CHAPTER THREE

I have always been somewhat skeptical of claims by people of the supernatural. I am always suspicious of those claiming mystical experiences. But there is one area of my life that would seem to lend credence to such things. It is the curse of minor inconveniences.

To explain, my bread or toast always falls butter or jam side down. I can drop a hundred pieces of buttered toast and they will invariably fall butter-side down. I can put a hundred dollars worth of quarters in a slot machine and lose the whole hundred dollars. This, of course, makes up for those who win. Without me, they would never win a dime. If my roof leaks, it will leak over my bed. And I learned long ago not to try to reach the next gas station when low on fuel, but to keep the tank filled. I am the guy who suffers all the minor inconveniences so the rest of you don't.

The more scientific reader might immediately think of Heisenberg's Uncertainty Principle and the statistics of probability. That would be perfectly acceptable. But for those whose minds run to mysticism, maybe it's a curse? I will lose a button off a shirt, suit or sweater at the worst possible time. When I am driving, a bug of horrendous proportions will always hit the windshield right in front of me, not off to the side.

I will have a box of 100 different screws. But the one I need won't be in the box. If I need a straight pin, I'll find a multitude of safety pins, but no straight pin; and vice versa. And I have never had a shoelace break at home rather than some place of convenience. If I need twenty bucks, the only visitors I get will be those also needing twenty bucks. Like Vivian in *Pretty Woman* I seem too often to be a bum magnet.

I go to the store and invariably amongst the purchases will be some item that was wrong or missing something. No matter the complexity or simplicity of the item, if it requires assembly at home, I have learned to open the package and check for every screw, bolt and nut before leaving the store.

Drive through fast food joints? I will be missing something or be given someone else's order. My car will start unfailingly until I am in the most inconvenient possible circumstances for my battery to give up the ghost. The same goes for flat tires.

Now the reader is going to be quick to point out that these are things that simply go with the territory of life. They happen to everybody. And most of these inconveniences are due to things like not paying attention to proper maintenance of your vehicle or simply not paying attention period!

But they remind me of insurance. Let us say that you have insurance to cover virtually every possibility. The premiums would bankrupt the average person. Which brings me to the subject of the wisdom of living simply; or to put it another way, the advantages of poverty.

In my travels in Southern states, I noticed the quality of poverty is far superior to that in California. But they have had generations of practice beyond that of the Sunshine State.

People on welfare and at or below the poverty level in California can't find housing at a cost anywhere close to what you can find in places like Arkansas or Alabama. And poor people in California have a tough time running trotlines for catfish.

The pace of life is slower in Georgia and the Carolinas, Tennessee, Virginia and Kentucky. There is a reason for the Southern expression: Y' gotta make a mark t' see 'im move.

But no matter where you live, one of the advantages of poverty is not having a sense of impending doom. You don't lay awake at night wondering if the Dow or NASDAQ is going to take a dump and leave you bankrupt. If you are going to be nuked into subatomic particles floating in the ether of space, well, you're no worse off than Bill Gates in a similar condition.

And you certainly didn't lose or leave behind what he will. Comforting thought, that. In fact, those in poverty can actually take some solace in death as the great leveler regardless the former station or circumstances of the departed. Neither poverty nor death are fun subjects. And I wouldn't be mentioning them if it were not for their being the subject of recent debate with some of the readers of TAP.

The actual basis of debate has to do with discussion concerning wisdom. For those who are poor, it is easy enough to consider death as a sour grapes issue in respect to people like Bill Gates. But the recent passing of Charles Schulz calls something altogether different to mind.

Will we mourn the passing of Bill Gates as we do that of Sparky? I doubt it. And the reason for the difference lies in the definition of wisdom being using knowledge to the best end.

But how, some ask, do you equate Charles Schulz with wisdom? My reply: Schulz not only had a genuine gift as a cartoonist, he had a gift of using knowledge to the best end. Gates? This is arguable. Both became wealthy using their gifts and knowledge.

But the legacy of Schulz is one of very human elements. Using his endearing characters, he taught things about us as human beings to which virtually all of us could relate. Everyone can relate to several of the little folks in Peanuts. But how do you put a human face on the technology of Gates?

Even granting the great benefit of computer technology, is it knowledge put to the best end? Nuclear energy held at the first great promise for the benefit of humanity. Now? And it takes the benefits of computer technology to go to the moon and target nuclear missiles on individual cities thousands of miles distant.

I am far from being a Luddite. I am grateful for the benefits of technology and would far rather have electricity, for example, than have to go back to my wilderness experience on the mining claim. But if I could wave a magic wand and have the simplicity of living I had then with the benefits of technology that would be the best of all possible worlds to me. So the question of wisdom arises. I maintain the world has never achieved wisdom because the world has never known peace.

***

I'm looking at a couple of books that I hold very dear to me.

One is a New Testament with Psalms my great-grandmother bought from the Jewel Tea Salesman when I was only about four years old. She bought two, one for my brother Ronnie and one for me.

She read both of them through, underlining passages that were especially meaningful to her. In the flyleaf, she wrote a precious message in both books that she prayed Ronnie and I would take these things to heart and always live for Jesus. I still have my copy, but Ronnie lost his somewhere along the way. I hold it and read these precious words in my great-grandmother's own so-loving hand:

"Donald darling. Grandma has read and marked passages she loves to think you and Ronnie will read someday when she is gone. But dear, grandma will love you even if she is not here and will always know if you are good boys and serve and love God and His son Jesus. Read it dear and follow its teaching, it's the true and only road to heaven and the Christ who died for you. God guide and keep you always honest and truthful. A world of love my precious boy. Great-grandmother Mary W. Hammond."

The other book is one of the hymnals my grandfather used in his little church. Ronnie and I first learned the music of the church from this hymnal. How I have managed to hang on to both of these books is a virtual miracle.

And as I struggle to make sense of so many things contradictory to the things I was taught as a child, things I taught my own children and others, one of the most difficult is looking at these two books and remembering that they represent what was right and good in the sight of those who loved me so much and would never have taught me things they believed were untrue.

Even at four years of age, the sight was so indelibly imprinted on my mind that I can still see my great-grandmother reading those two New Testaments in the light of a coal oil lamp and underlining those passages. She would glance up at me once in awhile and smile.

She knew she was doing something of great value for this little boy who, she hoped and prayed, would one day grow up into a God-fearing man who would preach the Gospel for which I was dedicated at birth and given the name Samuel.

Ronnie and I always called her grandma though she was our great-grandmother. And she was the greatest love of our lives.

How does one get past the feeling that you are betraying such love when you set your feet on the path I have chosen, forsaking the one that resulted in my teaching and preaching to my children and others the very things I now know are false?

I do believe grandma and my other loved ones including my daughter Diana now know the truth. This is my only consolation. That knowing the truth, they do not condemn my present course as one of betrayal of their love. And as I write with these two books in front of me and at my touch, I know the real truth they evidence is the love those like grandma had for Ronnie and me.

***

Just how harmful is it to swear an oath on the Bible? The question has a lot of merit.

Since my doctorate is in human behavior, such questions pique my curiosity. Just how has swearing an oath on a Bible effected history? And how does it still do so?

In my critique of *To Kill A Mockingbird*, I point out how neither Mayella nor her father had any reluctance to swearing to tell the truth in court, with their hands on a Bible, and then lied knowing their false testimony would send another human being to his death. Apart from Harper Lee's Pulitzer-winning novel, history is replete with actual cases of this nature, and the practice continues to this day.

We still hold to the hoary tradition of swearing in leaders to elected office with the oath of office taken by such leaders placing their hands on a Bible. William Clinton took such an oath, as have many others.

That many such people place no credence in such oaths and do not feel bound by them may have something to do with their knowing the Bible is a book of myths and fables, and therefore not to be taken seriously. And under such circumstances, neither is their oath of office or such an oath in a court of law.

There are millions such as the Ewells of TKM who will tell you they believe the Bible to be the very word of God. And then lie with their hands on the book. We may reasonably ask whether such people do, in fact, believe the book to be the very word of God. Which gave rise to the expression: I wouldn't believe him with his hand on a stack of Bibles!

While this use, and abuse, of the Bible has had a grave import in history, I do wonder if such a historical superstition and mythology continues to have an impact on our present day systems of judicial and government affairs?

That people like President Clinton, and the Ewells of TKM, do not feel bound to tell the truth under an oath in such circumstances, one should not discount the fact, and should consider it, that such people will defend the Bible as being the word of God, a holy book, the Holy Scriptures.

Then how to account for the discrepancy in fact by such people failing to practice what they say they believe?

We are keenly aware of the parental admonition, if not always spoken at least believed: Do as I say, not as I do.

It would be a mistake to take swearing an oath with hand on the Bible as simple hypocrisy, or even cynicism. It is far more than that. And it is far more than the formality of ceremonial tradition.

Many people believe, or would like to believe, that God has provided an instruction manual for humanity in the form of the Bible. Some believe the Koran to be such a manual.

There is a strong element of the need to believe which is implicit in such things. It is a most seductive thought, that God has literally given instructions to humanity, has actually spoken to men and women, and that these instructions and words of His are to be found in a book.

But underlying this need to believe, there is a strong element of doubt about such things, even among those who profess to believe. And there is also a large element of superstition, which treats of such writings much as a talisman, a charm or rabbit's foot. Believing in things like luck and various mechanisms to enhance chance, belief in astrology, all such things are in the same category as belief in books like the Bible and Koran.

With this exception: Charms, etc. are not usually treated with the fervor of religious fanaticism so closely related to supposed divinity and deity.

When a person declares: God said! God told me!, God says in his word!, The Bible says!, these declarations by people are much different than superstitions such as beliefs in lucky charms and amulets.

But a superstition of thousands of years duration which has been proven to be without any foundation in fact and is still found relevant to a nation's culture, society and leadership cannot be discounted as being detrimental to that nation's functioning in a rational and civilized manner.

It is, therefore, a legitimate source of inquiry as to the extent of the Bible's influence for evil in our system of law and leadership.

To a rational mind, the very idea that the Bible is, in fact, the word of God is repugnant. Still, the rational mind has to deal with the fact that multiplied millions still hold the book to be, if not holy or sacred, venerated in some fashion.

Taken as simply a book, albeit one of antiquity in some respects, but keeping in mind there are other writings far more ancient, the Bible has no more to offer in wisdom or philosophy than many others. And the claims of supernatural origins are not only patently ridiculous, but are in fact injurious as per the wars fought and millions killed because of such an ignorant and prejudicial superstition.

***

Enlightened Self-interest has a basis in fact. It is a fact that the ownership of property brings responsibility with it. Since it is obvious that the owner of a home is going to be far more responsible for its maintenance than a tenant, that property ownership encourages working and building for the future, that it encourages people to be involved in the political process in order to protect their interests and investments, it is to a society's benefit to encourage home ownership.

Since the facts in such a case are evident, wisdom would dictate the application of these facts to the best ends. That is, wisdom dictates the encouraging of the ownership of property thus encouraging personal responsibility for the benefit of a society.

Such a society is far more likely to produce statesmen, rather than politicians, since such a society itself is future oriented. But the politician looks only to the next election and how he or she can stay in office rather than working for the future good.

Many, including the Founding Fathers, have seen the connection between property ownership and responsible citizenship, between property ownership and freedom. A man or woman is far more attendant on things, which impinge on their freedom, when it is their own property at stake. Failing to recognize this is the fatal flaw of systems such as Communism in its various forms.

As America sinks ever more deeply into a system where the distance between the rich and the poor widens, we face the concomitant loss of freedom. As this widening gap evidences itself more and more, the lack of wisdom becomes ever more apparent as well.

It is not wise to promote either the acquisition of wealth through avarice or to encourage indolence. A requirement of good government, especially on the part of those who would govern themselves, is to ensure the personal responsibility of the private citizen through enlightened self-interest. That is, to encourage the private ownership of property while at the same time discouraging the kind of avarice that would promote a wide division between the rich and the poor.

While the facts of this are painfully obvious, the application of these facts in wisdom is painfully missing. And since the history of the human race has been one of warfare, wisdom has quite obviously always been missing.

Personal ownership of property must be that: Property ownership. Not being in bondage to moneylenders through excessive mortgages.

But it would take wisdom to avoid such a system of mortgages, which is as old as civilization. And such a system rightly calls into question the whole matter of just how civilized are we, really?

As to America, slavery was introduced early on. And this system of slavery was not, in spite of the wise counsel of men like Franklin, abolished by our Constitution at the beginning. But the reason it was not has its roots in very complex matters.

While it is easy enough to damn those who supported slavery on the basis of economics, not to mention the sheer immorality of such a thing, it must also be kept in mind that it was such an economy that produced much of the wealth that promoted our beginnings as a nation. The question naturally arises, would we have been successful in our beginnings without such wealth? The further question must be asked whether we should have succeeded on such a basis?

I know it sounds heretical, but suppose there had been no American Revolution? Suppose the Revolution had its basis more in economics than in the altruistic rhetoric of freedom?

In no wise discounting the noble motives of men like Washington, Jefferson, Franklin, Paine and others, we can question, as Franklin and some others did including Alexis Tocqueville and Thoreau later on, whether a system of government that countenanced and even encouraged slavery could possibly ever succeed on the basis of freedom granted to only those of a particular race?

And to take the high ground, one must go back even further to the very origins of slavery itself and trace it to its basis in America. If one take the trouble to do so, the lack of wisdom in human history becomes evident since wealth in the hands of a few has invariably required slavery in some form or another. Our own forms of wage and welfare slavery are acutely self-evident.

It is equally evident that it is impossible to be both ignorant and free. Thanks in the greater part to our universities our own form of government has degenerated into a system that promotes a widening division between the haves and the have-nots, and between those who are truly educated and those who are not. It has become a system that promotes ignorance and indolence. Or, to put it another way, it has become a system that promotes slavery.

One of the ugliest manifestations of this form of slavery is found in the multiplied millions who, in perverted definitions of freedom and democracy, are housed, fed and clothed by the efforts of others, and therefore brings the greater majority into bondage whether productive workers or drones. Wisdom would dictate that such a system is doomed since it increasingly steals initiative from those who do the work.

If wisdom does indeed consist of the application of knowledge to the best ends, it therefore falls to those in authority to make such application. But in our case, those in authority are politicians rather than statesmen. As a result, such leaders as I have said are not future-oriented.

But to change this would require an enlightened and educated electorate. And how is this to be accomplished?

As to a *Weltanschauung*, a world-view, wisdom dictates that as long as religious and political hatreds exist and are even encouraged, the world can never know peace. Wisdom further dictates that sophistries and arguments based on a priori presumptive ignorance avail nothing.

Without argument, some machinery of government is necessary for the collective and individual good. But such a government must be the servant of the people. And it cannot be so without just leaders and just laws. And these require wisdom, which in turn requires an educated and enlightened electorate.

But I have long maintained wisdom is impossible without including women in philosophy on a basis of equal value with men; for it is philosophy, The Great Conversation, which guides the course of nations.

At present, we in California face the fact of a corrupt police department in Los Angeles that is making international news. Without question, when a society degenerates into one where avarice, is the motivating factor, abuses of authority are inevitable. When a so-called justice system is so corrupt that it becomes, in fact, how much justice you can afford, the end of a society that encourages this is easily predictable.

And if ignorance and prejudice are encouraged in any society or nation, the end of such is easily predictable. Thoreau said of his time: Shams and delusions are esteemed for soundest truths, while reality is fabulous.

Have things changed for the better in this respect in the 150 years since Henry penned those words? No, they have not. As the popularity of astrology, belief in UFOs, angels and demons of every description prove.

I have written much about the wisdom of childhood. Of children, Thoreau wrote: Children, who play life, discern its true law and relations more clearly than men, who fail to live it worthily, but who think that they are wiser by experience, that is, by failure ... I have always been regretting that I was not as wise as the day I was born.

While my friend Henry never married nor had children, he was brilliant enough to discern the truth of the wisdom of childhood, the truth brought out so brilliantly in Harper Lee's To Kill A Mockingbird.

But Henry and Harper Lee both wrote better than they knew in this respect. The real wisdom of childhood rests in the fact that children recognize injustice and weep over it.

And while both writers recognized this, neither realized the foundation of such wisdom, which derives from the ability of children to recognize and avoid evil with an instinctive hatred of it. But adults will place their hands on a book of myths and superstitions like the Bible and swear to tell the truth, and then lie on behalf of injustice. In part because many recognize the hypocrisy of swearing an oath with their hands placed on such a book and respond in kind.

This is only one example of the many hypocrisies that are taught to children by adults whereby children, as they grow older, lose the wisdom of childhood.

***

It is very difficult to take a dispassionate view of some subjects, particularly when the subject is that of religion or politics. But a real love of the truth, the foundation of wisdom, demands such dispassionate objectivity.

Few would accept the criticism of their not being objective. Most people like to consider themselves objective rather than prejudiced to a point of view. For the fanatic, whether of religion or politics, the person actually believes he or she possesses the truth and therefore is objective.

But when a fanatical point of view is subjected to reason and facts, the prejudice is obvious.

The Jesus believer, for example, will cry quite loudly that their belief in Jesus is not religion, but the truth; as with the devout Jew or Moslem. But such religious prejudices remain just those, religious prejudices.

A dispassionate and objective view of things strongly believed is virtually impossible for the individual who is persuaded of such things and has chosen to believe in spite of reason and facts to the contrary.

To speak of Albert Schweitzer or Mother Teresa is to speak of people who exemplify the goodness of self-sacrifice for the benefit of humanity. But to view the goodness of these two people in the light of the fact that their sacrificial goodness has not made the world better or safer, has not made the world less dangerous, is difficult to accept. But it is the truth.

The dispassionate facts of truth and wisdom do not allow of the sentiment of the emotions to rule. While the goodness of some serve well as models to emulate, such models do not change the world or make it less dangerous.

How often it is said that to touch just one life is a matter of great significance. And true as this may be, to touch just one life will not save the world or change the course of history for the better. To do this requires an idea that will touch and change multiplied millions of lives, not just a few.

History is replete with examples of ideas touching millions of lives that have resulted in hatred and bloodshed. Stalin and Hitler were idea men of this nature. The ideas of Jesus and Mohammed, though espousing peace, resulted in the slaughter of millions. And continue to generate hatreds and prejudices.

But no matter how the original intent of ideas may be distorted and twisted to evil ends, the fact that an idea that can persuade millions remains.

Such an idea, which would be embraced by multiplied millions, must be, by its very character, revolutionary. Emerson and Thoreau, even Napoleon, dreamed of a revolution without cannon or musket. But by denying women an equal voice in philosophy on the basis of equal value, such a revolution that would lead to world peace is impossible.

Opinion is our natural state of mind. Problems arise when opinion, too often uninformed, willingly or unwillingly, degenerates into prejudice or bigotry. We do in many instances decide what to think.

The choices of what to think in a given instance about any subject or person are the product of our circumstances of family, education, those we choose as authority sources, personal experiences, and society.

The religion or political ideology into which a person is born, for example, often plays a vital role in that person's deciding what to think as he or she grows into adulthood. The person's choices concerning the many issues of life, unless that person becomes well educated, will likely be prejudiced in harmful ways.

But as is abundantly clear, even a good education is no guarantee of overcoming prejudices. One must have an appetite, if you will, for a certain subject in order for that person to study and master that subject. Whether it is an appetite for art or science, without the appetite, the compelling desire to learn of the subject and pursue it to the length of mastery, it is a distasteful thing to be avoided.

Addiction is the result of unwise choices. The person, for any number of reasons, many quite complex, decides to think wrongly. Of the various problems with an addiction is that it can become so powerful that the person literally lives for it, their lives become totally devoted to satisfying the addiction. In this way, the person becomes utterly selfish with no consideration for anyone or anything that gets in the way of satisfying the addiction.

The religious or political fanatic is an addict of passions, which overrule logic and reason; and, in many instances, any vestige of true conscience or compassion. The addiction to a belief can become so powerful it literally overrules what we would call civilized behavior. In this way the fanatic is no different from a person addicted to drugs.

The decisions one makes as to what to think are complex in the extreme when analyzed concerning their roots. Using Roman Catholicism as an example, particularly if the person is born and raised into it, has many conveniences such as the Confessional to expiate what the system considers sin. If, because of the choice of what to believe, what to think, results in an easing of what we call conscience, the reason for choosing to think in this fashion is obvious.

But when such a choice, a decision to think in a particular way, is used as a mechanism to excuse what would be considered criminal behavior such as molestation or murder, the rational mind finds the use of such a mechanism as the Confessional as a means of easing conscience repugnant.

No less is the mechanism of the Protestant version of the Confessional subject to such a use for selfish ends. To say a sin, a criminal act such as molestation or murder, is forgiven and washed away by the blood of Jesus is no less repugnant to a rational and civilized mind. Particularly when no demand is made on the conscience for real contrition and restitution for the sin, the crime, committed.

Along with the circumstances of birth, we choose in large part what we want to believe based on our interpretation of what we want the world to be. We may believe it should be a Methodist, Catholic, Republican or Democrat world. In far too many cases, such beliefs are no better than placebos.

People are quick to put their faith in placebos, like the efficacy of magnets for sore joints, without any benefit of science such as double-blind studies.

Quacks turn a quick buck by preying on the need of people to believe. There are few things as true as the poster of Fox Mulder: I want to believe! And whether it is the Bible, Koran, space aliens and UFOs, the need to believe too often transcends science or even common sense.

Recently, some quack was making quite a lot of money by selling vials of liquid for twenty dollars each. They were advertised as being Stabilized oxygen molecules in a solution of distilled water and sodium chloride. That this is only salt water didn't deter people from sending in their money. The charlatan depended, rightly, on the ignorance of people and their need to believe.

Physicist Robert Park has a web site "What's New?" that debunks much of this kind of thing. But few want what they choose to believe challenged, let alone debunked.

When a person makes the decision to think in a certain way, and that way is colored or distorted by choosing a belief over rational facts, the result is a prejudice. Just as many tried to justify slavery in this nation by choosing to believe it was morally correct to own other human beings as chattel, the choice to believe in such a thing is no less repugnant to what is rightly called the rational and civilized mind.

If someone tries to justify the deification of a human being such as Jesus or Mohammed, if they say books like the Bible or Koran are the very word of God, such a choice to decide to believe in such things repugnant to reason are as much the result of addiction as anything else. Whether the prejudice is one of religion or politics, the results of such addiction to belief over reason are just as harmful to humanity as a whole.

While examples of such addictions can be multiplied, suffice it to say that the rational mind always finds addiction repugnant and harmful.

****

With all the political rhetoric surrounding gun control, politicians are ducking the real problem, and that is the decades-old attack on families. I know politics is the profession of avoiding specifics because dealing with specifics foments controversy and puts the individual on the spot. As a result, glittering generalities are the norm in politics.

In spite of oft time appearances, I know the great majority of politicians are intelligent and educated people. As a result, I write and act on the assumption that these people know the facts. But we have evolved a political system that places elected leaders at risk to acknowledge the truth.

The recent murder of little Kayla Rolland in Michigan is not a gun issue. And I believe the elected leadership knows this. It is a family issue. It is the disintegration of families that is the root and origin of such evil in society. As a consequence, there are literally millions of children at risk in America.

One of the most brilliant men who ever lived, and one of the undisputed greatest essayists, Charles Lamb, told a story of his childhood that virtually every one of us should take to heart.

He said that when he was a small child, he saw a woodcut in a book that portrayed the Witch of Endor summoning the prophet Samuel from the grave. That picture, he said, impacted his mind so dreadfully he could no longer lie in bed at night without a lighted candle. Even as an adult, that picture haunted him and robbed him of sleep. He said he fervently wished he had never been exposed to the picture as a child, and he warned parents to

65

protect their little ones from such a thing, that it would continue to impact their lives as adults.

I had a similar experience as a child when my mother took me to see the film *The Picture of Dorian Gray*. I was only five years old and that film had the same impact on me as a small child that Charles Lamb describes.

It isn't that adults, that elected leaders, don't know that the horrors on TV and in films, the violent cartoons and sexual license, are harmful to children. But they fail to act on this knowledge. And if a woodcut, relatively innocent by today's lack of standards, could so impact Charles Lamb as a child, how monumentally more destructive to children are the things that pass as art and entertainment to children today!

But if adults, and most especially our elected leaders, know this, the legitimate question is why they do not address the problem in specifics? The answer has to be that family and children are not the priority of our society that they should be.

It is my conviction that America has the responsibility above all other nations in proving its concern for children and the family structure that is the foundation of all civilized societies.

It is my further conviction that the proposed amendment will evidence this concern on the part of Americans, that it will carry the message to the world that we are concerned for the future of children and intend to make them our proper priority. I also contend that whoever become our candidates for President, these two men must select a woman as their running mate.

These two things, the amendment and the selection of a woman in our highest elected office, send the right message to the world. And it is a message desperately needed by the whole world, a demon-haunted and dangerous world, which is hungry for such a message of hope for a future.

Having taught in the Ghetto of Watts and the Barrio of East San Jose, I am acutely aware of the abominable conditions surrounding children such as that of the child who killed another child in Michigan.

I write extensively of the problems confronting children. As I am a writer and publisher with a very broad background in education and Social Services, with three web sites and working closely with many organizations concerning child abuse, many people take my views on the subject very seriously.

Because of this kind of involvement and education, I know I have something to say of value in the following remarks

My recently having had to respond to a lady who was taking me to task for being an anti-abortionist, I was forced to reflect once more on the difficulty of being on the side of the angels. Not that I believe myself to be so since I do not believe in angels to begin with, but it is a false perception of me that so many have.

It is eminently logical to recognize the fact that abortion as a means of contraception devalues life. It is further logical to recognize the fact that women are their own worst enemies by encouraging abortion since the great majority of abortions throughout the world are of unwanted girl babies.

It should also be noted that irresponsible men find it to their advantage to encourage abortion as a means of contraception for obviously selfish reasons.

Nor should it be denied that women would like to have their cake and eat it too by their not adhering to standards of responsibility where sexual activity is concerned. The attitude seems to be that if boys and men are not held accountable, why should we be responsible?

Such selfishness and personal irresponsibility on the part of both genders produces the most innocent of all victims: Babies.

Logic dictates that abortion teaches children that life has no real value. And a society that encourages, even rewards, irresponsible sex at the earliest age and teaches that unwanted babies have no value has to be inviting the worst kind of behavior detrimental to civilized life.

I make far more enemies than friends because I will not excuse either men or women for their irresponsibility, particularly in regard to being bad citizens. If we have unjust laws and corrupt police, judges and legislators, it is because the average citizen is a bad citizen. We get the kind of laws, justice and leadership we actively support. That is fact, not opinion.

In addressing the origins of evil, it is apparent to me that people do not think about this issue. The proof of this is in attempts to deal with things like gun control and abortion.

If a child takes a gun to school, where did he get the weapon? Especially when that child is only six or seven years old? Obviously an adult is somewhere responsible for this happening.

Just law must look to the adult who is responsible for that gun and hold that adult accountable.

If a child is continually truant the parents must be held accountable. But I am as quick as any other parent to recognize the lack of means on the part of parents to enforce the necessary discipline to make a child go to school.

But suppose a few thousand parents began to be arrested and jailed on this basis? Suppose the responsible adults were prosecuted and jailed when a child takes a gun to school? Suppose the law made adults truly responsible for the actions of their children? Suppose adult parents had to bear the responsibility of the unwanted pregnancies of their children?

We would then be forced to face the fact that the very laws intended for the benefit of children have taken away parental authority. And adults, bad citizens, allowed this to happen.

Most certainly the recent illogical political posturing about trigger locks for guns is pathetic. Such devices would only prevent the legitimate use of guns by those threatened by criminals. Do not disarm the responsible, law-abiding citizen! Hold criminals, including those adults who do not effectively keep guns out of the reach of children, responsible for the abuse of guns. If the punishment were severe enough, if legislators focused on the criminal abuse of guns, the problem would be solved.

And what is it but political posturing when President Clinton says trigger locks would prevent tragedies such as that in Michigan? Does anyone of any sense think the criminals surrounding that child would have had a trigger lock on that pistol? No more so than in thousands of other like criminal environments surrounding children. And to point to tragedies such as that in Columbine as justification for such posturing is, to my mind, unconscionable!

The fact that I make more enemies than friends by pointing out things of this nature speaks for itself. Adults do not want to bear the responsibility for their own lack of being responsible, their failure to be good citizens. And when it comes to the origins of evil, there is none so evident as this failure on the part of the freest people in history failing to be vigilant in remaining so.

It is the lack of a responsible and enlightened electorate that has given government inordinate power over the people governed. It seems Americans long ago gave up the ideal of self-government into the hands of the state and federal government.

Nowhere is this so clearly demonstrated as in the willingness of people to allow government to make decisions detrimental to families, decisions that have encouraged the destruction of families.

What is needed is to bring this issue into open debate, to discuss the real causes, the real origins of the kinds of evil that have proven so destructive to our children, and our entire society.

This is one of the primary goals of my proposed amendment for the protection of children from child molesters. As a society, we must honestly face the very low priority given to our future, our children.

The battle for the rights that Negroes fought for here in America are insignificant compared to the battle for the right of a child to an innocent and protected childhood that is the most basic and fundamental of all human rights, a right beyond any consideration of those denied on the basis of gender, race, religion or politics.

I have gone to extraordinary lengths to understand and obtain primary source material concerning the issues of racial hatred and prejudice. I have gone to extraordinary lengths to encourage women to face up to their responsibility in forming a philosophy of their own which would give them a voice on the basis of equal value to men.

But in none of these has the issue been so difficult as that of getting people to face their failure to give children the priority they not only deserve, but also must have for the sake of our future as a species.

In all of the rhetoric permeating the political posturing of candidates, one thing will be conspicuous by its absence: Wisdom. None of the candidates have, or will, point to the universities being guilty of the dumbing down of America, of being guilty of producing the leaders in the schools, government, the judiciary and entertainment industry who have been taught that there are no moral absolutes, no absolutes of civilized behavior.

Virtually all tyranny begins and surrounds itself in the rhetoric and guise of freedom and liberty. In this way, perversion becomes alternative lifestyle and to criticize it makes the critic a bigot. Freedom of expression becomes license to promote perversion and violence. The most violent of so-called cartoons for children, exposing children to continual sex and violence by the entertainment industry, is excused on this basis.

With enough of this kind of propaganda, as Hitler and Goebbels so well knew and practiced, a nation becomes inured to every kind of lie and begins to accept the lie and deny the truth.

The truth of the case of a small child without any semblance of conscience murdering another child can be found in a society that not only lacks wisdom, but also promotes perversion and violence in the high-flown rhetoric of freedom and liberty but also denies any culpability for consequences.

Where, I have to ask myself in all reason, are the black leaders who are denouncing the racial characteristics of murders like those in Michigan and Philadelphia? They are too busy denouncing white racism because that is politically correct and fomented by the universities, the media and politicians.

A large part of the problem impinging on that shooting of the little girl, Kayla Rolland, in Michigan, apart from the obvious environment promoting racism and criminal violence of the boy who shot her, is the fact that there is so much violence on TV where every dispute is settled with a gun.

Every cop show tells children that shooting people is ok. Yet 95 per cent of police never draw their weapon during their whole time of service. But this misperception excusing violence has a bottom line, and that bottom line is ratings, which means money.

The entertainment industry is as much to blame as the drug environment and failed systems of justice, education and social services for what happened in Michigan. And as I point out, it is the universities, which preach there are no standards, no absolutes of civilized morality that produces the leaders in the entertainment industry as well as the Clintons, et al.

In my critique of To Kill A Mockingbird, I make it plain that it is our indifference to children throughout the whole of society that has taught our children we care nothing for them or their future. The truth of this fact is played out now on national and international TV where children are killing children. What is this but a reaction to the indifference of a society towards its children?

It is a fact that a nation that does not cherish its children has no future as a nation. Nor does it deserve one!

***

When it comes to our children, there should not be any politically sectarian boundaries. And whether you agree with my proposed amendment for the protection of children or not, I know you will agree that our children are suffering from a failed system of public education.

It was in another life it seems that I sat with California State Senator Ed Davis in his office in Sacramento. We had established a warm correspondence when he was LAPD Chief of Police and I was a fledgling freshman teacher at David Starr Jordan in the Watts district of South Central Los Angeles.

By the time of this meeting, I was no longer the naive young man who thought the problems in education would be relatively easy to fix. The travesty of the sixties in education such as Innovative Designs In Learning that cast out the things that had worked and instituted the things that made no sense whatsoever had done their dirty work. Children were going to pay the price of the adult abrogation of responsibility for their education.

The sacred cows remain the same, the universities which produced a failed system of public education which were untouchable then and are equally untouchable today in spite of the damning indictment of them through research and writing like that of Professor Reginald G. Damerell and so many others including myself.

I focused on Accountability in Education in my own Ph.D. dissertation only to discover it was such a hot button no publisher would touch it. Only one ed. publisher at the time was honest enough to tell me that the material in my dissertation was such an indictment of the schools he didn't dare publish it!

I discovered that the school systems from the universities on down are so rife with corruption and such cronyism and nepotism as to be inbred to the point of impotence. Then I discovered that legislators were dedicated to asking the very people who created the problems in education for answers to the very problems they had created! Insane on the face of it!

And while I would never accuse the educational hierarchy of the purposeful destruction of public education, I do say they could not have better designed a system for failure had they done so intentionally!

I found that schools are not held fiscally accountable because of such creative bookkeeping it is impossible to audit them and the money is embezzled at will in the amount of countless hundreds of millions of dollars every year throughout California alone. The fox that guards the henhouse, the State Department of Education, has its reasons for not wanting this publicized, not the least of these being the public outcry it would cause together with the potential loss of so much federal funding.

I discovered first hand how tenure was abused to the point that the worst teachers who wouldn't have been allowed to continue to work a week in the private sector were guaranteed jobs for life in education, especially in the universities, and children and college students paid the price for such incompetence and lack of accountability throughout the entire system of public education.

I was at ground zero when Special Education began to be the cash cow for schools, a blank check no one questioned, and as empire building at its very worst became the norm in the public schools. Had I not personally witnessed what I have in this system alone, I don't think anyone could fictionalize the enormous boondoggle of this single education bureaucracy!

I began to try to tell parents and legislators like Ed Davis and Gary Hart, governors like Pete Wilson, that the problems for children in education were not as bad as they thought, they were far, far worse!

I saw our classrooms being filled with teachers, products of the universities, who could not spell or do arithmetic and no one dared say anything about it! Why not? Because virtually every leader throughout society is a university graduate and would never criticize the institutions on which their own academic credibility and future success were based!

And teachers such as me with industry backgrounds knew the Ivory Tower mind-set was incapable of preparing children for real life. And most teachers who witnessed the terrible destruction of education would not speak out for fear of losing their jobs or becoming pariahs.

It has become the stock in trade of politicians to talk about educational reform. But politics being the trade of generalities does not deal with specifics and politicians always evade answering in specifics because they do not have any specifics when it comes to educational reform (or a host of other problems)!

No one knows better than I the enormity of the problems in education and the enormity of what will be required to fix them.

But as long as our children are defrauded of an education because politicians refuse to deal with the specifics, or even worse, have no idea of what the specifics are, I will continue to be a voice raised against the tragedy of ignorance that has invaded America and become the legacy of so-called educators and their crony political quislings passed on to our children.

Governor Gray Davis saw fit to pass my critique of To Kill A Mockingbird on to State Senator Gary Hart, the head of California's Education Committee. Senator Hart sent me a kind Thank you note.

Politicians have always been very gracious in thanking me for my concerns about our children and their education. But not a single one has ever followed through by doing the hard things my own research and experience proves need to be done. One school board president who tried to institute just a couple of the needed reforms I had suggested lost in the next election because of this.

In spite of my cautionary words, he didn't believe the furor this would cause among teachers who actively campaigned (illegally of course) against him in their very classrooms, even sending flyers produced in the school audio/visual department home with their pupils and taking out ads in the local paper against this man for re-election.

Of course, things were made pretty hot for me as well. I was betraying my kind and biting the hand that fed me.

It is easy to do the trend-forecast of where the present concerns about the latest enormously expensive and tragic boondoggle of education, that of Special Education, will lead. Nowhere. Once the noise dies down, it will be back to business as usual. The educational hierarchy from the universities on down depends on this.

Oh yes, audits there will be. A few arrests may even be made for blatant offenses and thefts that cannot be hidden regardless the creative book- and record keeping. The lawsuits will proliferate and taxpayers will foot the bill as usual while the guilty in the schools from the universities on down will wring their hands and refuse to accept any responsibility.

But like the IRS and California's Social Services, particularly Child Protective Services, the enormity of the task will make any meaningful audits virtually impossible. The educational hierarchy knows and depends on this to, as one principal told me, do their own dirty laundry and not expose it to the public.

His refreshing candor reminded me of that of a Downey Chief of Police who told me in an interview: We're not here to help people; we're here to slam the door on them!

Like expressed concern about child abuse, the problems in the Evil Empire of Special Education will sell papers and make for News at Eleven and political rhetoric for a while. And then, quietly fade away until someone sees a way of making headlines and political hay of it once more.

Harper Lee addressed the failure of the schools in Thirties' Alabama. I witnessed it as a teacher in Sixties' California. And not just during my tenure in the war zones of the ghetto of Watts and the barrio of East San Jose, but places like lily-white Castro Valley and throughout Stanislaus County; and, of course, my home county of Kern, the target of Edward Hume's Pulitzer-winning book.

It was in my home County of Kern that I had a group of high school seniors applaud me for telling them: Any real education you get here will be because you earnestly desire and work for it, not because this school is really prepared and dedicated to giving you an education.

These seniors knew the truth of what I was telling them. Their applause was for my being the only adult school authority that had made such a bald and honest confession to them of the failure of the school system to provide them the opportunity for an education, had in fact defrauded them of an education.

The applause caught the attention of teachers and administrators. When they discovered the reason for it, I was not invited back. But I knew that would be the result. I've always been known as a high roller on behalf of the kids against the system. It is one reason I have worked in so many different school systems in spite of reaching tenure in two of them.

Tragically for our children and young people, my words to that group of seniors would apply with equal truth in schools across America. And while young people like the class of seniors mentioned know the truth, and will applaud me for telling it like it is, it doesn't win me any friends among those adult authorities who should be my friends for telling it like it is.

The enormous fraud of Special Education has succeeded because those outside the system have no idea of what it is really all about. To understand how this is possible, you must understand that the field of education as a whole has its own manufactured language, a foreign language if you will that admits of no outsiders learning it.

Unlike true academic subjects, education is lacking any empirical body of knowledge itself and has borrowed wholesale from legitimate disciplines in an attempt to legitimize itself. The resulting language of education is to be compared with a corrupt kind of pidgin; a virtual gobbledygook best compared with meaningless psychobabble and its own kind of fraternal understandings available only to members of the club.

The system of Special Ed. particularly is a Byzantine labyrinthine monstrosity of nonsense within a larger system of nonsense. The language of Special Ed. is representative of the whole *Alice in Wonderland* field of education that reflects the language of the Jabberwocky. But unlike that children's piece, the nonsensical words and phrases of Special Ed. make the pretense of sensibility.

In no other field of education is this smoke screen of pretended expertise of knowing what you are talking about when you do not through an invention of the imagination so evident as in Special Ed.

If things are ever going to take a turn for the better in education, they will only do so when leaders such as you take on the responsibility for confronting this enormous fraud and call it what it is: An Enormous Fraud!

The entire system of education must be called to account and held accountable. But it will take leaders of rare courage and a genuine concern for the welfare of America's children to bring this to pass.

We knew in 1954 that the bottom 15 per cent of college graduates were going into the field of education and nothing was done to correct this. Those responsible in the universities did nothing to change this and encourage the best and brightest to enter our classrooms. Today, we live with the result of this failure on the part of the universities to act and be responsible.

***

Very few people outside the systems of entertainment and the universities know of the inordinate power of homosexuals within these. But when you wonder at the violent cartoon shows on TV, these are the products of the power of homosexuals who have taken over so much of children's programming.

The agenda of homosexuals is to promote their perversion and their target audience is children. The TV show Park Place is a perfect example of this.

You may well wonder at the part violence plays in this since the perception of so-called Gays, who are anything but gay in the correct use of the term, is one of non-violence. Thanks to Tom Hanks and Leonardo DiCaprio et al, every pervert is a sensitive artist.

Nothing could be further from the truth. Yet Hollywood and the universities promote this Big Lie. And since perversion has infected so much of our state and federal legislatures, it explains why so many in these institutions support the homosexual agenda.

As a deist, I believe in God but I despise systems of religion as superstition and no better than things like astrology, and having done far more harm than good throughout history. So I can hardly have a personal religious bias myself in regard to perversion.

But I do have a logical basis, one not dependant on whether one believes in God or not, upon which to confront homosexuals for the bullying tactics they employ. For example, how is it that a perfectly logical and normal revulsion to perversion is now called homophobic? Who made this a politically correct term? And for what purpose? One only has to look to the universities and the propaganda tactics of Hitler and Goebbels to understand this.

Thanks to the universities, the judiciary and Hollywood, it is politically correct to support perversion and incorrect to support family and family values. It is correct to attack white racism and incorrect to attack minority racism.

While racism on the part of whites against those of color is rightly denounced, where are the mobs of protesting marchers denouncing the racism of blacks against whites? A little white boy is dragged to death by a black man, a black man goes on a killing spree shooting white people loudly proclaiming his intentions of seeking out white people to murder, and a black boy murders a white girl at school. But there is no outrage on the part of black leaders against these criminal acts. Why is it that Jesse Jackson, Al Sharpton, Louis Farrakhan, and Alan Keyes are not denouncing these criminal acts of blacks against whites and asking for demonstrations against such racism on the part of black people?

It should be patently obvious that this is a rhetorical question. It is politically correct to denounce and demonstrate against white racism, but not black or Hispanic racism. And all the evidence, which is quite substantial, of racism on the part of white people does not excuse its parallel on the part of non-whites.

As I have pointed out to these black leaders, they do their own people a great disservice and cause grave harm to their own cause by not denouncing and demonstrating against such things in their own ranks. There is a monumental loss of credibility as a result. You simply do not denounce unfairness and injustice on the part of one group without attacking these things with equal fervor among your own and rightly expects to be taken seriously.

Religion, Race, and Politics are the predominant causes of an increasingly dangerous and demon-haunted world. Even as I write, the tensions between China and Taiwan, between India and Pakistan grow increasingly dangerous. North Korea seems determined on a nuclear arsenal. The conflicts in Ireland and Africa show no signs of abating. And in each of these cases, the propaganda of political correctness holds sway, and is often rooted in religious prejudices such as those of India and Pakistan. And in Israel, moderate politics is threatened by religious fanaticism, which finds its match in the abominably cruel and totally uncivilized fanaticism of the Moslem Taliban.

Just recently Bill Bradley in his concession speech quoted Vince Lombardi: Winning isn't everything, it is the only thing! And for fanatics, this is absolutely true! And whether the fanaticism of race, religion or politics, winning is the only thing! But far too many people supposing themselves to be good people don't get the message. And that message is very direct and eminently logical:

Evil can only be overcome by the good when the good confronts the evil with equal determination to win!

It is politically correct to attack gun owners and incorrect to support the rights of law-abiding citizens to protect themselves against criminals who abuse the use of guns. It is politically correct to attack legitimate, law-abiding gun owners instead of making the criminal abuse of guns the legitimate goal of prosecution.

It is politically correct to make the use of marijuana a crime and continue to leave tobacco and alcohol legal drugs. And in all reason we must ask why alcohol has not been attacked with the same fervor as tobacco? We need only look to the drunks in Congress to answer that one. Why is the drug war one that the leadership continues to pursue yet knows cannot be won? Here, as usual, follow the money is part of the answer. I say part because the rest has to do with power over the people and influence in the major drug-supplying countries like Mexico and Colombia.

Why is it politically incorrect to address the extreme abuse of law and taxpayer expense of illegal aliens when it is patently obvious that no other nation in the world puts up with this insanity, when logic dictates that no nation that cannot control its borders can survive? Follow the money; and the building of political agendas and empires. And how did it become politically correct to refer to these criminals as immigrants instead of what they are in fact: criminal illegal aliens? As with the bullying propaganda tactics used by perverts to advance their cause, call all those racists who oppose illegal, and by definition criminal, aliens entering America.

Lincoln could not understand why the free black leadership opposed sending ex-slaves to a country of their own after the Civil War? But anyone who has read historian Claude Bowers' definitive work The Tragic Era knows the answer: Money and power. Those black leaders had it made and were not about to sacrifice what they had and their hopes for having even more for the freed slaves.

Why is making English the national language politically incorrect? Again: Money and political power.

It continues to be politically correct to arrest and prosecute women as prostitutes but not the men who hire them. But what makes people like J.F. Kennedy and W.J. Clinton exempt from treating women like prostitutes and jail women for prostitution? What kind of message does this send everyone, children as well as adults? No, I'm not that naïve, but I know it still isn't right. Anymore than it makes me naïve to know we have a justice system that is one of how much justice you can afford.

Why isn't the murder of a child of equal gravity to that of a politician or policeman? Why is molestation not treated as a crime of the very gravest consequences to the whole of society? And why is it that the black leadership never addresses this issue which is pandemic in black communities and leads to the early puberty of black children, something that the CDC and medical community at large knows but wont mention? Talk about politically incorrect!

With over a quarter-million accidents a year caused by those that run red lights that disagrees that cameras that record these drivers and enables a system that sends them a ticket is not a good idea? It won't be those whose cars, even lives, are destroyed by these law-breakers. Too many of whom are not even licensed or insured! Will anyone disagree who has had to bury a child killed by these law-breakers?

As politicians wring their hands and posture with endless rhetoric over the murder of a child by another child, where are their concerns properly directed at an entire society of their making which has exhibited little but indifference toward children? The history of lip service by politicians that is only given for the reasons of an election or staying in office, not out of true concern for children, is evident to all.

I would be the last to say that addressing the real evils in society is an easy task. But I would also be the last to say that we have an elected leadership capable of addressing these evils.

But I won't let average citizens off the hook either. If you are not politically knowledgeable and active, you are a part of the problem as well. We get the kind of leadership we actively support!

Reform in education is impossible when the very people who created the problems are asked for solutions. But these people who created the problems in education are the very same who will say a six year old boy does not know what he is doing when he shoots another child to death. I would ask the reasonable question of these people: At what age does a child become aware that shooting another child to death is wrong? The so-called experts have no answer to this. But they are very quick to say it isn't six years old.

I totally disagree. I have known children this age that are fully aware of their actions. But such things are generally seen in their cruelty to animals and later acted out toward people. In such cases, where are the responsible adults who should be held accountable for their children?

But the experts in the schools, law, psychology will make every excuse to keep from being held accountable when the cruelty and bullying behavior of some children results in the murder of another child. Why do we not hold these experts accountable for their developing a system that creates victims in our schools and never holds the victimizer accountable or their parents?

Then we come back to the origins of an evil that has done so much to destroy families then denies any culpability for the consequences; it is truly an insane system, which continues to create victims, and does nothing to effectively remove the bullying predators of whatever age or for whatever reason they are so.

But there is one inescapable fact that the great majority of thinking people accept: No child, regardless of environment, genetics, or whatever, who bullies and threatens other children should be allowed to put other children at risk. The family and the schools should be held responsible for not allowing these kinds of children to put other children at risk!

We are now hearing India and Pakistan saying that their possession of nuclear arms is a rite of passage and a Coming of age! And I cannot help but think of that six-year-old boy shooting another six-year-old child to death. Accountability? Where do we see that? Not in any society which will excuse all manner of insanity and irresponsibility. Accountability is the purview of a civilized society that has absolutes of civilized behavior.

But as surely as k+w=p, k-w=a (the a standing for Armageddon). And what will be the result of the conflict between China and Taiwan? Israel and Moslem nations? North and South Korea?

We live in a world where three billion people have never received a phone call, where there are far too many unproductive mouths to feed, where superstitious nations are unwilling to practice birth control and mutilate children by circumcision and are willing to commit nuclear murder and even suicide in the name of their peculiar God!

We are surrounded in America with social epidemics of every description. Too many are professors and teachers who should not be, too many police who should not be, too many judges, legislators, etc. who should not be. Thanks to the universities and the lack of an enlightened electorate, our social and legal institutions are a shambles.

As physicist Michio Kaku and others have warned, nuclear annihilation looms. And as I keep pointing out, we will either attain wisdom or the logical end of humanity will be Armageddon!

CHAPTER FOUR

Two of the most endearing qualities of a child are trust and imagination. They will believe in magic, they thrill to stories of fairies and enchanted lands. Christmas, Santa Claus, the Easter Bunny, stories of birds and animals, enchanted islands and forests; these are the domain of childhood.

We don't forsake these things in adulthood. We continue to want our Merlins, Camelots, and enchanted glades. As parents, we enjoy making things like Santa and his elves and reindeer real to our children. All too quickly, we grow up and learn of the fantasies of childhood but the intent of parents in wanting their children exposed to the myths is the innocence of goodness.

Santa is the ultimate angel to a child. There isn't the slightest trace of evil connected to Santa; he could never do anything wrong or anything to hurt a child. Santa believes in children, in the innocence of childhood.

Our desire, as adults, to believe in angels follows the same pattern. We grow up and have to leave the myth of Santa, but we desperately want to continue to hold on to what he represents.

The history of Santa Claus is interesting. He is generally thought to derive from Saint Nicholas, the bishop of Myra about the end of the 4th or beginning of the 5th century. But no written document attests of this.

Legends surround the bishop who became the patron saint of children and sailors. These legends and devotion to the saint penetrated into every part of the world.

Early Protestant Dutch settlers in what was to become New York replaced St. Nicholas (Sinter Claes in Dutch) with Santa Claus. The change to Father Christmas began in Germany and extended into other countries through the Reformed Churches.

No other saint of the church has the popularity of St. Nicholas when it comes to children. And none other made the transition through the Reformation to acceptability in Protestantism, though not, of course, in the tradition of Catholicism. But it would be of interest to pursue the question of why both systems of religion find Santa acceptable?

The emphasis of Santa relating to children is the basis of his enduring popularity. He personifies the love of children and the best of childhood as no other figure, historical or mythological.

Yes, Virginia, there is a Santa Claus. Who will forget these words to a little girl written by Francis Church for the New York Sun in 1897?

His concluding words to little Virginia:

"Alas! How dreary would be the world if there were no Santa Claus. It would be as dreary as if there were no Virginias. There would be no childlike faith then, no poetry, no romance, to make tolerable this existence...the eternal light with which childhood fills the world would be extinguished... The most real things in the world are those that neither children or men can see. Did you ever see fairies dancing on the lawn? Of course not, but that's no proof that they are not there. Nobody can conceive or imagine all the wonders there are unseen and unseeable in the world. Thank God! He lives, and he lives forever. A thousand years from now, Virginia, nay, ten times ten thousand years from now, he will continue to make glad the heart of childhood."

Do I believe in Santa Claus? Of course! I couldn't be a poet otherwise; I would lose the best part of the man that makes me so, the child within.

The Christmas season with the distinctive music and decorations, the buying of gifts, the celebration of the hope of peace on earth, is something none of us would like to see disappear.

Singing Jingle Bells, Santa Claus is Coming to Town and reading 'T Was the Night Before Christmas celebrate the season. Children write letters to Santa and hang stockings with care and we watch A Christmas Carol, It's a Wonderful Life and Miracle on 34th Street. We have added The Grinch to the story of Scrooge, there is now a Charlie Brown Christmas, Frosty the Snowman, The Little Drummer Boy, Rudolph and so many more with all the innocence, charm and fantasy of childhood.

The story of the North Pole, Santa's home and the workshop of elves, the magic of Santa's being able to visit every home with a child in a single night, going down chimneys, his Ho, Ho, Ho, children leaving cookies and milk for him and, very important, Santa knows if you have been bad or good, naughty or nice.

Believing in Santa is as natural to a child as faith and prayer. George Beverly Shea sings a beautiful song: If I Could Pray as a Child Again. How many of us, as adults, haven't wished for this?

Childhood is of so very short duration, such a short time in which to teach and encourage children in the things that will prepare them for adulthood. The whole concept of Santa is one of the things that will do this. We know that all too soon our children will face the realities of the denouement of Santa. But the lesson of goodness and the memory of the magic and innocence of childhood, like the healing power of a mother's kiss, should remain.

Of the greatest importance is the fact that Santa loves all children no matter the physical or mental differences, the race, religion or geography. This is what children learn from Santa.

The non-Christian world recognizes the jolly old elf, separating him from sectarian religious beliefs. He is welcome in Turkey, China, Cuba, and even Iraq!

And unlike the cruel religious wars of Christianity, Judaism and Islam, none have ever been fought over Santa Claus.

To my Christian friends I would say Santa is not the enemy of Christ. Quite the contrary. Santa epitomizes the very essence of the Gospel. Don't you make Santa the enemy of Christ! How I wish the emphasis of Santa on children was practiced in the churches!

One Christmas, a store displayed Santa hanging on a cross. Many people were outraged but the storeowner said he was only trying to make people aware of how commercialized the season had become.

The philosophical aspect of this revolves around the substitution of Santa for Christ. People would yawn over a crucifix; but Santa? Perhaps, I say to myself, this may be the result of the virtually non-controversial universality of the goodness of Santa versus an image that separates people and one that has been steeped in controversy and bloodshed for nearly two thousand years and is still on going?

Some of you will remember a song, Green Christmas, by Stan Frieberg years ago that satirized the season. Many radio stations would not play it. But Frieberg was only following Charles Dickens' A Christmas Carol that made the name Scrooge a household word. But many religious people reviled Dickens because the emphasis of the story, as with Frieberg's song, was on the spirit of human goodness rather than Christ. The larger view of an entire humanity to which the Gospel makes a universal appeal is lost to such people.

It isn't surprising then that these people make Santa the enemy of Christ. It would be interesting, indeed, to know the thoughts of that early Bishop of Myra about this turn of events. But, of course, Santa turned out to be an expression of goodness, hope and belief that transcends all sectarianism chiefly because he is the champion of children and childhood.

Children are the basis upon which the peoples of the world can come together and coalesce for the common good of humanity. Once they are made the proper priority of humanity.

Far be it from me, as Rhett told Scarlet, to disabuse of the religious instruction of childhood, but it is far past time that humanity grew out of and overcame sectarian hatreds. Santa represents what the attitude of all adults should be toward children and childhood devoid of any evil.

Henry Adams said: Politics, as a practice, has always been the systematic organization of hatreds. Had it not been for the time frame, I think Adams would have included religion in the statement. But only a poet or a child would point to Santa as another direction for humanity.

THE AMERICAN POET

DECEMBER 7, 2000

It is without fear of contradiction one of the most dreary and thankless of tasks to confront Emerson's "sluggish mind of the masses, slow to the incursion of reason." The Presidential election of year 2k provides a perfect example of Emerson's indictment.

Some years ago I learned the truth of "A wise man lives simply" and began to subscribe to Thoreau's evaluation "... a man is rich in proportion to the number of things which he can afford to let alone."

But because of my many years of working with children in the schools, some of those years spent in the worst possible environments such as the Watts District of Los Angeles, I find there are some things I can't seem to "let alone."

If we can safely assume, as many writers and philosophers have, that the home and family is the foundation of a society, we can easily see where America has gone wrong. In 1902 Jacob Riis wrote of ... the vicious cycle of poverty, inadequate education and limited opportunity. "The homes, the family, are the rallying points of civilization. The greatness of a city (or nation) is to be measured, not by its balance sheets of exports and imports, not by its fleet of merchantmen, or by its miles of paved streets, nor even by its colleges, its art museums, its schools of learning, but by its homes."

It is the home, as the foundation of society, which is expected to produce the kind of leadership that will be dedicated to the advancement of a civilized society. And where homes fail, so the failure of a society.

The real failure of America, thanks in large part to its amoral universities, has been the failure to promote good homes. This failure can be traced directly to our universities that long ago began to teach that there are no moral absolutes, no real standards of behavior or academic accomplishment.

The universities knew in 1954 that the lowest fifteen per cent of college graduates were going into education. Nothing was done to change this. We live today with the results known as "The Dumbing Down of America."

Didn't the leaders of America, all products of the universities, know that rewarding illegitimate births was counterproductive to good homes, to a good society?

Didn't these leaders know that the continued lowering of standards in the schools would lead to an electorate that could neither read nor write?

Didn't these leaders know that abortion on demand would lead to a devaluing of life and concomitant violence?

Didn't these leaders know that countenancing, and even approving, perversion as an "alternative lifestyle" would lead to every kind of permissiveness counterproductive to good homes and a good society?

No one need be a "moralist" to recognize the pragmatic truth of the fact that a lack of standards of behavior and achievement, the approval, even the rewarding, of a lack of standards of personal responsibility and achievement cannot help but lead to the degradation of a society.

But university led propaganda of "elitist, racist" and "homophobic" appellations have silenced the voice of reason.

"Follow the money" is usually good advice. Whose interests are being served by allowing wholesale illegal aliens into our country? Whose idea is it to reward these illegal aliens with medical and welfare services, education, and instant citizenship for the babies of illegal aliens?

Whose idea is it that reasonable standards for citizenship such as ability in the English language and knowledge of American history and political structure be set aside? Who decided ballots should be in languages other than English? Whose interests are being served by fighting an un-winnable war on drugs? Whose interests are being served by the emasculation of our educational system? Whose interests are being served by approving perversion, even to the teaching of it in our schools? Whose interests are being served by the destroying of all vestiges of normal standards of behavior, of normal standards of right and wrong? Whose interests are being served by abrogating standards of justice through allowing pleas on the basis of drug and alcohol abuse, by not holding the criminals accountable for restitution to their victims?

Affirmative Action was a disgrace and a travesty. Big Brother, encouraged and aided by the universities and Hollywood, decided that the sins of fathers of the past would be visited upon the children of the present, that injustice would be corrected by instant fiat of law. The result has been the filling of countless positions of power and authority, even Superintendents of Education and university professors that could neither read nor write, with unqualified individuals on the basis of race. Whose decision was it that ignorance and poverty, inequities, were to be vanquished, even rewarded, instantly by fiat of law? A thing virtually insane on the face of it!

Morris Berman in his excellent book The Twilight of American Culture cites many of the things I have mentioned. The result of these literally insane decisions on the part of the universities, courts and government has been a nation that grows increasingly illiterate and irresponsible, a nation without any national identity or purpose, a nation, as the Russian poets have pointed out, without a soul.

Rather than attention to what should be the "soul" of a nation, our homes, we are a nation dedicated to conspicuous consumption and ever increasing Big Brotherism... a nation that no longer reads books that stimulate or challenge the thinking processes, that is dedicated to sports and entertainment rather than healthy and growing minds.

And as to the esthetic senses, the arts and music, the schools concentrate on sports instead of stimulating the fine arts and science. We have, as I have said many times, evolved a society that behaves as though it actually hates children... and children are fully aware of this.

We are a society where the rich get richer and the poor get poorer. But without standards, the poor will accuse the rich for being responsible for their poverty without accepting any responsibility themselves. Our courts, the universities and government have taught the poor and underprivileged that ignorance and poverty are the fault of others.

It is true that the rich will always ensure that their children will do and have better, that the children of the rich and privileged will have a good education. The danger lies in the universities, the courts and government, teaching the poor and uneducated that it is the fault of the rich that the children of the poor and uneducated are such and have a right to demand of the rich that which they will not attempt to correct for themselves by accepting personal responsibility for their impoverished condition. And the poor and ignorant would, in large measure, far rather feed at Caesar's table, thus being Caesar's dogs, rather than accept personal responsibility for their misery.

But what kind of "homes" has Caesar encouraged- Those that have single, teenage "mothers" with no sense of personal responsibility. "Homes" where no father is present or held accountable;"homes" where violence, drug and alcohol abuse are commonplace, "homes" where welfare is in its fourth generation and molestation is pandemic, "homes" where criminal behavior is a way of life.

If we get the kind of leadership we deserve, it can easily be seen that our citizenry, our nation, has fallen on hard times. Reason dictates that good homes would be the solution to this miserable condition. But where is the political will to do the things necessary to encourage good homes, to encourage a good, enlightened electorate that would result from good homes?

***

On January 1, 1831 William Lloyd Garrison began publishing the "Liberator," dedicated to renouncing slavery, in a small room on the third floor of Merchant's Hall in Boston. This was shortly after he was released from jail, having been imprisoned as a result of his outspokenness on the issue of slavery.

It would be twenty-one years later (1852) that "Uncle Tom's Cabin" would appear in book form. This was the book that galvanized anti-slavery sentiment and provided the emotional foundation for the Civil War.

On the basis of having spent a night in jail for not paying his taxes, Thoreau later delivered to the Concord Lyceum an address entitled "The Relation of the Individual to the State." In 1849 Elizabeth Peabody published the lecture in the single issue of her periodical "Aesthetic Papers" under the title "Resistance to Civil Government." Later reprints carried the title "On the Duty of Civil Disobedience." It is now best known simply as "Civil Disobedience."

Thoreau's friend and mentor, Ralph Waldo Emerson, in his address "The American Scholar" made the statement: The sluggish mind of the masses; slow to the incursion of reason."

And so it would seem to be, proven by the absence of wisdom throughout history, wisdom defined as the application of knowledge to the best end, a lack of which that has been the basis of unremitting warfare.

It would be thirty years after beginning publication of the Liberator before Garrison would see the war to end slavery. He had early made the statement: A few white victims must be sacrificed to open the eyes of this nation. I expect and am willing to be persecuted, imprisoned and bound for advocating African rights.

At the time he made this statement, he had no idea such a thing would eventually cost the lives of hundreds of thousands. Nor did Harriet Stowe have any idea of the enormous role her book would play in causing the Civil War. Nor did Thoreau, nor could he, have any idea of the enormous impact his little discourse on Civil Disobedience would have in cases like that of Gandhi and Martin Luther King, Jr.

In 1852 John Henry Cardinal Newman stated in his "Idea of a University" that virtue and decency were in the minority. The history of humankind being a history of unremitting war would seem to prove his dismal assessment. On this date of my writing, November 6, 2000, the day before our presidential election, the statements of Emerson, Thoreau, Garrison, Newman, et al have an inescapable timeliness.

We would hardly credit our presidential candidates as exemplary of virtue and decency, for example. But we would credit them with "relative" virtue and decency. Neither is guilty of murder or molesting children.

But "moral relativism" has a high price. The price throughout history has been paid by the lives of countless millions killed and maimed that had no idea why they were being killed and maimed. But the price is inevitable due to the lack of wisdom, the lack of enough of the good, the virtuous and decent, willing to confront determined evil with equal determination to win!

It took the decades-long efforts of those like Garrison for this nation to see an end to slavery. That he was a willing, living martyr to this cause may not be to his credit on the basis of self-sacrifice since he seemed to be compelled to do what he did, as did John Brown. And one can hardly give or claim credit on the basis of a compulsion.

In this sense there is no credit of nobility of cause or purpose to be given; what he did was the right thing to do makes no claim to nobleness of purpose. But the battle against slavery was a long one. We might say that lesser men than Garrison would have given up. But I think Garrison himself would disagree that he was any whit a better man for not having done so. The cause was right, and once given to that cause, he simply followed through. And this kind of perseverance, I believe, distinguishes the good from pretenders.

Having said that, it is equally apparent that the evil is quite able to persevere as well; proving Thoreau's statement that there is never an instants truce between vice and virtue.

The problems in the Middle East for example, hatreds, prejudices of such antiquity, certainly give one pause whether wisdom will ever overcome such dark evil. We do know that something believed "Holy" or "Sacred" is not amenable to any intrusion of reason. The very idea that a city can be thought "Holy" and be the cause of such misery and evil, even war and murder in the name of God, is a contradiction to reason, let alone wisdom.

Garrison, Whittier, Thoreau, Emerson, Stowe, Lincoln, could not know the minds of Negro slaves. But they had enough humanity to know that slavery was evil. More than that, they knew slavery was a reproach to any calling themselves "good" that did not oppose such an evil.

Yet Robert E. Lee, being morally opposed to slavery and most considering him a good man, led the armies of the Confederacy. His allegiance was to Virginia and the South; his morality misguided to the point of rather than determined opposition to slavery, prosecuting a war in its favor.

Virtually no one would attempt to discredit Lee's avowed Christianity and morality. Still, in spite of such Christian morality, he prosecuted a war that, if won, would sunder the Union and retain slavery.

We are asked to excuse Lee on a number of points: His integrity and virtue, his sincerity in his beliefs. But, to quote Lincoln: If slavery is not wrong, nothing is wrong!

If Robert E. Lee is to exemplify anything, it is the fact that even the best of good people may be sincerely wrong, that this great man and general of the Confederacy is proof of my equation k+w=p. For the one thing lacking in the beliefs and thinking of people like Lee is wisdom.

Would any disavow the Christian morality and sincerity of Cotton Mather? But how many would approve the Salem Witch trials?

In 1886 Henry Grady in his address The New South accused the leaders in the South of committing Southerners ...to a cause that reason could not defend or the sword maintain in the light of advancing civilization.

But those Southern leaders paid no heed to reason; there was nothing of reason or wisdom in their defense of an evil institution such as slavery. But there was a good deal of religion used in the defense of this evil cause, not just a corruption of State's Rights.

And if the evil of hatreds and prejudices continue to prevail and oppose advancing civilization as they do in the Middle East, such evil can only prevail on the basis of Cardinal Newman's observation that virtue and decency remain in the minority.

I have paraphrased Lincoln's statement *If slavery is not wrong, nothing is wrong* to say: *If perversion is not wrong, nothing is wrong.* For as long as children suffer at the hands of perverts, they remain ever bit as much in bondage as the Negro did under his slavery. As long as children continue to suffer without the protection of the proposed amendment, so long do they do so in opposition to advancing civilization.

No greater accolade has been given Lincoln as that of William Grady's assessment of the Great Emancipator as ...the first typical American, the first who comprehended within himself all the strength and gentleness, all the majesty and grace of this republic - He was the sum of Puritan and Cavalier for in his ardent nature were fused the virtues of both, and in his great soul the faults of both were lost.

Shortly after his second inaugural address, and only about five weeks before his assassination, Lincoln said: Men are not flattered by being shown that there has been a difference of purpose between the Almighty and them. To deny it, however, in this case (slavery), is to deny that there is a God governing the world. It is a truth that I thought needed to be told; and as whatever of humiliation there is in it, falls most directly on myself, I thought others might afford for me to tell it.

To arouse social conscience to the point of action is very difficult. And as Garrison and others found out, there was no polite or easy way of doing so ... It was not enough to discern evil, action was required. And while no civilized mind would applaud the course of John Brown, neither can the scholarly mind fail to recognize the circumstances that resulted in his course of action, including that of religious fanaticism.

The civilized mind will not accept the dictum of "The end justifies the means." So it is that we call upon wisdom and reason, we hearken to Socrates and Thoreau's "Civil Disobedience" in the hope that the continued questioning of amoral, evil authority and passive but questioning resistance to such will multiply into the millions required taking a stand against the evil and overcoming it. But it will require these millions who go contrary to the historical fact of virtue and decency being in the minority to change things for the better.

It takes only a handful of evil martyrs, fanatics, to wreak havoc on the innocent. The threat of a nuclear suitcase bomb going off in America is very real. And what makes America the target of such evil fanaticism? It is the lack of wisdom and virtue in America.

The Russian poets long ago described America as a nation without a soul. They were right. America has no identifiable national purpose, no identifiable major group of millions dedicated to the betterment of all humanity. We are no longer claimants of scholarship or literary greatness ... We are seen by religiously fanatic nations and leaders as "Godless," given to hedonistic materialism. As for wisdom, where does America exemplify this most necessary and essential virtue?

Make no mistake, religiously fanatical nations and leaders do believe themselves possessed of virtue and godliness. To many in such nations, to be the enemies of America is to be the friends of God.

The citizens of these nations have only to look at what America produces on TV to be confirmed in their minds as to the lack of virtue and decency, let alone godliness or wisdom, in America. And the choices the citizens of America produce for political leadership speaks for itself.

Like the abolitionists of over one hundred and fifty years ago, I have one cause: The abolition of molestation. I am a fanatic dedicated to the freeing of children from the slavery of molestation... a fanatic dedicated to giving children the legal right to an innocent childhood by our foundational charter of government, our Constitution. And I believe that had our Founding Fathers been able to foresee present conditions in regard to their posterity, the children, they would have included the proposed amendment in that venerable Bill of Rights, for what is more basic and fundamental to all the rights of humanity than that of a child to a protected and innocent childhood?

There had been "Holy men of God" quoting their "Holy Book" in favor of slavery for centuries. Such men persisted throughout our Civil War, claiming God's approval of an unholy and "peculiar" institution. There are those now in Israel and Arab nations that believe they are justified in murdering the innocent on the basis of beliefs as erroneous as those that died in America defending the evil of slavery.

There are those now who decry my stand for children in much the same way, claiming such a thing as the proposed amendment is contrary to "freedom" and "tolerance," that it is "bigoted" and "prejudiced" - The same people, most in the universities and Hollywood using these as their unholy pulpits, that use the propaganda techniques so successful for Hitler to make heaven into hell and black into white, that manufacture terms like "homophobic" while the truth is "heterophobic," the same people who sold America on the use of the term "gay" instead of the truth of "pervert."

It is without doubt or controversy an increasingly dangerous and demon-haunted world. But until America and the rest of the nations of the world make children the priority they must become, there is no hope of peace; there is no hope of wisdom and reason ever prevailing over religious and political hatreds and prejudices.

The proposed amendment brought many things into focus for me that caused Benjamin Franklin and Samuel Clemens to despair of humankind; that led them to wonder if the species were worth preserving? Such common frailties as greed and avarice are an indictment that deserves consideration. Those things that result in political corruption and religious chicanery being commonplaces are certainly an indictment of our species.

But the most troubling of all are those things that led Cardinal Newman to the conclusion that virtue and decency are in the minority.

I asked myself, is this because the bad people outnumber the good? No, I do not believe this to be the case. But I do believe that far too many good people do not involve themselves, do not trouble themselves, to do their fair part in confronting and overcoming the bad.

For example, over the past ten years I have had many articles and letters published in our local paper. In the great majority of cases, I have had people call me or come by and thank me for these articles. But they had never troubled themselves to write the paper to express their views in my support. But those that opposed me did write.

The same can be said for my correspondence with legislators. Such people can depend on good people doing nothing, on virtually never writing. But those that support bad legislation, legislation to curry favor or some selfish interest, these will write ... and in far greater numbers than good people.

Are homosexuals proper role models in the classroom teaching our children? I say no! But when it came to a vote in California when Reagan was governor, he vetoed a bill that would have excluded homosexuals as teachers in our classrooms. And people like John Wayne supported him in this view. Why? Because of the Hollywood interest and connection; and as with the case of Anita Bryant in Florida, Reagan knew good people would be conspicuous by their absence. Those few good people that did speak up were called "intolerant, homophobic, bigoted" and "prejudiced."

This was an instance where millions of good people who should have spoken remained silent. As a result, the will of a few thousand prevailed over those millions. And the real victims would be the children who would be taught that perversion was perfectly acceptable, that to oppose perversion was to be "intolerant, homophobic, bigoted," and "prejudiced."

The tail will always wag the dog when good people fail to do their part in opposing evil. But throughout history the case has been a failure of good people to actively oppose the evil ... hence the assessment of those such as Franklin, Clemens, and Newman.

Nobel-winning Physicist Michio Kaku has pointed out the very real danger the world faces because of nuclear proliferation. There is no denying the substantive evidence of such a threat. But it will take leaders of great knowledge and conviction to confront and overcome the obstacles to peace.

I call your attention to the fact that women are conspicuous by their absence in the UN. I ask you, can wisdom ever be achieved by the exclusion of a full half of humanity in the decision-making processes and leadership of nations?

Yet I have pointed out to women, and I believe most would concur, that their historical exclusion from the King of Disciplines, Philosophy, the discipline that guides the course of history and nations, must be overcome in order for them to have such a voice.

During all the turmoil of the years preceding our Civil War, a few women like Elizabeth Cady Stanton and Lucretia Mott were active abolitionists. But because they were women, they were refused admittance to the Antislavery Convention in London held in 1840. The commentaries of Sir William Blackstone held sway and continued to enslave women to their historical status as legal and political nonentities.

But Mrs. Stanton and some other determined women were resolute in changing their "slave" status. So it was that in 1848 the Seneca Falls Declaration of Sentiments and Resolutions came into being. Patterned after the Declaration of Independence, these women cited their grievances and asked for justice, especially in respect to the franchise.

But it would be another seventy years, 1920, before women won the right to vote. And only one woman, Charlotte Woodward Pierce, of that original meeting in Seneca Falls would live to cast a vote for President.

It is to America's credit that our nation would fight such a horrendous war on behalf of freeing slaves, though other major factors such as state's rights as well as the accidents of history, avarice and egos, are to be considered also.

It is to America's credit that such a meeting as that of Seneca Falls could be held and widely publicized (though most certainly unfavorably many times) ... This in spite of the fact that it would take seventy years to accomplish the purpose of that original meeting in 1848.

I find it a curiosity of history that the two, abolition of slavery and woman suffrage, should be so intertwined in time; but perhaps, given the similarity of the causes, not so curious. And I would point out that the battles of Civil Rights and Women's Rights would boil over and still be fought in the recent history of the sixties.

But in spite of the passage of time, even to this date, it cannot be said that women have achieved equal status with men, either in America or any place else in the world. For this to be accomplished requires wisdom, the kind of wisdom that denies prejudice and bigotry and leads to equal value, something not to be confused with equal rights and something not considered during the Seneca Falls meeting for women or by Martin Luther King, Jr. on behalf of minorities.

It will take the kind of perseverance evidenced by those like William Garrison and Elizabeth Stanton to accomplish the task of equal value. More, it will take exceptional women like Stanton and Mott, as diverse, educated and intelligent as Susan Anthony and Elizabeth Cochrane (Nellie Bly) and others, to develop a philosophy distinctive of women that will meld with that of men and, through the compatibility of differences correcting the errors in the philosophies of men, thereby making for a complete philosophy on the basis of equal value.

I give America credit for being a nation that considers fairness and justice of such great importance, a nation that fought a war to end slavery, a nation that would advance the cause of justice and fairness toward women. And we are a nation that has a history of being charitable beyond that of any other nation towards other nations, especially following WWII and in many other instances. We are a nation that in spite of many failures such as our treatment of Native Americans has a generally proud heritage of fairness and justice.

But my overriding concern is the fact that no nation in history can survive that does not cherish its children. I ask further: Can a world survive that does not make its priority its children?

Children, their future as the future of our species, should provide the basis of dialogue between nations. But we have never seen this happen.

It is my conviction that America, given its historical character and as the freest nation in history, has the obligation to lead the way in this dialogue, to open it by way of the proposed amendment through being the first nation in history to make such a commitment to children by its foundational charter of government, our Constitution.

And while it doubtless requires the kind of perseverance evidenced by those already mentioned as examples, like the abolition of slavery and women's suffrage the amendment will prove to be the right and wise thing to do.

I cannot think of anything of greater import or impetus that would restore the soul of America; that would create such a noble national identity and national purpose as a people than the proposed amendment.

CHAPTER FIVE

AMERICA'S MEMORIAL WALL OF SHAME!

I have started my own version of the Viet Nam Memorial Wall. But mine has the names of the children, the little victims of the monsters that have tortured and murdered them, names like Megan Kanka, Polly Klaas, JonBenet Ramsey, Melissa Russo and Julie Lejeune.

And while a memorial wall to such little victims, I want it to be a Wall of Shame and Disgrace to Americans who think themselves civilized and are not doing all in their power to rid society of the monsters who prey on children!

Melissa and Julie are the little 11-year-old girls who were locked in a dungeon in Belgium by Marc Dutroux. The little girls were raped repeatedly, videos of the rapes being made for distribution for Dutroux's pedophile network. These little girls were made to die of thirst by this monster, Dutroux.

He tried to blame his wife, who cooperated with his stealing and the filming of his raping the children, with failing to check on them. She said she couldn't bear to see them dying. So she locked the door to the dungeon and left them to die. Dutroux couldn't have cared less. There were plenty of other children available.

What can civilized people do when confronted by such inhuman, bestial cruelty? Raping little girls then leaving them to die of thirst, locked up alone in a dark dungeon! Did the little girls go insane as a result of the constant rapes or while their tongues swelled for lack of water? Would any civilized people allow an animal to die such a tortured death as these children?

These children prayed. They must have prayed! They must have shrieked and screamed out to God as they were brutally raped, as their tongues swelled up from thirst to the point where they couldn't scream or even whisper a prayer for death to deliver them!

Did they, in the end, try to drink their own urine as those dying of thirst often do?

But God couldn't help them. I had to eventually confront the fact that if God is Love, He can't possibly derive any pleasure from the torture and murder of children. If this is so, He cannot deliver these children from the monsters that torture and murder them!

But we can! And that is our responsibility, not God's.

There are things God cannot do, that are our responsibility, not His. Ridding civilization of the monsters like Dutroux and his wife is such a responsibility of civilized humanity.

The mere patron of virtue may call themselves civilized yet not be bothered by the monstrous deaths of children like Melissa and Julie.

As I worked with children over the years in the schools, churches and Child Protective Services, I came to realize that while people in general professed a concern for children, most were merely patrons of virtue.

Was I one of them? This is a question I had to finally confront in my own life. I didn't like the answer.

So what turned me around that I finally took up the cause of children; that I decided to take on this crusade to guarantee children the right to a constitutionally protected and innocent childhood? Nothing that I can name.

When the Apostle Paul said that the only thing that counts is faith expressing itself through love, it was obvious that he was reflecting the teaching of Jesus that faith is a growing thing and as faith grows, the love grows by the works of faith.

By the increasing awareness and sensitivity to my own failures, by confronting my own shortcomings, I was learning to be forgiving of the failures of others. Working with children teaches such things; especially working with your own children. But by confronting, repenting and confessing my own failures and lack of compassion, faith and love, with my increasing sensitivity to such things and my beginning to learn something of compassion especially, the nightmares began. I faced the fact, finally, that I had no right whatsoever to call myself a civilized man when I was only a patron of virtue.

My anger toward those who abuse the trust of elected office, my hatred of the bully, my anger toward organizations like the churches that fail to meet the needs of the very gospel they preach, my anger toward those who persecute and murder in the name of God began with the anger toward myself for being just the kind of person represented by these others.

The best I have been able to come up with so far is that the increasingly persistent nightmares of children like little Melissa and Julie finally forced me to take action, to quit being a mere patron of virtue.

I talked a good fight for years. Now, I was being compelled (Of God? The nightmares? What?) to walk the walk I so easily talked and preached.

Then the questions began to flood my mind. Why weren't the nightmares of children like Melissa and Julie common to all that call themselves civilized? Why weren't such nightmares causing all civilized people to take action against such monstrous evil, to rid humanity of these beasts, these spawn of Satan in the form of humans?

There is no question of why the parents of tortured and murdered children live a life forever after of a living nightmare. For the rest of their lives such living victims of the beasts that simply cannot be human will never be able to shut out the shrieking screams of their children, as those little ones died such indescribably horrible deaths.

My God in heaven, I have cried out, why aren't the screams of those children heard by the whole world? Why isn't every civilized human being in the world tortured by such a nightmare?

But civilized people sleep peacefully in spite of the evil, there are no nightmares filled with the screams of the children dying so horribly.

If I am compelled to do all in my power to answer the screaming prayers of these little victims, how can others sleep without doing all they can as well?

How can we call ourselves civilized and fail to do all in our power to rid the world of these beasts of evil incarnate in the form of human beings?

Someone recently told me the reason I was having so much trouble sleeping was that I was too involved with child abuse on a daily basis. It was said as an accusation, as though I were morbidly inviting the nightmares.

I will never be able to explain to such people the compulsion I work under; if it were a matter of stuffing my face and getting fat as compensation for depression that would be easily understood. A lot of people fall into this category.

If I turned to the bottle so I could face the ugliness and cruelties of the world through the bottom of a glass to anesthetize myself that would be understandable, even acceptable in some circles. But to lose sleep over the screams of children, children not even related to you, even children in other countries like Belgium, Asia and Africa? No, that's not explainable or acceptable.

The question remains; as long as I am compelled to deal with this issue on a daily and nightly basis, am I doomed to the nightmares? I don't know. But I know the absolute truth of Thoreau's statement: There is never an instant's truce between virtue and vice. Goodness is the only investment that never fails.

Ellie Nesler shoots the beast that molested her son and is in prison dying of cancer. The governor, Pete Wilson, has never responded to pleas of clemency for her. Is this the best a society can do, to put the mother in prison when justice fails and she is compelled to take the law in her own hands, knowing this beast will be coming after her and her son when he is allowed to go free?

It is well past time that God quit being the whipping boy for our failure to take action against evil! And that is just what religious people excel in, blaming

95

God in prayer for letting such evil go unpunished while not being confronted by us, blaming Him for not doing that which is our responsibility!

How many people tell me they pray for children and yet do nothing to stop the torture and murder of these little ones. I think the prayers of such people go into the pit where they belong, not up to heaven.

As to other patrons of virtue, there are the single, unwed mothers who let the booze and drugs; the various bums in and out of their lives destroy their children. I know of far too many such patrons as these.

The young woman is a boozer and drug user. She had three children and gave up one to adoption. She has lived with a number of men, worthless bums who sponge off her welfare check, and inevitably one of these is going to abuse and molest her little girl.

Can you say such a so-called mother loves her children? I don't think so.

A friend was telling me of a case he knew of where the man was raping the woman's little girl repeatedly and the mother would even watch! Tragically, not a new story to me. There are women equally vile compared to any man like that one. And equally monstrous, equally deserving to be put out of society permanently!

But my sympathy and understanding for such sorry and pitiable creatures ends where it impacts the children. At that point, both the men and the women can go to hell for all of me. There is such a thing as eventually accepting adult responsibility.

Child support and deadbeat dads. Yes. Where are the fathers of the children like those of this so-called mother?

But going back to the lady who called me concerning her research paper about child abuse, there is a tragic loophole in the procedures followed by Child Protective Services.

For example, a typical *Child At Risk* scenario is this:

The mother was molested herself as a child. Lacking any value to herself as a person, her life has consequently been one of alcohol and drugs, living with numerous men who are alcohol and drug abusers, usually with criminal records.

These men seek women who will provide a welfare check to support them and their alcohol and drug habits.

From an actual case with which I'm personally knowledgeable, the mother and her children live with the woman's grandmother and her boyfriend. The mother, grandmother and the grandmother's boyfriend are alcoholics and drug abusers. The man is just out of prison where he served time for beating both the mother and grandmother.

The children have grown up with nothing but a parade of such men in their lives; the real father's whereabouts are unknown. No child support has ever been paid for the children.

The ex-felon, now on parole, lives off the welfare check of the mother and the grandmother's disability payments (due to the alcoholism and drug addiction).

One night there is a big fight and the mother is jailed because of the grandmother and her boyfriend accusing the young mother of attacking the grandmother. The charge is simple battery. When she is released, she goes right back to the same environment.

The young woman was arrested just a month prior for drunk and disorderly, for getting into a fight at a local bar. This previous arrest leads to the officers treating the woman as a jailbird. They are getting to know these people. So they take her in on the word of another jailbird and the grandmother.

Another contributing factor is that the grandmother is the legal resident of the rental where they all live.

The children are exposed to all this violence, the drinking and drug use, the sight of their mother being arrested and hauled off to jail.

The mother knows she is placing her children in harm's way. Repeatedly.

Her little girl, a beautiful child, is only eleven-years-old. The man will eventually molest her and the mother knows this. But where can she go with her children?

She meets her men in the bars. She takes up with an ex-felon on parole (just like the grandmother) that is a known thief, alcohol and drug abuser. Both the young mother and the man have criminal records; a very limiting factor concerning their options for employment, etc.

The man used to live with another woman before he went to prison. There is long list of being a deadbeat tenant, of flopping wherever he can and living off the welfare checks of other women.

Now, if you call Child Protective Services and describe all these circumstances, including the scum the young mother is now living with, if you know because of these circumstances that these children, especially the little girl, are At Risk! you know what CPS will tell you? There is nothing they can do!

When such a scenario that blatantly shows children at risk and in spite of the fact that such men and women are supported by the taxpayers and receiving aid from a panoply of social welfare programs from food stamps to you name it, you are told there is nothing that can be done to protect children in such an environment you know there is something drastically wrong with the system.

Yet the system has signs all over with 800 numbers to report children at risk, to report child abuse and even suspected child abuse, and you call only to be told there is nothing they can do under the circumstances I just described, just who is kidding who?

Now multiply the actual case I have described and multiply it by the millions of children at similar risk in order to get an idea of the magnitude of the problem. And the children continue to be molested, beaten, tortured and murdered.

This is the best a civilized society can do to protect children? I can't, I won't buy that!

I watched a young mother with four, small children trudging along the road. It was afternoon and the temperature was 96 degrees. The smallest child was only a toddler, about two-years-old. The sun had already burned her little cheeks.

They had walked a long distance into town. I was returning from taking another young mother to the welfare office. I stopped to give them a lift. The older three children sat in the back of my truck, it has a camper shell, and the mother and the toddler sat up front with me. As I drove them home, I asked myself the question: When she loses her welfare check, what man will want her and four children?

I told the young mother that we have 30 sex offenders registered here in the Valley. Thanks to the information we now have available to us due to California Attorney General Dan Lungren we know who they are. But this is only those who have registered. We can multiply the number by a factor of ten to get an idea of the actual number.

One of the worst of these, a man with multiple convictions of lewd behavior with children, is living nearby to this young mother and her small children. I warn her of these facts. She is horrified to know about this and asks what she can do?

Keep the children close to you at all times. That's all I can tell her.

A new scenario presents itself with pending welfare reform. The bum will ask the mother how many months of welfare she has left before he moves in with her. What? Only two months! Forget it! What'll I do for beer money when you lose your check?

And what will the option be? Orphanages? What else?

But putting children at risk because of booze and drugs, because of the "freedom" of parents that could care less about the price of real freedom, self-discipline and responsibility?

I just painted the name of little Traci Conrad, 11-years-old, on my wall. Kevin Duane Galik Sr. molested and murdered her. He suffocated her with towels wrapped around her neck and face with duct tape holding a sock stuffed in her mouth. Her body was found in a pottery kiln in this monster's back yard a month later.

It's the first of the month. The welfare checks are in and the post offices are crowded early- Then the grocery stores. And the drug dealers will get paid; usually before the trip to the grocery store- Business as usual in Welfare Valley. And when the welfare stops, all hell is going to break loose!
　　***

I had just finished adding the names of two more little murder victims, brothers, Keith and Kurt Billie to my wall and came back in the house when there was a knock at my door. The beautiful young woman whose boyfriend beat her so badly was there with her children, three little girls.

They shyly give me a handwritten Thank You note. It's two pages, torn from a spiral notebook, the edges jagged from tearing them from the notebook. One corner of the back page is smudged with dirt. The pages are held together with a blue shoestring through the holes in the upper left corner.

On the front page, written in red it says in bold letters:

A Special Thanks To You!

The inside page reads:

To Sam,

We want to thank you for being there for our mommy when she needed someone.

We also want to thank you for all the help you gave her while we were gone.

You will always be in our hearts and in our prayers.

God bless you.

The children's signatures followed.

I think of this kind of gratitude and compare it with that shown by most adults I have helped, like the woman I picked up recently at the Sheriff's facility when she had no one else to help. There was never any appreciation shown by her, not even a hug, and she went right back to the kind of life that led her to jail in the first place. But such people provide a stark contrast to the children who make what I do worth everything.

But then there never has been anything to compare with the gratitude of a child. They mean it. I can think of few things I will treasure more than this Thank You of genuine and unfeigned gratitude from three little girls whose mommy was hurting and needed someone. And I thank God I was the one to receive such a priceless honor from three little angels. It will make the nightmares easier to endure.

NCPCA gives a figure of nearly one million substantiated cases of child abuse for the year 1996. This averages 14 children out of every 1,000. And that figure is only for those cases, which were substantiated. This means you can use a factor of 10 to get the true number, more like ten million children.

For those not disposed to dry statistics but do read Ann Landers, look at the column of August 1, 1997 for that seemingly improbable factor of 10-to-1 of cases substantiated versus the probable actual number. To repeat a point made many times: Children are not capable of telling adults of molestation or many other forms of abuse. The woman in the Landers column is typical. Molested at age 7, she didn't make it known until she was sixteen. And, as I have pointed out repeatedly the molest resulted in the woman turning to drugs and alcohol, and she suffered the ruined relationships that invariably result from molestation.

She says it took her 18 years to reclaim her life. Many never do. Many are like some of the women I meet in the bars and Walk the Boulevard here in the Valley where I live.

Another very important web address for the National Center for Missing and Exploited Children is:

(http://www.missingkids.org/childsafety.html).

Divorce: One of the most hurtful and contributing factors to molestation. A reason being that virtually 50 per cent of children left with only a mother will be raised in poverty as opposed to only 10 per cent raised with both a mother and father.

By its very nature, the amendment stresses the employment is the key to responsibility factor. When a father can bring home a livable paycheck and a mother can nurture children at home, molestation's by stepfathers and live-in boyfriends and others will plummet.

Politicians try to avoid the employment aspect of the amendment while paying lip service to the need of good jobs in order to give children a proper living environment.

The amendment holds the fire to the feet of these hypocrites who shout Family Values and do nothing substantive to improve employment opportunities beyond part-time jobs and flipping hamburgers. And by their back door deals even contribute to shipping our industries overseas encouraging slave labor and the exploitation of children in other countries.

Our elected leaders must be held accountable for this and nothing will be as effective as the amendment in holding them accountable and making them put their money where their glib mouths are; but to return to the other subject before I diverted myself.

Karen raises Rottweilers and is a professional trainer, winning many shows with her dogs. She trains them for the blind, for police department use and home protection.

Just recently, one of her dogs saved a young woman from a potential attack by her own husband who has a violent temper. The dog placed itself between the young woman and her husband. That is good training. And the young woman is divorcing the abusive husband.

This is why Karen won't sell her dogs cheaply or to just anyone who has the money. She does a good profile check on prospective buyers to determine their suitability for such dogs. She especially won't sell a dog for a lower price because as she pointed out, such would-be buyers don't appreciate the training that goes into such dogs, and probably want such a dog for the wrong reasons. It's sometimes a case where, as Karen put it, the potential buyer is more stupid than the dog.

Knowledgeable buyers know what goes into this kind of training; they know the temperament of these dogs, their usefulness and purpose and don't haggle on price.

This explains Karen's calling the above information to my attention concerning deaths caused by dogs as opposed to child abuse. Virtually no properly trained dog, especially Rottweilers, will attack a person without provocation or ordered to do so by virtue of such training.

But in nearby Merced, I learned of a molester, James Michael Flaherty, who was arrested for annoying children in the public library. Turns out this pervert was loose after serving time twice for sex offenses against children. One of the conditions of his parole was that he was not to have any contact with children.

So where do they find him? Trying to pick up on children in a library. Rehabilitation? You've got to be kidding! These monsters have to be expunged from a civilized society permanently, they cannot be rehabilitated and their behavior cannot be changed. And since the molested often becomes a molester, the chain of molestation must be broken! And only the amendment will accomplish this by a national, uniform one-strike code of justice!

During my last conversation with Karen, I was suddenly caught up short by the stunning realization that she was a very mature adult, now preaching the message against child abuse with the same evangelistic fervor as her father! She is passionate, well informed and very articulate in making well-reasoned points. I couldn't be prouder of her and I want everyone to know this. She has truly become a Momma Bear in respect to children.

And it is such Momma Bears, unlike men in general, that will cause action to be taken to protect children because in spite of the fact that there are some women equal to the vilest of men, women in general continue to be far more sensitive to the cries of the children.

I was visiting a friend recently; a Jewish woman named Monica, who had just returned from a trip to Germany. She's an exceptionally intelligent person with an acute understanding of human nature.

She showed me the stunning photographs she had taken and we got into a good philosophical conversation about the WWII era.

Neither of us is naive about the chicanery of the politicians and the dirty politics of that era on the part of both Axis and Allies. We are quite aware and well informed concerning the propaganda of the era.

She has a deep interest in my proposition that if a generation of children can be raised in protected innocence through the auspices of the amendment; anything is possible for them as adults. Even the elimination of violence.

We discussed Hitler's Germany, of course, and the fact that good people turned their eyes away from the persecution of others under his dictatorship.

I said to her, suppose there were signs posted throughout the cities of Germany at the time saying IT SHOULDN'T HURT TO BE A JEW, A GYPSY, etc.

She was startled at that.

Then I pointed out the obvious. People do not want to be confronted with the ugliness of indifference. My Wall Of Shame with the names of murdered children, my IT SHOULDN'T HURT TO BE A CHILD! signs are treated as obscenities by good people who do not want to be reminded of the atrocities being committed against children.

People do not want their faces rubbed in the dirt of their indifference to what is happening to children throughout the world. A virtual holocaust of abuse estimated by UNICEF at two and one-half million children a year (due to gross underreporting of abuse for many reasons, this figure is very likely closer to ten times that amount) is taking place and people who consider themselves civilized are turning their eyes away and by their indifference and inaction against such evil, are allowing it to happen at an accelerating pace.

In short, it is the same old *I Don't Want To Know* syndrome. And my wall, my signs become an obscenity of constant reminder to those that *Don't Want To Know*!

Monica saw my point and immediately agreed.

But the amendment, the Wall, the signs, go far beyond what I have described. These things get to the root of the evil among us; including the evil of good people that don't want to know; those good people to whom the wall is an obscenity.

The history of the human species has been one of constant hatreds, conflicts and warfare because of this root of evil. If we can begin by making children such a priority through the amendment that the evil of men and women is exposed, we can begin to have hope in ultimately triumphing over evil and violence completely.

Yes that is truly revolutionary, an idea to transform humanity from its history of hatreds and warfare by the mechanism of making children the proper priority of the species and then to reach out to the stars in world cooperation.

(The foregoing became the text for one of my columns in the newspaper)

***

Many readers expressed concern for the young woman I wrote of in the last issue of TAP who was beaten so badly by her boyfriend. To give you all an update, she will have to undergo reconstructive surgery for her left cheekbone and her jaw. Fortunately, it looks like her eye is going to be all right.

I wrote last month about my learning compassion. But lest the reader misunderstood, compassion doesn't mean being stupid about people.

The polarizing of opinion is necessary to accomplish my goal of creating the essential dialogue by which people will begin to understand the enormous complexities of the amendment and the absolute need of guaranteeing a protected and innocent childhood to the age of sixteen.

Many vilify me for their concept of state's rights. They would like the states to pass the laws protecting children. But this is not a state's rights issue; it is an American issue, a national issue, and a world issue.

Most of the states give the molester a slap on the wrist and turn the monsters loose to prey on children again. We have over 200 of these living in the Valley.

But all too typically, many governors and congressmen want to be the head honchos and not take a back seat to Constitutional law. They put their petty egos and political ambition ahead of the children for whom, in their political posturing and mouthing of meaningless platitudes, they say they are concerned. Preachers and Politicians.

The amendment, my Wall and signs are obscenities to such hypocrites. The average person could put a small sign in their front yard. They could put bumper stickers on their cars.

It's after 10 p.m. when there is a pounding on my door. It's D-, a woman I know well. She's an alcoholic and drug user. She used to be a beautiful woman but the alcohol and drugs have taken their toll and only the vestiges of a once beautiful woman are left. At 45 she looks a shop worn and tired 65. Tragic.

She's staggering drunk; crying, speaking incoherently and I wonder how she made it to my place in the dark. She is telling me about a 13-year-old boy who has been raped for over three years by a man she knows. The man is the boyfriend of a woman friend of D-'s, and this friend and mother of the boy knew what was going on yet allowed the animal living with her to continue to rape her own child.

The boy finally went to the local police after a particularly brutal rape, which had torn his rectum badly. D- couldn't stand it so she got thoroughly drunk. In her alcoholic state, it came into her mind to visit me to try to ease her pain, to help her understand how these people could do such a thing, how this friend of hers could actually allow this beast to do such monstrous, unspeakable things to her own child?

While she is so drunk, I can't say much to her. I make up the sofa sleeper, again, and put her to bed. We'll talk in the morning when she is sober and has enough coffee to function rationally.

D- wishes she didn't drink and has tried to quit many times. She would like to turn her life around but having lost her youth; the depression of her situation is too much for her. Her life is pretty much over and she knows this.

But she loves children. She wishes everyone in the Valley had my signs in their yards and bumper stickers on their cars. She can't understand how these monsters can do such things to children, how women like her friend can allow such torture of their own children.

I try to explain that we aren't dealing with normal, rational people when it comes to molestation, men and women treating children as things for sexual gratification. It is behavior not subject to either the understanding of normal people or rational treatment, and such monsters can only be removed from normal, civilized society permanently by the amendment.

D- will pass out fliers for the amendment. What has happened to this child she knows personally has shaken her badly. And by people she thought she knew! D- is now a convert to the necessity of the amendment and while most of the people she knows are alcoholics and drug abusers, many know what it is to love a child.

I hear about Frank Alvarez, the murderer of 5-month-old Tyler Ransom and 4-year-old Dylan Vincent, being beaten twice by Lerdo jail inmates. He shows up for pretrial with four missing teeth and wearing nine stitches in his head. The molesters and murderers of children find people who love children even in jails and prisons. And they hate monsters like Alvarez. Yes, a criminal, an alcoholic or drug addict can love children.

And who knows but given some hope that something can be done, is being done for children, some like D- might be encouraged to turn their own lives around. A cause like this for children really can help people like D- and others.

A part of alcoholism and drug addiction is a background of molestation in many cases. The amendment gives these people hope that something can be done to protect children from what happened to themselves as children. And in being encouraged to help with the amendment, they just might find a cause that will give them the will and the courage to change their own lives.

Speaking of a beast like Alvarez reminds me of the treatment given one Ali Kordiyeh in Iran for murdering nine women. He was lashed 214 times then summarily hanged. There was no ten years of appeals while being housed and fed at taxpayer expense; would that we could have such speedy and like justice in this country for the murderers of children like Alvarez.

In Delaware, Ohio a convicted child molester, five women attacked Rodney Hosler, 27, in his home. They wrestled him to the floor, pulled out scissors and sheared his head and pubic hair, assaulted him anally with a cucumber and put heat-producing ointment on his genitals.

The women included Hosler's wife and mother-in-law who feared he was again molesting the same child he was convicted of molesting in 1994.

Hesler will undoubtedly return to prison since he failed, as the majority does, to register with local police as a sex offender.

Like Ellie Nesler, these courageous women took the law into their own hands when perverted laws released this monster after only a brief stint in prison to prey on children again.

I will inform my readers when I find out how the law treats these women. I pray they fare better in Ohio than Ellie has here in California. Governor Pete Wilson didn't even have the courtesy or decency to reply to my request for clemency for Ellie.

But Ellie had the bold effrontery to shoot the beast that molested her little boy in the courtroom where he was being tried. And since judges have a God complex, how dare the common people exact real justice in their courts! The system, which includes the governor, found that an unforgivable offense and affront to their august personages and offices.

There are many good people here in the Valley. Once they come to have hope that something can be done to rid society of the Alvarez's, they will begin to take action. Of that I am convinced.

So the Valley becomes my ideal sociological laboratory in which all the necessary mechanisms and ingredients of revolution are found. All the elements are here to gain national attention for the amendment and open the necessary dialogue where reason has a chance to prevail over violence.

***

A recent study concluded that the early hominids had tough going when it came to a food supply. But apparently they could eat anything that didn't move too fast to catch as well as the fruits and various plants available.

I know a fellow who teaches survival courses for the military. He described the lengths some of the men he takes out in the field go to in attempting to kill birds with rocks, etc. just to try to get some normal food as opposed to the various insects available.

These guys will wear themselves out trying to get a bird when the only food they need is plentiful, he told me. Of course he was referring to the various lizards, snakes, grubs, worms, grasshoppers that he was trying to get them to eat.

He said the hardest thing he had to eat were cockroaches. The wings, he said, got stuck in his teeth. And he was dead serious about this. I was more than willing to take his word for it.

But being a poet of a philosophical bent of mind, I make a correlation between the hardships of those early hominids, my friend eating cockroaches, and learning compassion. Huh?

That's right. I see a connection between the two.

If the situation is extreme enough, I suppose I could eat grasshoppers, grubs and cockroaches. There are cultures today that consider beetles a delicacy and others that eat things that we, as Americans, say ugh with a shudder to.

But I'm an American with fairly typical American taste concerning food.

However, I could learn to eat things as foreign as insects if the situation demanded it. Like the difference between living and dying of starvation.

But the connection between this and learning compassion is: If the situation was so extreme that the choice was between life and death.

Now suppose it was a matter of my eating insects in order that one of my children could live? I would eat insects.

Compassion, I have discovered, is learned by extreme circumstances. There are things I can now do out of compassion that would have been unthinkable years past.

For example, I have learned through the betrayals of my love and trust to be compassionate. In the old days, I would have liked to take a gun and kill the SOB, man or woman.

Not that I have changed my mind that there are definitely some people that need killing, like child molesters. But I don't consider these creatures' people.

No, the compassion I have learned is for those that through their own desperate circumstances seem to have to practice deceit. I've learned compassion for women that have to rent their bodies to provide for their children. I have learned compassion for those who suffer alcohol and drug addiction. I have learned compassion for those who are so lonely and so without hope that they take their own lives.

In other words, I have learned I can eat insects if I have to.

But there is no room for compassion for the Judas's; especially those that betray their marriage vows, for those that betray the love and trust of others and those that betray the innocence of a child. Neither God, I believe, nor I have any compassion for these betrayers. And there is such a thing as righteous hatred of those that do evil, the children of the Devil.

A so-called mother, one Debbie Lowe, 29, in Fresno, California leaves her 6- and 20-month-old babies alone for FOUR DAYS in a sweltering apartment where they die of dehydration and heat. They were slowly roasted to death.

She is being arraigned on murder charges. She says she is devastated by the deaths of her children. I believe Hell has a hotter spot by far and of eternal duration for such creatures to suffer than her babies suffered as they died so horribly.

As an important aside, I had to call the Fresno Coroner's Office to get the names of the two babies. The article in the paper didn't include their names. Shouldn't that have been of real importance? Or didn't the reporter consider it significant? Too much of the attitude of society in that flagrant omission.

The 6-month-old baby's name was Myisha Tolbert. That of the 20-month-old was Ebony Whitfield. Note that neither of these little victims carried the name of the mother. This too, is a part of the tragedy and a searing comment on a callous society that perpetuates such crimes against children by not holding adults accountable for what should be basic standards of morality for any society calling itself civilized!

Robert James, 2, was shot and killed in Hesperia during a traffic incident involving his parents Travis and Wendy. A six-year-old sister of Robert survives.

24-year-old Amoret Powell is in jail in Tucson, Arizona for the first-degree murder of her 7-week-old infant Eve Powell. How did this woman murder her baby? With breast milk so full of heroin that it killed the baby.

A 13-year-old boy, Justin Kennedy of Oklahoma City, was arrested for the murder of his 3-year-old stepbrother, Deangelo James. He clamped the little boy's head between his knees holding him under water in a swimming pool while jokingly asking people around the pool as he was drowning him: Do y'all know where he is?

The names of these little victims have been added to my Wall, victims of the drugs and violence permeating our society.

But what of the estimated 60,000 North Korean children who will die of starvation within the next few weeks? Thank the greed and egos of those in political power in that country.

As it always is in such cases whether North Korea, Africa, Asia, the Middle East, Bosnia, etc. the wickedness of those who fanatically espouse religious and political ideologies of superiority or conquest freely sacrifice children.

The Modesto Bee had a piece recently about the CDC's finding that prenatal care has a profound effect on IQ. It is now believed this has far more to do with development than genetic factors.

Now it never did take a rocket scientist to figure out babies that are breast fed (provided the mother isn't an alcoholic or drug addict) cuddled and cooed over develop into healthier and more intelligent adults than those that miss these things. Kathleen Parker wrote an excellent article on this.

Getting your toddler a simple keyboard and helping him or her develop musical ability, reading to them and prompting them toward good literature rather than using the box as a baby sitter does promote intelligence and the ability to use that intelligence.

And speaking of the infernal machine that has had so much to do with teaching doctrines of demons reminds me of something Marianne Williamson said recently:

There is no amount of money I can make which could buffer my daughter from the horrors that will explode in our society if we do not address the huge amount of suffering in our midst.

Marianne Williamson has a six-year-old daughter that has caused her to focus on the things I have been writing about for years, the things that have, like TV and noise that pretends to be music, such a profound, detrimental effect on children.

She goes on to say that America has only five to ten years to decide its' fate. Now that is a really pessimistic view. Or realistic?

I have quoted Marianne several times, especially the following that I placed in the Forward to my Birds book:

Another of the many How To books on the market, this one written by a woman, Marianne Williamson, includes this statement: 'Some men know that a light touch of the tongue, running from a woman's toes to her ears, lingering in the softest way possible in various places in between, given often enough and sincerely enough, would add immeasurably to world peace.'

Two things: This may not, in fact, be overdrawn and, removed from erotica to the purpose of God in men cherishing their wives, it is a valid statement. It is at least a shade ironic to find a woman making my point for me in this respect. The point being that if men and women would give attention to those things which bring out the best in each, undoubtedly the world would be a lovelier and safer place, especially in the cherishing of children and family. How could it be otherwise when, in fact, a man and woman cherish each other? Compatibility, as God intended, not Competition, is the antidote to the plagues of divorce, adultery and the destruction of family and family values.

Since Marianne penned those words, she has had time for much reflection. Her little girl has made her reflect.

I still agree with her basic premise, but she misses the mark in respect to the priority for achieving world peace. That priority has to be children.

Marianne would be the first, I believe, to agree once she thinks it through. She should have realized that preaching a message of empowering women through emphasizing the spiritual misses the mark of having to do actual battle with the evil directed at our children.

But even Einstein was wrong on occasion.

***

I recently told a reporter that when people ask me why I am doing what I am in regard to children and the amendment I tell them I don't know. And that's the truth.

In many ways, I consider myself one of the most improbable people imaginable to be doing this.

When the thought first began to frame itself in my mind concerning a U.S. Constitutional amendment to guarantee children a lawfully protected, innocent childhood, I rejected it out of hand.

But it kept pressing itself on my mind; I couldn't get rid of it.

And the more I thought about it, the more sensible, even imperative such a thing began to be to me.

In the beginning, I had no idea of the enormous and profound complexities legally and socially such a thing would have on society. But I was well qualified to examine these things and the more I studied this approach to begin the process of making children our proper priority, the more logical it appeared to be.

Even granting the seemingly Draconian aspects of re-educating an entire nation to cherish children, to give them the most essential and fundamental of all human rights, the right to a protected and innocent childhood that word Draconian still stood out; yet nothing in the Constitution, the Bill of Rights or any of the articles following specifically addressed children; perfectly understandable within the historical framework of the Constitution when the needs of children could safely be assumed to be met by parents and society. But circumstances have changed dramatically in this regard and such a thing is desperately needed now!

If an amendment was needed to free people from slavery, to enfranchise women, wasn't it logical to recognize the human rights of our smallest citizens, to give children the right to freedom from molesters by the very same mechanism?

This is not a state's rights issue. This is a national, a world issue. Trying to solve the problem by a piecemeal, state-to-state process has resulted in the molester serving an average of only 2.2 years in prison for this most heinous of all crimes against humanity. It has resulted in monsters like Lawrence Singleton, Richard Allen Davis and Jesse Timmendequas being set free after imprisonment to go on to murder women and children. And this, I have to tell myself, is not only a flagrant miscarriage of justice, it is virtually insane!

There is at present no uniform way of dealing with the problem. On the contrary, too many such attempts by the individual states to do so has only resulted in many instances of laws that actually pervert the cause of justice as in the cases of Singleton, Davis and Timmendequas. A uniform code of justice is desperately needed. The amendment is that solution.

If discrimination in many different forms needed amendments, why should it be asking too much for Americans to grant children this most fundamental of all human rights by the same process?

But given the reasonableness of this approach to the problem, the truly revolutionary aspects of such a thing intruded incessantly on my mind. I was asking a nation to do something that no nation in history has ever done, to make children a priority by its most fundamental charter of government, something no nation in history has ever done!

I allowed myself to begin thinking what a generation of children raised under this protection, this mandate of cherishing our young, might be capable of as adults? Even the eventual banishing of violence from our society? Possible, I told myself.

And where do we start in the hope of banishing violence? Why of course, we start where the people of the world find common ground and agreement! We attack evil at the most basic and fundamental root! Why hadn't I thought of it before? Slow learner.

I saw myself addressing a stadium filled with a million people of every nationality, creed and religion and I ask the question:

Would all of you in favor of the molestation of children please raise your hands? And not a single hand is raised!

At last! Something that people the world over could agree on; something that could be the basis of understanding and dialogue among the community of nations, a place to start where we had complete agreement. Astounding thought! And with America leading the way by the amendment, where might such a thing lead in pursuing peace by making the cherishing of children the proper priority in our own nation?

My work with children and families over the years, the writing of research papers, articles, columns and books coalesced in the amendment. It, by itself, was not the answer to the world's problems. But it was the beginning of the answer. And, as such, like the multiplication tables to mathematics, absolutely essential, basic, foundational to pursuing other answers to the woes of humanity.

And America, I believe, has the responsibility to lead the world in making the cherishing of children an absolute priority; if we are to preach peace, our concern for children, how better to make it plain that we are not playing the hypocrite as the leader among the family of nations?

As to the improbability of my being the author of the amendment I have to remind myself it's true that I have spent most of my life working with children in the schools, churches and even Child Protective Services. I have worked and taught for years in the war zones and killing fields of places like Watts and East San Jose.

I've witnessed terrible, dreadful things done to children. I've had to have parents and others arrested for the abuse of children.

My degrees and credentials are largely oriented to working with children and young adults in many different capacities.

And I've single parented. That's an important dimension of understanding the problems parents face in raising children. Unexpected divorce taught me other dimensions of the problems.

On the face of it, I may be the ideal candidate to address the issue of child abuse and do something substantive, like the amendment, to solve the problem.

But these things are the qualifications of duty and responsibility, things most civilized, educated people understand and respond to.

But to actually carry out such an obligation of duty and responsibility in the manner in which I am doing, that is inexplicable to me.

I could blame the nightmares I have because of the murders of children like Melissa Russo and Julie Lejuene in Belgium. I see them and hear their screams until, tongues so swollen from thirst; they couldn't even whisper a prayer for death to deliver them when their prayers to God didn't avail.

I live with the daily images of little Megan Kanka, Polly Klaas and JonBenet Ramsey screaming and there was no one there to help them.

I came to the conclusion that confronting such evil was not God's job but that of good, civilized people. And frankly, we were failing to do the job.

Even more, I began to believe that God couldn't help and it was our responsibility, not His, to overcome such evil. An old maxim continued to plague me: It isn't enough to discern evil; action is required!

111

So it is that the good seems too often impotent in the face of determined evil simply because the good does not meet the evil with the same determination.

Could Hitler or Stalin have achieved such success if the vastly superior numbers of good, civilized people had withstood them? But good people too often lack the same determination. We Don't Want To Know!

In this way, my amendment, my signs, my Memorial Wall with the names of the little victims become obscenities to good people who don't want to know lest in their consciences they are asked to assume responsibility to meet such determined evil against children with equal determination, by action to overcome the evil.

I worked for years for educational reform only to witness the situation for children continue to deteriorate. We say we love children but we live in a society that seems to hate them.

And the words of Alexander Pope come forcefully to mind:
Vice is a monster of so frightful mien
As to be hated needs but to be seen;
Yet seen too oft, familiar with her face,
We first endure, then pity, then embrace.

So, little by little, we become jaded, inured to evil by not confronting it.

My IT SHOULDN'T HURT TO BE A CHILD! phrase isn't meant to change evil people. It's meant as a reminder to good people because only good people have a conscience concerning children. And if that phrase pops into their mind before they discipline a child in anger, if it gives them pause, more parents wouldn't hate themselves for losing their tempers and more children would be disciplined correctly.

To spank or not to spank has been a topic of dissension for a very long time. And while I generally agree with the study showing spanking to have a mostly detrimental effect on children, the study failed to address the causes of the behavior in a child that results in spanking; a kind of chicken and egg problem.

But suppose an entire nation placed such a priority on children, on families, that the entire society cooperated in the raising of children in protected innocence? Within a generation such a thing as spanking would become a moot point!

But in raising consciousness and sensitivity in this one thing, that it shouldn't hurt to be a child, other things involving children come to mind. There is a domino effect, if you will, by keeping such things before people. Advertisers know the importance of this in selling products.

For example, the recent series of articles by the Californian, the coverage of child abuse by KBAK-TV and radio KERN is here today and gone tomorrow.

There must be a constant reminder of the evil. If people are to be stirred to action, the fire cannot be allowed to go out.

I have elected the 2x4 method of getting people's attention by my signs and my Wall, my articles in the newspaper. I have chosen to make myself odious to the community by rubbing people's faces in their indifference and apathy toward children and families.

My Wall and my sign are obscenities to good people that Don't Want To Know! But justice demands that the screams of the little victims of beasts in the form of men and women be heard, that they not be forgotten!

So my Wall becomes a Memorial Wall in one sense and an indictment, a Wall of Shame and Disgrace, an obscenity to those that Don't Want To Know!

But as I asked a German Jewish friend, suppose the good people of Germany had placed signs in their cities IT SHOULDN'T HURT TO BE A JEW, A GYPSY, etc. when the Nazis first began to intrude themselves, would a Hitler have ever succeeded in the persecution of such people if good Germans had done this?

So I want the good people of America to be shaken in their conscience and take a stand against the monsters that prey on children, to put the signs in their yards or in their windows, in their places of business and bumper stickers on their cars IT SHOULDN'T HURT TO BE A CHILD!

A Constitutional amendment is a gargantuan undertaking. Knowing full well what would be required to accomplish such a task, I had no illusions from the start that the fight for such a thing would be easy in any way.

It is, primarily, an educative process requiring a great deal of time and effort. President Clinton, the various governors and senators being the intelligent, educated people that they are, have been quick to grasp the immensely profound and complex issues, socially and legally, such an amendment brings into focus.

The amendment requires an entire society to face itself on the basis of whether we do, in fact, recognize the necessity of cherishing our children, the hope of America.

President Clinton referred the amendment to the U.S. Department of Justice. As a consequence, I have been in correspondence with that body of our government.

The governors have invariably referred it to their various legislative review bodies. These people recognize how enormously and profoundly complex such a thing as this proposed amendment really is. In fact, how truly revolutionary such an idea is.

But to be the first nation in history to make children such a priority is truly mind-boggling. The very idea is so huge and grand in scope that it is no wonder that it will take a great deal of time to educate people to what the amendment actually represents in its tremendously numerous and various facets.

My approach to getting people to recognize the necessity of the amendment, to study it, is to begin the sensitizing process by the simple mechanism of making children the focus of our society. The phrase IT SHOULDN'T HURT TO BE A CHILD! is that mechanism.

When that phrase begins to take hold across this nation, it will serve the purpose of making children the proper priority of America; it will keep the fire of genuine concern for our children burning.

When enough rational dialogue begins as a result of such a campaign, it is my prayerful hope that the logical, empirical and pragmatic need of the amendment will evidence itself and become the Law of the Land.

Because of a number of incidents like the warning sign in my yard, shouted epithets in the night by rowdies driving by as I sit out front, threatening phone calls, our local paper decides to do a front page story on me and the amendment. This will include photos of the signs. I'm grateful for this.

The interviewing reporter asks a question about which I have been troubled myself. What is going to happen to the work I've started if I catch a stray, or otherwise, bullet or shotgun blast? Or become the victim of a sore loser who is better with a knife or gun than his stick when I'm shooting pool at one of the pubs?

In other words, there are no guarantees no matter where I am or what I'm doing. That's true for all of us.

But I'm not trying to be glib or nonchalant. This is serious business and I know it. What will happen to the work in such an event of my early demise?

It is my hope and fervent prayer that in such an event, the momentum of the amendment will have caught on, the signs and bumper stickers will have proliferated, the media will keep the issue burning and WE THE PEOPLE will have been writing legislators telling them: We've had enough! Pass this amendment!

When that begins to happen, whether I'm around or not, it isn't going to matter much. By that time, I hope to have done my part and the rest of the work will be up to others to carry on.

CHAPTER SIX

Mother Teresa and the People's Princess, Diana: the two most loved women of the century. But I believe Mother Teresa was the happier of the two.

It is easy to relate to the tragedy in the case of Princess Di. Too young and too much left to do with her life. Mother Teresa lived hugely and long, a full half-century longer than Princess Diana did. The world is so much the poorer for the loss of both of these ladies who proved one person could make a real difference in the world.

But I'm left asking, as I'm sure many of you are as well, who of the stature of these two women are on the horizon to take their places? I find this an intellectual curiosity and an emotional tragedy. There is no one. At least no one I can think of. Are we allowed so few in a century?

This isn't to say there are not many with their heart for the poor and needy, but it is peculiar that so few capture the hearts and minds of humanity as The People's Princess and Mother Teresa. That, admittedly, is strange.

And I'm left asking: Why so few such people who make such a difference?

***

The young man has been over a few times and asked for water. He fills a five-gallon, plastic jug and takes it to the trailer. Sometimes he has to make two or three trips so they can at least take sponge baths.

The other day as he was filling the jug, he walks up to me and tries to hand me a five-dollar bill. I refuse telling him I can't accept it. He looks at my sign, the names on my shed, and says "Please, Sam, this is for the kids." I took the five dollars; and thought immediately of the Widow's Mite of Scripture.

***

But sometimes I have to remind myself of a fact I have pointed out many times. We can admire genius while even despising the character of the person. In that respect, it wouldn't matter if Attila the Hun, the Marquis De Sade, Stalin or Hitler authored the amendment; it wouldn't make it any less worthy. And to my own credit, I haven't yet attained the stature of those gentlemen. Well, depending on whom you ask, of course.

I recently learned that Marilyn Vos Savant and I use the same mechanism to try to get to sleep. She says to start thinking about whatever you would like to dream about. In other words, start dreaming. Marilyn and I both call this Virtual Dreaming.

After a year and a half of working for the amendment, of dealing with so much abuse, torture and murder of children on a daily basis you find a way to sleep or go crazy. Unless you do, at the very least you become unfocused and too tired to be effective.

Pills, though suggested and necessary in some cases, were not an answer for me since they might make me sleep through a 3 a.m. phone call. And those kinds of calls sometimes literally mean the difference between life and death for some people.

Before the work became so consuming mentally and emotionally, I would use that mechanism of virtual dreaming. And it usually worked.

But once the nightmares began in earnest, it became ever more difficult to conjure up the necessary pleasant thoughts. The struggle to shut off my mind and try to sleep was causing me to wake up tired and with a headache. With enough coffee and an hour to get on track, I learned to deal with it. But I still resent losing that precious hour in the morning.

Most importantly, I learned to meet the physical and emotional needs by becoming mechanistic. That's right, I have become a mechanic; so much for Saint Sam.

Most of the work I needed to do was simple mechanics, a job. The need to analyze the amendment and its effects in its constituent parts, pragmatically and logically and write about these things was a matter of simple mechanics of the mind.

Painting the names of the little victims on the walls of my shed has a large, mechanical component. I have to assemble the stencils, tape them to the wall, tape protective covers around them and spray the paint. Then remove all the materials, let them dry and store them back in the shed for the next day's efforts and finally remove the paint from my hands and fingers with paint remover; all mechanical. Unless I dwell on the name and the particulars of how the child was murdered.

I do my best not to do this. Falling into morbidity is not conducive to mental health. So, mechanically, I am learning to cope by the very demands of the job. I try to focus on the job; not the mental pictures that so stir the emotions as to leave me incapacitated for the necessary work, the job.

I admit to a problem with the photographer assigned to the story about the amendment and me in the local paper. He had me pose in front of the shed. And then he asked me to smile.

The very incongruity of the request almost made me smile. I'm thinking; Here I am standing in front of all the names of these murdered children, children I have become intimately acquainted with, children I am trying to memorialize by my Wall, the little victims of unspeakably monstrous acts of cruelty and this guy is asking me to smile for the birdy? And some think I'm a nut? I didn't smile.

***

L- comes over late at night. She asks if she can please use my bathroom to wash. She is dirty from working on the fire-damaged house next door and there is no water over there.

I came to know her quite well from her sharing her childhood nightmares of having been molested. Her life ever after has been one of drugs, alcohol and failed relationships with men. But at nearly 40 years of age, she has never accepted responsibility for her life and keeps looking for men to care for her.

But the drugs and alcohol have taken their toll and she has virtually nothing to offer a man. Like most in her situation, uneducated, lacking saleable skills, she has spent a lifetime on welfare and letting bums leech off her welfare check to the detriment of her now grown children.

Now, she no longer has any welfare check and her own children, understandably, don't want anything to do with their mother. They carry too many scars, themselves, because of the selfishness of their mother and her permitting, even aiding, so much abuse in their lives.

Her boyfriend and owner of the fire damaged house, D-, had kicked her out some time ago after they had lived together about eight months. He had taken up with an eighteen-year-old blond. D- is 47.

But, as I wrote in my Birds book, men like young women and there is no changing the species (men) in that regard. This is one of the reasons single women over 40 have only about a one per cent chance of marriage.

Ok, another characteristic of the species is lying to women. D- had sold the teenager viz adult on his having money and property. Nothing wrong with a woman wanting a man with those things going for him provided he isn't lying about them. Certainly has made many an ugly man handsome to some women. Fat and/or ugly is ok if the bank account is equally fat and beautiful.

But, as dreadful as it sounds, I have discovered women are capable of lying as well as men. Fortunately for us men, if she still has them and fat, wrinkles, age, booze, drugs haven't depleted them, the major assets of a woman to a man are more easily seen and enjoyed.

L- discovers through papers she collected when she packed her things that the girl is wanted back East for passing bad checks and has a number of aliases and a few other sordid secrets she failed to share with D-, some of which the police are enjoying sharing with him when they pick the girl up.

117

So D- comes whining back to L-, pledging his undying love if she will only forgive him the small deviation from his previous position of undying and eternal love for her and take him back. His bed is cold.

So here is L-, all aglow, cleaning up the burned house for D-, so happy that she got the better of the young upstart. I'm so happy Sam, She tells me.

I know better. I know D-. But it isn't my place to disabuse L-. She wouldn't believe me anyhow. She wouldn't want to believe me.

It's late at night, two days later. There's a pounding at my door.

He kicked me out again, Sam! I can't believe it! He just wanted me to help clean up for him and sleep with him till he could raise that slut's bail!

The bail, I learned, was $4,000. But I had met the girl, J-, and had to admit she was a real beauty, con and jailbird notwithstanding. And men are really stupid when it comes to beautiful, young women and sex; nature of the beast and not subject to change.

In all of this, I'm thanking God there are no small children involved. So I can take a rather detached view of the unfolding drama.

L- does have other problems like an older son that is due to start serving time in the local lockup next Wednesday.

But L- is now virtually homeless. I give her my couch for the night.

She has boxed her things up and in the morning asks if I will use my truck to move them to storage at her brother's place. So I help her load the things and take them to her brother's house.

But he wants the things she already has stored out of his place. Her brother has had it with his sister's bouncing back and forth with D- and with the cops coming around he just wants to wash his hands of the whole matter and L-.

I arrange a storage locker for her and we spend the better part of the day moving all her things into it. Stuff happens.

Once the things are moved, she still needs to do some laundry and have some of her clothes at hand so she can dress properly, then, back to my place.

It is easy for me to sympathize with her, but only up to a point. And I'll do all I can to help, but only up to a point.

As long as these women do the booze and drugs, as long as they keep shacking up with bums like D-, they are on a losing track.

L- has another friend, C-, who has just left an abusive boyfriend who has threatened to kill her. C- has an old van and the two women will stay in that down by the lake until they can figure out what they are going to do for a place to live.

L-, like so many, has no vehicle and isn't likely to get one. Even if she had one, she will never be able to afford the insurance and like most in the Valley, would drive without it. Or a license, as C- does.

L- and C- will shower and keep a few things at my house until they have some place of their own. I give them permission to use my phone number as a message center. I've done this for several in their circumstances.

Many such people have a P.O. Box. They can't get their welfare checks without one. Most of them have learned not to have house delivery since they have had their checks ripped off by others staying in the places they commonly share, especially the men who don't get welfare and leech off the checks and food stamps of the women. But a phone is beyond most of them.

L- wants to cooperate with the police concerning D-'s young love since she is wanted out of state for floating bad checks and L- has some specific information she thinks would be helpful in the prosecution. She thinks if she can get rid of the little hussy, she will get D- back.

Bad idea, I tell her. If there are wants or warrants and the girl doesn't skip bail leaving D- with a $4,000 reminder of his liaison (Which I suspect will happen. Especially when the girl learns D- has lied to her about having a lot of money and property), the police are going to pick up on this before she appears for trial here locally.

And even at that, though there would be no point in telling L- this, D- would just use her again until he found someone he wanted more. Nor can I tell L- that she has lost her own looks and figure because of the boozing and the drugs. Most certainly she is no competition for the young beauty D- is chasing. It wouldn't do any good to tell her, she knows this and is becoming desperate, desperate enough to think if she can get rid of J-, D- will take her back and be faithful to her; not very good thinking and a definite sign of her desperation.

L-'s friend, C-, does try to tell her these things but L- isn't listening.

L- had a bunch of jewelry she said D- had given her and asks me to look at it. The pearls are paste, the diamonds are glass, and the silver and gold trinkets are a cheap alloy. The only thing of any value is an antique watch. I try to tell her the stuff is nothing but junk. She won't listen.

She calls later and tells me she pawned the stuff. She got a total of one hundred dollars. This primarily for the watch. She was beside herself after learning the stuff was just what I said it was. Junk.

You would think women would be more intelligent than to take some man's word that the things he is giving her are really valuable.

I'm at the club on a Friday night and sitting with K-. We enjoy each other's company, the music and dancing. She's a beautiful woman and she knows the parties involved in this scenario, an altogether familiar one to both of us. D-, in fact, has tried to hit on K- several times.

But K- is sharp. She's not an alcoholic or drug user and comes from an old established family with an excellent pedigree.

A common interest to K- and me is computers and computer marketing. She is very involved with this and has her own business. She has brought several books on the subject and loans them to me. I give her copies of my latest writings and will profit from her critique.

You know, Sam, she says, someday you are either going to win the Nobel Peace Prize, a Pulitzer or be canonized, maybe all three. Of course, that presumes you live long enough. And you aren't cooperating very well in extending your life span (K- knows some of the enemies I have made and about some of the threats against me).

I laugh and she takes my hand and places it on her lovely, shapely bare leg (her short skirt facilitates this maneuver). I give her satin-like, soft leg a friendly pat and squeeze and tell her that as long as I enjoy playing with the legs of beautiful women I don't think the Pope or Nobel Committee is too likely to be impressed with my credentials for Sainthood or Humanitarian of the Year.

That sets her off in a paroxysm of laughter. The band starts and we get up and dance. I'm grateful for the chance to get rid of the bad taste of such human misery that I deal with on a daily basis and lose myself in holding K- and moving to the lilting rhythm of the music, thanking God for the music and women like K-.

***

It was certainly heartening to learn that the U.S. Appeals Court recently upheld New Jersey's Megan's Law. The law requires sex offender's register with the state, and that the state notifies communities where they live. The court held that this was a permissible measure that offered important protection to families.

The downside of Megan's Law is that only about ten per cent of such perverts register. And to quote most police departments, including the one here in the Valley where I live: We just don't have the time or manpower to keep track of these offenders.

There are 30 such perverts registered here in the Valley. And our local police department can't keep track of this relatively small number of sex offenders. The actual number is undoubtedly over 200. And if the police can't keep track of 30, what could they possibly do with over 200?

This is a common complaint of most police departments. And since keeping track of sexual offenders is a low priority of the police, the great majority of these perverts take full advantage of this.

There reasoning can't be faulted. If so many states have laws that don't take the sex offender seriously, if the general population gives such crimes such a low priority of concern, why should the sexual predator not take advantage? Why should these monsters register?

In Arkansas, the police acknowledged that of 1,500 sex offenders, only 50 registered! And half of these gave false addresses. That means the police only knew where 25 out of 1,500 actually were! But who expects criminals, especially perverts, to be law-abiding; thus the extreme weakness of such mechanisms as Megan's Law.

A Dinuba, California woman, Epilida Aguirre, 23, was recently convicted of trying to flush her newborn daughter down a toilet. The little girl, no name given, is in foster care.

At her sentencing, this woman had the temerity to ask the judge to reunite her with her little girl, claiming that her actions stemmed from her drug and alcohol problems.

In spite of the woman's attorney pointing out that she had no previous record and shouldn't be sent to prison, the judge sensibly said no and gave the woman four years for felony child endangerment.

The conscienceless act of this woman and her case before the court is too typical. The utter lack of self-discipline and personal responsibility, the attitude that she could abuse drugs and alcohol, be sexually permissive and had no responsibility for the results, a human life, is exactly that; too typical.

No, I do not know the woman personally, I do not know what her background is and the circumstances that led to her despicable act of trying to get rid of, actually murder, her newborn daughter.

So I am not able to act as the judge of her motives or to judge her personally in respect to the circumstances that might explain her behavior.

But such an explanation leading to understanding will never excuse such an action. And the excuse these people try to use of drugs and alcohol for every kind of irresponsible and criminal action has become all too commonplace.

Society must accept its share of the blame for such things. If a society is encouraging virtue, you have that kind of society. If it encourages the lack of virtue, lack of self-discipline and lack of personal responsibility, you have that kind of society.

I have said many times that we have become a society that acts as though it actually hates children. There is too much evidence of this to think otherwise.

For example, we can point to the permissive attitude toward abortion. This attitude, expressed by the findings of courts, the apathy, ambivalence and conflict surrounding this most vital issue of basic morality on the part of the general population, cannot but lead to moral confusion and a devaluing of human life.

We can point to the general lack of character and integrity, of virtue in our leaders of virtually all institutions of education, the churches, government and business as another proof of not caring about children. After all, as they grow up children eventually reflect the character of the leadership of these institutions. And these leaders cannot be so stupid as not to realize this. So, do they really care about children, the future of humanity? I think not!

We can easily point to the teaching of the entertainment media that sex, even perverted sex and a total lack of sexual responsibility, is an acceptable way of life. Profit and the promotion of perversion are the concerns of the entertainment media, not children or the future of humanity.

The pervasive violence promoted by the entertainment industry takes its toll by thoroughly desensitizing children and young people to the value of life. The battle over abortion certainly greatly contributes to this. When the courts and people are saying it's all right to end life by abortion, the results in the thinking of society, of the children in such a society, is easily predictable.

When the leadership of the churches is in dispute over whether perverts can be ordained to the priesthood and ministry, the mixed signal adds to moral confusion and the erosion of the ability of religious institutions to preach and teach morality.

There are individual ministries, especially those of televangelism, that have been so disgustingly blatant in immorality, robbing people in the name of God and shaming Him by their theatrical efforts to gather viewers that children cannot help but be exposed to this message.

The problem in religion is human beings that tell other human beings they have risen above being human. It won't wash and never has. Children learn from this as well.

I rarely attend church anymore. And when I do, it is one that has a ministry of really helping people, like Calvary Chapel in Modesto. But even churches like this one suffer from believing they are making a real difference when they are not because they are insulated from the larger problems of society and the world.

By the mechanism of in-breeding, of associating with only those of their own kind, even the best ministries delude themselves that because they genuinely care, are seeing gratifying results on a local scale; they are doing a great work. They even come to believe that God is doing great things through them and other ministries like theirs across the country.

Not so.

If they were correct, we would see substantial changes for the better taking place in crucial areas like government, the schools and the entertainment industry. It isn't happening.

Self deluded that they are making a real and substantial change for the better, these ministries continue on blindly believing they are doing real battle against evil.

A part of the weakness of such churches is the belief that God can do anything. He can't. The responsibility to confront and overcome evil is ours, not God's. And you would think this is so obvious that good people couldn't miss it. But they do.

For example, the leader of the Southern Ku Klux Klan is a Baptist minister in Arkansas, Tom Robb. Who's responsible for confronting him if not good people claiming to be Christian?

I was largely responsible for pulling the teeth out of the prejudice and violence of the International KKK, then called The Invisible Empire, under J.W. Farrands. But the story belongs in another book that I won't write until I'm sure the innocent won't suffer as a consequence.

And, of course, we have Richard Butler at Hayden Lake in Idaho, the leader of the Aryan Nations who claims to be a good Christian and leads prayers with a Nazi salute and a large picture of Hitler in the background. I met with Butler face to face during the Randy Weaver affair and interviewed him at his headquarters compound.

We have Carl Franklin, a disciple of Butler's whom I also met, who left Butler and has started his own little Elohim village in Noxon, Montana dedicated to his own vision and version of Christianity. All of these men have one thing in common: They alone have a plan to save the white race and Christianity. And they generate a lot of mailings to that effect.

In a school in Brundige, Alabama, teachers have forced three Jewish children to bow their heads during Christian prayers, talked openly of converting them and fellow students have drawn swastikas on their lockers and beaten them up. Who but good people should confront this kind of evil and child abuse?

But no: Let God do it; it's not our responsibility! Say the good people.

Got a bulletin for all you good people and patrons of virtue; God can't! You, me, we are responsible for confronting such evil, not God!

In my personal fight against bullies and fanatics my cajones haven't gotten any smaller and I'll still jump in and mix it up in the mud, the blood and the beer if I have to. I'm still just as willin' as I've ever been but at my age, I keep reminding myself, my hide doesn't heal and my bones don't knit as fast as they used to.

Naturally I don't expect everyone to be as crazy as I am or purposely set themselves up as bait and targets to flush the insects and reptiles out from under their respective rocks. As dear Walt Kelly put it so well: "Ain't no future in bein' bait."But see how many fish you catch with a bare hook.

And I recognize that a part of such blindness to personal responsibility on the part of good people is the enormity of the task. What can we really do to change things? They say. They throw up their hands, go to church and blame God for not making the world right. Even worse are those who are waiting for Jesus to come and do their job for them.

Of course, such people don't see their prayers and church attendance as blaming God or copping out to Jesus. But when you are trying to make God or Jesus responsible for those things that are your responsibility, what else can you call it?

I have actually heard people ask God in prayer to bless the children of the world, to guide and bless our elected leaders, to overcome the evil in the world, to care for the hungry and homeless.

Yet these same people may never have so much as written a letter to their local, elected leaders (if they, in fact, even know who they are), know virtually nothing of the actual evil being perpetrated against children or even know of someone truly hungry and homeless. Such people are, in fact, no more than patrons of virtue, rather than possessors of virtue.

It is a simple matter to get the world report on child abuse that resulted from the conference in Stockholm, Sweden last summer. I even gave the details and the address in TAP at the time. It is a real eye-opener. Want to guess how many good preachers and churchgoers have requested this report? I don't want to know! Could be written on their foreheads.

Now that the issue of the Swiss gold is wide open it is, again, an issue of I don't want to know.

The Allied and Axis powers both did business with the Swiss during WWII. Since Switzerland was a declared neutral nation, many persecuted people trusted Swiss banks to care for their money and other valuables. When the people disappeared, so did most of the bank accounts.

The Swiss argument is that they had no choice and no chance if they defied Hitler and refused to do business with him. And they are probably right.

It is well said that in the conflict between good and evil, neutrality is morally indefensible. And, to paraphrase Thoreau, there is not an instant of a lack of vigilance between virtue and vice.

I won't be the historical, armchair quarterback. But I do know that evil is always the winner when Pope's Monster of Vice is allowed any incipient beginning as he warned.

Only when good people decide to confront evil head on with equal determination of the evil will the good be able to overcome. Or, in the end, you wind up wringing your hands, like the Swiss, and say: You had no choice and no chance.

Folks the amendment gives you a choice and a chance; please don't try to get out of it by indefensible neutrality or a lame I don't want to know!

When the president, when leaders in congress, state and local elected representatives of We the People are not held to standards of virtue, of morality, an entire society suffers. And the children learn.

Women are beaten and won't press charges against their attackers. In far too many cases, there are children at risk in such situations. But the women allow this violent behavior to continue in their lives and sometimes they die, and their children, because of this.

The battered woman faces a society that seems to excuse violence, even approve it. This makes it all the harder for such women to make the rational choice to leave an abusive, often a dangerously abusive, relationship.

And too many stay in such a relationship because of booze and drugs. And children die.

Such a society naturally produces Elipida Aguirre's.

Molestation is endemic to poverty. But since the poverty stricken inner cities particularly are comprised of minorities where welfare, drug and alcohol abuse is also endemic it is called racist to draw attention to the extremely high numbers of molestation in such areas.

They call her Girl X. And that is the name I painted on my Wall. She is nine-years-old.

She lived in a Chicago ghetto and on January 9 of this year, she was found unconscious and raped, her T-shirt wound around her neck in an attempt to strangle her. Foam was coming from her mouth from an attempt by the rapist to poison as well as strangle her. Gangster graffiti was scrawled on her abdomen in black ink. At last account, she had come out of a coma and was conscious, but unable to speak.

Girl X didn't make the news. Another little victim, a white, golden-haired child beauty queen, was making headlines: JonBenet Ramsey.

As one member of the community where Girl X was so horribly brutalized, Patrick Murphy, the Cook County Public Guardian put it:

No one is surprised when an underclass kid is raped or killed. I think we expect these kids to be killed. It's not that people don't care. It's that they yawn; whereas if it's a blond-haired, blue-eyed kid, they all go crazy. I've seen it a million times.

Mr. Murphy, I purposely put Girl X with JonBenet's name on my Wall. I go equally crazy whether the child is black, brown, yellow, red or white.

Children are children no matter what their parents or a society try to make of them to the contrary and regardless of whether the locale is Harlem or Beverly Hills!

But I advise the members of minority communities, the ghettos and barrios, the war zones and killing fields where I have taught and worked, to come clean about the extremely high incidence of molestation in those communities. It is not racist or discriminatory in any fashion to deal with facts and bring the needed attention to the brutalizing of children in those communities.

And if the leaders in such communities would tell the truth about this, maybe people would stop yawning when they hear about the little Girl Xs.

Another dimension of the problem is the ubiquitous tube. The message of violence and perversion carried by TV reaches into the ghettos as well as Rodeo Drive.

The Globe, The Inquirer, Star, the Tabloids. No question about their unabashed use of titillating headlines that attempts to get you to pick them up at the newsstands.

But, like the Readers' Digest, People Magazine and others, if you want to keep your finger on the pulse of the public, if you want to stay informed, print media in its varied forms is the way to do it.

Dear Meg is a column in Star. She recently wrote:

Even the American Medical Association has said that mounting violence among our children is endangering society. Although many libertarians argue against it, there is no question in my mind that TV violence, even more than on film, desensitizes young children so quickly that by the time they're eight or ten, murder, child abuse and sexual activity are seen as everyday occurrences.

Yet judge Bork is pilloried for pointing out the devastating effect of TV on children and calling for sensible censorship. Folks, we are not going to be able to have our cake and eat it to about this issue. Somewhere along the line common sense, moral absolutes are going to have to prevail or the results are going to be anarchy or totalitarianism!

I maintain that the amendment is the logical place to start in turning America to sensible and indispensable morality. This is where, for the sake of our children, our future; we must say: Here is where the battle line against evil is drawn! Cross this line and you give up any right to inhabit a civilized society!

Part of my doctoral studies involved trend forecasting. If enough data is available, it is relatively easy to make such forecasts.

Certainly enough data was available in 1955 to forecast the failure of public education and the reasons why. But the situation deteriorated in spite of the availability of the data. One of the major reasons for this was using the data to ask the same people, many with worthless doctorates in education, who created the problems to solve them. Insane!

Together with this kind of insanity one cannot help thinking we need fewer lawyers and more real people with real life experiences in the various legislatures and Congress. In this sense, there is little difference between the fields of education and politics.

But, to continue, it seems that there has been a reversal, which should have been easy to forecast, in the main concern of college students. In 1967, university and college students were concerned about learning the meaning of life, of who is God?

Today's main concern is to be very well off financially.

The last thirty years mired in so much economic uncertainty, has caused this major shift in values. Students today have become much more materialistic with little concern for the meaning of life or knowing God.

This shift from the spiritual to the material has certainly shown itself by the major changes in women especially. The study concluded they are now more likely to smoke than men, that they now drink as much as men, and are as career minded as men.

In short, women have fast lost the home and hearth mentality that made them the soft and gentle nurturers and the antithesis to war.

As a romantic, a poet, I don't want to believe that a woman would rather be a doctor or lawyer than the inspiration for the best efforts of a man in poetry, art and music. I still want her to be that inspiration, the softness and gentleness that compliments my necessary and male toughness, the resulting alloy being much more durable and flexible than either too hard or too soft.

But I stop short of saying that a woman cannot be a doctor or lawyer and fail to be that kind of poetic inspiration to me as a man.

Still, I live with the consequences of those thirty years of obfuscation and confusion of the proper roles for men and women in society.

Trend forecasting could have easily predicted the fact that women outnumber men when it comes to Road Rage. Such aggressive women drivers are typically under 34 and undereducated according to the study. Women, as they mature (read: losing their youth), are becoming increasingly angry with their lot and working out their anger and frustration behind the wheel and increased alcohol and drug abuse.

But keep in mind that the dangerously aggressive drivers remain young, uneducated, unmarried males with criminal records.

***

Kevin Galik raped and murdered 11-year-old Traci Conrad of Hanford, California. He then suffocated her with towels wrapped around her neck and face and used duct tape to keep a sock stuffed in her mouth. This monster then stuck her body in a pottery kiln in his backyard where it was discovered a month later.

A jury recently found this beast in the form of a man guilty of little Traci's brutal murder. He was then sentenced to life in prison where the taxpayers can continue to feed and clothe this monster while the parents of this little victim can spend the rest of their lives living the on-going nightmare of their little girl's screams, knowing her torturer and murderer is still living... and, as taxpayers, helping to pay to keep him living. So it is that I fully understand the cry of so many for the death penalty.

Keeping in mind that fully one-half of girls are molested in one way or another in America, I want you to carefully consider the ramifications of this in the following in order to get an idea of how this tragically shameful and disgraceful, dirty open secret of our nation impacts the whole of our society, both morally and financially. These are the usual results of the molested female child:

Early pregnancies and abortions, welfare dependency, physical and mental disorders from childhood on, poor school performance and high drop out rate, lesbianism, drug and alcohol addiction, prostitution, nymphomania, attempted suicides, repeatedly failed, intimate relationships with men and social friendships, multiple divorces and dysfunctional children resulting from dysfunctional marriages or live-in relationships, inability to focus on activities that lead to achieving goals, criminal activity, especially involving drugs, prostitution and shop lifting, expensive long term counseling for those that can afford it or paid by taxpayers for those that cannot. And this list is only the tip of the iceberg in the effect on society as a whole.

I once told my readers that if I were to ever see, hear or be visited by an angel, I would tell them about it. Well, it finally happened. I can only suppose that at this stage of the battle for the amendment God knew I needed an angel and sent her to me.

She appeared as an extraordinarily beautiful, petite young woman in her twenties. But her message was a horror story of a life that was a living nightmare from earliest childhood.

Her stepfather was molesting her with the knowledge of her mother. Once more, normal people cannot grasp how any creature calling himself a man can do such a monstrous thing or how a mother can be equally monstrous in allowing it to happen, to continue to happen!

No one who has not experienced such horror as this young woman can possibly understand what it is like as a child to be lying in the dark, waiting,

waiting and wondering if that creature that calls itself your father is going to come into your room in the dark and hurt you this night.

How long does such a child lay awake, night after night after night in fear of falling asleep, lying there in the dark in fear of that monster attacking? She curls herself up in a ball, tiny knees to her chin, hugging herself tightly with her tiny arms, and prays: Oh, please God; make him leave me alone tonight!

Some children pray for death to deliver them from such a living nightmare. And some kill themselves.

If the little girl lives, as she grows older the nightmares never leave. She may go into counseling or, if the circumstances permit financially, professional long-term therapy.

The majority, however, will never be able to avail themselves of such treatment but will follow the path of drugs, alcohol, failed relationships, early pregnancies, etc. that I have outlined previously.

But should such a victim of molestation be able to enter treatment, what the professionals will not tell her is that there is only one way the nightmares will ever end.

But I will tell her. If she finds someone who truly loves her, who understands her pain, someone in whose arms she can abandon herself in absolute trust and the security of the love she was denied as a child, then, and only then, will the nightmares cease!

Because I know how powerful love has been in my own life, I accord it the most powerful force in the world, powerful enough to overcome and heal the worst nightmares imaginable.

It is the lack of love in people's lives that makes life a living hell for so many. Our children, our young people are growing up without love. The hurt and pain, the anger and frustration of this is evident all around us. As I keep repeating, we have become a nation that seems to hate children!

The angel who came to visit me was totally unexpected as, I suppose, all such visitations are.

She was a very small angel, the top of her head not even reaching my chin. But there was no mistaking what she was. It wasn't just her extraordinary beauty or the sound of her voice; it was something indefinable about her that shouted unmistakably: Here is an angel!

The angel had driven into my yard; an angel driving a car.

At the sound of a vehicle pulling into my yard, I had gone out to greet whoever it was.

She got out, came up to me and said: "I had to meet the man who has painted the names of those children on this shed, who has put that sign on his house IT SHOULDN'T HURT TO BE A CHILD!"

She put her small, child-like hand out to me and I took it in mine.

We went in the house and she told me her story. For the first time since I undertook the work for the amendment, I felt like I could finally cry. I have wanted and needed the relief of tears many times and have been unable to cry.

But it has been years since I have had such release from the psychosis of grief. Not since the death of my oldest daughter, Diana.

As she told her story, this little angel was fighting for control of herself. I could tell she was fighting the tears, struggling not to break down. At one point, she rubbed her arms and legs vigorously to control her trembling and chills.

But unlike Sue and so many others I have met and written about, this little angel had the spark of determination and the courage to do battle, to carry the fight against molesters into the enemy's camp. She hadn't, like most of the others, had this spark beaten out of her.

So-called professional counseling had done its usual harm. She had been told she must find a way to forgive the monster that had stolen her childhood and made her life a living hell.

Forgive? NEVER! Those who counsel such a thing have never lain in the dark as a child, night after night after night waiting for the monster to come in and rape them! Forgiveness for such satanic monsters! Not in this life or the one to come!

If there is anything to justice in an afterlife, it will include the deepest and hottest part of the pit of hell for such Spawn of Satan! There is such a thing as healthy and perfect hatred for all such monsters that prey on children!

What of the monster in Cairo, Marzouk Ahmed Abdel-Rahim, Egypt who beheaded his own daughter, Nora Marzouk Ahmed, on behalf of the family's honor? Her crime? She had eloped. Thus the superstitions of religion and so-called culture continue to plague humankind throughout the world. Like the so-called parents in this country who deny medical care for their children based on religious superstitions. Forgiveness for such monsters? NEVER!

My little angel understood the vital importance of the amendment in meeting and overcoming the evil done to children, in overcoming the evil men and women who prey on children.

I have met so many like this angel with the same story, the same nightmarish story of being denied a childhood, of a living hell, in nighttime terror, the horror of the monster who kept attacking her and treating her as nothing but a thing to satisfy the hellish, unholy lust of such monsters!

Why did I feel I could at last openly weep real tears in her presence? I haven't cried real tears since the death of Diana those years ago. Why now?

Maybe because she is an angel- As I watched this angel struggle so hard to control her own tears, struggle not to break down in front of me, I wanted to reach out and take her in my arms and weep with her, to comfort her as I have comforted others.

Maybe my being unable to do so was part of the tears I felt I could finally let flow but had to control for her sake. I didn't dare reach out to her; I didn't dare let the tears come. How many men in her young life have taken advantage of her, pretending empathy and understanding for her only to betray her trust? I couldn't risk taking the chance of being perceived as one of those to her.

I have had the experience of earning the trust of many people. I have had the birds, squirrels and raccoons come to my back door and eat from my hand. The angel was like a small, wounded animal that desperately needed someone to trust, someone to help her. I couldn't risk moving too quickly no matter how much I wanted to reach out to her. Trust is an earned thing among all of God's creatures. We humans are no different in this respect.

Because of the constraints of time, she couldn't stay long. But we had talked; we had established an unspoken communication and understanding between each other simply looking into each other's eyes that guaranteed we would see each other again.

As I walked her out to her car, it seemed right that we share a light embrace and that we should kiss in the tenderest way, quickly, lightly as the brush of a butterfly. It was another part of that unspoken understanding we had reached. She knew instinctively that I wouldn't betray her trust. That is a humbling thing, to have the trust of an angel.

She had appeared so unexpectedly that I couldn't have been less prepared for meeting her. I was taking care of a friend who had tried to kill himself. I had gone without much sleep during the week I treated and cared for him. I was a mess, unshaved, hair uncombed, wearing an old shirt and shorts and no shoes on my feet, only open sandals. But the angel didn't seem to care.

It was only after she was driving away and I was walking back to the house that it came to me, why this angel made me want to cry again after so many years with nothing but the tears in my heart. It was something I had written some time ago after re-reading Bill Mauldin's Up Front that he wrote during WWII:

THE PAIN OF GOD

When my brother and I were very small, if we were hurting from some accident or illness our great-grandmother would tell us, Oh, sweetheart I wish I could take your pain on myself.

She couldn't of course. But she did hurt. She hurt because she would far rather suffer herself than to see my brother or me hurting. That is the love of a parent for a child; or, in this case, a great-grandmother.

How many of us, as parents, wouldn't far rather take the pain of our children on ourselves if it were possible? It is dreadful to see a little one suffer.

As a child, I wondered at my great-grandmother saying such a thing. It was a mystery. I didn't doubt her for a moment. I knew she meant what she said. And I loved her all the more because of it. And I knew how much she loved my brother and me. But I also knew she couldn't take our hurt to herself and spare us the pain.

Then there is the pain of having to discipline the child. How many parents, myself especially, have gone to bed hating ourselves for having to discipline a child? There is a lot of truth to: This is going to hurt me more than it is you!

Can there be any joy in pain? Yes.

I know my great-grandmother would have been praising God if she could have taken the hurt of my brother or me on herself. She would have rejoiced in such suffering.

When I had children of my own, I gradually came to know how our great-grandmother felt. How I would have been praising God and rejoicing in the pain if I could only have taken it on myself in those cases with my own children!

It was in coming to an understanding of this that led to my understanding how Jesus could rejoice in the pain of the cross.

If the suffering of Jesus, if his sacrifice for us is to have any meaning, it must have this meaning above all else.

That greater love he spoke of is to rejoice in helping others, in protecting the weak and the innocent from evil. Even to the taking of the pain on ourselves.

Folks, if you don't suffer when you see a child suffering, there is nothing of God, or even humanity, about you! If you can use your religion as an excuse for not waging war against those wicked people who are the cause of such suffering of children you are of a different species than humanity! And you know nothing of God or the love and pain of God!

I mentioned Bill Mauldin last month. His Willie and Joe were important to us during WWII. There was another cartoonist named George Baker who created Sad Sack. The Sack, like Willie and Joe, portrayed the life of GIs in a way that the grunts could relate.

Much of the dark humor of war is found in the work of men like Mauldin and Baker. Then, there was the art.

James Jones, the author of From Here to Eternity, put together a book of which I have a copy, of WWII art together with a commentary that led Joseph Heller to call it, The most stirring and lucid account of WWII that I have ever read.

One example of this commentary should suffice:

It's funny, the things that get to you. One day a man near me was hit in the throat, as he stood up, by a bullet from a burst of MG fire. He cried out: Oh, my God! In an awful, grimly comic, burbling kind of voice that made me think of the signature of the old Shep Fields' Rippling Rhythm band. There was awareness in it, and a tone of having expected it, then he fell down, to all intents and purposes dead.

I say to all intents and purposes because his vital functions may have continued for a while. But he appeared unconscious, and of course there was nothing to do for him with his throat artery torn out. Thinking about him, it seemed to me that his yell had been for all of us lying there, and I felt like crying...

This is why the angel made me want to cry, made me feel as though I could finally, after years, find some healing in my own soul through the release of real tears. Her pain was the pain of all those like herself, it was the pain of a child who cannot understand and is still living in the shadow of that monster who lurks in her nightmares and every waking thought! The vital functions are there, but the victim is only alive to all intents and purposes, the pain makes living a living death!

So the pain that was so easily seen in the angel, in her voice, her manner, her eyes, her eyes above all else, made me want to cry, made me hope I could cry. She was all the children in one whose pain and suffering, whose torture I was dealing with on a daily basis. And I needed to cry. The child within her was yelling Oh, My God! And no one had heard her cry. And if God did, he hadn't been able to save her any more than he had been able to save that soldier or little Melissa Russo and Julie Lejeune.

She called the following night to thank me for the literature I had given her including my book IT SHOULDN'T HURT TO BE A CHILD! She was so very enthusiastic about helping with the amendment that my own heart soared. Here was an angel with all the qualifications I didn't have to help with the battle ahead, an angel who had the spark and determination to carry the battle into the enemy's camp as a Momma Bear, who hadn't allowed that spark and determination to be beaten out of her!

Most importantly, she said she was going to come see me again and let me explain to her how she could help with the amendment. And maybe at our next meeting, we will be able to share our tears.

One of the most important elements of fighting the battle for the amendment, which I anticipate sharing with my little angel, is summed up in something I shared with my readers in the beginning phase of the amendment:

"So soon as an earnest conviction has cooled into a phrase, its work is over, and the best that can be done with it is to bury it."

God hates your sneakin' creturs thet believe
He'll settle things they run away and leave!

James Russell Lowell, the devout abolitionist and supporter of Ralph Waldo Emerson wrote both of the above.

As to the first, I have received so many letters from elected leaders using the phrase: Our children are our most important responsibility. They must be a matter of a national priority!

Yet nothing is getting any better for children and what should be a conviction followed by the appropriate actions of conviction, has cooled into a phrase and might as well be buried. But ACPC will not allow this to become a phrase to be buried!

And God hates such sneakin' creturs that believe He'll settle things they run away and leave! From the Biglow Papers.

Business as usual blaming God for that which is our responsibility. Nothing new under the sun? Not so far as recognizing the need for action. But there better be something new for the human race as to what that action should be! We have gotten nowhere fast by following the same path on a treadmill toward Armageddon!

If the same problem persists and defies solution in spite of enormous effort, you are obviously on a false trail.

So I propose something new, something truly revolutionary! And the whole world gasps and says: This is something new! It has never been done before! It cannot be done!

But I also have proposed in a couple of my books that attempts at a solution that denies the input of an entire one-half of the human race cannot possibly reach a solution. You ladies of the world are that one-half of humanity who have been steadfastly disenfranchised by men who ignorantly, prejudicially deny you access in the decision making process of a solution!

You ladies are far more sensitive to the cry of children than men. You do not bear children to sacrifice them to the lust and wars of men! The amendment is the chance for you to make your voices heard!

If I die, will you love me?

I only had to hear of an abused child asking that question once for it to impact my life.

Deborah Elizabeth Reynolds, 33 and 180 pounds, assisted by two other women, Julia Ann Olivas and Esther Griggs, beat her daughter, 5-year-old Breeann Spikard, to death to drive the demons from her. This monster calling itself a mother beat the little girl to death with a large wood paddle.

All three women had children who they regularly beat with the paddle. The little victim's 8-year-old brother when testifying in court said he could hear the screams of his little sister as she was beaten to death.

Evidence indicates that the 180-pound monster stomped up and down on the little girl as well as beating her.

And I ask myself, how can we call ourselves a civilized nation of laws when we allow, under the guise and hypocrisy of religious freedom, such monsters as Reynolds to torture and murder children, to murder them by denying them medical attention, to warp and twist their minds to hatreds and prejudices against others?

Yet, when the president suggests religious tolerance guidelines in the workplace, those calling themselves patriots vilify him.

Ellie Nesler is finally released though pleas for clemency were ignored by California Governor Pete Wilson. As I said some time ago, Ellie made the mistake of exacting justice in the courtroom by executing her son's molester. Had she done it in the street, she would not have gone to prison. But judges and governors, being lawyers first, were incensed that a member of the great unwashed, a commoner, should seek justice, personally, in their courts.

Mr. Governor, your refusal to grant clemency for Ellie will long be remembered by the electorate!

A little girl's body is found buried in a trashcan in the yard of a house in Ironton, Ohio. The little girl's dog was buried with her. The family, Volgares, had moved away and workers who were doing repairs to the property made the discovery. The family's whereabouts is unknown at present.

Little 4-year-old Heather Jackson here in Kern County is in a coma from being violently shaken. There were also burn marks on her feet. The prognosis is not good but even if she comes out of the coma, doctors expect the little one to never be more than a vegetable. And another Kern County name goes on my Wall.

The mother, Sandra Dee Stewart, and her boyfriend, Martin Vincent Carillo Sr., have been arrested. The monster calling herself a mother has three other children, ages 6, 10 and 12.

10-day-old Joy Baker dies slowly roasted to death in summer heat in the car of the monster-mother, Gail Baker, while she played video poker in a Columbia, S.C. casino.

12-year-old Benjamin Rodriguez is shot to death while watching TV in his Modesto home, a random act of violence by a drive-by shooter. Police say that at least five shots were fired into the home.

Susan and Gene Mitchell starve little 2-year-old Jeffrey Mitchell in Paducah, Kentucky to death. He weighed just 10 pounds at death.

Two other children were found starving to death as well. Jeffrey's little sister, Melanie, age 3, and didn't even have the strength to hold her head up when police arrived. Yet they all lived in a nice, well-furnished house. The parents have been arrested.

A 2-year-old girl and her 4-year-old brother were found bound and gagged in a motel room in Montebello, California. God only knows what was in store for these two children.

An Oildale couple, William and Lucy Stewart, have been arrested for the stepfather's molestation of the woman's daughter. The girl's mother agreed to the molestation. The little girl was 12 when the nightmare began. She is now 15. The couple's defense? They wanted the girl to give the monsters another child!

A child slave operation has been exposed in Lagos, Nigeria and neighboring Benin. Hundreds of children were rescued from being sold into slavery. But other hundreds continue to be missing.

This attitude toward children throughout the world has a great deal to do with what is becoming increasingly called a global explosion of incivility. When people become callous and apathetic toward children, they quickly begin to lose civilized manners in other areas.

It is a well-recognized fact that when governments do not address the issues concerning children and families and makes the home the priority of a society, people quickly begin to lose the sense that they are in control of their governments. Are you watching your elected leaders in this respect?

Education is an emasculating profession for men. One reason being it attracts a large number of perverts and the universities that train teachers are riddled with homosexuals and child molesters. After all, the schools are a magnet for molesters and they need the universities to become teachers. And the schools are where the children are.

Have you heard about the convicted molester, McClendon, who was cured and is now running for the school board in Denver, Colorado? It seems convicted felons in all categories of crime except molesters are excluded, but not convicted molesters. If anything makes it clear about America's apathy and lack of concern for this most heinous of all crimes, this does.

Only the amendment will put these monsters away permanently and do away with the piece-meal efforts of a state-to-state boondoggle of trying to deal with the problem. Only the amendment will solve the problem of these monsters ever being released back into society where such vain attempts as Megan's Laws only make the situation worse.

Why should a convicted molester ever be released? This is the mockery of laws such as Megan's Law. Such laws mock the little victim, Megan Kanka! I believe this little one is with the Lord. And I believe she knows there is no justice yet for her. But, Megan, Americans for Constitutional Protection of Children are fighting for justice for you and all the other little ones you represent!

I am often asked why a Constitutional Amendment instead of trying to get Congress to pass a federal law?

I'll tell you. A Constitutional Amendment is We the People speaking. It gives you and me, as citizens of America, the chance to make our voices heard as opposed to Big Brother making laws for us.

I have little to be proud of when it comes to the direction our government has taken in regard to children and family. I want, as an American, to take my rightful place as a citizen to make it clear to politicians that they are on my payroll, not me on theirs; that they are to represent We the People, not their own interests.

By the amendment, we declare to the world that we are, in fact, a nation that cherishes its young, that we are a nation of people that does not need a corrupt government, a corrupt court, congress or president to tell us what is good for us, by the amendment we tell that government that in spite of the wide-spread corruption and cynicism of such leadership we are able to act as a people in the interest of our most cherished possession, our children! We tell the world that we can act as a people in spite of the thoroughgoing cynicism and corruption of leaders, that we can do for ourselves what is right and noble, that we are Americans with the proudest tradition of personal liberty and personal responsibility of any nation in history!

It takes an idea that appeals to the masses to accomplish revolution. I believe the time has come in the midst of so much violence in America and the rest of the world to address the issue of the most fundamental of all human rights, the right of children to a lawfully protected and innocent childhood.

The literally brilliant genius of the amendment is that is addresses this right at the most fundamental level where the peoples of the world agree. It transcends all nationalism, all creeds of politics, religion and race.

But genius always has a very complex nature. This has to do with the enormous complexities built into the amendment sociologically and legally. It is truly revolutionary in every sense of the word. And, as such, once intelligent people start figuring this out and understand the position standing up for the amendment places them in and the demands it makes of them to make a commitment, they tend to back-peddle.

Kathleen Parker, the noted columnist, is an example. Like many others, she was very enthusiastic at first. But as she became increasingly aware of what was really involved, of how sweeping the changes would be once the amendment is the law of the land, she backed off. Or, and this is a real possibility, she was scared off; perhaps by publishers or one or more of the influential homosexual groups and lobbies.

Even discounting such influence, once the enormity of the amendment and the demands it places on a nation's accountability to its children sinks in; it is daunting to many people and organizations.

Shari P. Geller touts zero tolerance of molesters; and has even written a book of this nature. Yet she has never replied to my letters concerning the amendment. Nor have many others like James Dobson, Oprah and Pat Robertson. Scared?

It is only to be expected that as the battle for the proposed amendment gains more attention, there are many unscrupulous people and organizations that will want to get on the bandwagon for their own purposes. I have steadfastly refused to have ACPC connected in any way with any of these.

But I know how the game is played. Some organization will claim an affiliation and, in some of the worst cases, even try to solicit funds.

Be it known to all that ACPC does not solicit or have any affiliation with any other organization no matter how worthy. This is a grass roots WE THE PEOPLE movement. Every single citizen is invited to take part. And the only organization legitimately involved with the amendment is Americans for Constitutional Protection of Children.

The only thing I ask of people, the citizens of America, is to get involved in the political process, which will lead to the passing of the amendment.

These are some things We the People, every citizen, can do in support of the amendment:

Write the president, your governor, your U.S. representative and senators in support of the amendment.

Let your local radio, newspaper and TV station know of the amendment. Write letters to the editor of your local paper.

Get petition signatures and pass out flyers in support of the amendment.

Put a sign in your yard or window and/or the bumper sticker on your car: IT SHOULDN'T HURT TO BE A CHILD! You can even have T-shirts made; then tell people this is the phrase ACPC is encouraging to bring attention to the amendment.

You can do a similar thing with the sticker: Americans for Constitutional Protection of Children. The ACPC is in red and the rest of the letters in blue against a white background. In smaller, black letters print Dedicated to Zero

Tolerance of Child Molesters. This is the format of the official ACPC cards, stationary, signs and stickers. I mention this because many people have the computer capability of making their own signs and bumper stickers. Spraying with a fixative will weatherproof ink jet copies.

By all means, tell others of the amendment and try to make presentations to your church or any organization to which you belong. Encourage discussion but please, and this cannot be emphasized too strongly, know what you are talking about! Study the literature of the amendment before you speak to groups especially. If you make yourself look foolish, you make the cause you espouse look foolish as well.

For example, people will ask about false accusations of molestation leading to imprisonment. This is not a legitimate question since the constitutional guarantee of Due Process applies to all criminal trials equally of whatever nature. But you must be prepared to answer people who are concerned about such things in good faith.

For those with the computer capability, use a web site and the various chat rooms to advertise the amendment.

Part of the game unscrupulous people play is to use their organization to call someone world renowned for the sake of publicity, the old scholars-quoting-scholars ploy. By plugging each other, they build a circle of usually spurious wannabes.

That is the mechanism of propaganda. Tell a lie often enough and people begin to believe it. Call a pretender and charlatan an expert often enough and uninformed, intellectually lazy and ignorant people begin to believe it.

What's the difference between a man and a battery? She asked.

The battery has a positive side.

Well, I take exception to that. A man's positive side is like gold, I tell her.

OK, that means it's hard to find, she replies. Guys, we can't win.

It's called Divorce Barbie. It comes with all of Ken's stuff.

Scientists have recently discovered a food that greatly reduces sex drive. It's called wedding cake.

Universities are notorious for lying propaganda. For example, it was recently noted that college textbooks are actually pessimistic, even inaccurate, about marriage and marriage statistics. That's right. By trying to make perversion an acceptable lifestyle, since there are so many homosexuals in the schools, the universities have gone out of their way to denigrate marriage.

One researcher on the subject, Norval Glenn, says many such texts make marriage more of a problem than a solution to personal relationships and places the emphasis on divorce, problems of child-rearing, domestic violence, etc. This is the way of propaganda.

I'm a well-trained academic and researcher. I have the degrees, credentials and experience to support these positions. And my qualifications are open for all to inspect.

So when some person or representative of another organization wants to attach himself or herself to ACPC or wants to make it appear that ACPC is supportive of them, you better ask me if this is true.

Some very unscrupulous people are already trying to make it appear that I approve their organizations and movements in the name of ACPC. They lie!

While I often applaud the efforts of others in the battle against things like pornography, abortion, perversion and violence in the entertainment and print media, the abuses in government and the schools, ACPC has only one single purpose and focus: The U.S. Constitutional Amendment directed toward ZERO TOLERANCE OF CHILD MOLESTERS! This, I repeat, and this alone, is the single purpose and focus of ACPC!

But I do my best to make it clear to these others that the battle for, and the passage of, the amendment will have a monumental impact, a domino effect, in these other areas. Much of my writing is directed to educating people to the far-reaching and profoundly complex implications of the amendment legally and sociologically.

Another favorite mechanism of the unscrupulous is name-dropping. For example, it is the most difficult of tasks to get a politician to commit him or herself in writing.

Because of the very seriousness of the amendment, I have had phenomenal success in getting responses from the president, governors and others. But I'm used to not getting any response or say-nothing, non-answer responses as well. That comes with the territory.

But a person can get a response, a say-nothing response, and claim to others, "Why, yes, senator so-and-so dropped me a line the other day in regard to my proposition, my organization," etc. Such people often take a paragraph, a sentence, a phrase or even a single term out of context in order to make it appear that the senator supports the person or organization.

I recently received material from an organization making great claims for itself to the benefit of children. Among the copies of claimed support by well-known personalities was one from Dan Quayle. His letter didn't even acknowledge the organization or direct a single comment toward its support.

But those in the organization could say, and even had the stupidity to print, the letter and claim Dan Quayle supported them. It is surprising how stupid such people in these organizations think others are. But they fool enough often enough to get the money. And for such organizations, that is the bottom line.

There are just too many scam artists out there for anyone to be so naive as to take any organization's word for anything. Learn to ask for facts, documentation, before sending any of them your money or take their word that they have the recommendation of influential people.

Small wonder that politicians become extraordinarily cautious in written communications; I have to exercise the same degree of caution in my own responses to inquiries that I receive.

A famous scientist, Karen Wetterhahn, died from a single, small drop of dimethylmercury that inadvertently fell on her latex gloves. She had worked with many extremely toxic materials for years and assumed the gloves protected her.

But neither she nor any others knew this form of mercury was actually promoted into the bloodstream through latex. That one, small drop killed her.

It only takes that one small lie, couched in the bulk of truth; to promote a personal agenda built on that lie.

For example, we all know of the lie that Madelyn Murray O'Hare was getting the FCC to ban all religious broadcasting. Millions of mailings were made to the gullible promoting this story. The FCC spent enormous amounts of money refuting this lie.

But a few unscrupulous people profited by getting the gullible to send them money to counter this attack of Satan.

And we all know of the myth, the lie perpetrated against Procter and Gamble and its logo of the moon and stars as a satanic symbol. Again, a few unscrupulous people profited by this scheme.

So when I recently received a mailing that railed against The Convention on the Rights of the Child (I've received many, by the way), it was immediately apparent that it fell into the same category as the myths of O'Hare and Procter and Gamble.

Reading this material and comparing it with the actual Convention, you have to wonder: Have these people even read the Convention for themselves? Or do they, as so many do, simply parrot the preaching of the ignorant and misinformed, the propagandists, without doing their own homework?

And in too many cases, the answer is a dismal Yes.

For those who are really concerned about this, simply write UNICEF, as I mentioned previously, and request a copy of The Convention.

For those who have been lied to, especially about the supposed loss of parental authority and control of children, you are in for a very big surprise when you read The Convention for yourself.

Those of us who have been through WWII and the Cold War know the threat Communism once posed. But a few of us were aware that it was a doomed system.

There is no question that America is the leader of nations. It remains a question of how that leadership is to be exercised. If patriots like myself can come to the logical conclusion that such leadership requires setting an example of morality above all else, that means an end to the lying politics that has so infected our leadership.

Other nations, the UN, are not stupid. Pressure has been brought to bear for the UN to reorganize and cut costs. This is good and necessary. But if America is to lead in this area, it must cooperate as well with other nations.

The key to this cooperation and leaving off lying, of not being the hypocrite in preaching human rights, is the passage of the amendment. If America proves it is willing through a Constitutional Amendment to make such a commitment to making children the priority they must become in order to achieve cooperation and peace among nations, this will have a domino effect.

The UN, UNICEF, the Convention on the Rights of the Child, these are key elements to achieving this goal of world peace. If well-meaning individuals who exercise their prejudices in lieu of really doing their homework, that is read and talk to others besides those who only reinforce their prejudices, will approach this problem fairly, they will be amazed at the lies and false propaganda they have been subjected to.

I have many good friends who consider themselves good Americans and good patriots who damn the UN, UNICEF and the Convention and know nothing about these things first hand. Instead, they have been willing to blindly follow leaders who have an agenda of America First, My country right or wrong and only add to the problem rather than doing the hard work of going to primary sources. This, of course, is not only intellectually lazy but can be deadly to anyone who considers themselves knowledgeable about the subjects.

Bottom line, as I tell people who want to work for the amendment; know your subject. In the words of Scripture: Study to show yourselves approved. It was with good reason that my soul brother, Thoreau, who was our best example of civil disobedience, said: God spare me from well-intentioned people. He was, of course, referring to those who thought they knew the subject but were, in fact, only the apostles of ignorance and prejudice.

I receive reams of material from organizations and individuals filled with glittering generalities and meaningless platitudes. What does it mean, for example, that Children are our most precious resource; they must be given a national priority? Not a damned thing unless accompanied by specific courses of action!

But the organizations, leaders and politicians who mouth such meaningless phrases, I remind myself, are of the category of those who decided you could put men and women together in the military and not have sex. So I am convinced that it is better by far that We The People should take the matter of children and family in our own hands when it comes to doing something of really substantive value for them.

And I have to continually remind myself that there are those people who want war, not peace. Much of the so-called patriot literature is directed toward fomenting conflict rather than reasoned and reasonable resolutions to the problems. Many are making big bucks off the gullible by beating this drum, not unlike unscrupulous TV evangelists.

Too much such preaching falls into the category of *My way or the highway!*

I'm getting used to being roundly condemned by those who think that America has such a message and it needs preaching. But I will maintain with all my heart that unless such people, themselves, start putting children first, and I mean the children of the world, they are preaching a false gospel and are no better than gospel-peddlers.

As long as I'm on the subject of liars, holy or otherwise, do you know that the medical profession has been guilty of covering up countless cases of child abuse and infanticide over the years by listing such deaths as Sudden Infant Death Syndrome?

An article in Pediatrics comes clean about this monumental cover-up. Some outrageous things have been discovered such as the videotaping of some mothers, suspected of abusing their children, actually trying to strangle and choking them! Many such deaths, the Pediatrics journal stated, have been written off as SIDS.

A book about this, The Death of Innocents by Richard Firstman and Jamie Talan is in most bookstores now. And I have to ask myself: If it weren't for the courage of Firstman and Talan, would Pediatrics have admitted to this?

Last Saturday was a full day for tragedies and violence in the Valley. Two little girls, a 3 and 6-year-old, are dead

Our weekly paper, The Kern Valley Sun, had a lot to handle and the editor/publisher, Bret Bradigan, did a very sensitive editorial concerning the tragedies of the two little girls. Coincidentally my column in the paper dealt with the guilt of society because of apathy, neglect and indifference concerning the violence directed toward children and adults.

One little victim, 3-year-old Denamica Duniphin, drowned in the canal that runs through the Valley because of the indifference of society toward the plight of her home environment, a home from where the little girl had already been removed once by Child Protective Services.

The little girl had been spotted walking along the canal and had been returned to the mother by sheriff's deputies that very day she drowned. The deputies warned the mother to keep a closer watch on the little girl.

It was 6:30 that evening when she was reported missing again. The following morning her body was found in the canal.

Six-year-old Amanda Kuhar was killed by a selfishly irresponsible young man, Vincent Marcy III, who lost control of his adult toy, a souped-up Mustang, as he passed another car in a no passing zone crossing the double yellow line on a blind curve and lost control of the car. It rolled and struck Amanda as she was sitting with two other little girls on a rail fence at the Jochin Ranch.

The killer was well protected, however. He was well belted in and the Mustang was equipped with a heavy-duty roll bar. The car, it was discovered, was fueled with racing fuel.

These tragedies led to the following column I wrote for our local paper:

There's an old saying among bikers that if you ride long enough, they'll get you.

The *They* are the selfishly irresponsible, dangerously aggressive drivers, typically young males with no license or insurance.

One of them got me when I was 30 years old and the kid pulled out of a blind intersection without stopping or looking for traffic. Virtually every bone on the left side of my body (I had instinctively torqued the bike to the right in an attempt to avoid the car) was broken with numerous compound fractures nearly causing me to bleed to death before the ambulance arrived.

Had I passed out and been unable to apply pressure with my still good right hand to the worst damage to my left arm, which had smashed out the window of the kid's car, I would have bled to death on the spot.

I spent over three months convalescing, transitioning from full body cast to a wheelchair to crutches; a lot of physical therapy for months.

The kid was fined $17.50 for failure to yield the right of way. I wondered if the fine would have been $18.50 if he had killed me?

My insurance company went after the kid and his family only to discover they had nothing worth suing for; a whole family's irresponsibility resulting in high premiums for those of us that buy insurance and own our own homes.

It was less than ten years later that my eldest daughter, Diana, was killed on her bike in Torrance.

It doesn't make sense, of course, why I lived and she died. And the great majority of parents spend the rest of their lives wishing it had been them instead of their child.

But the root of such tragedies is an apathetic society that encourages selfish irresponsibility (whether it's the dangerously aggressive driver, typically uninsured and with nothing worth suing for or the dangerously selfish irresponsibility of adults who don't supervise a three-year-old child) or encourages by both apathy and its perverted and violence-promoting entertainment media the shot-gunning of a bar.

I've said many times that we have become a society that acts like it actually hates children. Having worked for years in the schools and finally for Child Protective Services, I know all too well the kind of policies that, coupled with public apathy, handicaps those who genuinely care about the welfare of children.

As long as We The People continue to promote such selfish irresponsibility by our apathy, We The People must continue to shoulder our share of the blame for such tragedies that have hit the Valley so hard in such a brief period of time.

***

Joel L. Swerdlow writing for The National Geographic (February, 1997) about New York comments about one man riding the subway who was attacked while 20 other people simply looked away; the New York PD keeps no statistics on indifference of bystanders. What would you do, I ask some of my fellow travelers, if you saw someone being assaulted? Most ignore the question. Those who do answer reply: Nothing!

Mr. Swerdlow, while the police keep no statistics on the indifference of bystanders, they are there for any knowledgeable person to read for themselves in the daily abuse and murder of children and accidents like the recent ones in our Valley.

It is the indifference, the apathy, of a whole society that makes up these statistics and caused me to start my Memorial Wall of shame and disgrace to such indifference and apathy on the part of good people.

A personal note; the pastor of the church where the grandparents of little Amanda attend and where her funeral is to be held tried to comfort them and the parents. That is his duty as the pastor.

But at the same time, he was also holding the hand of the selfish, irresponsible idiot that killed their little girl! And this killer had no tie to any church, let alone the one the grandparents attended!

The parents and grandparents were understandably angry with the pastor. How could he be so insensitive as to do such a thing?

Christian charity! If I weren't the Southern Gentleman and civilized man that I am I would say to this pastor, loudly in his face, B--- S---! You take your warped idea of the consolations of religion and stick them where the sun never shines, you hypocritical idiot!

Are we to show ourselves merciful and civilized to the monsters and killers of children or to the victims, the living and the dead, of the heinous, even criminally selfish and irresponsible acts of such monsters?

No! In this case let some other bleeding heart take the part of the killer and hold his hand. All my sympathy, and it should have been the position of this pastor as well, goes to the victims of this SOB's monstrously selfish and irresponsible actions!

This was not a tragic accident. This was a cold, calculated act of utterly selfish, irresponsible behavior that killed a child! Just as the drowning of little Denamica was not a tragic accident, it was the cold-blooded callousness of uncaring neglect on the part of the adults who were responsible for the child!

Yet people will attempt to escape the part they play, their own guilt through apathy, in such tragedies by the mechanism of calling such things accidents.

There is a place for justice tempered by mercy; there are accidents where the innocents suffer. But the examples I have given are not in this category. These examples cry out for Justice for the little victims. Showing sympathy for their killers is not, in any sense, justice in these cases nor do they in any sense deserve mercy in any form!

On the contrary, what they deserve is the contempt of all civilized and truly compassionate people.

I'll reserve comment on the case of the little 3-year-old girl who was strangled by an electric car window in Delano, California while her mother and another man of the cloth, a traveling tent-meeting evangelist, were too busy in the front seat of the car to notice what was happening.

An autopsy has confirmed that the electric car window strangled the little girl, Jazleen Salou, to death while her mother was busy in the front seat with this traveling evangelist. Her death may yet be ruled accidental!

There is such a thing as civic responsibility, a duty of citizens to practice restraint and exercise responsibility for the sake of a society. A glaring breach of this and the damage it can cause a society is found in the following example:

By now many are aware of the line of candy and soda being produced by one Steve Corri that mimics drugs like cocaine. The candy is packaged in surplus medical test tubes with names like Avalanche, White Lie, Cloud Nine, DOA, Crave and BrainWash.

When confronted by parental concerns about this overt glorification of drugs under the guise of selling candy and cola Mr. Corri responded:

Hell, these parents are like sheep. They're nothing but uptight, narrow-minded, self-righteous, mentally constipated hypocrites, afraid to have fun. We don't care. We did it (put these products on the market) 'cause we wanted to do it.

As an adult, been one for quite some time now, I believe I should take responsibility for my own actions. If those actions lead to unpleasant consequences at times, that comes with the territory.

I only mention this in passing to make a point. It would be deadly for the cause of the amendment for me to be perceived as some altruistic do-gooder. Nothing could be further from the truth. I get out there and mix it up in real life with real people. And in doing so, I get into some very human predicaments (like interfering when a man is threatening a woman, sometimes resulting in my paying a visit to a doctor).

Admittedly, writing of such things provides some vicarious titillation to a few of the good churchgoers who wouldn't dream of doing some of these things but thrill to my doing them. And they are free to self-righteously condemn me when things don't quite work out. Like my trip to the doctor's office.

But such incidents, like shooting pool at Sluggers Saloon on Friday or Saturday night, put a very human face on the man behind the amendment. He's definitely no angel.

But to repeat something I recently wrote a very beautiful woman, the last thing I can afford to have is for people to idealize the man behind the ideal of the amendment. I am far too frail and weak a mortal man for that to fly.

The Holy Grail of physics is the Grand Unification Theory. So far, a balanced equation has escaped physics. But I believe it will eventually be found.

The Holy Grail of world peace requires a balanced equation as well. And through the amendment as a starting place I believe it will be found.

One of the missing components of the equation has always been the exclusion of women in the process of seeking solutions. You don't discount an entire one-half of the human race and hope for a solution.

Another missing piece of the equation has been the failure of humanity to give children the proper priority. These two things alone have been more than enough to doom the world to a history of conflict and continuing warfare.

I used to be very religious. As such, I prayed long and often. But I never got an audible reply in response to my much praying. I always wished God would answer audibly, that I could be certain of a yes or no to my requests. I would pray for wisdom and guidance and ... nothing.

I've wished for a messenger angel to tell me: Hey, Sam, God just got your latest request and here's what you're supposed to do. Nope; never happened.

Why couldn't I have a burning bush or Damascus experience? Why didn't God speak to me as He did my namesake, the last Judge of the Old Testament?

Was God mad at me? Surely I gave Him reason enough many times.

It wasn't until I wrote the HEY, GOD! book that things began to come together for me.

I really poured out my doubts and reservations of those things I used to believe, in that book. It was not only an intellectual exercise, finally discriminating between what I knew as opposed to what I believed, it was a catharsis of religiosity, a cleansing of much hypocrisy and religious prejudice in my own life that I confronted honestly in the book.

So I began to consider this lack of communication between God and myself. Was I praying or talking to myself? And if praying why no answers?

Gradually I began to consider the other guy who writes this stuff that goes under the name of Heath. I've always known it wasn't me; it was that stranger with whom I, at times, only have a reserved and polite acquaintance.

As I lay in my bed at night, I would pray. Nothing. But a new thought began to form. Was God replying or was I carrying on a conversation with myself, talking with myself?

Now I talk to myself frequently. I long ago realized that if I wanted an intelligent conversation, I would have to talk to myself.

But I have never heard voices. I may be nuts but I'm professionally qualified to know what that means and I'm not quite ready to be committed. Not yet. Sure 'nuff workin' on it though.

Well, I asked myself, suppose those conversations required God's input? I often come back to myself while talking with God with questions and answers of which I may not, in fact, be the author; a considered possibility.

And if I'm not the author of such ideas, questions and answers, then who is?

I have never understood the compulsion to undertake the amendment. The idea presented itself and while at first rejecting it, the more I considered it, the more pragmatically and logically it became the only way to begin the process toward world peace.

Certainly I could look at my background and experience working with children and understand trying to do something for them. I've spent my life working with and for children; but a U.S. Constitutional Amendment? And one that would cause America to begin the revolution leading the world to peace?

The more I examined the profound implications and complexities of the amendment, legally and sociologically, the more convinced I was of the very genius and originality of it, a genius I couldn't claim for myself leading to something no nation in the history of the world had ever done through the foundational charter of its government.

The genius of the amendment, in large part, lay in the fact that it does, indeed, transcend all national characteristics and boundaries, it addresses an issue on which all people of the world agree. For the first time in history it makes America, the world, face itself with the question of whether or not we do cherish children as the hope of the future of the world, of an advancing civilization.

Another part of the genius of the amendment is the fact that there was a love and caring in this of which I could never dream of being capable. At the very least it had to be the work of that other guy if not of God.

But I'm not about to say God made me do it, that the idea is His. When people ask me what I know about God, I tell them honestly: Nothing!

But ask me if I believe in God, emphatically YES! Ask me what I believe about God and the time would fail in my reply. That was a part of my own conversion away from religiosity, learning to separate what I know from what I believe.

But who is that other guy, for example, that in spite of the many betrayals of my love, in spite of having my heart stomped so many times, keeps trying to stick up for women?

Who is that guy who keeps a romantic mindset, who is sensitive and caring, who seems to love children when I want to tell the world to go to hell and leave me alone while I go fishing?

He seems to be there in my conversations with God. He seems to be there when I'm ready to throw in the towel and tell the world to go to hell and leave me alone.

This other guy doesn't seem to know when he's licked. And he refuses to become bitter, hard, cynical, callous and unbelieving. Who is this guy who seems to take over just after I've been pouring out, quite angrily and loudly at times, my complaints against and to God and others?

Well, whoever he is, he is relentless. I can't seem to escape him. And I've certainly tried to.

I've described him, at times, as the best part of the man, the child within who has the wisdom and innocence of childhood that the man lost along the way.

But there's a kind of maturity, at times, that this child seems to possess, a maturity I don't have that enables him to examine and reflect on things I would never be able to think of. It's as though he can delight in the seemingly erratic flight of a butterfly yet find a logical pattern in it. But such things have no practical value to me.

I ask myself at times whether I'm responsible for protecting this child? And, if so, how? But wouldn't I far rather be rid of him? It would, again at times, sure make my life a lot simpler and easier. For example, I know when I'm beat, when to give up. He doesn't.

He delights in the great musicals of the theater, the great works of poets and philosophers who encourage things like love, romance and chivalry. He delights in the compatibility of differences between men and women, in the peculiar differences between mother and father in their relationship between each other as husband and wife and their different relationship to him as mom and dad, of the differences between his boy companions and girl companions.

There is fascination, mystery and charm, even adventure in those inexplicably strange and marvelous creatures called girls that are so very, very different to him as a boy.

There is a totally non-understandable, mysterious yet exciting promise about them of something future. But what is that thing? It intrigues the child-boy. Part of the indefinable mystery of it all is the lack of the boy's ability to think of much in the way of future beyond tomorrow. This is a time when the two weeks before Christmas seems an eternity.

He may even try to impress these marvelous creatures when he is in kindergarten. But he could never explain why he felt he wanted to. He wouldn't even talk about it and would be terribly embarrassed if someone should accuse him of doing so.

Part of his embarrassment would be the inability to articulate a reason. If he doesn't understand it himself, how can he possibly explain it to others?

But another part of his embarrassment remains a mystery into adulthood. A large part of this lack of understanding will carry into adulthood, an adulthood plagued with thousands of books written by other adults who don't understand either.

I think I was looking for the other half of myself. I was, as she, incomplete without the other. Of course, how could any child understand or articulate such a thing?

I frequently refer to the great works of literature and stage and often read such books and watch the movie productions over and over. I read, among others, Thoreau's Walden and Harper Lee's To Kill a Mocking Bird at least twice a year.

Then there is William Inge's Splendor in the Grass. I very much appreciate Natalie Wood's artistic genius in playing the role of Deanie, a tormented young woman, with such extraordinary sensitivity. I will always believe Natalie knew personally the tragedy that Deanie suffered.

But it is the ending of the story that always affects me so deeply as she and Bud (Warren Beatty in his introductory role) ask the question of each other: Are you happy? Each replies that they don't think about that much any more. And they don't need to speak of the heartbreakingly grievous pain of such thoughts; it needs no words spoken. It is understood.

As a society, we are not happy people. In fact, I don't meet many people who have ever known real happiness, at least not in the sense of Inge's story. I write of this at some length in my Birds book. The loss of the best of innocence in childhood that would lead to real love and romance for the adult in a society carries a heavy price.

Most people now are best described in the words of Bud: I guess you just have to take whatever comes along.

But both Deanie and Bud realize they lost something precious, something priceless, and will never be happy again because they once knew happiness and it would never be there for them again. They have the standard of real happiness against which all the experiences of the rest of their lives cannot escape comparison and be found wanting.

They will spend the rest of their lives loving others without that kind of happiness again. Ever.

The Splendor in the grass will never fade. It is a haunting thing once you have known it and lost it. This is the tragedy of betrayed love and innocence.

As Deanie leaves after seeing Bud for the last time, the lines of Wordsworth's poem, Ode: Intimations of Immortality from Recollections of Early Childhood come to her mind:

What though the radiance which was once so bright

Be now forever taken from my sight,

Though nothing can bring back the hour

Of splendor in the grass, of glory in the flower;

I leave the Ode at this place because of the way Inge used it and because it best makes the point here without going on to grim reality or vain attempts to justify such monumental loss of profoundly innocent love and happiness by supposed lessons learned.

Better to have loved and lost than never to have loved at all? Or, Better never to have known love than to have loved and lost?

Inge leaves the question unanswered. Indeed, he had no answer. He magnificently poses the question but knows better than to attempt the answer.

Of course, can you miss something you never had, something you have never experienced? You can if someone else tells you they have had such a thing, such an experience. You can recognize the hollowness of your own heart in response and never have found love and romance in your own life.

But if you knew the pain of the betrayal and consequent lost love and innocence Inge presents beforehand, who in their right mind would opt for such a thing? Yet it requires such experience to warn others, to be a poet, to be able to separate the diabolical from the divine for the sake of others. The genius of such a system is the survivor alone knows whether it was truly worth the pain in order to save and keep the innocent from such pain in his or her own lives.

There is a desperate need for civilized manners in our society, for protocols and proprieties to be observed. There is a need for chivalry and the encouragement of protecting the weaker, of ridding society of bullies and predators of children. There is a desperate need of encouraging the ideals of childhood and adolescence.

The betrayal of the ideals of youth and innocence is not the price of reality and should never be misconstrued as such. When I write and speak of the absolute necessity of guaranteeing children a lawfully protected safe and innocent childhood, too many react as though reality carries just such a price. Such people may well have never experienced real love and romance, may never have experienced the splendor in the grass Inge so movingly presents. Such people cannot know the price paid for real love and romance, the price our children pay for such a chance being ripped away from them.

I have learned many things from the betrayal of my love and trust, the betrayal of my innocence. But they are lessons I would far rather not have learned. Life may well be too often a bittersweet waltz. But it needn't, shouldn't be. Children, young people, know this.

As adults, with vaunted mature thinking, planning and, yes, plotting, abetted by never knowing the best of the ideals and innocence of childhood in too many cases, we have become a callous and hardened society that acts like it hates children.

If such a society thinks itself adult, sane, then it does indeed take a madman like Boo Radley (To Kill a Mockingbird) to strike the necessary balance and save the children though his actions in doing so be considered unsuitable to the laws of a civilized society. There is a higher law such madmen recognize that must be obeyed or we are lost, the prey of those whose callous bitterness, lust and hatred knows and recognizes no civilized laws of humanity.

And, in fact, when such laws, no matter how well intended, deny, even thwart, justice, and only such madmen as Boo can hope to bring society to its sense and understanding of justice.

The madness of the amendment is of the nature of Boo's madness. It is a call to justice, justice and protection that has been denied children throughout not only our history as a nation, but also the history of the human race.

The root of the insanity of our society is the lack of a willingness to risk loving. By cheapening love through perversion of every description, whether pornography, abortion, the entertainment media, and literature that pretend to extol reality at the cost of innocence, we are becoming a hardened and callus, violent people.

My eldest son, Daniel, was visiting once and, as usual, there was the music. My children were raised with music.

But singing is a very special part of the music. I love to sing and was performing for audiences as a child.

As an adult, I loved singing for women. After all, they were the inspiration for my singing as a man.

I told my son that I would try to pick out a beautiful woman in the audience and sing to her, to make love to her by singing to her. It never failed to inspire me to sing my best.

This is a part of the softer and gentler aspect of real romance. I loved teaching songs to my children and singing to them. Children should be raised with music. But it should always be the kind of music that moves the heart to the fun, joy and romance, which the best music inspires.

The harsh, ugly noise that promotes perversion, sexual license, drugs and alcohol abuse, this has not a little to do with children who, as Jesse Jackson recently pointed out, would choose juvenile detention centers, jails, over the kind of environment they have in their so-called homes.

But as I have often pointed out, you can't make people care.

I recently asked a woman, a woman very active in her church and other social organizations, if she had read of the mother in Los Angeles who beat her little 5-year-old daughter to death. The woman replied that she thought she had but usually only skimmed the papers for articles of interest to her.

Yet this very woman will tell everyone, including me, how very concerned about child abuse she is.

I asked a man, an ordained minister in a position to know and who professed his whole-hearted support of the amendment, if he had any information on a recent case of a tortured and murdered child?

His response: Oh, yes, I think I heard something about that.

I asked if he would please get me the details of the case.

His response: Oh, well I don't think I'm going to have time to do that.

I was so angry with this hypocrite I could have spit nails.

Folks, you simply cannot say you believe children to be the closest thing to the heart of God and live as though other things have the priority.

And you cannot pretend or fake a burden for children you do not, in fact, have. That is hypocrisy, plain and simple. Don't even try to put a good face on it; it won't wash. You really care and evidence it in your life or you don't. As Jesus pointed out, there is no middle ground concerning evil. Particularly the evil perpetrated against these little ones.

Failure to discriminate between knowledge and belief (opinion) has been the bane of humanity. Religious, racial, political opinions confused as knowledge and preached and taught as such have led to some of the greatest crimes, including wars, against humanity.

For example, the bishops of the Roman Catholic Church at a national conference are now saying homosexuals can't help being what they are and should not be discriminated against. They further state that love and compassion for perverts should come before the established, doctrinal position of the church.

There are several obvious reasons for these bishops taking this totally unscientific position of perverts not being able to help being what they are. First and foremost, it offers justification for perversion against children in the ranks of the priesthood of this religion. Recent lawsuits against molesters in the RC church have brought this to the fore and perverts in the church are looking for a way out.

It also reinforces the common religious dogma of the Impurity of Women doctrine found in the major religions like Christian, Moslem and Jewish. The dogma of celibacy in the priesthood of the RC church makes it peculiarly susceptible to perversion and the denigration of women throughout its history. Hence, another compelling reason for attempts to justify perversion.

Lacking any scientific basis for their position, these bishops hope to make a belief, an opinion, and a basis for their teaching of a doctrine that only serves to promote acceptance of perversion. The self-serving objective can't be missed in this situation.

But other beliefs in lieu of or confused with knowledge are far more subtle; but often equally harmful, even deadly; for example, beliefs that lead to propositions and dogmas of racial superiority. Hitler was enormously successful in this area.

***

I believe God is a civilized gentleman and a romantic. How else would I have been so blessed by the recent visit of Professor Boyko Stoyanov to Bodfish?

To explain that, here is the column I wrote for our local paper that resulted from his visit to me:

Itinerary:

Oxford, London Sept. 7; Seattle, Washington Sept. 15; Bakersfield, California Oct. 4; Los Angeles, California Oct. 11.

Professor Stoyanov and I became acquainted three years ago through a mutual acquaintance connected with The International Congress on Communication and the Arts who knew of our common goal of working to achieve world peace by making the children of the world the priority of nations.

Over that period of time, our correspondence and phone conversations made us realize the increasing urgency of meeting face to face. Boyko's deep interest in the amendment I have authored and our mutual agreement that America must take the place of leadership in making children the proper priority of all nations was a fundamental reason for our need to meet personally.

Boyko's heavy schedule of performances in Japan, England and Europe kept him from coming to the U.S. until this September.

Once he knew he would be able to make the commitment to come to the U.S. for a Pacific Coast Tour, a primary focus was being able to meet with me so we could spend some time together discussing how his music and my writing could be used together to benefit children.

Since I was trained as a classical clarinetist as a child and kept up with the music as a professional musician and singer, Boyko and I also had some common ground in music for our relationship. My music teacher, Mr. Willard Swadburg, and I used to tour Kern County giving performances.

I explained to Boyko that it would be a good idea for him to give a performance in Bakersfield since it was becoming an increasingly important city. Since he and his daughter, Julia, would be staying with me and I could put something together with relatively brief notice, he agreed.

The task of making an impromptu concert come together was helped tremendously by the efforts of Byron and Gladys McHaig here locally. Gladys is a member and Dean of the Kern County chapter of the American Guild of Organists and plays The Great Organ of The First Baptist Church in Bakersfield. This organ is world famous and was moved to the church from Harvard University. It has an astounding total of 8,531 pipes!

The church also boasts a concert grade grand piano used by Arturo Rubenstein and the acoustics of the auditorium that boasts the piano and organ are superb.

Dr. Phil Dodson, head of the music department of the church, gave permission for Boyko to perform in the auditorium, which seats 1,200 people.

With the further help of Mrs. Jean Baughman who heads Young Audiences of Kern County, advertising of the event was accomplished.

Boyko gave a superb performance. The solos from Mozart, Chopin and Bach were interspersed with solos by his daughter Julia, a very accomplished pianist in her own right. Then, they did some duets, which were punctuated with Boyko's improvisations that were especially composed for children. Thoroughly delightful.

After Saturday's concert, I took Boyko and Julia to Kernville, which was hosting the Rod Run that weekend. They were fascinated by the display of old cars and took many pictures. They were delighted with the charm of the town and the beautiful park and river with the mountains all around.

We watched from the riverbank and the bridge as fishermen reeled in trout and kayakers were trying to negotiate the rapids. The clarity of the water of the unpolluted Kern was especially thrilling to Boyko and Julia.

I was able to tell them stories of the old days in the area before the lake went in and I had the whole Sequoia National Forest and the river as my personal wilderness and before the new towns of Kernville and Isabella existed. Boyko, being from Bulgaria and a world-traveler, tales of local folklore and history are of great interest to him.

Boyko has a marvelous sense of humor, which is invaluable when working with children. One of the stories we will both enjoy sharing with others will be his navigating from Japan to Bodfish, especially Slugger's Saloon!

It was about 8:30 Thursday evening when he arrived in the Valley. He knew he would have to call me in order to find my place. Now, at that time of the evening in Bodfish there aren't many places from which a stranger to the area can make a call.

So when the call comes, where is Boyko calling from? The one place you can usually depend on to be open at that time of night and the one place where the people would know me well enough to welcome a stranger in my name; Slugger's Saloon! Boyko and mine's, thanks to my friends at Sluggers.

Boyko and I fervently hope he will be able to return. Next time, there will be plenty of advance planning and Kern County will be able to boast of a composer of international reputation including the Valley and Bakersfield in his planned itinerary.

And Boyko confirmed what I have been trying to tell parents: Good music greatly enhances intellectual development in children.

CHAPTER SEVEN

So, in obedience to that duty and responsibility, I have to tear myself away from the humor and the softer and gentler things of which I would so very much like to devote my life. And with cruel effort assisted by a very special kind of madness, I give my mind to the agony of dealing with the ugliness, the evil committed against children, those things of which I am a most unwilling and well-qualified expert. And only this special kind of madness enables me to live daily with the knowledge of such evil.

And in doing so I feel once more as I shared with a friend, that I've lived too long and learned too much.

As others have pointed out to me, only a madman would be putting the names of tortured and murdered children on his property for all to see. If Lincoln was chosen of God to do a specific work as he claimed, it isn't a choice of the man or woman, but a compulsion (a madness?) that leads to obedience to the calling.

Since I do not understand such a compulsion on the part of either Lincoln or myself, a compulsion that invites enmity and derision by so many and separates from the comfort of friends, from joy and happiness, I am not going to attribute such to God. Therefore, what better answer than a special kind of madness?

The issue of slavery in this nation was one of profound and monumental proportions. Lincoln was going contrary to thousands of years of human history that had approved slavery in many nations.

Lord Charnwood, being an honest man, accepted the role of England in bringing slavery to the early colonies thus sowing the seed for the Civil War.

But, as Truman said of the Presidency, the buck finally stopped with Lincoln. And in the end, there was the blood of over 500,000 men on his hands. At the second election of Lincoln, the comment was made that if the Union dead had been able to vote, they would have voted for him.

The comment was intended to comfort Lincoln with the thought that these sacrificed dead would have felt they died for a noble cause.

But Lincoln replied: The dead vote for me? No, not the dead! Never!

So Lincoln realized and accepted the enormity of his decision and it may have been this that gave him the prescient conviction that when his task was done, he would be murdered.

Historically, we legitimately ask why, if God had shaped and was in control of Lincoln's destiny, He didn't intervene to save Lincoln to complete the program of Reconstruction? Even some leaders in the South gave homage to Lincoln by expressing deep sorrow over his death, realizing that this great man would have promoted healing between North and South rather than the punishment and plundering they knew would be their lot without him.

Perhaps God decided the South should be punished. After all, if Southern leaders like Calhoun and Davis hadn't blasphemed God by preaching that the perversion of slavery had His approval, the war wouldn't have taken place.

Perhaps God couldn't intervene to save Lincoln. But Lincoln had survived other attempts on his life. By God's intervention?

Or, perhaps it was the kindness of God to spare Lincoln the final indignity of becoming totally mad? It would seem this was the direction he was headed. The pathology of this possibility is easy to determine. As it was, Mrs. Lincoln was declared insane in 1875. My feeling is that Lincoln would not have been able to survive this indignity to his wife let alone continue to live with the knowledge that he had been the instrument of the deaths of those half-million.

A Stalin or Hitler wouldn't have had a problem with this. Their madness was one of egomaniacal centrisim. Lincoln was just the opposite. His conscience kept the responsibility for those hundreds of thousands killed ever before him. And in spite of the necessity of the cause, in spite of the lack of cooperation by those who should have come together to prevent such a blood bath, in spite of the obvious confluence of historical events which left no other path before a man like himself, those dead at his hand were ever before him.

The Gettysburg Address clearly reveals Lincoln's innermost thoughts on this subject. You can clearly read his own epitaph in this most sublime poetry.

I ask the reader to be patient with me as I attempt to shed some light on the work for the amendment by this historical analysis of Lincoln and his work. As I wrote in the last issue of TAP, there is no clearer blueprint for the amendment than that of the Civil War era and Lincoln's work in ending slavery.

I would further ask the reader to study the life of Lincoln together with that all-important era of the Civil War and its aftermath to get a clear understanding of the blueprint and why the proposed amendment is the logical extension of the work Lincoln undertook.

***

When it comes to barbaric culture and violence against women, one Francisco Sanchez of Bakersfield must have taken lessons from the Taliban in Algeria. He shot his wife because, as he told police: Ok, I shot her. I had to do it. She was rude to me. And he did this in front of the couples' little 3-year-old girl as she cried: Daddy, you kill mama!

The mother, Martina Sanchez, is expected to recover… but the little girl watching in horror as daddy shot mama?

Speaking of barbarians, America and Algeria aren't alone. What about the recent massacre of 65 tourists, men, women and children, in Egypt by animals in the form of humans? And they laughed and danced while they shot and stabbed their innocent victims! What can you say about societies and so-called cultures that produce such monsters?

You call yourselves militants! I'll tell you what you are; you are conscienceless monsters that (not who because that would give you human status) have, like child molesters and child murderers, forfeited any right to exist in a civilized world! And the sooner all you vermin are exterminated and cease to exist, the better for all real human beings!

Many such animals preach they are good Moslems, Jews, Buddhists or Christians; or good Mexicans, Americans, Serbians, Irish, English, Japanese, Chinese, etc. Religious, Ethnic, Political, what is the difference to the murdered whether they were murdered in the name of God or Nationalism?

Speaking further of barbarians, Michael and Angeline Rogers of Chilton, Wisconsin were arrested when their 11-year-old son showed up shoeless and coatless at the police station asking help for his little 7-year-old sister. The parents were keeping the little girl locked in a 24 X 17-inch dog cage in their cold, dark basement. There are other children ages 9, 6 and 16 months and it is reported that the father regularly hit the children for violating rules of the household.

But few such inhuman cruelties compare with the unspeakable act of Ivan and Veronica Gonzales of San Diego, California in the torture-murder of little 3-year-old Genevieve Rojas. These beasts literally scalded the little girl to death in a bathtub. The medical examiner said she died of thermal burns.

Apart from the heinous and inhuman actions of these monsters, it may make legal history because the main witness against them is their 8-year-old son. He testified against his parents telling the judge that he watched as these torturer/murderers kept pushing the screaming little victim into the scalding water until she stopped screaming.

These monsters have six children ranging in age from four to eleven. Little Genevieve was their niece. The boy testified that she was starved, beaten and forced to sleep handcuffed to a hook in a closet ceiling.

My daughter, Karen, sent me the news clipping of this torture/murder of little Genevieve and suggested I include her name on my Memorial Wall. It was done the very day I got the clipping.

Karen asked about the trauma of the little boy having witnessed what he did and having to testify against his own parents, the testimony together with the forensic evidence resulting in the death penalty for his father, and, perhaps, the mother as well.

I could only tell Karen, among other things, that, in time, the boy will grow up to know he did the right thing and this will help him deal with his nightmares.

We read of such things and righteous anger wells up in our hearts and minds. How can these monsters do such things to children! We shout. So it is that the death penalty is the only real justice we can give the little victims of such inhuman action by these monsters.

It is my belief that God alone can make the punishment fit the crime. Still, as I shared with Karen, it is our duty in the name of justice to rid civilized society of such inhuman monsters by the death penalty.

Recently, a 14-month-old boy, a toddler named Damon, was saved from a burning building. The child's mother, one LaDawn Jump, had left the child alone for five days without food or water.

An article by Kathleen Parker makes the point that with the throwing of babies into toilets, dumpsters, plastic bags, etc. we have become a society that seems to place no value on life. A point I have made many times myself. We can thank the university-trained judiciary for this as well as the judicial support of abortion as a means of contraception. Don't want it? Kill it or throw it away! After all, it isn't a person; it's only a baby! So with university-trained judge Zobel and his decision about the murder of little Matthew Eappen.

But with the vicious, conscienceless torture, neglect and outright murder of children like little Genevieve and Damon, the throwing of babies into toilets and dumpsters, the tragedy of little Alexes and Deziree and so many others, I have to ask a fundamental question, a question that is virtually never asked: Where are the fathers?

The answer is that these so-called fathers rut like animals and have virtually no thought of responsibility toward the children they father. But as Lincoln said of slavery: It is not a sin of the South, but of a whole nation!

And that, folks, is a responsibility that we, as a nation, have refused to accept! The devaluing of life is not a sin of these mothers; it is a sin of an entire society!

We can paint such women as the Legrees but it is acceptance of perversion on a monumental scale that leads to the devaluing of life. But as I wrote Kathleen and several elected leaders, nothing is going to change for the better until some in Congress have the moral backbone and integrity to stand up and announce:

If perversion is not wrong, then nothing is wrong!

Once our elected leadership takes that stand, all these other things will fall into order. But this is where it must start!

As a writer, I know the power of the pen. As Lincoln said upon meeting Harriet Beecher Stowe:

So you're the little woman who made the book that made this Great War.

Lincoln was a political realist who had learned the power of the pen. And it was Charles Sumner who said that without Uncle Tom's Cabin, there would have been no Lincoln in the White House.

This is not to beg the question whether slavery would have been abolished without the book, it undoubtedly would have been. But the book both polarized and galvanized people to take action. Men like Benjamin Lundy, William Lloyd Garrison, John Greenleaf Whittier and Bronson Alcott were men that took abolition seriously and, like Lincoln, believed in the power of moral suasion to move the hearts of the common people.

I can only hope and pray that the book I'm working on will be as successful as Stowe's was in moving the hearts of people to take action.

If perversion is not wrong, then nothing is wrong! Is the message we should all be shouting.

***

Janet Leigh made an appearance at the venerable Fox Theater in Bakersfield, which was showing the original full-length wide screen version of Psycho. A few, brief scenes were shot on highway 99 near Bakersfield.

A Bakersfield judge, Skip Staley, was among those standing in line to see the film. He is quoted as saying he was going to have to attend a judges' meeting and felt the film would be good preparation in getting along with his fellow judges. Hmm.

Perhaps he was thinking, also, about the woman, Jackie Robles, who is suing for $20,000,000 because her two little girls, Alexes and Deziree, were killed by a train while she and a young man were asleep in the woman's apartment.

To add insult to the deaths of these two little girls, the biological father of one of the little victims, one Fernando Soto, is filing a $10,000,000 claim as well. The attorney for these two sorry excuses for parents, one Arden Silverman, must be an ambulance chaser of the very worst sort!

I cannot imagine such a flagrant abuse of law by creatures like these in attempting to profit from their own negligence and thoroughgoing lack of personal responsibility! But with lawyers like Silverman and an infamously, notoriously litigious society, such abuses must happen. Folks, it is out of control when these kinds of lawsuits can take place! But as we all know, there is nothing like the scent of money to draw vermin out from under their respective rocks.

There is a local joke going around about a busload of lawyers going off the canyon road and all were killed. The real tragedy was that there were three empty seats in the bus.

When one thinks of the Silvermans, it isn't any wonder we laugh at such jokes and wistfully wish they were true.

One out of five children in America (a full 20%) will spend at least part of their youth being raised with an alcohol or other drug-abusing parent! And some of these so-called parents, these scum, will, like Robles and Soto with the help of the Silvermans, try to make money from their own abuse and negligence of their own children.

The daily and nightly prayer of a little girl, 10-year-old Ashley Bryan: Just once, give me something good. Please make life get better.

L.A. Times, Sunday, November 16, 1997.

Well, Sweetheart, ACPC is doing something that will make your life better and is going to do something good for you and all the children like you. Just don't give up and please keep praying; but a great hindrance to little Ashley's prayers is found in the following:

President Clinton vowed to name five perverts to top White House posts. October 1 he chose former Catholic nun, lesbian activist Virginia M. Apuzzo, to run the White House management shop thus making her the highest-level open pervert in a U.S. administration.

Rather than God, We The People and children like little Ashley, the president is trying to win the approval of Hollywood, San Francisco, American Airlines, PAW, Gary Trudeau, Tom Hanks, Chastity Bono and Ellen. Well, since GLAAD reports this fall's network prime-time lineup will increase the number of openly pervert characters by almost a third, no wonder Bono's daughter is ecstatic.

Mr. President, you are certainly making your mark in history. For your consideration, I have recently sent the following letter to my California Assemblyman, Senator and Governor. You should find it of interest to yourself as well:

Learning of the action by the U.C. Board of Regents in approving benefits for perverts the words of a biographer of Lincoln, Lord Charnwood, came to mind:

Every honest Democrat who then refused any action against slavery must have regretted it before three years were out, and many sensible Republicans who saw no use in such moderation might have lived to regret their part too. Nothing was done. It is thought that Lincoln expected this; but the Proclamation of Emancipation would begin to operate within a month; it would produce by the end of the war a situation in which the country would be compelled to decide on the principle of slavery, and Lincoln had at least done his part in preparing men to face the issue.

By this time in history, Lincoln was able to express to his cabinet and for posterity this simple dictum:

If slavery is not wrong, then nothing is wrong.

Building on this foundation I would add:

If perversion is not wrong, if the molestation of children is not wrong, then nothing is wrong.

A course of deadly moderation regarding slavery led to the Civil War. With the murder of Lincoln, America fell into what Claude Bowers called The Tragic Era, that time of so-called Reconstruction that led to corrupt Big Government and corrupt Big Business named the Gilded Age by Samuel Clemens.

Regarding the churches of his time Lincoln wrote:

In great contests each party claims to act in accordance with the will of God. Both may be and one must be wrong. God cannot be for and against the same thing at the same time.

The truth of this sentiment of Lincoln brooks no disagreement. But the churches long past gave up any authority as the moral arbiters of America. This is now the purview of the universities, which, since The Tragic Era, have preached a gospel of There Are No Moral Absolutes.

Because of this doctrine of the universities, the leaders they produce all across the spectrum of American society in education, industry, government, the judiciary, and entertainment and even in many churches, we face a crisis of morality in America.

It was on the basis of morality that Lincoln held firm to his simple dictum concerning slavery. Scholars of the period know the agony and grief this caused this righteous man in holding firm to his conviction so simply yet eloquently expressed.

As opposed to this great man, we have a president who has set his approval to perversion. The homosexual lobby would have us believe that the heart of America is the heart of a pervert and has been enormously successful, far beyond the merit of their numbers, in advancing their cause of perversion.

Yet where in history has such a thing been the proud monument of any nation? It has been, rather, the moral rot and shame of nations that has led to their destruction!

Now I would ask you, as a political leader, how is it possible that this small number of perverts can so advance their cause in the universities against the will of We the People? Has the political leadership of America become so sensitive to being called homophobic that it has been thoroughly emasculated?

Or are political leaders such a result of the university doctrine of no moral absolutes and so far-gone down this path that they fear taking a stand on basic morality? How has it come to pass that our political leaders in California and President Clinton, a Rhodes Scholar, come to bow to Ellen, Tom Hanks, Elizabeth Taylor, Heather Has Two Mommies and Daddy's Roommate?

History has long vindicated Abraham Lincoln. But he had the integrity to face his foes and stand on a principle. But we look in vain to find a holy trinity of Hendricks, Thurman and Bayard in Congress today. There is no Cato or Henry Grady to act as the voice of moral conscience for We the People in confronting the self-serving hypocrisy and lack of moral integrity of those in high office.

But Thaddeus Stevens, Grant and even Balzac are well represented and have made, and make, their continuing contributions to the fait accompli of the universities in becoming the enemies of moral absolutes.

In the words of Lincoln: We cannot escape history.

I ask you as a leader who is sworn to represent We the People; do you think you will be the exception to this?

And if you believe you are doing your best to confront the evil of perversion, history will be your final judge and there will be no escaping that judgment whether you believe in God's judgment or not.

A most honorable man, Benjamin H. Hill of Georgia, wrote during the infamy of the tragic era of so-called Reconstruction under the tyranny of Thaddeus Stevens, of carpetbaggers' and scalawags' intent of punishing and plundering a defenseless South and creating the very enmity between white and black with which we live today:

Ignorance is more easily duped than intelligence, and ...knaves have always been advocates of conferring power on fools; and so fools have generally thought knaves their best friends.

The universities hold sway in America today. They produce the leaders who dictate America's role in the world. Granting we suffer from a lack of an enlightened electorate it becomes all the more important for good men and women in positions of leadership to confront the knaves in the universities and take the stand Lincoln took on principle. There are moral absolutes and some things are patently wrong!

I urge you to take an unmistakable stand on the basis:

If perversion is not wrong, if the molestation of children is not wrong, then nothing is wrong!
Samuel D.G. Heath, Ph. D.
Americans for Constitutional Protection of Children.

***

The case of Mary Kay LeTourneau points up a very real double standard in cases of molestation. A schoolteacher, she got a six month jail sentence for having sex with one of her pupils, a sixth grade boy. In fact, she had a baby girl by the boy.

Child advocates are rightly angered by this slap on the wrist. If it had been a man teacher and a girl pupil, there is no way such a so-called man would have been given such a light sentence. And rightly so.

It cannot be denied that humanity has a mindset concerning this double standard. I've made the point to ultra-feminists that the logic of their position would lead to having to wipe all the laws concerning rape off the books. Yet, in spite of the logic, they are, understandably, opposed. Still, the extreme position of sexual equality demands such a thing.

So, instead of taking an illogical position, I point out the need for the compatibility of differences to be emphasized, giving due honor to those differences which, in spite of emotional aggravation, are undeniably real. But I invite you to read my Birds book for elaboration on this theme.

***

My position on the UN continues to result in mailings and phone calls from those who want to educate me about their brand of truth of the Great Satan of the New World Order. Several people sent me information about congressman Ron Paul's (R-TX) H.R. 1146 directed toward the U.S. leaving the UN

A few of you even called attention to the congressman having a Ph.D. But, as usual, none even bothered to check where he obtained his degree. Again, as usual, those without a university education don't know how vital it is to check on the credentials of such people. But educated people know the relevance of this all-important information.

The Great Gatsby would tell people he graduated from Oxford. What he didn't say was that this particular Oxford was a small high school in a small town and he lied by not telling the whole truth. But he counted on the intellectual laziness of people not to check his credentials. And it usually works.

But this is the major reason I have my degrees and credentials hanging on my wall for anyone to see and I invite anyone to check them out. I've had a few reporters do this. And I say good for them.

When faced with religious leaders supporting slavery Lincoln said: I suppose the Almighty is as able to speak to me as well as to you. But obviously God was talking out of both sides of His mouth if you had to accept both sides as the Word of God. And folks, like Lincoln, I don't think God speaks out of both sides of His mouth!

And I do think God spoke to Lincoln in no uncertain terms when that great man, reflecting the heart and mind of God, finally said: If slavery is not wrong, then nothing is wrong! But in so doing, Lincoln called down the wrath of those espousing slavery having the approval of God.

So it is that I call down the wrath of people like those who preached God favored slavery when I tell such people they better study the UN from primary source material not taking the word of others second hand, that they better start working on making the UN a better organization rather than wasting their time and resources trying to tear it down. Like those slavers of old, they will not succeed. All they can do is wrap themselves in the flag, Bible, Torah or Koran and die a self-righteous death after causing all the misery they can.

When I consider those people who are still making buggy whips in a computer age I always think of Thoreau's story of the Indian who was so angry when no one would buy his baskets. After all, he had gone to all the time and trouble of making baskets. Therefore, in his thinking, people owed it to him to buy his baskets!

The problem was that people didn't need or want baskets. They needed and wanted clay and metal utensils and cooking ware. For these, in a more modern society, there was a market. And if only the Indian hadn't been so ignorantly prejudiced, he would have acknowledged the superior quality and versatility of these other implements as opposed to his baskets.

The Indian wouldn't change and died miserably in poverty, roundly cursing those who owed him a living. Folks, if you're trying to peddle baskets or buggy whips when the world and the enemy are using computers, go ahead and die cursing those who wouldn't buy your baskets, go ahead and die cursing those who took the trouble to become computer literate and world knowledgeable, those who paid the price of getting a real education and as a result left you to your stock of unsold baskets and buggy whips.

In the end, you will have earned the disdain of truly educated and civilized people. And your epitaph of history should stand with that of Clay and Calhoun!

I'm a qualified gunsmith. I was raised with a gun in my hands and was reloading my own ammunition when I was twelve and used to deal in firearms. I am an avid supporter of the NRA and the rights of citizens to bear arms.

But if I had it in my power to eliminate all guns throughout the world, I would do so. If I had it in my power to eliminate all landmines, etc. and weapons of mass destruction, I would do so.

Because I'm a pacifist, a bleeding heart liberal? Far from it. But given the choice of peace or war, I opt for peace.

And not peace at any price! But a peace that would guarantee I would not become a victim of altruism.

Folks, the UN is the only world body that has this potential for working for world peace. But it needs our help, not destructive criticism. I try to do all I can to cooperate with UNICEF through the UN because I believe we must do all we can for the children of the world, not just America.

They say charity begins at home. And they are right. There is much we must do to clean up our own act at home in America. But planet earth is our home as well. In this age of phenomenal scientific advances, it is the highest form of dereliction of duty for Americans not to cooperate in doing all we can for those less fortunate worldwide.

I was fortunate beyond words to have been born in America. But that carries with it a responsibility to those who were not so blessed. And I never take my birth in the freest nation in history for granted. I have a duty to my nation. The proposed amendment has its roots in the recognition of that sense of duty to the posterity, the future of America, our children.

But education freed me from the tyranny of parochialism, of the narrow view that my duty stops with the children of America; that it stops without an understanding of other cultures, other nations and other points of view worldwide.

Sadly, in America, an education seems to have degenerated to knowing Rick didn't say **again** in Casablanca and in the surfeit of epitomes how the word Monty is presently used. Bret Harte and Sam Clemens, not to mention Lincoln, would find this tragic and fill them with foreboding.

I strongly recommend that those who consider themselves patriots get a real education and start attacking the real enemies of America and the world: The universities and religious ignorance, superstitions, bigotry and prejudices!

A large part of my thinking that is in contradiction to so many well-intentioned but ignorant people has to do with my daughters. It occurred to me some years past that in spite of my being able to enjoy blasting away with a gun or mixing it up in a real brawl, I just didn't fit the Neandertal (no h, by the way) image.

I could not countenance the prospect of my girls running around with nary a deep thought in their pretty little heads. Vacuity was not an attribute or an option because they were girls. I accorded them the best of ability to think and do as well or better than any boy.

I did encourage them to be little ladies and the boys to be little gentlemen. It was never a competition. Apples don't compete with oranges. But they can compliment each other.

By extension, I came to confront my own prejudices. My girls had to face many grim realities such as being the prey of predatory men. As a boy, I didn't have to face the problem girls did. Realizing this, among many other things, gave me a different slant about many things men without daughters don't have.

To further extrapolate, many adults find themselves trapped in a mindset from which it is only with the greatest difficulty that they can be released. An open mind is needed.

But how many such people are willing to admit they have a closed mind? Not many. It is not an admirable characteristic. But as Lincoln pointed out: *Men are not flattered by being shown that there has been a difference of purpose between the Almighty and them.*

Now whether you are a Mason, a Baptist, Catholic, Mormon, Jew, Moslem, etc. you have prejudices that have to be overcome. Some of these prejudices place you in the category of Us vs. Them and you can even find yourself lying, cheating and stealing in the name of your supposed god or version of patriotism. Real education should disabuse such people of their self-deceptions but it is too often a case of being too opinionated, as was said of Horace Greeley, to be honest.

And when good people set out to do battle against such evil prejudices and self-deceptions, they better get at least an equal education to that of the enemy and you good patriots better heed the sage appraisal of Greeley.

I fervently wish good people would take the position of being threatened by an invasion from space. If such an invasion or a virus threatened the world, wouldn't they be forced to cooperate? The world is threatened. And we Americans have the greatest power for good to meet the threat; but how much better if we could come together willingly to lead in cooperation rather than wait until some cataclysm forced cooperation.

Suppose for a moment that Saddam really believes in what he is doing. Try putting yourself in his place. He has a fervent, and to him, holy hatred of America. He believes in his righteousness, that he is the arm of God to destroy Satan America.

No one is going to lead such fanaticism to reason. But look around you, right here in America. We have our own fanatics of the stripe of Saddam right here!

You can see them on TV, you can listen to them on radio, and you can, like myself, and receive their hate-filled and doomsday literature.

But if I were in Iraq, I could pick up any baby or two-year-old and love that little one. And that little one would respond to my love. Ask yourself what it is that produces the Saddams of the world.

Then consider the message the hate mongers right here in America are preaching and I challenge you to tell me the difference between them and Saddam. Both will look you right in the eye, wave their flag and holy book and tell you they are the instruments and true prophets of God!

Lincoln's famous speech, A House Divided, is one we in America would do well to heed. As he said, our country could not endure half slave and half free. It would become all one thing or all the other.

Either the opponents of slavery will arrest the further spread of it and place it where the public mind shall rest in the belief that it is in course of ultimate extinction, or its advocates will push it forward till it shall become lawful alike in all the states, old as well as new, North as well as South.

Lord Charnwood added this incisive thought:

It may perhaps be said that American public opinion has in the past been very timid in facing clear-cut issues. But, as has already been observed, an apt phrase crystallizing the unspoken thought of many is even more readily caught up in America than anywhere else.

And what was that apt phrase of Lincoln's to which Lord Charnwood was referring? A house divided against itself cannot stand!

With this phrase borrowed from Scripture (Matthew 12:25) branded into the minds of Americans opposed to slavery, they did take up that apt and crystallizing phrase. And from that point on, slavery in America was doomed.

But Lincoln had another phrase burning within him, one that he had thought on since he was a young man:

If slavery is not wrong, then nothing is wrong!

And it was this phrase that compelled him to finally sign the Emancipation Proclamation, thus fulfilling in his own words: My promise to myself and to my Maker:

We are a house divided. And a house divided cannot stand. And here is that apt phrase which will crystallize the unspoken thought of all good Americans:

If perversion is not wrong, then nothing is wrong!

There is no middle ground between obvious good and evil. There is no gray area between the two for as Lincoln pointed out concerning slavery, the leadership of the South as per Jefferson Davis and others would settle for nothing less than an admission that slavery was morally right and socially

169

elevating, the South was not going to settle for anything less than national recognition and approval of this.

If you cannot see Tom Hanks and The Philadelphia Story and pervert activists and sympathizers and the support of president Clinton in this mirror reflection of those supporters of the blasphemous perversion of slavery, you are as willfully blind as those in the South who held so jealously to their perversion and even tried to promote it as glorifying to humanity and to God Himself!

I feel so strongly about perversion in America for the same reason Lincoln expressed his hatred of slavery:

I hate it because of the monstrous injustice of slavery itself. I hate it because it deprives our republican example of its just influence in the world-enables the enemies of free institutions, with plausibility, to taunt us as hypocrites.

Far removed though Iraq is from free institutions, if Saddam has a just criticism of America, it is in America's being increasingly perceived as a nation with the heart of a pervert together with the hypocrisy of preaching its concern for children and families both here and abroad!

This Janus-faced sermon cannot bring anything but shame to America and it is small wonder other nations increasingly view America with suspicion as a consequence.

The universities, Hollywood and the president of America, glorify perversion while the judiciary and even some churches approve it and Congress fears opposing it. And the nations of the world look on and judge America accordingly.

It is a curiosity that so many good people who believe they are really fighting the good fight cannot even get their U.S. Representative or Senator to get up in Congress and make the simple statement:

If perversion is not wrong, then nothing is wrong!

But they hail the idiocy of Representative Ron Paul getting a bill to the floor to get the U.S. out of the UN as a victory! Talk about the success of the Enemy diverting attention away from him! And there is nothing the Enemy would like more than to get the U.S. out of the UN, to get America isolated from any influence for good it might be to other nations, to remove America from the just criticism by other nations of our own hypocrisy!

We are a House Divided. It is the goal of the Enemy to make sure our House does not stand. America possesses the foundation, thanks to our Founding Fathers and men like Washington and Lincoln, to bring peace to the world. This is the greatest fear of the Enemy, that America will fulfill its destiny in this regard.

Thanks to Lincoln, the major flaw of our Constitution was corrected and the perversion of slavery is no more. But we are a House Divided as long as we are going down the road of compromise with the perversions of homosexuality and abortion, easy divorce, the perversion of a growing lack of personal commitment and responsibility, the growing overall lack of any moral absolutes.

Lincoln went to his knees before God to ask for a victory as a sign of His approval before signing the Emancipation Proclamation. And while it may be argued whether Antietam was that victory, there is no doubt in my mind about God moving the heart of Lincoln to sign with the further proof of His approval in giving Lincoln the final victory in the war and the passage of the thirteenth amendment.

It doesn't take a literary scholar to appreciate the Gettysburg Address. There is no more sublime work of literature in the English language.

I've made the point in the past that no mere politician could have written such a masterpiece of poetry. It took a very great poet to do this. And Lincoln's place as such a poet was thus assured in history.

It took a poet of Lincoln's stature to make the connection he did in his speech A House Divided. It took a consummate poet and statesman to keep the Union together, to choose so wisely, to learn from mistakes and profit from them, to take a moral stand in the face of so many detractors who would compromise with obvious evil in the name of peace.

We The People have our role model in Lincoln in facing the compromisers and glorifiers of perversion. It is in the hands of We The People to take this next and necessary step toward fulfillment of our destiny in passing the proposed amendment, which will end the enslavement of our children, of our society, by those who would glorify, evil using the very same arguments of God's approval and the high-flown rhetoric of those slavers of old.

The question is legitimately asked whether God is an intervener God. And I believe He is. But, to repeat what I mentioned earlier, not in either the traditional or orthodox way of thinking. I believe there are things God cannot do, things that are our responsibility as the adult children of God to do. But I believe God intervenes in the hearts of people, to move hearts and minds to do right.

I think God needs our help. If America is to fulfill its destiny of righteousness to the world, as the beacon of hope to the world, We the People, not God, have that responsibility. It then only remains a question of whether We the People will accept that responsibility and act accordingly.

At a time when we are hearing so many mixed signals by the leadership, tobacco and drug abuse are wrong but you can murder by abortion, have and kill babies with no penalty or stigma attaching, live together with no commitment to each other or society, let your children wander off to be killed and sue for $20,000,000 because of your own negligence, etc. ad nauseum, submit a bill to Congress to get the U.S. out of the UN but don't stand up and say: If perversion is not wrong, then nothing is wrong! Our work is cut out for us.

Especially when governors and those in Congress have the unmitigated gall and temerity to tell me that in confronting perversion, in protecting our children by guaranteeing them the most fundamental of all human rights, the right to a lawfully protected and innocent childhood: Well, it's a good idea; I just don't think a U.S. Amendment is the way to go!

Back in November 1996, the 15 justice ministers of the European Union led by Belgium approved an initiative to fight the sexual exploitation of children by pursuing producers, vendors, distributors and owners of pornographic material that features youngsters. We should be doing all in our power here in America to follow the example of the EU. And the amendment should be America's example to the world!

One of the first names on my Memorial Wall with the names of murdered children was that of little JonBenet Ramsey. That was a year ago. Many names have followed; the little victims of violence and beasts in the form of human beings.

Two candlelight vigils were held for little JonBenet (though the reporters outnumbered the participants). Said one woman, a neighbor: I am really frustrated no one has been arrested. I think they (the Ramseys) are too rich. As to comments about only having circumstantial evidence another neighbor, a man, said: They convicted Terry Nichols on circumstantial evidence.

It is widely acknowledged that wealth and power made the original investigation a bungled affair, purposely or otherwise. It has been an affront, an obscenity of justice to see how the Ramseys have been handled with kid gloves by authorities from Governor Romer on down.

The two most essential items of the case, a thorough, independent autopsy and a DNA determination of paternity/maternity have yet to be done or told of. Immediately after the murder, I informed Governor Romer of the necessity of these things in such cases. He never replied. Cover up? We all wonder.

It's been over a year now since little JonBenet's murder. The infamous anniversary date of Christmas has passed. But during the Christmas season, I looked at my Memorial Wall with the names of so many children and the thought crossed my mind that there should be a Christmas tree or Christmas wreath, some holly or some lights and decorations for these little ones. They will never see another Christmas but couldn't I, shouldn't I do something for them?

But would such decorations be an obscenity? How would the hundreds who pass the Wall interpret such a thing? Yet, the idea haunted me. I wanted so badly to have Christmas for these little ones who would never have another Christmas. Santa lives for millions of children but none of these little ones would ever hang another stocking or open a Christmas gift. And, in some cases, they never had.

I've lived long enough to question my own wisdom and decided that if only one other person would suggest such a thing for these little victims, I would go ahead and do it. Not a single person made such a suggestion. What could I conclude from this? That I was the only one who thought it was a good thing to do or I was wrong in thinking of such a thing?

The purpose of the Wall is to make sure these children are not forgotten. A further purpose is for it to be a Wall of Shame, pricking the consciences of Americans into action against the beasts that murdered these children.

Maybe some of you will respond, maybe next Christmas there will be a tree or wreath, lights and decorations for these small ones from whom all future Christmas's was inhumanly stolen. Maybe their angels will appreciate it. There were two candlelight vigils and many decorations in Boulder, Colorado for little JonBenet. People remembered her.

But most of the names on my Wall are unknown to the majority, they are the little forgotten ones with whom little JonBenet is now joined, whose parents were not wealthy and for whom there are no candlelight vigils or decorations.

And I ask myself, was little JonBenet embarrassed, even ashamed, at all the attention she received this past Christmas while so many other little victims were ignored? I most certainly don't know, but I do wonder...

***

Every once in a while, I have to clear the air concerning some issues, even at the expense of being misconstrued or cast in the role of Mencken. Here goes.

If I was still teaching college courses, or even some high school courses, I would make Carl Sagan's book A Demon Haunted World and Michio Kaku's book Visions required reading.

To myself I seem to have been only like a boy playing on seashore, and diverting myself in now and then finding a smoother pebble or a prettier shell than ordinary, whilst the great ocean of truth lay all undiscovered before me.

When Newton surveyed the vast ocean of truth that lay before him, the laws of nature were shrouded in an impenetrable veil of mystery, awe, and superstition. Science as we know it did not exist.

With these words Kaku introduces his book. His point is well made. I have the distinct advantage of having been a student of the Queen of Science, Theology, for years. After all, until the dawning of the age of science, Theology was the predominant study of the universities.

It takes just such a background to understand and fully appreciate the profound significance of the present state of science, to understand and appreciate why philosophy is the guide of the power of the discoveries of science for good or evil.

I find myself just like Newton. In considering the profound and complex issues of the proposed amendment, the whole gamut of history, art, theology, science and human behavior presents itself as that great ocean of truth. And yet, each pebble and shell has its part.

The amendment presents itself as a syllogism wherein all these other factors find their proper role. As with any balanced equation, there is a beauty of symmetry once each pebble and shell is placed in its proper niche. The quantum of the amendment is far more than the sum of its separate parts.

But the evil that people still do is a part of the whole and prevents a balanced equation. Ignorance is a real killer. The amendment offers a foundation for the behavioral equivalent of the Grand Unification Theory in physics. Just as the revolutions in quantum physics, DNA and computers leads in the direction of Einstein's dream of a theory of everything, so the amendment utilizing the synergism of physics, chemistry and biology leads in the same direction for a philosophy which will direct such revolutions in science for the good of humanity as a whole.

It will take Renaissance thinking to pull these ideas and discoveries together. The amendment is based on such a Renaissance view. The ethical and moral considerations which revolutions in science present us are of enormous magnitude and only such a Renaissance Philosophy as that of the amendment is capable of a balanced equation leading to the peaceful use of these scientific revolutions.

Imagine if you will that the discoveries in science eventually present humanity a chance to grow organs like livers and kidneys; then, entire bodies. Futuristic as it sounds, these things are going to happen. Then, as we develop the science to make full use of the Sun's energy or other energy discoveries, coupled with continuing advances in physics, biology and chemistry, we face the possibility of merging molecular machines, true creations based on photon processing of organic, molecular computers, with human consciousness!

With computers already capable of the incremental processing of differential equations in nanoseconds, models of prediction will lead to making artificial intelligence a reality which in turn will lead to computers capable of making decisions based on real, though insentient, intelligence.

Beyond that frontier lies the fantastic prospect of a sentient and compassionate immortality itself through a merger with molecular machines! Cyborgs?

Such a merger could conceivably accomplish star travel unless some method of accomplishing speed approaching the speed of imagination is discovered in the meantime thus enabling humans, without modification, to do this.

Computer simulations in virtual reality will soon enable us to explore the brain and understand the mechanisms of the birth and the exploding of a star, the processes of creation. Cyber science, a combination of the experimental and theoretical, will answer questions of enormous magnitude opening the door ever wider to wonders we can scarcely imagine!

But what of the nature of sentient, compassionate consciousness: God Himself? While we may well discover the nature of life, this does not in and of itself answer the ultimate question of intelligent and sentient, compassionate consciousness, the I Am, that which constitutes the human being created, I believe, in the image of God. For myself, I'm content to look to God for that answer. Yet, I do believe that all these other discoveries have the potential for a universal agreement concerning God. And it is impossible to have world peace as long as people continue to kill others in the name of ethnicity or God!

Science is not a religion regardless of the devotion of some to it. Nor is real science a threat to religion unless religious people create a miasma surrounding it with superstitions and ignorant hatreds rather than crediting God with being the source of true science. Ideal science is invariably proactive as opposed to religion that, historically, is reactive.

Science, in and of itself, has no power to change human behavior. Only philosophy has that power. For example, the cure for pellagra was made scientifically obvious but the philosophy of the time, based on economics and prejudice, refused to accept the findings of science that a chronic vitamin deficiency was the cause of the disease.

I place the emphasis that I do on philosophy because its ideal, uncorrupted by economics and prejudice, like that of ideal science, is etiological. All ideal philosophical searching for truth is based on consciousness. Some within the scientific community are of the opinion that science will never discover the mechanics of consciousness, that it will remain the domain of God.

Thoreau honestly admitted that he wrote so much of himself because he knew himself better than he knew anybody else. A great deal of my writing falls into this same category. As a writer, philosopher and poet, how could it be otherwise? The search for truth begins with and has its primary focus on our own consciousness of ourselves. It is this that enables us to move on to a consciousness of others, of thoughts that weigh the consciousness of others against that of ourselves.

In respect to sentient, compassionate consciousness, I believe that only God can provide the motive force for moral behavior, for putting the discoveries of science to work for the good of humanity. But only the general acceptance of God as Creator of all can accomplish such a thing in my opinion. I further believe that making children the priority they should be worldwide can accomplish this.

I believe only a generation of children raised in lawfully protected innocence can accomplish the goal of humanity being all that it has the potential of being. We rightly dream of the time of Isaiah where a little child will lead the wild beasts, when all of creation is at peace. Only a generation of such children raised to be the best adults possible will be able to properly utilize the discoveries of science. And I continue to believe children to be the closest thing to the heart of God Himself.

Trying to understand the nature of God is the most profound of all subjects. This was the purpose of my Hey, God! book to which I would refer the reader rather than attempt any discussion of the subject here. Suffice it to say that general agreement on the nature of God is one of the most critical of all things leading to world peace.

Kaku rightly points out that knowledge and skills will be the commodities of the future rather than manufacture. As the world becomes Hawthorne's electric head, McLuhan's true global village due to the revolution in communications, thus giving people throughout the world a chance of understanding one another, in the sharing of common hopes and dreams of the future for our children, it will become ever more evident that the majority do not want things like war and prejudicial ignorance to rule their lives.

If I were to write a computer program for world peace and cooperation based on the present status of nations steeped in ignorance and superstitions of race and religion I would face a screen scrolling: Does not compute; Does not compute; Does not compute!

At present, Douglas Lenar is working on a Common Sense program that will enable computers to incorporate things like a sense of "Time and Nothing can be in two places at the same time." We need the equivalent Common Sense program in our own brains and psyches to overcome prejudices.

Imagine, if you will, the complexity of this example contained in Kaku's book:

Mary saw a bicycle in the store window. She wanted it. Lenat asks: How do we know that she wanted the bicycle, and not the store, or the window?

This, as Kaku points out, requires understanding the nearly complete set of human likes and dislikes.

Likes and dislikes are human traits requiring nearly astronomical bits of data which our brains process. Can you imagine the difficulty of writing such a program for the present generation of computers? Let alone a program that can incorporate causality in its conclusions; that would give a machine learning capability? At this point, what it means to be human may be the choke point where only the photon-processing molecular computer, the generation beyond Artificial Intelligence, will be able to do the job with the brain's ability and accuracy.

As to "Does not compute" there is no chance for a balanced equation for world peace until the Common Sense program can be written on this basis:

There will never be any true hope for enduring love and peace until men and women throughout the world regard each other as of equal value on the basis of honoring the compatibility of differences between them, and children are given their proper priority.

This Computes! But this cannot be accomplished as long as racial, political and religious hatreds hold sway in the world. This computes as well!

For America to be the leader in peace, to be the leader for the peaceful use of revolutions in science, Americans are going to have to reverse the present trend in America toward mounting ignorance and illiteracy.

As talk of improving America's schools continues, I can't help thinking requiring high school pupils to read Sagan and Kaku as well as Emerson, Hawthorne, Melville, Thoreau and Rousseau would help some of these children make the transition from being pupils to becoming real students. A mark of present illiteracy is using the two terms as synonyms.

The present Asian financial crisis is rooted in ignorance, greed and avarice. Capitalism is relatively new to the Asian community. Family and government cartels have raped the financial markets and the fallout is occurring.

A cultural gulf still presents itself and is clearly seen in what is happening between Eastern and Western philosophies of gathering wealth. America has had its Morgans, Carnegies and Rockefellers but the leavening influence of democratic ideals has been there throughout to blunt the force of financial dictators.

Asia, along with many other nations such as Iraq where the people are pauperized while a despotic dictator accumulates billions in personal wealth does not have this leavening influence to protect the common people. To cross that cultural gulf, America has the responsibility of the leadership of instruction in the democratic process. The communications revolution provides the opportunity to do this. But many societal problems must be solved in America before such a thing can be accomplished.

A Renaissance of enlightenment, legally and sociologically, is the promise of the amendment. Since it will take a generation of children raised in protected innocence to be the best adults humanity can produce to reach the stars, to develop a philosophy of world peace and cooperation in order to fulfill our promise and potential as human beings, it becomes ever more critical to America's role as the leader of nations to make the amendment a part of our foundational charter of government as quickly as possible.

Kaku describes a delightful scene of children with Ph.D.s at MIT playing with robots. Such playfulness on the part of those with real genius gives hope that in making major scientific advances, what makes us human remains a part of such advances. Robots with the names Odie or Attila (the insectoid pattern for the Mars Sojourner), a Yellow Brick Road leading to a computer named Oz, a high-tech Santa's workshop where the major themes of imagination, curiosity, fun and humor, love and romance are not lost in such an environment of genius. How could they be when the best of genius is motivated by and involves tribute to such things? Funny, but the Scripture perfect love casts out all fear comes to my own mind in such an environment.

My particular emphasis for some years, scientifically, has been on the impact of subatomic particle research, believing as I do, that discoveries here will explain PSI, the paranormal. Now it appears that I have been correct in this emphasis. It will undoubtedly be the quantum theories and discoveries in this area which will provide the needed cross-fertilization of quantum physics/DNA/computer, where superstring theory will coalesce with understanding the relationship between neurons and atoms, between pleasure and pain principles of civilized behavior, to fashion the next age of science with ultimate computers that can dream, all these things working together providing the mechanism of reaching the stars and all that this implies literally and figuratively for humanity.

Serendipity will, I have no doubt, play its part in the new, scientific revolution that will result from such cross-fertilization. But it is unlikely any Minerva will be born full-blown of Jupiter. All of this work will require intense, disciplined, scholarly dedication as well as genius. But it is gratifying and cause of much hope for humanity that, as at MIT, the fun and joy of play, humor and romanticism have their major roles in the process, providing a paradigm for scientific achievement that borrows from and utilizes all the best of what is human, including trial and error.

If so much of humanity seems hard-wired for violence and children are the real antithesis of war, it seems only logical that the need to satisfy human needs of danger, risk, excitement and exploration be applied to reaching the stars. And this, of course, will require global cooperation, a cooperation that will require the satisfaction of working toward the goal of humanity as a whole rather than self-gratification at the expense of others. And this will require that generation of children raised to be the best adults possible. This Computes.

Learning, in quantum physics, is the process of finding the lowest energy. John Hopfield applied this attribute of the atomic lattice to the neurons of the brain. In doing so, he bridged the gap between the two sciences. While the two sciences working together will, I believe, explain PSI we still have a long way to go in understanding the brain and subatomic physics.

Yet, this lowest energy principle seems to be too literally true of human beings when it comes to real study and learning. Too many remain intellectually lazy or subscribe to some Royal path to knowledge nonsense.

So much of my writing has to be dedicated to education that fifty years ago would not be necessary here in America. For example, the following would be common knowledge to pupils having taken only a high school biology class back then:

Haploid: The chromosome number of a normal gamete that contains only one member of each chromosome pair. In man, the haploid number is 23.

Genome: All the genes found in a haploid set of chromosomes.

Gamete: A mature germ cell (male or female) with haploid chromosome number.

But I can no longer take it for granted that even college graduates know these things now. Yet people bandy about words like gene, genetics, cloning, atom, even computer as though they had understanding of such things! The vast majority does not.

Scientists have made such amazing discoveries and science has progressed to such an advanced state that Kaku can say we are approaching an understanding of Einstein's dream: The Grand Unification Theory, the theory of Everything!

Three things, as Kaku points out, give hope of finding this Holy Grail of physics: The quantum revolution (atom), the DNA revolution (biomolecular) and the computer revolution.

These three things open the door to the new age of science that will make us, as Kaku says, pass from being observers of Nature to being active choreographers of Nature. The quantum revolution will open the door to manipulating and choreographing new forms of matter at will.

To rightly understand this, you need to know, among many other things that the photon is a quantum (packet) of light… that subatomic particles have properties of both particles and waves.

But, philosophy being guide to the power of science, even if everyone was an accomplished physicist it would do no good unless there was a philosophy that would properly guide in its use.

Science made the power of the atom available to America against Japan. But philosophy directed the use of that power. And philosophy created the situation of the nuclear arms race.

For America to fulfill its promise of leading in world peace, of leading in democratic ideals and transcending corruption in government and the historical prejudices and hatreds based on things like racial and religious ideologies, we must look to the laboratory of history itself.

But to do so requires a Renaissance mode of thinking in order to transcend parochialism, to transcend the deadly view that cultures are phenomenal rather than challenges to be overcome in their detrimental aspects such as the Chosen People syndrome (based on the power of suggestion and idolatry rather than fact), and discover what is truly germane to ridding humanity of the demons that still haunt and plague the world. So I turn to such an example in the laboratory of history at this point. I trust the reader to make the necessary connection of relevance to the whole. If America is to fulfill its promise of proper world leadership, it is imperative that we learn the lessons of history.

It took some of my readers by surprise to learn that Indian leaders like Geronimo jumped the reservation because of General Crook's mandate against wife beating and liquor. Because of the propagandizing by the universities together with relatively recent Hollywood productions, too often the greed and abuses of whites against the Indians have been made the prominent factors in a revisionist history of the period.

The resulting Noble Savage image has been propagandized virtually to the exclusion of the barbaric savagery practiced by Indians against whites, each other, and especially against their own women.

In films, Gene Hackman's Geronimo and Dustin Hoffman's Little Big Man are representative of such distorted views. And, unhappily, we live in an age when far too many people are educated by film and TV rather than scholarly books (during the sixties, it became politically incorrect to produce a film showing an Indian man drunkenly beating his wife).

To compound the matter, even books must be read with an understanding of potential bias among experts in the subject. The educated man and woman know you don't read just one book on a given subject, you read several to gain a discriminating perspective before trying to draw conclusions. And it's imperative that you know the pedigree of your authors!

Human nature being what it is, it isn't surprising to find instances of barbaric cruelty and even massacres practiced by both whites and Indians against each other during the time period of the Indian wars.

For those of you who want a better grasp of the Indian wars in the West, one of the books I recommend is Frontier Regulars by Robert M. Utley. The author gives a fairly even-handed and well-documented treatment of the subject.

It is important to gain understanding of several things that were working during this period of American history. One very prominent thing is how successful guerrilla warfare can be. Up to a point.

In countless instances, a very small band of Indians wreaked havoc far beyond what their numbers would seem to command. Superior forces of the Army were often of no avail against this kind of guerrilla action.

But those superior forces, eventually, overcame. The side with the most cannon won. And the Indian paid the price for his inability to match such organized warfare.

Conservative America needs to learn the lesson of the Indian. The most cannon and organization will always overcome guerrilla tactics. You can fight innumerable small battles, you can fight and win harassing skirmishes, even terrorize, but the larger, well-organized army will eventually overcome all these things.

After Antietam Lincoln pointed out the North would win because the South would run out of men and the North wouldn't. That was logical, pragmatic fact devoid of any God-is-on-our-side rhetoric. Every battle, every war of attrition has proved Lincoln's point in spite of the argument of some scholars whose bias (or just plain penchant for argumentativeness and contrariness for the sake of trying to call attention to themselves or prove their bias) sometimes blinds them to this fact.

Like the role of Negroes in the Civil War on both sides. Some obviously self-serving experts have tried to muddy Lincoln's image as the Great Emancipator by making the role of Negroes during the war, a relatively small issue, that of a major issue. Not true. The North would have won the war whether Negroes played any part in the fighting or not.

This does not, in any way, detract from individual acts of heroism and sacrifice on the part of some Negroes during the war. But understanding and wisdom come from historical facts of truth, not revisionist myths.

This is the basis of what I wrote in one of my books: There are three things you never discuss in a bar: Politics, religion and the Civil War. Far better to stick to the number one topic in such an environment: Women (never could understand why any man would ever prefer to talk about other sports).

Seriously, not that the subject of women isn't enormously important, it is; but you don't discuss the Civil War in the context of today's culture and mores; those not educated in the time frame of the Civil War will invariably argue from a vast amount of assumed knowledge, i.e. prejudicial ignorance.

But no matter how erudite the arguments, even apologetics offered by the knowledgeable of the religious, political, cultural and economic raisons d'etre, the bottom line of the Civil War is summed up in Lincoln's words: If slavery is not wrong, then nothing is wrong! And nothing can detract from the moral and courageous position of Lincoln, a position he took against immensely formidable forces at the time, a fact unassailable apart from either ignorance or prejudice of some nature.

Most certainly the ideas of a Balkanized America or Trans-Mississippi Confederacy were issues Lincoln had to take into consideration. And he did. But the courageous and moral bottom line of Lincoln's stand remains.

To attempt to make Lincoln equivocal concerning emancipation and its importance to all other considerations, especially the preservation of the Union, in any way is to show a profound lack of knowledge of the man and the time period.

Admittedly, Lincoln may well have been often heeding Andrew Jackson's words, as I do myself: If the hair on my head knew my plans, I'd cut it off! Many enemies and few friends surrounded Lincoln.

It is well said that the power of the purse, the power to tax, is the power to destroy. You raise armies, among other things, with such power. The Indians lacked such organized power and they lost. They didn't even have a common culture or national holiday around which to organize.

Which brings me to a pronounced weakness; I'd even compare it to a cancerous disease, infecting America. The exaggerated emphasis being placed on celebrations of cultural distinctives by some groups; which is destroying the sense of being an American in favor of racial or religious affiliation.

It would help immeasurably if the universities, groups and organizations would shut up about race and religion and focus on being good Americans! Why emphasize the things that make you a better Baptist, Jew, Catholic, Muslim, Buddhist, African, Mexican, etc. if, in the process, you lose the primary emphasis of what makes you a better American?

It isn't racist to decry the celebration of things like Hanukkah, Cinco de Mayo, Kwanzaa, etc. in America. The celebration of a race or culture in some instances may be well and good. I qualify this statement because no civilized person would call the barbaric savagery of religio/racial fanatics in Africa, Algeria and Bosnia anything to celebrate.

But when such things as Hanukkah and Cinco de Mayo are made a source of racial or religious superiority, of distinctive separateness and discrimination against America and being Americans as the proper priority, they become counterproductive. You're proud to be Irish, a Jew, Negro or Mexican. Fine. But you are not in the freest nation in the history of the world because of Irish, Asians, Jews, Negroes, Mexicans or Muslims and Buddhists. Neither are you here because you are an Atheist, Agnostic, Catholic or Protestant. You're here in the freest nation in the history of the world because of Americans irrespective of whatever race, creed, religion or culture.

Immediately the reaction is: Hey, look at what this (fill in the blank) race, culture, etc. has contributed to America! This begs the statement; it has nothing to do with the statement. And no one who knows the early history of America could possibly, apart from ignorant prejudice, take exception to the statement.

If this rankles, why don't you go to Israel, Africa, Arabia, India, Pakistan or Mexico if you are fixated on those only of your kind? You know why not just as well as I do. It is well said that if America should open its borders, many other nations would be drained of population.

I always get a laugh out of poor, long-suffering Tevye's line in Fiddler on the Roof when he says to God: I know, I know, we're the Chosen People. But, God, couldn't you choose someone else once in a while?

The myth of a Chosen People of whatever race, religion or culture is exactly that, a myth. And far from being funny, it's a deadly myth with unnumbered thousands of victims to its hateful and despicable credit! No Jew, Arabian, African, Mexican, Asian or European of whatever description belongs to a Chosen People. It isn't politically correct to point out the similarity of thinking between a fanatical Hitler and a fanatical John Bircher, Jew, Moslem, Hutu, Tutsi or Irish Catholic or Protestant. But there it is. The same holds true for fanaticism of every description.

The self-delusion of this myth of a Chosen People, including some militant God and Country types in America, is the grounds for the barbaric savagery and murder in the name of some god or holy book throughout history and still on-going in the world today. Carl Sagan's book A Demon Haunted World has its roots in just such demoniacal thinking.

And if you are something else before you are an American in the best historical meaning and privilege of that name, you're at best a victim of a deceived sense of the priorities. At the worst, you are an enemy of the liberty and freedom you enjoy at the expense of those who gave everything even to their lives for you to have the liberty and freedom of this nation!

I'm not waving the flag by saying these things. It isn't racist to point out the truth. America has a huge responsibility in the world. I'm not a My country, right or wrong so-called patriot. You won't find a greater critic than me concerning the failings of America in being what it should be.

But for America to be all it should be, the internecine rivalry of racial, religious and political ideologies must be overcome. Or, like the Indians, we will be destroyed. We will become Americans first and anything else second or we will never realize our potential for good as a people.

For those who believe America should be a continuing beacon of hope and an example to the rest of the world, this is only logical. And just as only perverts would speak in favor of perversion, only those perverted in their own thinking will argue with this logic.

Pride of race and intellect is ignorantly, prejudicially misplaced. Gratitude and thankfulness are more appropriate to such things. These are things properly called accidents of birth. Not a single one of us chose to be born to or with either. But pride of achievement; pride in making the best of yourself as a human being irrespective of accident of birth, that is something else.

I don't think and write as I do because of my being a WASPM (White Anglo-Saxon Protestant Male). I think and write as I do because I am a human being before I am anything else. But we all have at least that much in common and that has virtually no bearing on what makes me distinctive. The distinctiveness is my being born in America. Overcoming the hurtful and harmful strictures of racial and religious prejudices and separating what I believe from what I know achieve further distinctiveness.

Learning to be human, learning that all humanity has a common bond in children, that is the lesson I have learned and want to promote. Being an American with the enormous freedom and liberty such a birthright has gifted me, together with the concomitant responsibility, gives me distinct advantages in being able to promote this lesson for all humanity.

Not the least of these gifts bequeathed is the freedom of expression I enjoy as an American. Virtually no other nation in the world enjoys such an extensive privilege.

As Americans, we have the opportunity to be citizens of the world far beyond that of those in any other nation. And that, I believe, is a part of our responsibility as Americans.

But being neither naive nor altruistic, I am fully aware of another gift and privilege I have as an American, the right to keep and bear arms. An armed citizenry is the only thing that enables us, as Americans, to keep our other liberties. Make no mistake, we have had would-be despots and dictators in the past right here in America; we have them now and we will face them in the future.

As to home and personal protection, I'll gladly give up my guns when there is a guarantee virtually no one else can have one either- And not until. As long as America and the world are dangerous places, I choose not to be an unarmed victim. In this, I bow to the wisdom of those founding fathers and our Constitution.

Propagandizing such as columnist Herb Benham's and others against guns is the most hurtful kind of thing. It displays a prejudicial ignorance like that of demonizing tobacco.

What civilized person doesn't wish that neither guns nor tobacco were in the world (and let's not forget to include nuclear weapons in the list)? But I can grow tobacco in my backyard and I can make a gun with nothing but a grinder and drill press. For the foreseeable future, we are not going to rid the world of either guns or tobacco.

I'm sure Mr. Benham wouldn't try to match his intellect and wisdom with that of Jefferson and others that rightly saw an armed citizenry the strongest deterrent to the tyranny of government. And until human nature changes, I choose not to be an unarmed victim of the tyranny of an individual or the state.

When I was a boy, the fourth of July was really celebrated. But children memorized things like the Preamble and the Gettysburg Address in those days. I wonder how many children today know these things, much less Whittier's Barbara Fritchie?

We have a national heritage of The Star Spangled Banner, My Country 'Tis of Thee and God Bless America, Sousa and the Statue of Liberty, memorials to Washington and Lincoln of which we have no fear of ever being ashamed.

Good men and women gave the last full measure of devotion to secure and guarantee our freedom and liberty. And what nation in history would ever sacrifice over a half-million of its own, brother against brother, in the cause of moral justice as America did, even granting the cause of Union in the conflict?

No nation in history has had so many truly great men and women of whom to boast! Like Lincoln, I want to make a contribution to the greatness of what America represents historically, not an iconoclast who would tear America down with nothing better to offer!

We are not a nation that celebrates titles and lost causes and has to take refuge in past battles for the sake of nobility. We are winners, not losers. But a large part of what has made us winners is our sticking up for the underdog, of the extreme measures we have taken to picking up a fallen enemy once he has been beaten. We have proven ourselves to be a compassionate and giving people as Americans.

There is every reason for gratefully celebrating America as Americans. There is no reason for anyone calling themselves American to put race or creed above this noble name. By all means take pride in foreign ancestors and heritage where this is justified. But Americans have a duty first and foremost for allegiance to being Americans rather than race or religion with all that that name represents, an allegiance not to be usurped by worshiping foreign gods as though they had something nobler to offer than what America represents.

This is not to be misconstrued as denigrating, in any fashion, what other cultures have to offer. Cultural Anthropology is a fascinating study of mine and I have taught it in college. But different alone does not make anything better by virtue of being different.

Our greatness as a people is in what America represents in the ideals of the value of the individual in equality, freedom and liberty and our historic and righteous hatred for the bully, tyrant, despot and oppressor. These are the qualities that make the enemies of these things in America so onerous to us as a people. The true American believes in the ideals of justice and fair play, in the democratic ideal of individual value, liberty and responsibility. These are the things De Tocqueville and others saw and applauded about America. And when scurrilous thugs abuse their positions of power and influence, true Americans are enraged!

As De Tocqueville so well said, as long as America remains good, so long will she remain great.

We are allowing, as Americans, to have our goodness and ideals debased by the enemies of America, those who are flaunting perversion of every description in a grotesque, twisted, distorted and perverted caricature of equality, freedom and liberty. They do so without the conscience and cornerstone of equality, freedom and liberty: Personal Responsibility! The last thing such perverts, charlatans, and Judas's have any claim to is the noble name of American!

The hyphenated American- Where did this come from? The universities; where else? An idea so stupid only the universities could credit it and politicians use it! Just who are these talking to when they preface their remarks: My good Italian-Americans, my good African-Americans, my good Mexican-Americans, my good Jewish-Americans, my good Asian-Americans, my good Irish-Americans etc., ad nauseum?

If you are red, yellow, black, brown or white, don't you think I know that? Ah, but are you an American? That is quite something altogether different. And why should it be of any real import to an American if you are a Jew, Catholic, Baptist, Buddhist or Moslem; unless you make such a thing more important than being an American?

Being a U.S. citizen, an American, makes you the envy of the world. Not your being anything else regardless of your race or religion! Because of this, I am keenly aware of my duty and responsibility, as an American, to the world. I have a duty as an American beyond that of the children of America, a duty to the children of the world who have not been so blessed by accident of birth.

I will exercise that duty, not because of being a WASPM, but because of being an American and all that that name represents quite separate and apart from anything else.

I am a patriot of the ideals of America, of what America should represent of the best attributes of personal responsibility, equality, freedom and liberty.

Therefore, as such a patriot, I am the harshest kind of critic of those things that betray or denigrate those ideals my flag represents.

And unlike the egotistical and self-serving flaunting of a Whitman's Song of Myself (and I appreciate the genius of Whitman but don't excuse his faults), I'll sing of what makes America great: Americans!

This past Christmas season, the American Atheists organization based in Austin, Texas endorsed a display by Jerald Lasky in Bryan, Ohio. Lasky was protesting the endorsement of religion by the city. This confrontation has led to a spokesman for the Atheists, Ronald Barrier, saying "We hope next year to execute a full assault on public property in every state."Everywhere there is a religious display there will be an atheist display.

Now some Jews want a Menorah everywhere there is a crèche on public property; equal time in the name of religion. There was a real furor over a holy Crescent representing Moslemism put up in D.C. and it was vandalized. What does all this have to do with being an American? Are these people agitating for America to be Agnostic, Atheist, Christian, Jew, Moslem or Buddhist? Let's not deceive ourselves that any of these are for equal rights. The proponents of each believe themselves to be advocates of the one true way.

Let's look at it this way. Our Constitution not only guarantees freedom of religion, it equally guarantees freedom from religion. Fairly and logically, if any form of government from the lowest to highest endorses any single religion, it flies in the face of the Constitution.

This is why I am unalterably opposed to any representative of government forcing his or her religious (or anti-religious) views on others through the abuse of office. Some judge wants to call out the National Guard so he can keep the Ten Commandments on the wall of his court. Insane! This is not only an abuse of authority, but it is imminently unfair and unjust (I can't help but be reminded in saying this of the insanity of the recent law in California making it a crime to smoke in bars).

No American should ever feel he has the right to force his religious views on others. If there is a single consensus to be found among the framers of the Constitution, it is to be found in keeping America free of such religious tyranny!

Because of this wisdom of the founding fathers, we do not have massacres in the name of God in this country. Look at what is happening in Algeria where religious hatred has already claimed 75,000 lives, India, Africa (with well over 100,000 murdered), Burundi, Ireland, Egypt, Bosnia, Mexico, Iran, Pakistan, Afghanistan, etc. and then try to tell me you want the same thing to be happening here in America! And there are few things so successful as religious and racial hatreds to make such a thing happen!

Did you know that Islamic fundamentalists practice genital mutilation on women? That's right, female circumcision. This same kind of mutilation is common in Africa as well. Do we really want the hands of thieves cut off? Do we believe any culture has a right to call itself civilized that practices such cruel barbarisms?

The Islamic court in Iran ordered a man's eyes to be gauged out because he was guilty of blinding a co-worker. Prisoners in Dubai are freed if they memorize the Koran. Book worship, Book idolatry whether Bible, Torah or Koran!

And right here in America, in 1982, there was an attempt in Congress by joint resolution to declare the Bible the Word of God! Insane! For a real nightmare scenario, suppose some rabid TV evangelist should become an American dictator! We'd be right there with Algeria and Iran. Give me a plain old-fashioned thief or corrupt politician any day compared to would-be messiahs.

The leader of a Taiwanese cult in Texas is teaching God will descend to Dallas in human form on March 31. Should God fail to appear, the leader of the cult has promised to offer himself up for stoning or crucifixion. Airplane vapor trails are, according to this nut, supposed to be signs from God. I'm sure Jehovah's Witnesses are not amused. While California usually leads the pack in weirdoes, Texas certainly has its share.

I believe I'm still on speaking terms with God. And I cringe at the things done in His name. And I'm appalled at the things threatened in His name right here in America!

We are not a nation with a third-world suitable work ethic, which translates slave and child labor. Why do we tolerate those who would make us a third-world nation by attempts to enslave us religiously? You want America to be a Christian nation. By what definition? Yours? God forbid!

I'm not opposed to any nation being a Christian nation by the definition of the Gospel in the words of Jesus himself: Love God and your neighbor. Beyond that, don't demonize America by your religious beliefs of whatever nature! Real Americans should be better, must be better, than that!

Don't fly in the face of humanity, compassion, conscience or logic by consigning to hell everyone who doesn't agree with your own peculiar gospel of God, Jesus, Mohammed, Jehovah, Yahweh, Buddha, etc.! I believe God is better, and deserves better, than such gospels purporting to speak for Him!

What hope of world peace presents itself as long as there are people who are killing others, or even discriminating against others, in the name of God? Are you one of those who believe that God favors murder or tyranny, despotism and dictatorship in His name? If so, I call you an idolater and enemy of both God and humanity!

Further, how can such superstitions ever contribute to, or even be able to take advantage of, the beneficences of science? Such ignorance can never help mold a philosophy incorporating the best of science for the common good of humanity or make any contribution toward reaching the stars!

Of course, the plague of those who condemned Copernicus makes their contribution to a Demon Haunted World. But it will take world cooperation to deal with the demons. And nothing holds the promise of such cooperation as does making the children of the world our first priority.

I give America credit as a nation that has produced such great art, poetry, literature and music, a compassionate and giving nation of people who have helped so many other nations, to be able to point the way to world peace.

As I look at that star-studded canopy above us, that only measure of eternity I can grasp to any degree, I can't help thinking that is the inheritance and goal of humanity God has presented us.

Then, as I lower my eyes to our world, the future of our children, the dreadful poverty and ignorance that must be overcome world-wide for their sake, the abuse of our environment, the hatreds and prejudices, the murders of the innocent in the name of God, there are many grounds for pessimism. But I know these problems can be overcome by making children the priority of humanity.

So I lift my eyes and look toward the stars for continued renewal of purpose, living and working in hope that humanity is better than the record of those comparative few who would enslave and destroy, who would rob humanity of God's purpose for us and steal our birthright.

Surely the love I have for my children and grandchildren, multiplied countless millions of times by other parents and grandparents can withstand and overcome all evil. All we have to do is meet the evil with the same determination to overcome and win.

Music, play and laughter, fantasy and dreams are not the domain of childhood only. I worry about adults who have forgotten these things. Or worse, have never known them and fail in passing them on to their own children. To fail to pass on the adventures and excitement of Tom Sawyer and Huckleberry Finn, of Pathfinder and Swiss Family Robinson, of Fairy Tales and Camelot as well as Dr. Seuss and Santa is to rob of a childhood. And the seed of evil of every kind finds fertile soil in a missing childhood.

We have many problems of tremendous magnitude facing us throughout the world. But none are of the magnitude of the problem of countless millions of children who are denied a childhood. Children are the future of humanity. There is no future for a nation (or a world) that fails to cherish its young. Nor does it deserve one! This Computes. To have any other priority above this results in that scrolling screen: Does not compute; Does not compute; Does not compute.

Our failure to accept the logic of this and make children our priority will result in a final screen: End Program!

CHAPTER EIGHT

Lacking a functioning TV remote and edible food, I turned my attention to other pressing matters. In sheer desperation I was preparing to tune my steam calliope when I tried to warm up a cup of coffee by putting it in the microwave and then tried to light the contraption with a match. While holding the lit match and looking at the microwave, it occurred to me I wasn't exactly focused on task. This reminded me, naturally, of the time I tried to put the broom in the refrigerator (at least in this instance I wasn't trying to warm my coffee in the refrigerator).

Now before you start to laugh, which obviously isn't my intention, there was a perfectly plausible explanation for this. It was getting cold and I was thinking of lighting my gas heater. I simply got the two confused; could happen to anyone.

But it did make me think of mornings when you get up that develop into days when you confuse the shredder with the copier. Don't go there; especially not with your Picasso sketch.

I loved Yogi Berra's reply to his wife Carmen when asked where he would like to be buried "I don't know, why don't you surprise me."

My read on Yogi on Clinton: I didn't really say everything I said.

In spite of a great performance, there is probably no truth to the rumor that Hillary Clinton is being considered for an Oscar.

I can easily commiserate with Celine Dion, the French Canadian singer, when she was trying to learn English. Hey, mama, yo mama, yo, whassup? wasn't in the dictionary.

But at least we can thank Clinton/Lewinsky for teaching the general public a new word, a word that used to be the sole purview of Litt majors, seminarians and lawyers: Redaction.

Granting that the idiom of a language is the most difficult of tasks to learn, when that idiom sinks to such a depth of ignorance as to be virtually indecipherable and unintelligible, it bodes ill for the culture that allows it, reflecting as it does, the literacy and intellectual level of a given society. If English-speaking people bow to the language barbarians, the results are easily anticipated. Cause and Effect is not just an immutable fact of physics. Or, as Heath's Corollary states in regard to confronting evil: Nothing happens unless you make it happen.

But at least we aren't hearing any more about Ebonics. The usual idiocy we have come to expect of the educational establishment lost that round. Now if we could only do something about the language of so-called educators and their counterparts in politics.

I taught for nearly four years at a high school in Watts. An all black student body in an all black community. I was one of three white teachers in a school with a faculty of 107.

Looking back, I wonder how I survived. At no time did I patronize my pupils. My expectations of them were no less than I would have expected of any group of white pupils. And I did not even attempt to learn ghetto idiom any more than I would have expected them to learn the idiom of Oklahoma or Weedpatch. Instead, I brought my pupils up to the level of correct English if they wanted to converse. And they met that demand I made on them.

Oh, we could kid each other in the peculiar phrases and words of the Ghetto and the South, but when it came to learning that was always treated with the seriousness it needed and deserved. My pupils learned to respect that difference.

And I stressed the fact that a love of words will never substitute for knowing how to use them correctly.

The Hague, Netherlands reported to the UN that poverty is spreading even in the wealthiest nations. In America, this is the direct result of illiteracy.

We can expect such poverty in places like Afghanistan where the illiteracy rate is so very high. There are very few educated people in Afghanistan. The Taliban succeed in their atrocity-ridden and advocating religion because of this fact. To believe men wearing a beard or that circumcision, male or female, is essential to please some deity is proof of this ignorance. Engaging in public beatings, and even the murder, of women and children because of some infraction of a religious code is proof of a cruel ignorance and religion.

I have my moments of personal whimsy with Weedpatch University. I purposely cast my characters in roles where the issues and personalities are easily identifiable when parodied.

Why the parody of a university? Because the ignorance of superstitions, religion, and bigotry may very well carry the imprimatur of a Ph.D. or M.D. Even in Afghanistan as with Weedpatch University here in America. And God is not Irish; or Christian, Jew, Moslem or Hindu.

Belief System is a nice phrase but I've never known anyone in my life that was really systematic about his or her beliefs. Most such are a patchwork of ignorant opinions and anything but systematic.

As I sat with California State senator Ed Davis many years ago and tried to impress him with the dismal condition into which California schools had fallen, I was made quickly aware that things were not going to improve.

The legislative leadership was going to continue on the path of asking the same people (the products of the Ivory Tower) who created the problems for solutions. That this was obviously insane didn't seem to penetrate.

In fact, it was quickly apparent that the job of the schools was increasingly one of just keeping the lid on, not education. This being the case, what need of truly educated teachers? The schools were to be holding cells while parents went about their business; which was increasingly not the education of their children.

But I've been singing this song for so long it has become a real weariness to me. Besides, no one is listening.

Computer literacy in the schools? Not when the teachers aren't even computer literate themselves. And so it goes.

And while on the subject of illiteracy and computers, I enjoyed reading Roger Rosenblatt's criticism of the infernal devices. He won't use one. He's right; a stick with a small ball at one end that dispenses ink from a plastic tube is a real invention. And legal documents still retain the necessity for such a device for authentic signatures.

And so do love letters.

But, alas, the letters may now be done on word processors and computers. In some instances, unlike Roger, I find no particular fault with this.

As a poet, I love nature and I love to write of the many enchantments of nature. But it still takes a beautiful woman to bring out the best of my poetic sensibilities. And that's as it should be, the way I believe God intended it to be.

I disagree, however, with Roger's basic premise that the miracle of technology the computer represents leads to isolation. If it does in a particular person, that is the fault (or choice) of the person.

I don't surf the web; I hate the plethora of eye candy cluttering the screen (Alfred E. Neuman as a cursor?) and pray for the day when some order emerges in the multitudinous search engines. But this is a new technology and will undoubtedly improve in time as consumers make their likes and dislikes known via the dollars they spend.

And when I consider on-line surveys, tests, etc., I won't make the mistake the Literary Digest did in its 1936 telephone survey by thinking everyone has a computer and is on-line. The majority of Americans has little real pc knowledge and is not on-line. The media, politicians, and Hollywood seem unaware of this fact. This ignorance should make any thinking person chary of deductions and forecasts formed on this false premise.

Unlike Rosenblatt, I am very grateful for being able to use the word processing capability of a computer (which should not be mistaken or confused as computer literacy). It is an enormously timesaving device. But Rosenblatt isn't a poet; he isn't a writer of books, big books. He is, predominantly, an essayist. So, with short pieces, he can be anachronistic when it comes to writing and leave it to the flunkies to scan in his missives to accommodate the computers that, whether he is willing to admit it or not, keep him prominent and well-paid.

I'm grateful for e-mail and web pages. Just as I know what it is like to live with wood cook stove and coal oil lamps and without indoor plumbing and electricity, I'd rather not have to go back to such a lifestyle. It was uncomfortable and an awful lot of work. I have no romantic illusions of such. Try a few years on a mining claim in a wilderness environment before you think it is a bed of roses.

I'm grateful, in short, for both the ballpoint pen and the computer.

I taught myself to type at the age of 40. I never regretted it. I just kicked myself roundly for not having done it sooner. I've learned to accommodate myself to computers and haven't regretted that either.

So, my dear Roger, get off the dinosaur kick and stop saying the old was better in this case. Like rubbing sticks together to make fire, the outhouse, and the days before toilet paper, it wasn't.

It's been a long time since I first saw High Sierra. When it was released in 1941 our mother, who had just returned to the States after the attack on Pearl Harbor, took my brother and me to see it. She cried at the ending of the film and said she was sure the movie would make Humphrey Bogart a big star. She was right.

I just watched the film again the other day after an interval of many years. As a child, I didn't understand my mother's tears. But the ending of the movie did seem awfully unfair. Why was that beautiful, young girl being bullied and punished by the police? And why did the other one to whom Humphrey Bogart had been so kind treat him so badly?

The movie made me sad when I first saw it. There was just something terribly wrong with the way that beautiful young girl, Ida Lupino, had been treated. I remembered after seeing the film again, that as a child I had hoped she found someone later who would make things right for her, someone who would make her happy.

Maybe I became a romantic at that tender age. Maybe High Sierra was a focal point for me. Can that happen to so young a child? Sure.

Now, in my maturity (a pretty euphemism for old) I realize a lot of things that were happening in my mind as a child as a result of High Sierra and the books I was reading, books like King Arthur, Ivanhoe and The Talisman. These were not typical children's books. But I was reading them, along with a lot of Cooper, Gray, Harte, and Twain.

Over the years, I've learned to deal with being labeled a romantic in the derogatory sense of the term. Such people believe I'm now old enough to be respectably cynical, rather than a romantic, that in some manner I should be embarrassed by being a romantic rather than a cynic.

Well, perhaps they are right. The mirror doesn't lie. The miles show and I can't turn back the odometer.

But there is a difference, which I can appreciate between the child and the man watching High Sierra. As a child, the movie made me sad but there were no tears. The man watching the film could feel tears forming. But he stifled them. He knew what was going on; he knew things the child could only dimly perceive those years ago.

Now, the child within the man understands and could have cried but the man wouldn't let him. The man has enough nightmares to contend with and has no wish to add to them. But there are times when the man has enough good sense to let the child be heard and allow his feelings to come through to the man.

Hollywood has a well-deserved, well-earned reputation for being tawdry, shamelessly without moral restraint, a place where dreams are turned into nightmares. Tinsel Town; all show and glitter but rotten at the core.

Ida Lupino was a girl in High Sierra. She wasn't a woman. She was so effective in her role as Marie because she was a girl, not a woman. Her girlish dreams of knights in shining armor, her romanticism and girlish fantasies, hadn't yet been beaten and stomped out of her by grim Hollywood reality. The man watching the film now understands that. The child didn't those years ago. But he does now. And it makes him angry and want to cry at the unfairness, the injustice, of it all. Marie deserved better.

I'm visiting with a friend in Kernville. There are a couple of young women visiting as well. They are talking about The Hut, a local joint where a band plays every Friday and Saturday night. Loud. And bad loud.

It's nothing but a meat market, one is complaining.

I keep quiet but can't help thinking to myself: Then why go there?

But there's no need to state the obvious: Even if the wheel is crooked, sometimes it's the only game in town.

No one in their right mind dwells on how many germs and insects, how much dirt and fly vomit, they have eaten. These are ugly realities of life but we don't dwell on them; they fall into that category: I don't want to know!

I learned later this guy has been complaining and really resents the sign on my house IT SHOULDN'T HURT TO BE A CHILD! and the names of the murdered children on my Wall. Seems he has to pass by them every day.

Three school buses pass my place daily during the week. I watch them filled with children and think to myself: These children see my sign and the names on my memorial wall as well as people like this guy who tried to pick a fight with me. I wonder how many of those children will take courage from the sign and wall and speak up if they are abused who might not otherwise? And how many of these children are encouraged to see someone even cares about them?

And I wonder how many adults will think twice, seeing these things, before they lose it and lash out in anger at a child?

Later, while chatting with the barmaid, I told her: It's a wonderful thing to be a writer and be able to create your own world where things are beautiful and people are never mean or ugly.

It caused me to recall a TV drama in which an aging actress would pass her time watching her old films. They were filled with beauty, music, dancing, and all the hopes and dreams of youth for love and romance. Eventually, she actually entered the film on the screen. She was young and beautiful once more and all was right at last.

Maybe that's heaven? Maybe it's what Ida Lupino finally found? I hope so.

But in real life, things are not usually so beautiful and there are too many mean, ugly people trying to pick a fight. Still, who can blame anyone trying to escape from such fly vomit?

In fact, when I got home from the bar, I put on one of my favorite Ink Spots records and escaped into the music of a softer and gentler time. Because the plain fact is that some people need killing and I know it.

My job, my duty and responsibility, is to do my part in creating a real world where there are no people who need killing mixing with children, a world where children and young people, the Maries, can hope, love, and dream, a world where such things are not fantasies and are never called romantic nonsense. As I have told my children, their dad doesn't want much, just to change the world.

I miss taking the kids out trick-or-treating on Halloween. It used to be one of my favorite things to do. But this Halloween, a friend called and said that for the first time he and his wife were not going to hand out candy. He said they had made this decision because of a fear of being sued.

Suppose, he said, some child should fall down and be hurt coming to his door? These days, he continued, the parents might well sue them.

Paranoid? Maybe. But these days, I wondered how many other people were of the mind of this man and his wife? Bad enough we now have to contend with razors and pins or harmful drugs in candy. But fear of lawsuits? It boggles the mind!

But involving myself in the various cultural pursuits of the Valley such as the above, I'm constantly reminded of the problems facing children today.

I see many of their parents in just the kind of situation I have described. And who's minding the children as their parents are out having this kind of fun?

And maybe this is why my first novel has to have two children as the main characters?

I have written nine books now; large books and all non-fiction. I've simply never been drawn to writing fiction. I've always found real life surpassing anything I could fictionalize.

An exception to this is this first novel I'm now attempting. And I can't even explain the impulse to attempt such a thing. But over the past two years I have been working on it, it has taken on a life of its own.

The best I can offer as an explanation of such an effort is the need I feel to give children a voice, a voice they don't seem to have in our contemporary society.

Maybe watching High Sierra again after these many years led me to decide to share the following with the readers of TAP, I don't know. Maybe I'm still trying to get the bad taste of too many I Don't Want to Know's out of my mouth. But for whatever reason, I can only hope the reader will find something of value in this portion of the book I have decided to share.

In one part of the novel, Donnie and Jean, an Angel's Story, the boy, Donnie, is asking himself a lot of questions. He loves a girl, Jean. One of the characters in the novel, doctor Mathison, recognizing something special in the boy recommends he read Moby Dick and The Scarlet Letter.

These are most certainly not books normally thought of as children's books. Such books raise some disturbing questions. The following is a part of the narrative from the novel having to do with Donnie's attempt to deal with some of these questions. The year in which the events of the novel take place is 1948:

As I struggled with the questions the books had raised in my mind, I suddenly remembered an incident that occurred when Ronnie and I had first moved to our grandparents.

I was only three at the time. But I never forgot.

Our grandparents raised rabbits and I was in the yard looking at the bunnies. One was backed up against the rabbit wire and his short, small fluffy tail was poking through the mesh. I reached up and grabbed the bunny's tail. The rabbit immediately hopped away at the unexpected touch and left his small tail between my fingers.

I stood transfixed, holding the bit of fluff between my fingers and staring at it. I hadn't meant to hurt the bunny. It had just happened.

So many hurtful things just seem to happen to innocent people and animals. Why? They weren't all like my unintentional accident with the bunny; but some of them? Well, some of them just seem to happen. Can people hurt others just out of innocent curiosity like I had with the bunny? Of course they can. But I'd never really thought about it before; not really. And why was I thinking about it now? It had to have something to do with those books, I supposed.

I knew I wasn't a mean person. I had known, and know, mean people and I knew I wasn't like them. There were people capable of intentionally hurting a baby duckling, a bunny or kitten. And I sure couldn't do anything like that! But I had hurt the bunny.

Did plants, flowers, have feelings? When I would pick flowers for grandma, did the flowers feel any pain? I loved flowers and the beauty of them seemed to fit with how I loved grandma. She was always grateful when Ronnie or I would give her flowers. Flowers were beautiful and just seemed right to give people you loved.

But while the flowers looked so beautiful in a vase on a table, they eventually wilted and died. Did some things, some people, have to wilt and die after their beauty had been used to satisfy something more beautiful, something like using flowers to express my love for grandma?

A horrible thought suddenly crossed my mind! Jean! She was so beautiful. Was she somehow like a beautiful flower that might have to give up its beauty? What if her beauty, the beauty of a small angel, should be somehow taken away by something, someone, evil!

That was a terrifying thought! I tried to get it out of my head, to get away from it!

But I knew beauty could be hurt, corrupted or destroyed, by evil or evil people. Such people didn't pick flowers to sacrifice their beauty for something more beautiful. I had read many books with this theme. I recognized the envy and hatred of beauty by evil in some of these stories.

There was something in those books doctor Mathison had recommended that caused me to think about Jean in this respect. Was my knowing how beauty was envied, even hated, by evil the basis for the unexplained protective feeling I had about Jean from the very beginning?

Was my love of the beauty of flowers somehow connected with flowers having to grow and eventually die to satisfy some greater beauty? Could there be some harm threatening Jean that I might have to confront and be able to prevent?

I'd known mean, malicious children, even adults, who seemed to like destroying flowers, who didn't seem to have any appreciation of their beauty.

Now why should thinking of flowers in this way make me think of Jean?

I shuddered at the thought that anything, anyone, would threaten the little angel! Yet, there was that feeling that she was a beautiful flower and there were mean people who seemed to enjoy destroying beautiful flowers. That was real, terribly real.

The books. Could doctor Mathison have known how I would react to those books? Was this why grandma had acted so strangely about them? If so, what was the real reason the doctor had recommended them to me? And why had grandma been willing to have me read them? These were good people, grandma and doctor Mathison. They must have thought the books would be good for me.

It wasn't possible was it, that they both knew how I felt about the little angel? No, that wasn't possible. I hadn't even met Jean when doctor Mathison had recommended the books; and grandma...? Well, I had told her about Jean. And I knew grandma knew me well enough I didn't have to say much for her to know how I felt.

But doctor Mathison. He had directed me to Jean's house. He must have known I would meet Jean. Could there be some kind of plan in all this, even an unconscious plan by good people directed by God in some way?

Of course, I had no doubt God could so such a thing.

Suddenly I thought about the story of my other name, Samuel. The folks had said I was dedicated to God at birth. Could there really be something to it? Could God have something special in store for me because of the folks dedicating me to Him and naming me after the prophet?

I hadn't really thought about that before. Now I did. I had always thought it a sin to think you were somehow special with God and above other people. But could a person be special to God in some way that didn't lead to their getting swelled up and poisoned with pride?

Still, wasn't it perfectly natural that we would want to protect anything beautiful? Or anyone, even if there wasn't any visible threat? That didn't require anyone being someone special with God. There didn't have to be any plan for such a thing. Anyone who loved beauty naturally did all he could to protect it.

But what of the evil people who did their best to hurt or destroy beauty? There was always a plan in such things, an evil, wicked plan. Why shouldn't there be a plan by good people to protect against such things? Why shouldn't God have such a plan?

I thought about the bunny again. I hadn't meant to hurt the bunny. I would have to be very careful not to hurt Jean. If I could hurt an innocent animal without intending to do so, it was possible for me to hurt Jean in the same manner. I would just die if that should happen! I would far rather die before doing anything like that! I would have to be very, very, careful with Jean.

But at the same time I would love to be a hero to her somehow, to perform some heroic act for her. But never at the risk of her being in some kind of real danger from which I would save her. That had been a pleasant thought at first, but not now. Those first thoughts hadn't taken into account my realizing what I did now that there were very real dangers facing beauty; that a beautiful flower like Jean, a little angel, would be at real risk.

I tried to shake such a dreadful thought from my mind. After all, what bad could possibly happen to the little angel? She had her dad and brother, the church, Mrs. Comstock and doctor Mathison. What was I worried about?

Dang it!

Well, maybe grandma or doctor Mathison would be able to answer my questions about the books.

And I still needed to talk to grandma about angels, especially the small human one, Jean.

Whether of God or not, I had met Jean and that had changed my whole life. Now, I didn't know what I did without her in my life. None of my life before meeting her now seemed of any real consequence or importance. She had made my life meaningful in a way I had never thought possible. But, of course, before Jean I wasn't aware of this and couldn't really give it any thought.

Was I satisfied with my life before Jean entered it? I believed I was. But was I really? I thought I was happy before I met her. But she had brought a joy and happiness into my life that I had never been able to know existed.

I thought about the stories I had read of love and romance, the movies I had seen. And there was a thought. I had been aware such things existed. But somehow I never really related them to myself; not really. Sure, I dreamed of rescuing damsels in distress, I thrilled to things like Tom Sawyer rescuing Becky Thatcher.

But down deep inside, I always knew these were only stories; they didn't really happen to real people, but now...?

Jean had brought another reality to my life. She was real. Sure she was an angel, a little girl-angel, nothing would ever, ever, change that! But she was real; she was real in my life! She was My girl; My little angel!

Suddenly a very strange thought came to me. I hadn't had to do anything heroic; I hadn't had to try to impress Jean; in fact, quite the contrary. I hadn't had to rescue her from danger. I hadn't had to do any of those things I always believed you had to do to impress a girl and win her. Nothing of the heroic exploits of Errol Flynn or Deerslayer had been required of me.

There was simply nothing to justify her loving me. How did such a miracle happen without my doing any of the things the stories and movies always had the man doing to get the girl? That was a puzzling thought. There hadn't been any dragons to slay, Jean had never been a damsel, a princess in distress; with Jean there simply wasn't even anything remotely like I had imagined there would be to love a girl and win her love.

But Jean was everything, no, more than everything; I had ever imagined such a girl to be. She was more than a princess; she was an angel. She was far above everything I had imagined such a girl would be who could inspire men to heroic valor and selfless feats of bravery! Why hadn't this been required of me?

And the more I thought about it, the more puzzling it became; it was a real mystery.

Ordinary, everyday people did fall in love and get married without those things happening. But Jean was not ordinary; she was an angel. How could an angel love me without my doing something really extraordinary, something really brave and selfless, to earn that love?

I remembered my conversation with grandma. It wasn't right to question love or the gifts of love. But I still couldn't get past the puzzle of why an angel like Jean would choose me to love?

Or was it a choice? Was the choice of God? If he brought us together, then I supposed that must have been what happened. That, at least, made some sense. In such a case, it didn't require my doing anything brave or heroic; for whatever reason, God had put the love in the little angel's heart for me. A real miracle!

Who couldn't help loving a little angel like Jean? That was only reasonable; but for her to love me? It had to be a miracle of God. Nothing else made any sense.

Another thought. Was love, all love, a miracle of some kind? God is love; all that love are born of God. The Scripture was plain on that. And I was sure this was true.

I knew many loving people; grandma and grandad for example. Why shouldn't life be more like the music, the stories and movies? With such loving people, with Jean, it could be, it was.

But not all girls were angels. Did it take an angel to make life like the music, stories, and movies?

That was a perplexing, no, a distressing thought. If that were true, why weren't all girls angels like Jean? Of course, they couldn't all be as beautiful; no, of course not. But they could still be angels, couldn't they?

But what about boys? Was the trouble with girls, the boys? I hadn't ever thought about that before. There was something to this I was sure, maybe something like my attitude at first toward Jean wanting to be a doctor and my thinking it wasn't fitting for a girl? Maybe something like my thinking girls shouldn't have fun shooting and fishing or be interested in building a model airplane just because they were girls? I just didn't know. But it bore thinking about.

Jean's dad's sermon came to mind. There was something about this in what he said in his sermon, something about the equal value of women that men didn't take into account. Was that the reason I hadn't liked hearing Jean say she wanted to be a doctor or knowing how to do things I had thought only appropriate for boys? There had been something wrong in my thinking like this; I knew that now.

But until I had met Jean and this had resulted in my talking about it with grandma, and after hearing Jean's dad, I never thought there was anything wrong with my thinking in this regard. Did such wrong thinking on the part of boys contribute to preventing more girls from being angels?

Men were to take responsibility for women and children, for family. That was the way of things, it was normal and natural they do so. But they weren't to think any less of women and children or value them any less because of this. Was the failure to be properly responsible, the failure of men to properly value women and children, the reason for the lack of angels like Jean?

My girl. Jean. I felt so grown up, so happy and proud to be able to call Jean my girl. It was a miracle of God's love in my life! Why, now that I thought about it, how could anyone fail to see the supreme value of a little angel like her?

But there was a real and great responsibility connected with this, I knew that. All things of real value carried responsibility with them. That was what grandma had told me about the ring. And I understood that. Well, didn't love have responsibility; shouldn't love be responsible? Certainly. But did real love seek out such responsibility? That was an interesting thought.

Well, of course, it must. Love, like the Bible said, couldn't abide alone. But I knew the value of Jean, she was worth more than the whole world to me, and I couldn't be happier than to accept such a responsibility. Sure I had to keep reminding myself that I had to be very, very, careful with Jean, to be responsible, conscientious, and never do anything to hurt her. But I loved her; and it was only natural that I would never, never, want to do anything to hurt her! In a way it must be something like the way a mom and dad felt about a baby; that protective feeling I had about Jean.

I thought about my father and Jean's mother. Somehow, the lack of my father and the lack of her mother hadn't kept us from loving each other; it hadn't prevented Jean being a little angel.

But I had grandma, grandad, and Ronnie. And Jean had her dad, Mike, and Marianne. These were all very loving people. Maybe that was what made the difference?

Well, of course it was! That made sense. We had people who really loved us. That made the difference. If kids didn't have people who really loved them, how could they learn to love? How could girls be angels?

What was wrong with the world that there weren't more angels? What was wrong with a man or woman who would abandon their children? The evil of such a thing was so apparent and still confounded me! It was so inexplicable that anyone could be so selfish!

I remembered the stories of babies left on doorsteps. But the stories always made it clear that the mother was in such terrible circumstances that she couldn't care for the baby. That I could understand, like children that had to go to an orphanage because of the death of their mother and father and didn't have other folks like Ronnie and I did to take care of them.

But Jean's mother hadn't been in those circumstances. Why did she abandon Jean and Mike? Didn't animals try to take care of their babies? Why, just think of how a momma bear tries to protect her cubs and take care of them! How could any human mother do less or care less than an animal?

Then I thought about mom. She mostly left Ronnie and me for grandma and grandad to take care of. Why was this? I knew mom loved us, at least I believed she did, but why did she leave us so often? And why had our father left us? I had asked myself this question a thousand times. How could any man think of himself as a real man who would do such a thing? There couldn't be any real love in any man who would do such a thing! And how many such men, and women like Jean's mother, were there?

No matter how you tried to explain such things, it made the fact that much more clear to me that the world needed all the angels it could get, of this I was now certain. Maybe God could do more to help the world if there were more angels like Jean? Maybe the world war just past wouldn't have happened if there had been more angels?

Suddenly I realized I was thinking in terms of Jean's dad's sermon. What if God really did need our help for there to be more angels like Jean?

But maybe that required there being more men like grandad and Jean's dad and fewer people like my father and her mother? Another distressing thought; just what would it take for there to be more people like grandma, grandad, Jean's dad and Marianne and fewer people like my father and Jean's mother so there could be more angels like Jean?

I suddenly realized that was the problem with those two books. That is what had troubled me about them. They seemed to skirt around answers to such questions. The problem of evil was there and made so plain, but they didn't offer an answer to the problem. That was what was missing in the books! Why, if Hawthorne and Melville could see the evil so plainly, why didn't they tell how to deal with it?

I really needed to ask grandma and doctor Mathison about that.

Suddenly another thought came to mind. What if I asked Jean about this? Had she read the books? If she had, I would most certainly like to talk to her about them.

Or would I? Maybe not. The subject of evil was definitely not one I wanted to talk to her about. But wouldn't an angel know more about such a thing than me?

Now that was a kind of paradox. Could an angel really know about evil and still remain an angel?

I thought about the passage in Genesis: The man has now become like one of us, to know both good and evil.

God had cast Adam and Eve out of the Garden because of this. How was it different from an angel knowing such a thing? Because angels were created differently than Adam and Eve?

But a human angel, a little girl-angel, could she escape knowing about evil? No, I didn't think so. But even so, why didn't I want to talk to Jean about it? Even if she did know about evil, and she must, why did I feel I didn't want to talk to her about it?

I thought of the boy who had behaved so despicably in our church so long ago. And I thought about the boy, the son of one of the deacons, who liked to wear his sister's clothes. Sure there were such boys, but I definitely didn't like to talk about them, I didn't even want to think about them. Maybe this was in some way connected to my not wanting to talk to Jean about the evil in those books? Just knowing something wasn't always an excuse to talk about it, especially if it was something bad. Like bad or vulgar language, you could know it but that wasn't any excuse for using it.

Still, why did I feel like I could talk to grandma and doctor Mathison about those books and not Jean? I knew it had something to do with Jean being a little angel and one for whom I had joyfully accepted responsibility. Somehow, because of this, it was a subject I wanted to avoid with the little angel but I wasn't at all sure why this should be the case?

Thinking of grandma and Jean I wondered what made the real difference between the angels, Adam and Eve, and a little girl-angel? There was no way Jean, a little girl-angel, could ever do anything evil, any more than grandma could, even if she knew about such a thing! It was absolutely unthinkable! What was, what made, the real difference between Adam and Eve and Jean?

Guardian angels. What were they, really? They had to know about evil in order to protect us. But why hadn't there been such an angel to protect

Adam and Eve? The Bible said there were bad angels. But didn't the good angels outnumber them? And if so, why should bad angels win? And where were these good guardian angels when some children did get hurt or got sick and died, or even murdered?

But the Bible said Adam and Eve disobeyed God. And children could reasonably be expected to get hurt when they disobeyed their parents. There was some justice in that. But how about children who got hurt even when they were obedient and not doing anything wrong?

I thought about the bunny again. I hadn't meant to hurt the bunny. Could children get hurt in such a way, an innocent way, where the guardian angels couldn't help? That was a distressing thought.

I was glad I was out in the field far away from everyone. I sure wouldn't want anyone to hear me. I had been talking out loud to myself, thinking out loud I called it. It was a habit when I was alone. But I sometimes forgot myself and did it when others were about. It was always embarrassing when this happened. Fortunately it didn't happen very often. But when it did...

How had I even gotten into this frame of mind? It was most unpleasant. I had wanted to get away by myself to think about the wonders of Jean, the miracle of her as my girl, my little angel. Could it be that part of the love and responsibility of having a little angel in my life required me thinking of such things, was the natural result of Jean being my girl? Was thinking of such things somehow preparing me for the responsibility of loving Jean, of her loving me and saying she would be my girl, of my wanting her to be my girl and accepting responsibility for her becoming my girl?

I needed to put all these thoughts and ideas into writing. It always helped me to think things through when I wrote about them. There was just something about being able to look at the words on paper that helped me figure things out.

Most importantly, I needed to write about Jean. Now why hadn't I done this already? That was curious. It should have been the most natural thing in the world to do. But I hadn't. Why not? I usually wrote about anything I thought important in my life. I had written many stories about such things. But I hadn't written about Jean.

Come to think of it, why hadn't I written about the Red Ryder Carbine?

I stopped and stared at the BB gun in my hands. Why had I wanted it? Why had I gone door-to-door selling in order to get it? What had made it suddenly so important to have it? The same questions I had from the start. And now the only answer I had that made any sense to me was that somehow God had placed it in my heart to want it and earn it the way I had in order to meet Jean.

A word came to mind: Adumbration. It meant foreshadowing. I learned the word from the Scofield Reference Bible. Reverend Scofield used it a lot in his footnotes, kind of like the way Mark Twain used the word freighted so often. Had there been any adumbration, any foreshadowing of events of which I wasn't aware? None that I could think of.

But why hadn't I written anything about any of this? Normally I would have. Why hadn't I even thought to do so? It was a terrific story and I hadn't even thought about writing of it. That was so very unusual for me.

Was it because I had been waiting to see how the story would turn out? Could I have somehow known there was going to be more to the story? How could that have been? No, there hadn't been any adumbration, any clue of such a thing. Or had there been? Maybe I just missed it somehow?

But Jean? Why hadn't I written about her from the start either? The carbine was one thing, but Jean? Was it because I simply didn't know how to write about an angel? Was it being afraid that things would turn out badly? Was I fearful of profaning something holy, sacred, by mere words or, at the least, not being able to do justice to such a miracle?

No, the need to write about Jean wouldn't go away. I would have to try no matter what; I knew this. And now that I wanted to write about these things and about Jean, were they somehow an adumbration of the future? And if so, how?

A future without Jean was unthinkable! But what about all these other things, all these other questions?

I started walking again thinking, thinking hard.

As I walked, I kicked a small tumbleweed out of my path and watched as a lizard scurried rapidly into another bush. It was good to see the little fellow. He didn't have to think about complicated things. All he had to do was survive. Creatures like lizards seemed to have it all over people in some ways. They just had to watch out for predators like roadrunners and snakes.

For some reason, I always felt at home in wide-open spaces with nothing but the critters for company. I liked people, but I just seemed better suited for solitude than society. Maybe because I enjoyed thinking. And thinking was best done alone away from people.

But the best and most interesting thinking was about people. And you couldn't think about people without mixing with them.

I still wondered sometimes what it would be like to be a bird or lizard? I still wondered if animals really talked to each other? Oh, I don't mean just communicated, I mean really talked. But, all things considered, I'd rather be a human than a bird or animal, even if life were complicated for humans.

I realized I was trying to get my mind off those complicated and confusing things by thinking of the birds and animals. It was always nice to watch the birds and animals and think about them; kind of like seeing the lizard or a butterfly unexpectedly. These were nice things when you saw them in their natural environment.

And while I could enjoy catching a lizard or holding a butterfly, it always felt good to let them go. I had picked up a hummingbird once. It had dazed itself by flying against a window of the house. I held the tiny bird in my hand and marveled at the small, exquisitely delicate creature. It was one of those with emerald green feathers.

Shortly after I picked it up, it revived and stood shakily on its tiny legs, its tiny wings and tail feathers spread out on my palm to steady itself. We looked at each other, the tiny bird and I. Then, gathering its strength, it finally took off. It flew only a short distance and perched on the limb of a nearby bush. After a few moments, it flew off out of sight. I didn't suppose many people had ever held a hummingbird in their hands. Somehow, I felt privileged to have done so.

Thinking of the little hummingbird made me think of Jean and her telling me about Bull Run Creek. That had sounded like a really beautiful place. Jean had said it made her think of what heaven must be like. It would be wonderful for Jean and me to be able to go to Bull Run alone together, all by ourselves in such a beautiful place. That really sounded like heaven on earth. Like Adam and Eve in the Garden; just Jean and me at that beautiful trout stream in the mountains away from everybody but the birds and animals.

As I walked, I watched the heat waves rising from the alkali field, making distant images shimmer. This was always interesting to me. I had read that mirages were created by this effect of heat.

Gradually, my mind turned once more to the need to write about what had happened.

Whatever the reason, somehow I had known the things I wanted to write, however well or poorly I wrote about them, had to wait until I knew … knew what? Even now I wasn't sure. But somehow giving Jean my ring, her giving me the lock of her hair, our kiss; these things had made it all right for me to write the story, to write about Jean.

Now I could hardly wait to write about the little angel in my life, how it had all happened beginning with suddenly wanting the carbine. This was the most important story I ever wanted to write! And now I wanted to do it while everything was still fresh in my mind. Most of all I wanted to try to describe the little angel. I hadn't been able to describe her to grandma that first time. But now I wanted to portray her, to limn her in words, to paint her picture in words. I liked the idea of doing that better than even trying to paint an actual picture of her though I would most certainly like to do that as well.

They say a picture is worth a thousand words. And in some cases, I knew this was true. But in Jean's case, a picture could never really describe her. It could show the outward beauty of the little angel and, if done by a real master, to some extent even capture some of her inner beauty. But no portrait, regardless of how well done, could ever describe or capture her real beauty; I knew this as well. Only the right words could do such a thing.

I had often wondered if I might become a writer? I loved to write; I loved it as much as the music, perhaps even more. Maybe writing the story of Jean would answer this question in my life? Maybe if I could do her justice, if I could do a little angel justice by really doing it well, God might tell me this is what He wants me to do with my life?

But that made it all the more important that I find out everything possible about the little angel! We just had to find a way to spend time together so I could learn everything possible about her! And there had to be so very, very, much to learn about her, all those things that had happened in her life that had made her an angel, that had made her so very different than any other girl!

I shook my head to try to clear it of all the depressing, troubling and confusing thoughts and concentrated on the story of Jean, the story writing itself in my mind as I continued walking, letting the heat and bright sunshine, the empty space all around me, work on my mind to clear it of the troubling and complicated confusion I had fallen into about other things.

It was peaceful out here. And that is what I had come out here for, the peace and quiet, the solitude to think of the miracle God had done in my life and to thank him for it, the miracle of a little angel. Grandma was right; it wouldn't pay to go analyzing it too much. I needed to just be grateful to God for it happening; it was a gift of love from God. And I was, so very, very, grateful; grateful beyond anything I could possibly say or do!

I kept on walking, concentrating on Jean and thanking God until I finally managed to put these other things aside. I held on as tightly as I could to the wonderful miracle of the little angel in my life. I re-lived our holding each other, our kiss, her asking me if I wanted her to be my girl, if I wanted us to be kind of engaged and my suddenly realizing this was exactly what I wanted.

I thrilled to re-living hearing her say "Yes, I'll be your girl." I re-lived the thrill of her saying there couldn't be any other boy for her but me!

And then, putting the ring on her small, delicate, almost child-like finger, the gentle, soft and warm, innocent and pure, trusting dove in my hand as I did so, her obvious joy in my doing it. Could there ever be a happier or more joyous event in my life than that?

There were so many things I didn't understand, so many things I knew I had yet to learn. But because of a little angel, I would understand, I would learn.

I thought of Jean giving me her ribbon, of walking home feeling I had been given a lady's banner, her colors. But I had not become a knight and as willing as I had been, I hadn't had to slay any dragon.

I thought of the way grandma had reached out and touched the ribbon when I showed it to her and said that I was right, that Jean had meant it to be a part of herself; that she had meant to give me a part of her. But not only did I have the ribbon, I now had a lock of the little angel's hair.

I had stopped walking; I was standing in a vastness all around me and between heaven and earth, looking up through the brilliant, golden and pure, cleansing heat of the sun, lost in just thinking of the miracle of the little angel in my life, my little angel.

I took my billfold from my pocket and very carefully removed the small feather. Holding it in my fingers, I stared at the wonder of it in the bright sunlight, marveling at the shining beauty and softness of it. I closed my eyes and held it to my face, the fragrance and downy, feathery softness of it the wonder and essence of a little angel, my little angel.

Would life, could life, ever be sweeter than this?

***

Quite obviously Donnie is a romantic. But will life stomp this out of him? We can hope not, the world needs its poets and romantics; and more now than ever.

Recently I met another woman whose life is over at 40. She's overweight, divorced, isn't very attractive; she is undereducated and lacks job skills. I've known quite a few of these women, as my Birds book makes clear.

Bad choices, bad decisions, on the part of such women have led to looking in the mirror one day and realizing their life is over. And unless this woman learns to deal with the grim realities of her life and do something about them, her life is, indeed, over at 40.

I have to laugh at magazines like Modern Maturity that point to the growing field of older women as models coming into its own. Sure, if you wear as well as Ann Margaret.

Make no mistake; the wisdom that comes with age should be compensation for the loss of youth. But, and make no mistake about this either, it isn't necessarily a satisfactory substitute. I can still recall bending over and picking something up without asking myself if there isn't something else I should do while I'm down there (that's every time I have to bend down now and light that gas heater)? And nothing you do will make fat, wrinkles or cellulite pretty, man or woman.

I really respect the common sense of Doctor Dean Edell; except for his position on abortion, which I adamantly oppose without equivocation. But he is certainly wrong as well about men ever finding women with a posterior as wide as a gate ever being attractive. I have to suspect his motivation in even hinting at such a thing.

A woman with whom I shared a chapter in the novel having to do with Jean told me after reading it that she had forgotten what it was to have had such thoughts as a little girl. She marveled, she said, that a man could have written such material.

I had to confess that it was my daughters who taught me the softer and gentler things about women, who taught me the dreams of little girls. I hadn't learned these things from women.

The tragedy is that so many women were never encouraged or even allowed as little girls to think or dream as Jean. The further tragedy is that if they had, it had been stomped out of them.

But I ask myself, why hadn't this woman been a little angel? She said her life had started well enough but society was changing as she grew up. Being a little girl-angel had been discouraged.

As grandma points out to Donnie in the novel: All little girls were intended of God to be little angels, to bring out the best in boys as girls and the best in men as women.

I think Donnie is on to something. Maybe there would be more angels if there were better boys and men. As the man, the alter ego of the boy, I know men lead and women are forced to follow. I'll never excuse, as a result, the failure of men to encourage angels. Most especially those most precious of all little angels, the little girls who look to a father to lead them and encourage them in being such by setting an example of what being a real man is all about!

As long as the hardness of men who love war rules in nations without the leavening softness of women, so long will there be wars. And fewer angels. As long as there are men who teach their boys that girls are only notches on their belt, so long will there be fewer angels.

Thinking on this, I realize that as a boy I was never in the category of so many who are taught that girls are sex objects. This, together with the lessons learned from my daughters, prevented me from ever thinking in this way.

As to real love and romance, why should the hopes and dreams of girls and boys be any different? But just as children must be taught to hate, so they can be taught to love.

There's a lot of truth to Eliza Doolittle's comment that if you treat a flower girl like a duchess she will respond like a duchess. Cherish a little girl like a princess, a little angel, and she will respond. She wants to.

This has absolutely nothing to do with spoiling a child. Those who really want to do better will know the difference.

But it takes both loving parents and a loving society in cooperation to bring this to pass. It doesn't happen in a society that cares little for families and acts as though it hates children! Little angels don't come from such societies.

Children have a right to a protected and innocent childhood. Of all human rights, this is the most fundamental of all! And when a society fails to recognize and act on this most fundamental of all human rights, that society is doomed! As well it should be.

I'm often taken to task for my perceived attack on religion and the churches. This is usually in the context of my remarks concerning the failure of otherwise good people to take personal responsibility for confronting evil and their blaming God for not doing their job for them.

And yes, I sometimes tweak the noses of the righteous, both Christian and Jew, by letting them know of things like the change in the Masoretic text, Judges 18:30, of the name of Moses to Manasseh just to protect the honor of Moses (blame the redactors). So much for the *pneuma* of Scripture.

But to justify my criticism, my recent column in the newspaper concerning the death of a drunk, my friend Nelson, is an excellent example of the real point I'm trying to make.

After the column appeared, I got several phone calls and letters of appreciation for the column. Most of these were from recovering alcoholics and people who were living with alcoholics or had an alcoholic relative.

But not a single pastor of the 22 churches in the Valley called or wrote. And the Letters to the Editor from those defending booze ran ten-to-one against those who expressed gratitude for the column.

Now I have no doubt that the great majority of church-going people agreed with and appreciated the column. But they didn't write or call. The evil, those espousing drunkenness and addiction, quite overwhelmed the good people.

And this has been my experience throughout life in religion and politics. To make the point that I keep stressing: The good will never overcome the evil until the good meets the evil with equal determination to win.

The question Donnie poses is a legitimate one: If the good angels outnumber the bad ones, why do the bad ones keep winning?

But it's a little too much like the bitchers and complainers against our government who, themselves, are not actively involved in the political process.

Many of who can't even name their elected representatives of government, local, state or federal, many of who don't even vote or aren't even registered to vote!

Good people: If you are content with letting George (or God) do it, you are to blame for evil gaining the ascendancy over the good!

It is the apathy of good people that allows the tyranny of evil to prevail. And too many believe the evil is too great for an individual to make an impact.

But we will applaud the vigilantes like Bronson and Eastwood who blow away the bad guys. Why? Because as human beings we believe in justice; we feel good about the guy who comes in and cleans up the town, blowing away the bad guys with his quick draw and unerring aim. That is justice. But don't ask Mr. Average Citizen to try this.

But is this because Mr. Average doesn't have any guts? I don't think so. I believe it is because America was founded upon law. As such, we try to be law-abiding. It is the perversion of law that has frustrated Americans.

Too many of the Founding Fathers and other worthies following made this point and I won't attempt to improve on what they have already said. Suffice it to say that they warned in no uncertain terms what bad leadership and bad laws would do to America if its citizens became complacent about their liberty. What was won at the point of a gun will, if not kept at the ballot box, have to be won in the same way again! The cycle of the history of nations repeated endlessly. Unless a New Way for humanity is found. The Amendment holds the promise of being that New Way.

I know people who seem to favor revolution as a solution. But I don't know of any that talk of such a thing that would be willing to pledge their lives, honor and property to such a revolution (provided they have honor and property to pledge, which most don't).

Now I'm all for a revolution. But I want Emerson's bloodless revolution, one without need or use of cannon and musket, a revolution that will, for the first time in history, acknowledge the priority of children in society.

I don't want vigilantes running around attempting to fix things. But as I've often pointed out, when the law will not or cannot protect from bullies, where do you turn? Why should I be the one who has to move if I have a bully for a neighbor?

In To Kill a Mockingbird, Boo Radley fixed things for Jem and Scout. But he was a madman. So the law couldn't touch him for his meting out justice. But why should justice require the intervention of a madman? Because the law perverted justice!

Tragically, that is the society we live in. To quote Alexander Pope:
Vice is a monster of so frightful mien

As to be hated needs but to be seen;
Yet seen too oft, familiar with her face,
We first endure, then pity, then embrace.

If we have the chief law enforcement officer of the country (and his cohort Janet Reno) flouting the law and getting away with it, even rewarding him, we have finally embraced the monster and the perversion of justice is assured.

In HTTPD, the D stands for daemon. This is a UNIX term for a program that sits in the background and waits for a request. Have we, as a society, made such a request through apathy and complacency? Or worse, have we done so in an attempt to justify our own evil hearts?

7 Eagle Scouts in Salt Lake City refused to accept their certificates of achievement if signed by Clinton. To quote one 14-year-old Scout: The president's signature should be a thing of high honor.

Speaks for itself, doesn't it.

Speaking of the perversion of justice, why should a crime be more heinous because it involves a pervert, Jew or Negro as a victim? As a society are we saying: Go beat up on those ordinary white folks; there's nothing special about them and the crime will be less heinous? Shouldn't the degree of violence, the viciousness of the crime, shouldn't justice, be the sole determining factors regardless?

But special laws to protect special people do have one very pronounced effect: They make minorities hate the majority even more! They will make minorities feel justified in acting out that hatred on an ever-escalating scale!

A perfect example of the truth of this is found in rogue nations throughout the world today. Make a minority special by any means, and that minority will justify every kind of acts of hatred in return; even the use of terrorism and weapons of mass destruction.

And speaking of gangs, of which we are really speaking, the lack of individual self-esteem in such things is easily discernible. Group self-esteem is the basis of gangs. When you have nothing within yourself of which to be proud, join a gang. Whether the Cripps or Iraq, become a gang and now you can be proud and wear the colors and wave a flag!

But if Americans make the choice for the Amendment, if Americans decide it is children, all children, who must be made special, we can change the world!

The weather is moderating here in the Kern River Valley around Lake Isabella. It has been a beautifully mild day with abundant and glorious sunshine. This evening after sundown, I was able to take a turn around the grounds of my little cottage. An occasional bat would flit about the oaks while a coyote barked in the distance and was answered by some closer neighbor's hound. Doves, quail, and other assorted birds had roosted for the night. It

213

was time for the bats, raccoons, skunks, owls, and other nocturnal occupants of this small corner of my world to take their turn in company with me and begin their rounds.

The soft mildness of the evening following the mild weather of the day was a real tonic to me. It was good to be able to be outdoors so late and enjoy the reflective mood such weather and such an evening always calls me to. For some reason, I found my mind dwelling on Harper Lee's To Kill a Mockingbird.

As I watched the first stars begin to appear, a slight, night breeze began to stir the leaves of the trees with just enough hint of a chill to remind me that winter had not yet had its full say. In fact, a storm is being forecast for this weekend.

I most reluctantly went back inside, pausing only to look up once more at the stars through the now black-silhouetted branches of the tall, old pine next to the cottage, and settled down to the writing.

It is difficult to get back to work after such a tranquil evening, but duty calls so with prayer, and a pack of Zantac handy, I plunge ahead.

Kern County, especially Bakersfield, has made its mark again nationally. No, I'm not talking about Weedpatch University, Buck Owens, or the rock group Korn. This time it is a book by one Edward Humes entitled: Mean Justice. The Kern County D.A., Ed Jagels, is featured in the book (in a most unflattering way) and is not happy. Especially since so many ugly rumors continue to circulate about this D.A.

Admittedly Kern County has a deserved reputation for being tough on crime. And we have a lot of it to be tough on. From the city of Oildale being featured by Time Magazine as one of the top ten cities in the U.S. for racism, to the daily shootings among and between minority gangs over drug turf, Kern County is quite a mix of crime. Invariably, in such a milieu of wrongdoing, the cops catch a lot of flack. And it has become a commonplace to scream Discrimination! Racism! with the equally commonplace lawsuits to follow whether the cops got it right or wrong, whether in Bakersfield or L.A.

Books will continue to be written by well-meaning and not-so-well-meaning people with the various authors' solution to the problem. When welfare (in its many and varied forms of Bread and Circuses) and prisons are a nation's growth industries, the social problems are easily predictable.

But, like most books of the nature of Mean Justice, it doesn't tell the whole story, distorts some stories, and there is an observable bias. Still, as long as we have freedom of speech and freedom of the press, let the books be written. We need the gadflies of society to help keep us honest.

But I certainly don't intend to read Monica's Story nor did I watch her TV regurgitation to Bawah Walters. I hear enough self-serving stories and lies in the normal course of events. For the same reason, I wouldn't be interested in a similar Clinton's Story. Heard all I need to hear, and more, from him.

My favorite non-fiction book, as readers of TAP know, is Thoreau's Walden. But it has been a while since I mentioned my favorite novel, To Kill a Mockingbird. It, together with Walden, occupies a space on the table next to my bed. And perhaps it wouldn't be a bad idea to give both books to college graduates along with their diplomas.

One reason for my keeping Harper Lee's wonderful and masterful novel so close at hand is the fact that I was a contemporary of the era Miss Lee describes; and I was born into, and raised in, the identical culture with the identical kinds of people straight out of the Dust Bowl and Grapes of Wrath with the identical ignorance and prejudices all around me (and diet and idiomatic dialect), described in the novel.

And thanks to my maternal great-grandmother and grandparents, I am most familiar with the best of the values, sense of justice and fairness, good manners, and civil behavior so characteristic of the best of Southern people like Atticus Finch. And I am ever-grateful loving people so representative of him raised me.

But I am also well acquainted with what cruel poverty and ignorance can do to any people of whatever culture or race.

I repeatedly watch the film as well as read the novel, never tiring of the film with its marvelous score by Elmer Bernstein nor failing to gain inspiration from hearing the little girl's singing to herself, and her happy, giggling laughter during the introduction of the film, for there is no sweeter and joyful music this side of heaven than a child's singing and laughter. And I don't doubt God chooses children for His choir.

The poignant scene of a little girl drawing, and tearing, her crayon picture of the mockingbird accompanied by her singing and laughter, is an unforgettable adumbration of the events to follow, the ugly events which have been, without let throughout human history, so successful in inevitably stifling, silencing, the voice of children's singing and laughter.

God knows how badly, how desperately! children (and adults) need the Aunt Maudies and Calpurnias, the Heck Tates, and Atticus Finches. And we desperately need them far more than all the great men and women of history, far more than all the great philosophers and artists of history, none of whom, including all the manufactured deities, messiahs, religions and prophets, have provided the wisdom that would deliver the world from the continued abuse and murder of children or led the world to peace!

Few people know of Harper Lee's childhood association and friendship with another child, Truman Capote, and her using that childhood friendship in her novel. For that matter, few seem to know that Miss Lee's first name is Nelle.

Since I have gone into an examination of the novel in so much depth in time past, I won't repeat myself. But I have had some new thoughts about it that I would like to share at this time.

When I first read the book so many years ago (it was published in 1960), and then saw the film starring Gregory Peck, it never occurred to me that a madman, Boo Radley, would become so influential and important to me.

Long before I was able to fully appreciate the true social implications of the book, I was taken by the charm of childhood Miss Lee made so convincingly real through the eyes of little Scout. Nor was I aware when I first read the book that I would be going through a similar metamorphosis as Miss Lee in my own writing, trying to awaken the child both in myself and in others.

For those who have seen the film but never read the book, you have been cheated of some of the most important points that make it a truly great story told in a masterful way and you will never be able to understand how truly powerful the message of the story is, a message told in such a way that removes it far away from being the usual morality play. And told in such a way as to be so very deserving of the Pulitzer Prize Miss Lee was awarded.

This is not to denigrate the film, for the film is great in its own way. But the film is very, very far from the whole story Miss Lee has told in the book, a story that in its entirety was worthy and deserving of the Pulitzer. The film, while addressing the monumentally important issues of racial prejudice and injustice, could not, due to its brevity, tell the whole story in spite of Peck's Oscar-winning performance. Though if the Oscar were awarded to children, my vote would have gone to little Mary Badham who played the role of Scout.

I've said that Harper Lee wrote better than she knew when she used a madman to balance the scales of justice. Certainly she knew this of the children and Boo Radley, of Boo, Tom Robinson, and the evil Mr. Ewell. But she didn't see that such a madman as Boo would be needed to balance the scales of justice for the children of the world against all the Ewells. That would have been too far a reach. It would take a madman such as me to reach so far and Miss Lee was too civilized and anything but mad.

Then too, when it comes to such madness, far better a man such as myself than a lady like Miss Lee. The whole point of such madness is to free children so that boys can be gentlemen and girls can be ladies. And this is the responsibility of madmen, not madwomen, since it is men who bear the primary guilt of the decisions that prevent children from becoming ladies and gentlemen.

What inept civilized law and law-abiding citizens could not do in confronting evil with determination to win in order to protect children, only a madman could, and would, do.

So I credit Harper Lee, as well as Tolstoy and Dostoevsky, for planting such a thing in my mind, for driving me to such madness.

Mr. Dolphus Raymond does not appear in the film. After all, the makers of the film were not interested in saving the children of the world. Their attention was on the adult issue of racism apparently not realizing, or ignoring, the fact that it is a children's issue long before it becomes an adult issue.

But to let the reader know how important the real point of the novel is, here is an excerpt as little Scout relates it of Mr. Raymond:

I had never encountered a being that deliberately perpetrated a fraud against himself. But why had he entrusted us with his deepest secret? I asked him why.

Because you're children and you can understand it, he said, and because I heard that one-

He jerked his head toward Dill: Things haven't caught up with that one's instinct yet. Let him get a little older and he won't get sick and cry. Maybe things 'll strike him as being - not quite right, say, but he won't cry, not when he gets a few years on him.

Cry about what, Mr. Raymond? Dill's maleness was beginning to assert itself.

Cry about the simple hell people give other people - without even thinking. Cry about the hell white people give colored folks, without even stopping to think that they're people too.

Harper Lee knew there were things children understand that adults don't. She knew children weep over injustice and lose this wisdom as they grow into adulthood. Adults excuse this loss, this forsaking of wisdom, by claiming it is a part of growing up, a part of the real world, never realizing that their real world is a world of their choosing and making, a world that has ever failed to attain unto wisdom, the wisdom they, in fact, had as children. And having forsaken such wisdom, contributing so much to this loss is the resulting failure of good people to confront injustice, to confront evil with absolute determination to win!

Every child recognizes and resents a bully. This is because children have the wisdom to believe in justice and fairness.

Let's examine a very small point in justification of my criticism:

In my pious and devout, albeit thoroughly misguided, days of religiosity, I attended a church, North Redondo Chapel, which was fundamentalist orthodox.

We had a guest singer one Sunday who was very pompous and full of himself. He sang to the glory of God, of course, not himself. Just as so many preachers preach for the glory of God and the sake of others, not to be praised for their much speaking. Of course.

But wanting to impress the congregation with his range and the magnificent virtuosity of his voice, this fellow did Ol' Man River (which neither he nor Frank Sinatra should have ever attempted. If you ever heard Paul Robeson you know what I mean). But in order to make it suitable for such self-righteous people as he and the members of the congregation, including myself, he changed the word drunk to happy. Talk about straining at (out) a gnat and swallowing a camel!

Well, even being at least as pharisaically self-righteous as any member of the congregation, I was nevertheless critical of this sop to religious conscience in the singer's taking such advantage. I think in my more lucid and honest mind, I had recognized the hypocritical dishonesty of doing such a thing with the notion of supposedly making it more acceptable to God and the Elect. It was a lie! And it was a lie ostentatiously perpetrated against God Himself in the so-called House of God! And for the sake of one man's ego!

Sadly, even tragically, it was a lie I was to witness over and over again without the slightest exception in all the churches in which I worked (only I called it ministered in those days. Wonderful how you can excuse so much delusion and deception, not to mention poor theater, and blame God for it on the basis of this word ministry). And to my own shame, I participated in some of these lies; all to the glory of God and the work of saving souls. Of course.

Telling of this, I recall another singer who emasculated a lot of Elvis music for the glory of God with the rationale: Why should the devil have all the fun and good music? In fact, the guy was an Elvis wannabe and the only audience he could get was church congregations. Last I heard he was still making pretty good money doing this.

But I have written a great deal about the need for even the religious to get into Broadway and Hollywood but not having the talent to make it; and, as a result, providing insipid and even outrageously poor, when not downright insulting, theater in the name of God. This, of course, reminds me of the great majority of religious books written with the same lack of talent and for the self-glorification of the petty egos involved.

This has not a little to do with the loss of ethics worldwide, the loss of ethics, for example, on the part of the International Olympic Committee and our own Congress. As for the world looking to America as an example of ethics, well, we can forget that now. And, of course, it isn't all the fault of Clinton and Reno by any means. They just epitomize such a loss, a loss that evidences itself in the failure to bring the murderer of little JonBenet to justice, a failure that is so closely connected to politics, the kind of failure due to Caesar's lust for power that makes things like Ruby Ridge and Waco, bankrupting suits against businesses like Dow Chemical, tobacco companies and gun manufacturers, a part of his agenda.

Harper Lee, since she was quite well educated, prefaces her book with a quote from one of my favorite essayists, Charles Lamb: Lawyers, I suppose, were children once.

Granting the extreme difficulty we face in giving lawyers any credibility as being human, let alone once children, Miss Lee nevertheless chose Atticus Finch as the preeminent humanitarian and a man who kept the best part of the child alive in himself.

But Atticus had the extreme good fortune of having little Scout (Jean Louise) to keep him honest. It is Scout who, innocently, and because of such innocence that must be cherished, is the best part of her father's life and compels him to stand up and be counted for truth and justice. Being a good man, how could he ever betray such believing and saving faith, trust, and innocence as that of his little girl!

I haven't forgotten Jem (Jeremy) in this. But Jem is growing up. And Miss Lee gives Jem a lot of credit for his own sense of truth and justice. But Lee knows how little girls differ from little boys. As she has Scout say at one point "I began to think there was some skill involved in being a girl."

Harper Lee epitomizes the need to include women and children in The Great Conversation. There is indeed some skill involved in being a girl. And boys and men are in desperate need of such skill on the part of girls and women. The constant refusal on the part of men, who were once little boys, to accept women and children as of equal value to themselves is at the heart of the problem which has kept the world at war and without wisdom, and as a result, without peace, throughout history.

Harper Lee must have recognized this. But it must not have been as conscious to her as a grown woman as it was to her as a little girl. And how could it be otherwise when men still exclude women and children from The Great Conversation?

To say she has forgotten is not a criticism of Harper Lee. The little boy in me is far more aware than the man of the things Harper's little girl knows that she had forgotten as a woman, the things that are in fact the well-spring of intimations and hope of immortality.

The question confronting humanity is whether we will reach the stars or destroy ourselves? Unless the equation K+W=P is put into practice, #92 will do us in. There is no middle ground between the two, any more than there is between vice and virtue; humanity has run out of the failed options of the past. It will either be K+W=P or #92!

For example, it is obviously unwise to exhibit so-called adult themes such as the perversion of homosexuality, among others, in cartoons and cartoon characters that children mistakenly think belong to their world. But propagandists know their targeted audience: Children. China uses this format very successfully in indoctrinating children to various themes and issues. Joe Camel made an easy target on this basis. But we must ask why promoting perversion is excused on the same basis? Where is wisdom in such a thing?

I mentioned the social implications of Harper Lee's novel. But what was the real impact? Certainly it had an impact on me; both because of my own background and because it wasn't long after the book was published that I found myself teaching in Watts at Jordan High.

The results of the Watts riot were fully in evidence and I was a part of the whole milieu of that time in our history. You might say I was at Ground Zero during the 60s.

But decades after the riots, what has changed for the better? Nothing. If anything, things have only gotten worse in respect to Negroes in America; and for children; the future of America and the world.

Riots and rhetoric, films like To Kill a Mockingbird, A Woman Called Moses, Mississippi Burning, Ghosts of Mississippi, A Time to Kill, The Tuskegee Airmen, Miss Evers' Boys, and Amistad, have not changed things for the better. And the world lacking wisdom, how can they? Nor can Hollywood have it ways, pretending to fight discrimination on the one hand and supporting perversion on the other.

Nor can we ignore the fact that so many Pulitzer and Nobel Prize winning works have failed to make any substantial changes for the better, including To Kill a Mockingbird.

To quote the Chicago Tribune (one of many such sources of praise) about the book: Of rare excellence ... a novel of strong contemporary national significance. And as the reviewer for the Minneapolis Tribune said: The reader will find ... a desire, on finishing it, to start over again on page one; and so I have; many times.

Abundant and well-deserved praise was heaped on Harper Lee and her extraordinary novel. But far too often do great themes such as hers concerning inequities, injustices and discrimination, find the deserved applause and rewards of good people while never accomplishing the avowed goal of righting these inequities, injustices, and discrimination.

And one can go back into the furthest distant past to find the same themes being declaimed by good and wise men. There is nothing new in these themes.

Doesn't it puzzle you, as it did me, why this should be so? Since I have a pretty healthy ego myself (i.e.: I'm nuts), I think I know.

In Harper's novel, Tom Robinson was convicted of a crime that he did not commit and died by the ugly and hateful mechanism of racial prejudice in 1935. And sixty-three years later, more than a generation later, a Negro is dragged to death behind a truck driven by monsters posing as human beings solely on the basis of his being a Negro. Recently two others, one on the West Coast and another on the East, were unarmed but riddled by police bullets.

What, any civilized person has to ask him or herself, has changed for the better in this respect for Negroes in the last sixty-three years? Or since 1960 when the novel was published?

Before you say anything, I am fully aware of the problems Negroes have created for themselves, problems acerbated by Negro leaders not accepting responsibility for these problems and for speaking directly to them, problems like the necessity and encouraging of birth control, for example. Not the least of these problems is that of molestation which is literally pandemic in many Negro communities. But this is largely hushed up.

The sustaining of racial and religious prejudice is by no means peculiar to America. It is, in fact, far, far worse in other parts of the world where whites are killing whites, blacks are killing blacks, Christians kill Christians and Moslems kill Moslems.

Knowledge is abundant. But Wisdom is, as ever, conspicuously absent, an orphan from knowledge! Since true wisdom is derived from perfect love and compassion with a perfect hatred of evil, it isn't surprising that the world lacks wisdom and people continue to torture and murder for the sake of ideological differences and in the name of God. It should not be surprising that the same crimes and cruelties continue to be repeated without end in spite of all the great books and apologetics designed to overcome the hatreds, ignorance and prejudices that continue to make their contributions to an increasingly demon-haunted world.

Once more, my point that knowledge is confused for wisdom is made by even the best attempts to meld knowledge and wisdom without facing the fact that until women and children are accepted as of equal value to men, and until children become the priority of nations, wisdom will continue to be orphaned from knowledge and unachievable!

Nor should it be surprising that knowledge dictates we must become wise or we will most assuredly destroy ourselves! But at the same time we are reaching out to heaven, hell is abundant throughout the world, a world as much and even more of a demon-haunted world as it ever was on the basis of ignorant and prejudicial hatreds thousands of years old! Wisdom? Who's kidding whom?

I was in one of the local bars when a guy walked up to me and asked about the names of all the murdered children in front of my house? He didn't even recognize the names of Polly Klaas or JonBenet Ramsey; which only underscores the magnitude of my task on the behalf of children and the Amendment in the face of so much apathy and ignorance concerning the threats to children in America, of the actual evil being perpetrated against children because of such apathy and ignorance!

But then, such apathetic and ignorant people care nothing about the evil of such things as the corrosive social cancer of pornography which serves the Devil and Caesar equally well as their handmaiden to the destruction of sound minds and true morality, to the evil perpetrated against children!

On the appropriate holidays, I have displayed a small American flag on my Memorial Wall with the names of the murdered children. I do this in spite of an America that always talks a good game for children but fails to follow through.

The other day, a good-hearted friend brought me a larger flag. I was very grateful for his most thoughtful gift. I am fortunate to have such thoughtful friends.

But I am acutely aware that my greatest fight for the Amendment is a battle against the prejudices of good people. The overt evil is well known; that evil which possesses good people is far more successful in remaining hidden.

It is the kind of evil so well recognized by Benjamin Franklin in his friend George Whitefield, the Evangelist. When Franklin offered Whitefield lodging during one of his evangelistic crusades, Whitefield thanked Franklin on behalf of Jesus. Franklin would have none of it and rebuked his friend with the words: Make no mistake, my offer is based on my affection for you and Jesus has nothing to do with it!

Whitefield exemplifies the evil Franklin felt, in all honesty toward his friend and before God, he could not allow credence and had to rebuke.

And so it is with me toward such friends who would try to salve their consciences by blaming God in the name of Jesus for their apathy. Or even try to obligate both God and me through their gifts by giving anything in the name of the superstitions of religion.

There is always the hidden agenda of such good, religious people that they are glorifying God and making brownie points with Him by trying to obligate God and me to them by petty efforts and gifts.

And I know they often do these things in the deluded idea that they are somehow going to bring me around to their way of thinking. But that is their agenda all along, that through their petty efforts and deluded, often self-serving prayers and gifts, I am going to finally be drawn from my benighted state of unbelief in their peculiar deities, whether Jesus or whoever, because of their so well-intended, even sacrificial (?), efforts on my behalf in the name of God. They believe.

But such things are usually nothing but selfish ego at work and have absolutely nothing whatsoever to do with any love of God, let alone any love for me because of the work I am involved with on the behalf of children. Such people believe they will get their reward in heaven even if they fail to convert me by their good works.

For people to be so deluded that they can convince themselves that God has truly done a work in their hearts on behalf of children, and then practice such deceits in the name of God would seem to be the height of hypocrisy. But seldom do such good people recognize this in their lives, let alone repent of it.

I often have to point out the obvious to such people: If children are the closest thing to the heart of God Himself, how is it that you live as though there was something of greater importance? And all too often these other things done in the name of God are absolutely contradictory to the welfare of children! The time would fail me to list such things, things I have been guilty of myself!

Now, before you criticize me for such remarks, I know full well whereof I speak. Because I am expert in such thinking myself, having practiced the very same way of thinking for many years! Having worked for years under the very same self-delusion as that of Whitefield, I easily recognize it in others. It took extraordinary measures on the part of God, I believe, to get me to understand and accept Franklin's point of view and repent of my own dead and self-serving works in the name of God and Jesus.

So it is that my battle is most often fought against the good people who, in their deluded minds, think, as they have throughout all of recorded history, that if they do things in the name of their peculiar beliefs, God is somehow obligated to honor their good intentions, even their petty and back-handed gifts and efforts.

I have several friends and acquaintances that sometimes stop by for coffee and a chat. One of these always tries to intrude God in the name of Jesus into the conversation. And I feel my blood pressure beginning to rise. After he leaves, it takes me an hour of quiet time to get back to normal.

Though his visits are sometimes unwelcome because I know his not-so-well-hidden agenda so thoroughly, I still love this man and hope he will eventually come to his senses. But I also know there is slight hope of this. I might as well try to change the mind of the Pope. People who have come to believe lies, that have lived these lies all their lives, are not likely to change. As I said, it took extraordinary measures for me to change.

But my blood pressure goes up now because I know the real evil in them that prevents such good people from being effective in the cause of children and wisdom, the real evil of their living in the darkness of religious delusions and superstitions. And these have been the greatest obstacles to world peace throughout the entirety of human history!

Such good people, religious or not, will spend their time, money and energy stomping ants while the elephants rampage through the village. Every time.

Harper Lee makes some very good points concerning this in her novel. She also recognizes the religious animosity toward women for example. That of the Moslem and Jewish religions is patently obvious. But when Harper Lee points out the preaching of the Women are unclean and a sin by definition doctrine of Christianity, she hits the nail on the head! And most ministers would certainly get their backs up over her accusation that ministers are preoccupied with the subject. But I believe she, and all thinking people, realize why this is so.

Sex by any definition is still sex, whether cloaked in religiosity or not, whether God is profaned in the process of preaching such damnable doctrine or not. You think and preach that women and children are of lesser value than men? You take that kind of thinking and preaching right back to the pit of hell where it originated!

Yet good people, including women, are going to try to convince me that religions such as Christianity and Judaism are working toward world peace by denigrating women (when not each other or other religions)? Just who is kidding whom?

A fair and sensible mind, a rational mind, has to reject such deluded, self-serving and lop-sided propaganda. Just as the rational mind has to reject the claims of those who say they do good in the name of one they call the Prince of Peace, Jesus, when the misuse of that name by its deification has been the cause, and continues to be the cause, of so much divisiveness and misery in the world ever as much as the names of Mohammed, Allah, or the Jewish YHWH (Yahweh) or Jehovah.

I've often related the story of the old Indian I knew as a child. He had a pistol that he said had been used to commit a murder. Every night he would place it under his pillow. In the morning, it would be covered with blood. He would clean it, and the following morning the blood would be back again.

As a child, I had been taught it wasn't proper to contradict adults. So I didn't. Besides, the old Indian was a source of many marvelous and entertaining stories.

Did this old man really believe this himself? He certainly impressed me as believing it. And I have known many adults who believed such stories,

stories like blood coming from statues for example. Or believing stories like the talking donkey in the Old Testament, confirmed in the New.

We can certainly be understanding of the fantasies of childhood. But carried over into the adult, we call such things childishness; and for good reason for so they are.

In spite of the obvious point, at no time in history does humanity seem to have suffered so much separation anxiety over the loss of their brains from the beliefs in UFOs, astrology, to you name it.

As a consequence, the superstitious beliefs of humanity continue to be the bullies of humanity.

The wisdom of childhood causes children to separate from bullies if at all possible. Children will not play with bullies. So it is that so many good people evidence the lack of the wisdom of the child in allowing themselves to be bullied by superstitious beliefs that hold them in bondage.

And so it is that such good people are so representative of why the good has never been able to triumph over the evil! Such good people do not recognize the evil within themselves that they serve and to which they are held captive!

We are very often, as a consequence, the victims of the well intentioned. The result: God save me from the good intentions of others, from well-intended people! It is no wonder Thoreau said he would run away from any such person intending to do him good.

Benjamin Franklin, reputedly the wisest man in America of his time, refused to be bullied by the beliefs of people like his friend Whitefield. And so do I. But the reader can certainly appreciate the enormity of the battle to be fought against this enemy of humanity, the beliefs that hold so many in bondage to the darkness of their minds, a darkness that constitutes the real evil and is the enemy of enlightenment and the enemy of the liberty of wisdom!

In retrospect, there wasn't any real difference between the old Indian's pistol and many of the things I was raised to believe, there was no difference between the story of a bleeding pistol and a bleeding statue, a talking donkey, the parting of the Red Sea, tablets of stone written on by the finger of God, the resurrection of Jesus, or any of the other fabulous stories of the Bible. There was no difference in any of these and beliefs in astrology and flying saucers. The source of all such stories and beliefs is ignorant, prejudiced, self-serving, self-righteous, and superstitious ego.

We are all born with a desire to be the center of attention. And we will get that attention by any means possible. It is natural for a child to demand attention. Children need the attention of parents, for example, in order to grow up with essential and healthy self-esteem.

But far too many adults demand attention in childish ways. The charismatic churches, especially, are successful in allowing and encouraging adults to be childish. The childishness is no less evident in the liturgies, ceremonies, and various religious impedimenta of all churches, high and low.

As a formally trained behaviorist, I find it amusing, when I don't find it thoroughly repugnant, to watch grown men and women behaving in such childish ways, from the speaking in tongues to the mode of dress like men who love the vestments of holy office and wear their collars backwards, to the lighting of candles and repetitious prayers as though by their much speaking they honored God by believing and practicing superstitious lies.

Some will demand attention through various experiences, epiphanies, miracles, visions, and voices of angels and God. Some will have actually seen or have been abducted by UFOs.

But when such childishness with its stories and beliefs come into conflict with truth, fairness, and justice, when such stories and beliefs become confused with knowledge and become the enemies of wisdom, preventing wisdom, then they become the source of every kind of wickedness and evil!

It is a very disturbing fact that books about angels are the number one selling books in America. People actually want to be deceived.

I would disabuse anyone, no matter how noble they consider themselves, no matter how noble they consider their institutions and their beliefs or their efforts in the name of their institutions and beliefs to be, of the thought that they can hang onto lies for the sake of the truth; that they can ever attain unto wisdom by such.

Sounds sensible and logical enough; it is most certainly rational thought. But just try putting it into practice and discover for yourself what conflicts arise, some quite surprising!

I know I have used very strong language in confronting the myths and superstitions of good people, some even whom I love. And while I have explained my reasons for doing so, there is something else which motivates me. We are running out of time. I firmly believe this.

Because of the very real and immediate threat of #92 we have run out of time for the failed options of the past, we have run out of time for the polite civilities of: Well, you have a right to your opinion or But look at all the good he or she or the churches or this or that institution does.

We have run out of time to be polite to well-intended fairy tales and well-intended people and groups. We have run out of time for anything less than being absolutely and ruthlessly honest and truthful!

During the battle of Gettysburg, General Lee finally realized he was in the most important battle of the war. He desperately needed information from

Jeb Stuart but Stuart was late getting to Lee. The General upbraided him and Stuart offered his resignation.

Lee told him: There's no time for that!

The point was well made. At some point in time the war becomes such that the ordinary civilities and amenities have to be suspended. There is an abundant failure on the part of good people to recognize the fact: There's no time for that!

America cannot keep hordes of illegal aliens from entering our country. America cannot keep tons of illegal drugs from crossing our borders. And yet Americans are so naive as to believe that terrorists cannot bring a nuclear bomb into our country! It's just a matter of time. And we are running out of time!

In respect to the kind of madness that seems all-pervading and prevents good people from seizing the initiative in acquiring wisdom, in Harper's novel she has Calpurnia telling the children: You're not going to change any of them by talkin' right, they've got to want to learn themselves. And when they don't want to learn there's nothing you can do but keep your mouth shut or talk their language.

And sure enough most do not want to learn; they want to believe in angels and not only have no interest in talkin' right, they want me to talk their language no matter how ignorant or self-serving, to be polite to their idols, myths, and superstitions no matter how harmful to wisdom. The worst of these insist on everyone either talkin' their language or they will mount a jihad in order to destroy anyone who does not!

In spite of how very, even selfishly, ignorant their own language may be, they not only do not know better, like the ignorant Ewells of the novel, they have no interest in doing any better.

When the jury in the novel, because of ingrained, ignorant prejudice, finds Tom Robinson guilty of a crime he so very obviously did not commit, Dill and Jem cry. Scout would have cried if she had been just a little older. She was just old enough to realize a great injustice had been perpetrated, but still young enough to not understand and cry about it. She would learn to cry about such things later. And when Jem asks his father how the jury could have done such a thing, his father tells him, as Mr. Raymond told Dill: I don't know ... when they do it - seems only children weep.

It is, once more, the wisdom of the child that Harper Lee brings out so clearly, vividly, in her novel.

As an adult, I have a rather normal and healthy reluctance to being lynched or shot. Notwithstanding the target I make of myself by the names and sign in front of my house, and writing and speaking as I do, even mixing with some of the people I do. I am not a John Brown and would far rather go along to get along; I would far rather live peaceably without conflict and confrontation.

But good people filled with their inept and counter-productive good intentions and ignorant prejudices and beliefs will not allow of my doing so.

In spite of my wanting to live peaceably, I began to realize it was the prejudicial ignorance of good people, good people who believe lies ever as much as those good people who constituted the jury for Tom Robinson, who would be the most difficult enemy I faced in the cause of the Amendment. And so it has proven to be.

For example, when I first proposed the Amendment, many thought organizations like The Christian Coalition and men like Pat Robertson and Jerry Falwell would be in favor of it. I knew better. I used to be one of them. I know their thinking: If the idea didn't originate with them or someone like them, it couldn't have any real merit. Most especially since it came from a benighted infidel such as me who isn't even a Christian!

As a result, the Amendment has not suffered the kiss of death by bearing the imprimatur of such men or organizations. Just one more reason I am more than a little inclined to think the idea for the Amendment may very well have come from God.

If, instead of the names of murdered children, I had painted: UFOs! Inquire within on the side of my shed; I would have people, good people, flocking to my door. But no one stops by to inquire about the names of the murdered children or my sign: IT SHOULDN'T HURT TO BE A CHILD!

But I'm fully aware of why people don't stop and inquire. They don't want to know. They would rather hear about UFOs (or angels, the latest miracles, etc.). They are interested in UFOs, not what they can do to stop the molestation and murder of children, not what they can do in the pursuit of wisdom.

The foundation of effective teaching is repetition. The art of teaching is being able to practice this by not seeming to be repetitious. Being a well-qualified and experienced teacher, I know how vital it is to repeat essential points and lessons. As a result, some of these points and lessons occur with some frequency in TAP. My readers of some years will forgive this necessity of repetition knowing, themselves, both the purpose and necessity.

For some, the lessons are as obvious as slicker than spit on a brass doorknob or a large zit on the end of one's nose; or, as not forgetting to take your socks out of the oven before cooking your dinner of fish sticks and Tater Tots (this from my handy hints for bachelors with epicurean palates).

People do forget. Had a guy come by the other day that fancies he knows somewhat about being a teacher by virtue of the fact that he did some substitute teaching. He claimed to know what I was talking about in respect to the necessity of repetition from his college training, forgetting that I had told him this long ago. But he is one of many I know who cultivates a convenient memory.

And being so familiar with the schools of education on university campuses, I also knew he wouldn't have learned this from them, let alone have learned how to do it. The art of teaching fundamental lessons is in how to be repetitive without seeming to be repetitive. This isn't always possible, of course, but a teacher should always keep it in mind.

But this fellow conveniently forgets many things I have told him, not wishing to give me credit for them. He has a not-so-well hidden agenda of trying to put me down and convert me from my comfortable, benighted infidel state. But he's a likable sort and I tolerate him. Occasionally. This in spite of the fact that he invariably leaves feeling self-justified that he has been noble and pure of heart in his efforts to save my soul.

Over the years, I have become accustomed to people trying to take credit from me, even stealing ideas and writings of mine and claiming them for their own. But this invariably has come back to haunt them because of their lack of ability to follow through.

Recently I had one of these fellows come by and tell me that my equation for world peace K+W=P was in the Bible, a claim several people have made since I first came up with the equation. Of course it isn't, so I challenged him to show it to me and never heard back from him on the subject. What made this particularly rancorous is the fact that he knows I know the Bible from cover to cover and far better than he; I know perfectly what is, and what is not, in the Bible. But his prejudice insisted on being heard. He is representative of those who are going to give the Bible credit even if he has to lie in order to do it. I've known many such people and am used to such holy lying; done enough of it myself in time past.

I encounter a lot of this prejudice and outright theft on the basis of the Amendment and the Equation. Such people, being so egocentric, don't realize that I could care less as long as the message gets out there. To paraphrase the Apostle Paul: whether of good or evil intent, thank God the gospel of the Amendment is being preached!

Such people remind me of something Atticus says in the novel: Naming people after Confederate generals makes them slow steady drinkers. And there is nothing like naming someone The Pope, Reverend, Rabbi or Ayatollah to accomplish the same result of making men drunk with their own egos and self-importance.

Jem and Scout are only children. But they talk about people, about issues of life arising from the trial of Tom Robinson. They wonder why people can't get along together?

Jem suddenly says to Scout "I'm beginning to understand why Boo Radley's stayed shut up in the house all this time ... it's because he wants to stay inside."

Over the years, I have come to love Harper Lee; I have come to love Scout, Jem, Atticus, and Maudie. I lay in bed last night pondering this and talking it over with God.

Like Boo Radley, as Jem had it figured, I realize I would prefer to dissociate myself from many of those who think themselves sane. I most certainly wouldn't have gotten on with those who considered Cotton Mather a marvelous man. And I don't get along with those who consider Robert Schuller, Kennedy, Copeland, Robertson, Falwell, the Pope, et al. marvelous men. There is too much of the stench of Cotton Mather about them.

If I could be a child again wearing my bib overalls, walking barefoot in the alkali dust of a Weedpatch or Little Oklahoma road in Bakersfield, just kickin' it once in a while to make the dust fly, enjoying the honest warmth of it between my toes and just doin' nothin', how delightful that would be. Maybe I'd be carrying my Genuine Daisy Red Ryder Lever-action Carbine BB gun, the one I earned selling garden seed and Cloverine salve door-to-door.

I was really proud of this; though it was accompanied by the usual and familiar dire threat about putting out the eyes of all the children in the neighborhood. One of the mysteries of childhood was why adults thought the sole purpose of BB guns was that of shooting out the eyes of children. But, then, it did seem adults engaged in a lot of morbid preoccupations of this nature intended to either frighten us or make forbidden fruits all that more desirable.

Maybe I'd be thinking, like Scout, that there really wasn't much more to learn when I grew up than what I already knew except, possibly, algebra. And like Scout, nothing would be really scary except what I read in books.

The thing is, I have had this experience of childhood and I know what I am missing. I know and love Scout and Jem and Dill and I long to join them. I know they would welcome me. But I can't, and it makes me feel I've lived too long and know too much. There has been more to learn than algebra and I know all the scary things are not just in books.

Like Atticus of Jem and Scout, I wish I could spare my children, all children, the pain of growing up in a world with ugly, ignorant, and hate-filled prejudices and hypocrisy, a world that has little concern for children, their future, or the monsters that prey on them. But I could no more do that than Atticus could of Jem and Scout.

I don't want to write as I do of the pain and suffering of children; I want them to play and I want to write of their playing. I want to go play as I did as a child, I want my occupation to be that of child: to play.

But the ugliness remained for Jem and Scout long after the trial of Tom Robinson. It remains today and it hurts to imagine Jem and Scout as adults, facing a world that had not changed for the better no matter how hard their father had tried to make it a better world for them.

Like Atticus, I wanted to make it a better world for my children. But I finally realized this couldn't be done unless it became a better world for all children.

But to accomplish this, I can't be the child I long to be. I can't join Jem and Scout and Dill at play. I'll never be able to walk that dusty road again barefoot just doin' nothin'. I've lived too long and I know too much.

Humanity, as nature, remains red in tooth and claw. And as long as it does, I can't live just doin' nothin'. I have even had to give up the toys of adulthood, the things I used to play with that only filled the time and gave me the illusion that they were somehow of importance.

It's all well and good to comfortably intellectualize the truth of such a thing and it's been done many times. I've done it myself. It is easy to intellectualize the proverb: A wise man lives simply (unless you begin to deal with the fact that such sayings always exclude women and why. And don't try to make the term man generic when it isn't intended).

But it's hard to live it, this thing of putting aside the toys and focusing on the things of real importance. And this is new to me; I am trying to grapple with it, understand it, every day now. It's a hard thing and I fervently wish I didn't have to do it, that like Boo I could just stay in the house and avoid the ugliness outside.

But when the circumstances demanded it, Boo did come outside and face the ugliness, the real madness, of a society believing itself sane.

I do not believe in guardian angels. I believe adults have all the responsibility for children, no part of which may be sloughed off onto supposed angels in any way. As I do not blame God for my failures, so I will not accept the blaming of God or angels for the failures of others.

As Boo watched the children through cracked shutters from the confines of his lonely, dark tomb, their lives began to be a part of his. He became their guardian angel, a mad angel, from time-to-time placing small treasures for them to discover in that hole in the tree.

How was it possible for a madman to know the children were in danger? One has to suppose that such a madman can know and sense things sane people cannot. As the film Rain Man so well portrayed, savants are the product of some forms of madness.

231

Boo was a kind of savant in respect to the children. The genius in his madness made him their guardian angel, an angel who could plunge a knife into the evil Mr. Ewell who was intent on revenging himself by attempting to murder the children. And undoubtedly would have done so had Boo not been there.

The children never knew they had such a guardian angel until that moment in their lives. Nor should children be expected to know of such angels. They had, in fact, been warned of him, warned by dire threats and stories to stay away from him. He was the neighborhood bogeyman of their childhood. How very strange that a bogeyman, a madman, becomes an angel of light.

Scout was mistaken in her sadness that she and Jem had never given Boo anything in return for his love and gifts, his kindness to them, even saving their lives. The children had given a madman the most precious gift of all: A reason for being, a reason for living. Imagine that! Reason in a madman. And reason because of children. But then that has been my point all along, hasn't it?

But To Kill a Mockingbird is only a story. Well, at least it was only a story until the real message of it struck me and I finally realized that it would take just such a madman as Boo Radley to balance the scales of justice for all children. To personify the Amendment, it is the Boo Radley that children need as their guardian angel, an angel to protect them from all the Ewells who prey on children.

What loving parents wouldn't wish for their children such a guardian angel as Boo? An angel who watches over their children when circumstances, circumstances of which the parents are all too often unaware, puts them in harm's way?

I look at the computer with which I connect to the world via the Internet and web pages wishing it were someone else's task, that someone else had the job, not me. I never wanted the blasted thing in the first place.

But those things of duty and responsibility nag at a man. Especially a man who knows he has lived too long and knows too much. And just as Atticus could never tell Jem or Scout to be obedient to him if he failed to perform as a man, neither can I of my own children or others should I fail to do so. Children all too soon learn the difference between those who only preach and those who do as they preach.

I often enter the world of the novel and film and lose myself in them. The novel describes little Scout taking Boo home after he has saved her and Jem from Ewell. Boo has asked her to do this. It's as though he is a frightened child himself, frightened to be separated from the children, frightened to once more enter his dark and lonely place apart from them.

But Scout refuses to lead Boo home by the hand. She has him offer her his arm, just like a real lady and gentleman would do, and Scout makes sure that any neighbor who might be watching will see that the madman who has saved hers and her brother's lives is a gentleman. And she is a lady, a little eight-year-old lady, on the gentleman's arm.

And I think to myself: A little child shall lead them. But the prophet failed to recognize the fact that the "them" are madmen like Boo Radley. And how could he? Women and children were not, and never are, the equal of men to such prophets.

But little Scout on the arm of a madman, their roles now reversed; it is a scene that never fails to bring the sting of tears to my eyes and a lump in my throat as I realize it is the little ones like Scout leading me.

The producers of the film, the script writers, had enough sensitivity and artistry to have Scout walking Boo Radley to his house with her hand in his arm, as though he was escorting her, rather than her leading him by the hand like a child. I suspect Harper Lee may have insisted on this.

It was too complicated to explain the purpose of this in the film as Harper Lee did in her book. Perhaps the filmmakers depended on the sensitivity of viewers to catch this. But like the shadow of the heart in the courtyard of Gigi, very few do. You have to have read Harper's account in her book to understand the whole significance of little Scout realizing that to tell the truth about Boo would be kinda like shootin' a mockingbird, to understand how a little eight year old girl could understand the significance of insisting Boo offer his arm to her, rather than his hand, in order for her to take him home.

Even as I write of this, in spite of the many, many times I review this whole scene in my mind's eye; I always feel the sting of the tears and the lump forming in my throat. And I feel the longing to flee the man who has lived too long and knows too much, to flee back into a time when the boy, not the man, had such love and wisdom as that of little Scout. And a madman.

But when I put the book down or the film comes to an end, when I begin to write, the reality of Now is there to greet me. And I face the fact once more that it is, after all, just a story. There are no Boo Radley's; only children who die daily for the lack of them. And myself as the man who in his own madness is compelled to warn the world of the lack of them.

But speaking of a little child leading, what of the lynch mob little Scout disperses by the simple but ever miraculously profound ingenuousness of being a child? Don't adults need the leading, the love and wisdom of guardian angels in the form of children? Oh, how very badly, how very desperately, we need them! We need the saving faith of their love and wisdom when our own fails so miserably! How often the world appears to me as a mad lynch mob in need of the love and wisdom of a child to disperse it, of children to be the leaders of love and wisdom into sanity!

I believe the hope and optimism with which I greet each day is of God and is based on my belief that if good people know better, they will do better. If I could learn, so can others. If I can be led of a child to see and understand the need of the Amendment from Harper Lee's story and the cruelties perpetrated against children everywhere, so can others. If in spite of the hardness and darkness of my own heart I can be so moved and feel the sting of tears about such things as I have described, so can others.

I learned long ago through many futile attempts on my part that good people needed something to give them hope that they could actually do something substantive to change things for the better. Many good people give themselves to causes in the hope that this will prove to be the case. I needed such hope myself.

But I also came to realize that there were just too many things in need of change, that good people often felt impotent in the face of so many problems of ever-growing magnitude.

But why, as Thoreau pointed out, should there be a thousand hacking at the branches of evil to only one hacking at the root? But so it has always been. This is why the evil has always prevailed. Good people are too busy stomping ants.

It was when I began to really research the origins, the root, of evil that I realized what was needed, that I realized why so many were fruitlessly hacking only at branches, stomping ants. Women and children had to become part of The Great Conversation; they had to become accepted as of equal value to men. I began to write of this and book followed book.

Finally, the proposed Amendment came into being. It was the result of a very arduous and time-consuming process of many diverse factors coalescing into a single thing, a single thing that held the promise of good people coming together in concert with hope of success because it confronted a single issue, a single but most fundamental evil, on which all good people could agree. It had absolutely nothing in it of a divisive nature such as religion or politics.

I knew that all the people of the world have at least this in common: Parent's love for their children. If the focus of the world could be brought to bear on children, it could be the basis of dialogue between all nations of the world.

Granted, I knew there would have to be an enormous amount of time given to educating good people to the necessity of such a Constitutional Amendment and the domino effect it would have in overcoming so many other evils of humanity. This is a new thing, a thing never before done in all the history of humankind, working through the mechanism of making children the priority of a nation in its most fundamental and basic charter of government. As such an original, complex, and enormously profound thing, both legally and sociologically, I knew it would be first rejected out of hand, just as I had first rejected it.

But the Amendment addresses an issue about which all good people throughout the entire world agree. For the first time, I had an idea of an issue and something that could be done about it that held promise of good people coming together in common cause to fight for something good with hope of success! The enormity of that alone was truly mind-boggling!

But I also realized it was an issue that would not have the support of men; it would take women, the momma bears, to bring such a thing to pass. And, sure enough, men have stayed away from it in droves while women respond.

The equation recognizes this. Because wisdom is not quantifiable in the way of knowledge, love and compassion with a perfect hatred of evil has to be universal. And it cannot be so unless women and children are an equal part with men.

And this cannot come to pass as long as humanity is held in mind- and heart-darkened bondage to such a witch's brew of hateful prejudices, superstitions, and ideologies which in their various forms become ever more deadly to humanity!

But children can change this. And only children can change this!

I sow in hope with every book written, with every issue of TAP written, mailed, and posted on the Internet, with every letter and email to various columnists and politicians.

I do so knowing some will, flattering themselves, think I am picking on them personally. But I'm really not.

Harper Lee addresses many things in her novel which made the story and her way of writing it worthy and deserving of the Pulitzer, many things not brought out in the film and deserving of in-depth analysis such as the interactions of the various people involved with the courtroom proceedings of the trial of Tom Robinson and the real point of Mrs. Dubose and Mr. Raymond as characters in the book. But I have written extensively about these things and won't belabor them now.

Suffice it to say that the awarding of Miss Lee's Pulitzer was largely based on the social injustices she addressed in such a masterful way, not on the things I have shared with you about Boo and the children in this issue of TAP.

The world easily recognizes, and always has, though throughout history been impotent to prevent, such injustices as the crime committed against Tom Robinson. As I mentioned previously, it is a familiar theme throughout history.

But I believe the real story Harper wanted to tell was the one I have emphasized. I believe she was listening to the little girl within herself who was crying to be heard. And Harper responded to that little girl she used to be, who still cried out to be heard, in a most astonishing way! But the Pulitzer and Nobel are not awarded to children; nor are they given for the wisdom of children.

If this was simple cynicism, I could deal with that, I understand that. But the cynical blindness of humanity is beyond my capacity to heal, in any other, beyond the ability of any one individual or myself.

I will say that I believe my eyes have been opened somewhat because of what a little girl in a grown woman's book has said to me. And maybe Harper, consciously or not, was trying to reach men with this message.

And in my own plodding way, I fervently want to help that little girl to be heard. To do this, the little boy within me must have a voice. It is that little boy who perfectly loves that little girl and understands what she is trying to say. It is that little boy who understands the relationship between Scout and Boo Radley, the relationship between these two angels; each in a very distinctive way, the guardian angel of the other.

But isn't this the way it is supposed to be between all children and adults?

In the meantime, the civil war in Sierra Leone is heating up. Children as young as seven years old are being used in the fighting; if you can imagine an AK47 or an Uzi in the hands of a seven year old.

Not to worry, the U.N. is working on a treaty forbidding nations to use children as soldiers. They figure it might have a chance of passing, maybe, in about ten years or so.

And China really has no ulterior purpose in mind for the nuclear weapons technology they are plunging ahead on with secrets sold them by American scientists; or just given as a gift through Clinton's generosity and superior knowledge of foreign affairs.

Leaders with superior wisdom press for federal hate crimes legislation making it a more heinous crime to murder homosexuals, Jews, or almost anybody else than to murder plain old ordinary white people; or children. In fact, if these leaders have their way, such crimes will carry the federal penalties so steadfastly denied of crimes against children.

But I see Jem and Scout and Dill. Jem and Dill are on their clandestine and fearless mission in the night to try to get a surreptitious peak at Boo Radley. They have not yet discovered that it isn't a madman like Boo they should fear, it is the insanity of the world, the insanity of their own small society in Maycomb that will condemn an innocent man to death just because he is a Negro, a society that will do this and still allow the real monsters such as the Ewells to continue to run wild and prey on the innocent and defenseless.

Scout is afraid and I hear Jem telling her: I declare to the Lord, you're gettin' more like a girl every day!

As a man, I can laugh at Jem and still understand his aggravation. It will take time for him to grow out of his aggravation toward Scout and to appreciate girls, for him to appreciate what little girls become as they grow up.

But Jem has the advantage of a father who will teach him to respect girls, a father who loves his little sister and will teach Jem to show her due regard as she grows up. Not all children have such an advantage. But they should.

And should Jem grow up and become the father of a little girl? Oh, my! What he will learn about girls he would never learn otherwise. He will learn as a man what it is to cherish. But this is only for those like Jem to learn for only those like him are capable of learning such a thing.

But if little boys and girls are taught and encouraged to respect each other, they will grow into ladies and gentlemen. Provided they are given the love and affection that is their due as children and don't fall into the hands of real monsters.

All children should be able to have the advantage of mysterious missions in the night without fear, of play involving daring exploits of courage, of finding nothing scary but what they read in books.

I have so much yet to learn. But the children are more than willing to teach. As I reach the end of this issue of TAP I feel the melancholy of not putting the message of the children in the words they would use. But I live with the disadvantage of being all grown up.

Like dear Harper Lee, all I can do is try. And pray God and the children will still bless and overcome my shortcomings of age, overcome the many years of cynical disillusionment with so many of the dreams I have had, so many of which turned into the nightmares all parents live with.

It has been said that all children deserve better parents. And to a certain extent, I have to agree. But I believe this goes back to my thought that if good people know better, they will do better.

And maybe if I am ever successful in giving a real voice to the children, if I am ever able to get in touch with the loving wisdom of the children and can reach others with that loving wisdom, goodness will yet prevail over the evil.

But this presupposes that the message will be successful in preventing the Mayella Violet Ewells ever growing up so love-starved that they will put their hands on a Bible and swear a false oath condemning another human being to death.

The challenge the message of the children presents is that of awakening the consciences of adults to the all-too-often silent cry of children who cannot be heard.

What happened to a little girl that produced a woman like Mayella as opposed to a little girl like Scout and her so very different prospects as a woman? I know the Amendment confronts this monster and exposes it.

But the message can only be truly effective once it is able to find expression in the voices and language of the children. And the truth of that fact is, at times, almost more than I can bear.

CHAPTER NINE

I am pleased by Governor George Bush of Texas running for President. Though the office often makes the man and we can never predict the outcome, I have been encouraging him to do so as readers of TAP know. You also know of my urging him to ask Elizabeth Dole to be his running mate.

During the course of our corresponding, the Governor has acknowledged the value of Elizabeth Dole but has not yet indicated whether he will choose her for his Vice President. I can only continue to advise him to do so and hope this will happen. As I wrote him last, it is far past time that America had a woman in such a leadership position. And by having a woman Vice President, finally begin to acknowledge the value of women and the need to include them in this top representative position of government.

In my last letter to the Governor, I concluded with these words: It is too easy to miss the forest for the trees and it would seem that all the good intentions of good people will not avail until a new way, a new path, is taken by humanity. I propose America takes this new way and path by making children the national priority they have never been.

I have asked this question of good Americans and I ask that you consider it as well as you begin your campaign: If children are the closest thing to the heart of God Himself, how is it that good people live as though there were something of greater importance?

I hope the readers of TAP will write Governor Bush and encourage his asking Elizabeth Dole to run with him. It will, at the least, make for a most interesting campaign in the next presidential race. Whatever happens, whether you agree with me or not, we can hardly do worse than what we presently have in the White House.

I think Governor Bush choosing Elizabeth Dole as a running mate will accomplish flushing out some of the vermin. It would not only be good for America, but it would make those who only give lip-service to the equal value of women to men put up or shut up!

The present occupant of the White House is certainly helping people make a name for themselves. And money. The tell-all books and talk show appearances are giving Americans and the rest of the world a good look at the kind of people politics attracts. Like insects to a lamp in the dark.

The self-serving rats leaving the sinking ship of state and now trying to save their own backsides saying that if they had known what a rat Clinton was they would never ... Just fill in the blanks; it all has a familiar ring to it throughout the history of politics. Birds of a feather still flock together. One thing is abundantly clear: America better get it right this next time!

The fellow I mentioned in the last issue of TAP who came by to tell me my equation k+w=p was in the Bible still hasn't delivered. I reminded him of this recently, saying to him: The most reliable reports of late have it that Hades has not as yet frozen over but you may depend on it happening when you find the equation in your holy book.

I could have simply told him: Put up or shut up. But such people are immune to the obvious. And being a relatively civilized man, I try to keep sarcasm to a minimum.

And I don't usually resort to such sarcasm, but exercising the prerogative of age I find I have less and less tolerance for those who insist on being fools, treat it as a virtue, and expect me to countenance it as such.

It is such an attitude that sometimes leaves me as cantankerous as though someone set my outhouse on fire. And I was in it at the time. Not unlike getting up in the morning to discover your pet marmot has died or someone has called you some ugly name like Okie lover!

And speaking of being cranky, like any normal addict I have to get that first cup of coffee down in the morning in order to restore the power of speech. Should anyone call or come by before I get my fix, they are likely to be treated to my equivalent of expertise in the Mesopotamian dialect or what one would normally expect from the inarticulate and guttural sounds of your average mongoloid idiot.

But with the elixir of life doing its magic number on my tongue and brain, within an hour I face the day with the kind of exuberant speech and intelligence one usually associates with your average idiot.

I really don't mean to brag or boast, in spite of the praise I heap upon myself from the foregoing comments, but I've always said that if I want an intelligent conversation I'll talk to myself.

Now some carping and super-critical souls might find that statement somewhat egotistical. On the contrary, it is meant in the most self-effacing way. I'm one of the few people I know that loses arguments with himself in this manner.

Having lived alone for some years with only the occasional hiatus in my bachelor status, I've noticed that my conversations with myself have increased somewhat. Of course, I know that a guy who goes around talking to himself is not always a paragon of mental health. And while I don't hold it against anyone who has lengthy conversations with the resident cat, it has to be admitted that there are some eccentricities associated with living alone for an extended period of time notwithstanding the benefit of not bumping into things in the dark.

I have shared with my readers that the most used expression in my vocabulary is: I don't know. But I haven't mentioned several others that usually find their way into my conversations with myself. They are: What should I do? I wish I knew what to do? What can I do? Should I do anything? This last one is of particular significance because I have discovered over the years that there is no problem of whatever magnitude that, with very little effort on my part, I can't make worse.

These phrases are so common of my conversations with myself that no intelligent conversation with myself fails to include them. It seems they are repeated endlessly at times.

At that, I don't think I'm as bad off as the fellow who stopped by the other day, who has seen flying saucers. I know a few of these people but this fellow is exceptional. He is brilliant when it comes to computers, for example, and has been quite helpful to me on occasion.

But having a good mind and an outstanding education, or even being expert in computers, is not a preventive of self-delusion. Regardless of the mental equipment, training, and experience, people choose to believe what they want to believe. And, quite often, see what they want to see. For this fellow, it's flying saucers.

Since he is very intelligent, he does try to follow my explanation of how something a person wants to believe can become an experience to that individual. It works in the same fashion as the placebo effect. If you believe something exists or will be beneficial, it may become a part of your experience. And you will relate such things with great sincerity since you believe them; a person's belief in Tarot cards, astrology, and avatars of all description falls into this category along with all the myths and superstitions to which many people subscribe, including that of religions where similar beliefs become articles of faith.

I was raised with many fascinating and marvelous tales that were as much a part of my culture as hot water bottles, asafetida, Snuffy Smith, Li'l Abner, Brown's Mule, and Carter's Little Liver Pills. My maternal great-grandmother and grandparents were a fount of ancient lore and myths. The people of my childhood, many of them immigrants to California during the Dust Bowl era, were sources of many fabulous stories.

As a child, my imagination thrived on such stories and I couldn't get enough of them. If anyone was ever prepared as a child to later believe as an adult in flying saucers or hot steams, ghosts, witches, and goblins together

241

with Nostradamus, Edgar Cayce, the Resurrection, the Second Coming, and the miracle-working efficacy of Vick's Salve, I was.

I also had the benefit, thanks to my mother's rather heterodox marriage habits (she married six times), of being well indoctrinated in both the Protestant and Catholic religions. Somehow, in some mystical way, faith in a religion was different than being faithful to a marriage partner and my mother told me that I shouldn't confuse the two.

But I was only a child and had great difficulty with this. As an adult, ex-wives would later straighten me out on the subject.

The Catholics have it all over the Protestants when it comes to believing in myths and legends. But thanks to the charismatic forms of Protestantism, the Protestants are fast catching up.

In retrospect, I came to learn that I believed what I chose to believe. Like anyone else. I may now cringe at some of these things, but there is no denying I believed them and preached them as gospel truth to others.

In time, as a result of my confronting these myths in my own life, my conversations with myself began to take on a curious turn. I began to win more arguments with myself than those I lost. It didn't make me right, of course, but it has become a comfort to me.

When I began writing books, I quickly discovered that I was far more interested in writing than selling my books. It is true that a writer does not want to divert his or her mind from writing and, as a consequence, are poor promoters of their works.

When Thoreau bought back those hundreds of his book that did not sell, he wryly turned it into a joke. The Vanity Presses thrive on the gullible that think they have written books that are bound to be best sellers. But unlike Thoreau, such would-be writers are not likely to be appreciated after they die. And I'm not sure how much Thoreau himself is comforted by the fact that he has been vindicated and so much appreciated after his death. I told you so! May be beneficial to the living, but the dead? I'm still normal enough to want the flowers and the praise of my good works before I die.

Only the most sensitive, intelligent, and thinking people read TAP (place pat on back here). Therefore it is assumed on my part that such good and intelligent people are thoroughly conversant with To Kill A Mockingbird, that they have read the novel as well as viewed the film; and not just once, but also several times.

So naturally I write of my thoughts about the book and film with this assumption. This is a pretty thin veneer of attempted concealment for my real message of: If you haven't, you ought to be thoroughly ashamed and do something to correct such a monumental dereliction of cultural and intellectual duty and address the deficiency immediately!

With that off my chest, I return to the theme involving the novel that I introduced in the last issue of TAP.

A good book, as with a good film, can become a close friend. In the case of To Kill A Mockingbird (the book and the film), as with Walden, it has become one of my best and closest friends. As I love Thoreau, so I have come to love Harper Lee, little Scout, Jem, Dill, Atticus, Calpurnia, Miss Maudie, and Sheriff Tate. And Boo Radley.

A Pulitzer winning novel is always deserving of special notice, so much so that they become the subject of college and university seminars. But such a novel may not become a close friend. I am maintaining that Harper Lee's novel is especially deserving of our notice, even our friendship, that there are especially significant things of profound import in it, which will serve us well in love and friendship, in wisdom, if they are fully understood and applied.

A substantial part of the genius of Harper Lee was in her being able to present the monumental truths she was conveying in such a subtle and cunning way. The reader becomes absorbed in the simplicity of the story-telling format of the book, the simplicity of language and plot, and isn't really aware, at least not from the first reading of it, that these great truths are there.

This is the evidence of a work of real genius. And the Pulitzer committee was fully aware of this. Those on the committee are no slouches in the good brains department in spite of the fact that they occasionally hit the target and miss the real mark. Such was the case in To Kill a Mockingbird.

The Pulitzer was given Harper Lee for all the right reasons. At least all the right reasons adults were capable of knowing. But the real mark Harper Lee was aiming at was the story behind the story as I attempt to make clear. And it is this story behind the story seen through the eyes of the children, especially little Scout, that equates a mad guardian angel, Boo Radley, with the Amendment. And further makes little Scout the guardian angel of a madman.

In the last TAP I noted the fact that in spite of all the great books and philosophers, the world has yet to attain wisdom. The undisputable truth of this being that the world has yet to know peace, and wisdom is the foundation and the source of peace. I also noted that until women and children are included in The Great Conversation, wisdom is impossible of attaining.

There have been a number of books like Uncle Tom's Cabin that have changed the course of history but, in the end, have not led us to wisdom.

To Kill a Mockingbird is a great book. It stands right there with the best of Tolstoy and Dostoevsky in spite of its deceptive simplicity, a simplicity of real genius. Harper Lee did even better than these great writers, or any others such as Hawthorne, Melville, Hemingway, Steinbeck, Faulkner, Inge, Williams or Miller, in reaching my own heart and mind.

I would be drummed out of any Litt class for comparing Harper Lee with Tolstoy and Dostoevsky. But I don't mind. Having been a Litt major, I know the party line of the universities and would be the last to accuse them of much in the way of being a source of creativity or original ideas.

It is a commonplace of uncommon genius to be unaware of its own genius. Like all great writers, Harper was inspired to write better than she knew. Because of this, together with the fact that I am able to personally relate to the time and people of which and of whom she wrote and interact with their culture, speech, and manners, I felt I had a duty to attempt to explain some things that only the little girl in Harper Lee knew and the little boy in me could respond to, the things that are essential in leading to factual knowledge, wisdom, and peace.

I am able, for example, as a point of strictly critical literary analysis, to appreciate and understand why Harper Lee had to say waked up rather than awakened in the last sentence of the novel and it had to be used in the film. It takes an appreciation of the genuine charm of Southern culture and people to understand why Samuel Clemens had to say rose up rather than rose or arose. In this context, it led Sam to say: Some things are unlearnable.

And when it comes to some parts of Harper Lee's masterpiece, for some people some things are, in fact, unlearnable. But I write in the hope that the most important things she writes of are learnable to most people.

But in addition to things of this nature, I can also relate to little Scout's observation of Mrs. Grace Merriweather sipping gin out of Lydia E. Pinkham bottles. It was nothing unusual for, as Scout observes: Mrs. Merriweather's mother did the same.

When Scout's aunt Alexandra descends on the household in order to help Scout become a lady and she is asked by Atticus how she would like her aunty staying with them, she admits: I said I would like it very much, which was a lie, but one must lie under certain circumstances and at all times when one can't do anything about them.

Regardless her tender years, Scout is no fool. So when the reader encounters my remarks about the innocence of childhood, I am not talking about innocence of the foibles of life that come with the territory of childhood. As Scout remarks of adults by trying to comfort Dill at one place in the book: They don't get around to doin' what they say they're gonna do half the time.

Children maintain their marvelous, nearly miraculous, innocent wisdom in spite of such things, in spite of their keen observation of adults, which early begins to acquaint children with unfairness, injustice, and the typical hypocrisies practiced by adults; and taught to children as they grow.

A truly great book, because it is inspired, is in turn an inspiration to thinking people. It causes such people to analyze many things to which such a book relates. There are lessons to be learned from To Kill a Mockingbird. And I am a qualified teacher. In that capacity of teacher, I am learning myself. And it is my fervent hope that I will learn the lessons of the novel well and be able to pass them on to others.

Of great encouragement to me was the comment of a gracious lady eighty years of age who recently told me that the last issue of TAP had given her some insights, and thanked me. This is high praise and I felt rightly humbled by it. And I once more took stock of the truth of the phrase: You are never too old to learn. It made me wonder what I would be learning at eighty? Shudder.

But as we talked, we shared the fact that longevity is no guarantee of wisdom any more than it is a guarantee of continued marriage, only an opportunity. And at no point in life can we fold our hands and say: That's all there is.

Those fathers who are blessed as I am with daughters learn things about women not learnable in any other fashion. The intriguing little alien creatures are, undoubtedly, unquestionably, from another planet.

I am so taken by little Scout in To Kill a Mockingbird because she is so very much like my little girls Diana and Karen. They grew up. But daughters, unlike sons, never grow up to fathers. They always remain a father's little girls.

And I suppose this is why the change from daddy to dad and father left me with a melancholy. I never wanted to stop being daddy to my little girls. The compensation of little girls growing up to the need of a father rather than a daddy doesn't lessen the melancholy.

Because they were little aliens, I often found myself torn between cuddling my girls and treating them with the courteous detachment described of Scout's father, Atticus.

I don't think a man ever learns quite how to act with or around his little girls. Not surprising since they come from another planet.

But like my little girls, Diana and Karen, Scout required a great deal of understanding from Atticus. Harper Lee did a terrific job, as a woman, trying to make Atticus appear understanding. But since men will never be able to think as women about some things and vice versa, there were some problem areas for her.

As Maudie in frustration exclaims to Atticus at one point: Atticus, you're never going to raise those children!

Harper did create Atticus as a father any little girl might envy any child having as a father; particularly in a home missing a mother. But we have to face the fact that there are some things only mothers can do. Harper has Scout make the observation at one point that her father tried to do something that only women can do.

I might have done as well as I could as a man and father without a wife, but I failed miserably as a mother. Scout was right; there are some things that only women can do. But Harper did not intend this as a criticism of men. She understood all too well her own limitations as a woman.

Things are difficult enough for children when a parent dies and the other is left alone to do the job, as was Atticus. But divorce is quite another thing and easy divorce has done more damage to children by far than anything else in American society! Children are not thrown into a turmoil of allegiance between a dead parent and a living one; children are not left wondering as with divorce what terrible thing they did that drove their parents apart. And their natural fathers seldom molest little girls and boys.

But in respect to things that only women can do, this is by no means to say that there are not things that only men can do. And Harper gives full recognition to this.

It takes two parents to really do the job. I know this. But my girls always seemed to need a father in a very special way, somehow special in a way that could never be found in a mother. Harper makes this clear as well.

The biological facts of a mother and father concerned with differing roles and needs are there, of course; but there is far more to it than this, things of a nearly mystical significance in regard to little girls and their fathers.

One of the results of the way a little girl can really get into a father's heart differently than boys is that fathers have an especially difficult time in disciplining girls.

I was basic with my boys, Daniel and Michael. No slack. But the girls? The boys rightly perceived the girls got special consideration and treatment from me. It was the most difficult thing in the world for me to spank my little girls and I may have done it only twice, if that. And that was twice too much.

I think fathers are aware, in a way that mothers and boys are not, that there is a special treaty between fathers and that alien planet from which little girls come. No spanking. Boys are different. They were born right here on earth; as a result, no special treaty for them.

My girls, however, kept me afraid for them more than the boys. As a man, I knew my little girls were prey and boys and men the predators. Naturally, this made me far more protective of my little girls.

Tragically, we have evolved into a society that approves, even encourages, early sexual activity. And in spite of how you may love your children, in spite of the fact that such early sexual activity is destructive to girls especially, no lone parent can overcome such insanity of an entire nation's approving this destruction of our little girls and the babies resulting from this insanity!

As parents, you can sit your little girl (or boy) down and tell her: Early sex is wrong! But society, the schools, the government, Hollywood and the universities are telling her it is perfectly normal, natural, and if it feels good, do it. And to hell with what your mom and dad say! And these days, since parents have no way of legally enforcing discipline and responsibility, your child may very well tell you to go to hell! And if not in so many words most certainly by their actions.

In Scranton, Pennsylvania parents are going to jail for not making their children go to school. In the individual cases, the parents may very well be to blame. But the insanity of the situation is in trying to enforce laws of school attendance while at the same time the parents have no authority to make their children attend school! This is a situation of Caesar at his very best!

It has always been the peculiar madness of kings to consider themselves wise by virtue of position. Quite often the delusion of position becomes, in such thinking, the equal of wisdom. And lunatic kings are well known to populate history.

The leadership of America indulges this kind of lunacy. The leadership of America has proven it does not cherish our children: The leadership would continue in the insanity that children can be encouraged in early sexual relationships without consequence. Thanks to the universities, the leadership believes and teaches that moral absolutes are not necessary to prevent such destructive behavior on the part of children; or to the future of America.

This is one of the main reasons men oppose the proposed Amendment. Men would like to maintain the status quo of little girls becoming sexually active at the earliest age and being the hunting preserve for boys and men. As a consequence, the moral restraint and absolute of the Amendment is not to men's liking.

Men would like to maintain the status quo of it being a man's world, a world without the equal influence of women or the emphasis on cherishing children. The Amendment strikes at the heart of this as well. Men who lead religious empires, the Pope, Pat Robertson, Jerry Falwell, the churches, typically male-dominated, hate the idea of the Amendment for the same reason. If you attend a church or synagogue and doubt this, just try getting the leadership of your place of worship to support the Amendment!

This is why I keep repeating that it will take the Momma Bears to pass the Amendment. Men oppose it for their own selfish, licentious, and prurient reasons; even when these men try to cloak these reasons in quotations of scripture and other ecclesiastical impedimenta.

At one point in the novel, Scout starts using the words hell and damn. She thinks this will move her father to allow her to stop going to school. She has been having some real problems in school and tells Atticus she is picking up such language from this source. Hearing such words from Scout, Uncle Jack says to her: "You want to grow up to be a lady, don't you?" To which Scout replies: "Not particularly."

Scout is only about seven years old at this point in the novel. Lacking a mother, she is influenced more by her father, Jem, and Dill than by girls and women, and at this time in her life isn't particularly impressed by the role of ladies in her world. In fact, Scout describes her attitude about becoming a lady in the following words when her aunt comes to visit with this express mission in mind: I felt the starched walls of a pink cotton penitentiary closing in on me, and for the second time in my life I thought of running away (I'm sure Diana and Karen harbored such thoughts themselves).

Harper does a magnificent job in pointing out some of the failures of the school in its attempt at innovative designs in teaching and learning, beginning way back in the 30s. The destruction of public education has a long history in this country, a destruction designed in the universities.

Little Scout reacts to this by wanting to get out of going to school; as she puts it in her thoughts to herself, she doesn't think the state of Alabama really intends her to go through twelve years of unrelieved boredom.

Scout thinks events like Burris Ewell's squishing the cooties from his filthy, unwashed hair between his fingers and threatening their first grade teacher and calling her a slut might make school mildly entertaining.

But she rightly perceives that it obviously isn't an institution really intended for teaching children; except as a place of incarceration and to learn words like hell and damn, words only excused and acceptable from pulpits.

Scout fights and is always ready with her fists. Lacking a mother to settle disputes with Jem, she and her brother are quick to fight. She splits the skin of a knuckle on a cousin who calls her father a nigger lover and a disgrace to the family because of his defending Tom Robinson in court.

At one point early in the book, Scout describes her relationship with Dill in the following manner:

He had asked me earlier in the summer to marry him, then he promptly forgot about it. He staked me out, marked as his property, said I was the only girl he would ever love, then he neglected me. I beat him up twice, but it did no good, he only grew closer to Jem. Which only proves some lessons of childhood do not always carry over into adulthood.

Scout lived in dread of being called: Only a girl. She realized she was a girl. But not just Only a girl.

It took a lot for Scout, without the support of a mother, to sort things out to the point where she had the feminine wisdom of a girl, a little girl only eight years old, to become the lady who would refuse to lead Boo Radley to his home by the hand, to make him, for his sake, offer her his arm like a gentleman to a lady.

The film does not tell you of a madman's whispered plea to little Scout: Will you take me home? The film doesn't go into the thought processes of little Scout's realizing that while she could lead Boo by the hand like a child through their house and out to their porch where the Sheriff and her father are discussing the situation, once she took him home in view of neighbors, she has to insist on Boo offering his arm to her and their walking together like a lady and gentleman, the gentleman escorting the lady.

But as I pointed out in the last TAP, I don't think it was possible for the film makers to go into the profoundly complex things that led to Scout realizing she couldn't lead Boo home by the hand; certainly not without making the film much longer in length in order to do it justice. And many other points in the book would have had to be included to do this.

Harper's novel focuses on children. But I think the filmmakers knew an epic four hours or more in length about children wouldn't be saleable. Concentrating on sex and violence at epic length? Yes. Children? No.

And it would take a film of epic length to achieve what Harper Lee did in her novel culminating with Scout walking Boo home in such a fashion. Perhaps Harper herself didn't fully realize she had achieved the zenith of the romance of wisdom in describing this the way she did. I wonder if anyone ever commented on this to her? Whether or not, I have to believe this was the effect she was aiming for all along.

It is obvious to me that the deepest part of Harper's heart went into this part of the book, that at this point in her novel she exposed her innermost desire and yearning as a woman for the purity and nobility of the real love and romance of the wisdom of childhood. She not only wanted this for little Scout, she wanted it for all little girls and for all the women such little girls would become. Just as she wanted to make it plain that little girls like Scout, exercising the skill of being girls, were necessary for boys like Jem to grow into men like Atticus.

And I don't doubt those on the Pulitzer committee were moved by the way Harper closed her novel in such a fashion, whether consciously or not. But it isn't the kind of thing men like to talk about or even admit to recognizing. It hits too close to the point of the Amendment.

Children like Scout epitomize the love and romance of wisdom. And it attracts the monsters that prey on children like Scout, the beasts in the form of men who would destroy such innocence because they hate it so! It clearly and indelibly exposes these monsters for what they are!

My comments about this culminating part of the novel should not be taken as denigrating the film. It is a great film. And like all great theater, books, art, and films, it makes certain demands on the viewers. But my criticism of the film still stands. It exaggerates the adult view to the minimizing, and at times ignoring, that of the real emphasis and importance of the book.

To this extent, the film can rightly be called superficial compared to the book itself. But this just criticism does not take away from the value of the film in its own right. Having said that I still emphasize the fact that to have only seen the film is to miss the real import and real significance of the book, an import and significance that moves me to place it right up there with Tolstoy and Dostoevsky.

For example, the film does not address the following except in the most superficial way: At what point in a little girl's life does she begin to realize as Scout there might be some skill involved in being a girl? And more, when she begins to realize that she wishes to be a lady instead of not particularly?

As Eliza Doolittle pointed out, if you treat a flower girl like a Duchess, she will act like a Duchess. And as Scout was to discover, it often takes a little lady to make a gentleman.

As Jem begins to enter puberty, he is increasingly aware of his responsibility to Scout as her older brother. Harper Lee does a magnificent job of describing this transition and Scout's quite normal resentment of the change in Jem, of the change in their relationship as brother and sister.

Opposed to Jem's accusing Scout of acting more like a girl all the time, is Jem beginning to tell her to act more like a girl; admittedly very confusing to Scout and a source of resentment. It was bad enough to be lacking the talent to compete with Jem and Dill after the children's unexpectedly surreptitious observation of Mr. Avery's awesome performance when emptying his bladder; but Scout had to begin to accept some of the other facts of life that had condemned her to being only a girl.

But Scout is learning. And there are those like Maudie and Calpurnia to help her during this transitional period, to help her begin to understand and appreciate that there might be some skill involved in being a girl.

Little did Scout realize, nor could she, how much boys and men are in such desperate need of the skill involved in her being a girl.

She is beginning to acquire a dim understanding of this, however, when she thinks to herself that Atticus needs her presence, help and advice: Why, he couldn't get along a day without me, she thinks to herself at one point. Atticus has made his love for his little girl so plain to her that she feels important and needed by him. That, folks, is successful parenting!

But it was Scout's very skill as a girl that made her father the kind of man and father he was, the kind of skill that would make Jem want to be the very same kind of gentleman their father was, that would make Jem far prouder of his father as a gentleman than of his father's talent for shooting. It was this skill in being a girl that Scout was learning that had made Atticus a gentleman; that would cause Jem to admire his father and want to be exactly like him. It was this skill as a girl that would cause little Scout to both understand Sheriff Tate's verdict regarding Boo and to refuse to lead Boo home by the hand. And it would be this skill that would defuse and disperse a lynch mob.

In the last issue of TAP I brought up the point that it took a little girl, Scout, to disperse the lynch mob. And I mentioned my own view that the world itself seems a lynch mob that can only be dispersed by the saving faith of the innocent wisdom of children. If the world would only cherish its children, it wouldn't behave like a lynch mob.

When those men in the mob were confronted by the best that humanity holds promise of being in the form of a small innocent girl, each individual comprising the mob had to look at himself as an individual, something that lynch mobs are not inclined to do.

But once having done so, conscience had no choice but to bow to that innocence, an innocence in which fairness and justice rule with wisdom and where the Beast has no place of concealment; he is exposed and laid bare to those all-knowing pure eyes found reflecting the wisdom of an innocent child.

If the wisdom of childhood had ruled in that court and jury box, Tom Robinson would have been restored to his wife and children. Scout had saved her father from being harmed; she had saved Tom Robinson from being lynched. At that, it took the goodness of her brother Jem insisting on standing by his father to give Scout a chance to innocently confront the mob. But Jem alone could not have prevented violence. Only the skill of a little girl could do that. This is one of the things that separate girls and boys into what should be honored as the compatibility of differences.

Harper Lee knew with her feminine wisdom that men make war, not women. Women do not bear children with the idea of sacrificing them on the altar of the wars men make.

If it had only been Jem and Dill there with Atticus to confront the mob, this would not have worked. The all-male makeup of such a thing would only have acerbated the situation. Harper knew this. As a woman, she knew it would take the skill of a little girl, little Scout, to defuse the situation because there are some things that only women can do. Or, in this case, only a little girl could do.

This whole scene illustrates one of the most profound characteristics of wisdom. It is one thing to speak of wisdom being comprised of love, compassion, and an instinctive hatred of evil. Atticus and Jem are incorporating all the aspects of wisdom in confronting the lynch mob. But one thing is lacking, the wisdom of that other half of humanity without which wisdom is incomplete.

It is that part of wisdom, the instinctive hatred of evil that little Scout so well represents in a way that only an innocent little girl can, that accomplishes confronting the mob peacefully and successfully. Atticus and Jem know full well the evil the mob represents. But Scout is innocent of this. As such, her knowledge and confrontation of the evil is totally innocent! And, victorious! This is wisdom in action; this is wisdom at its best!

The genius of the Amendment is based on this fact. Once the mob confronts itself as individuals in the face of such representative innocent knowledge and instinctive hatred of evil as little Scout so well exemplifies, the mob will look into its heart on an individual basis and return to sanity. The melding of knowledge and wisdom is accomplished, and peace is the result.

But the world lacking in wisdom, neither Scout nor Jem (nor Atticus) could save Tom Robinson from a caste system and perverted judicial system of evil constructed stone by stone and brick by brick through the determined and dedicated labors of evil men.

In the case of Tom Robinson, it was a system that put even good people in a no-win situation. In fact, women were not even permitted at the time to serve on juries in Alabama and some other states.

If the jury found Tom Robinson innocent, it would be calling two white people liars against the word of a Negro. Unthinkable! The good people of that jury would be ostracized from their own society! And only madmen are capable of confronting the kind of sanity that leaves good people in this no-win position.

Some weeks ago I wrote of a girl I know who was pulled over by the local police and had to go to the sheriff's office where she was detained for over four hours before being released.

I knew she was beaten before she started. The police pulled her over at night for a broken headlight. But she had come from a bar and was with a disreputable fellow well known to the police. She was subjected to humiliating behavior from the cops, especially as they searched her and made sexist remarks like calling her Sweetcheeks.

But she was confrontational with the cops, a real no-no, even demanding a lawyer, and it came down to guilt by association. She admitted having been to a bar and she was with a guy the police recognized. Unfavorably.

The public defender seemed to be on her side. But when she appeared in court, this disreputable looking fellow she had been with was the only witness for her. And the jury looked at him and found the girl guilty.

There was little the public defender could really do. Police testified against her and the jury couldn't keep their eyes off the guy who was the girl's only witness.

Unfortunately, people are not educated to the facts of our judicial system. And when they are confronted by it, it is usually too late to get an education. Lacking money for a good attorney, the common people, the great unwashed, are at the mercy of a system that has little mercy for such people as this girl.

Let's face it: You are judged by appearances and you are judged by those with whom you associate. You are judged by your use of language, your vocabulary and your pedigree. And your money.

The girl will do seventeen days in jail and will be on five years probation. She is now in a system that will permit the police to pull her over at any time they choose, to search her and ask her anything they want. Her life is no longer her own. If she complained of having no rights as a citizen before, she is going to learn how little she really does have now.

In this manner, the system of the 30s that condemned Tom Robinson hasn't really changed all that much. But as I told this girl, until good people get together to confront it, those who have the authority of Caesar will pick them off one by one. Hang together or hang separately. This has not changed.

I freely admit that had I not known this girl personally and I had been on her jury, I would have found her guilty. I am no more immune to appearances than any other. And faced with having to choose between duly constituted authority and the word of this girl and the guy she was with, admitting having come from a bar and her demanding a lawyer instead of submitting to a sobriety test, or even requesting one (which she should have done if she had not been drinking), it would be, in my mind, a just verdict of guilty.

But the system is designed to militate against anything less than the amount of justice you can afford. It is designed to favor the rich against the poor. And that is why I bring up this particular case involving the girl. Guilty or not, given our judicial system, she couldn't win if Caesar really wanted her. To this extent, it was like shooting a mockingbird.

When that good man Sheriff Tate rendered his verdict that Bob Ewell fell on his knife, that it would be a sin to tell the truth, then abruptly leaves, Atticus looks at Scout and says (this in the book, not in the film) "Scout, Mr. Ewell fell on his knife. Can you possibly understand?"

Scout runs to him and hugs him and kisses him with all her might. She says to her father "Mr. Tate was right." When Atticus asks her what she means she replies "Well, it'd be sort of like shootin' a mockingbird, wouldn't it?"

As parents, we are never really sure of what our children understand of adult thinking. Little Scout is only eight years old now but she remembers what her father had said two years before about it being a sin to shoot a mockingbird. This was reinforced by another loving and responsible adult in the children's lives, Miss Maudie. And Scout is able to make the connection between this and the way fairness and justice could be best served in the case of the madman who has saved hers and Jem's lives.

The main concern of a loving father was that his children would misunderstand, how they might perceive the excusing of what amounted to vigilante justice in the case of Boo Radley killing Mr. Ewell in order to save them.

But Scout does understand. To tell the town that Boo had actually plunged the knife into the evil Ewell would, indeed, be a sin as Sheriff Tate had said. And children know far more of actual sin than do adults. It takes the innocence of a child to really recognize sin for what it is with an instinctive hatred of it. And in the two cases of Tom Robinson and Boo Radley, the hateful sin of killing a mockingbird.

The scales of justice had been balanced by a madman and Scout understands this, as only a child is capable of understanding it. Atticus had nothing to fear on this score. There would be no taint of hypocrisy to come back to haunt him in his relationship with his little girl. And it must have reassured him further to know his little girl had every bit and more the sense of fairness and justice he had himself.

An obvious conundrum presents itself in spite of this. Jem and Scout will be able to understand the necessity of not telling about Boo. But the case of Tom Robinson remains. That justice was served by a madman is something children can understand and accept. But for adults, it remains vigilante justice. The law required telling of Boo killing Ewell in order to save the children and the Sheriff and Atticus are civilized representatives of the law.

But these outstanding civilized representatives of the law could not save Tom Robinson. And they could not prevent the evil Ewell from stalking and murdering the children. Only a madman could do this and get away with it. But given the option of having all the ladies in Maycomb knocking on Boo's door and bringing him angel food cakes, Sheriff Tate and Atticus had only one choice: To ignore the law, to, in fact, become lawbreakers themselves!

This is a point I have hammered in time past. It needs another hammering.

Scout understands and accepts what was done in the case of Boo. She will never be able to understand and accept what happened in the case of Tom Robinson.

We will applaud the vigilante with the fast gun who comes in and cleans up the town. But we refuse to face the fact that it is perverted laws that make such a thing necessary! And as long as the vigilante remains necessary and is applauded, so long will the world lack wisdom. So long will Scout be unable to understand what happened to Tom Robinson.

I need to repeat a couple of quotes from the novel that I used in the last issue of TAP in order to make a point. Please bear with me:

Mr. Dolphus Raymond does not appear in the film. After all, the makers of the film were not interested in saving the children of the world. Their attention was on the adult issue of racism, not realizing, apparently - or ignoring - the fact that it is a children's issue long before it becomes an adult issue.

But to let the reader know how important the real point of the novel is, here is an excerpt by Mr. Raymond as little Scout relates it:

I had never encountered a being who deliberately perpetrated a fraud against himself. But why had he entrusted us with his deepest secret? I asked him why.

Because you're children and you can understand it, he said, and because I heard that one-

He jerked his head toward Dill: Things haven't caught up with that one's instinct yet. Let him get a little older and he won't get sick and cry. Maybe things 'll strike him as being - not quite right, say, but he won't cry, not when he gets a few years on him.

Cry about what, Mr. Raymond? Dill's maleness was beginning to assert itself.

Cry about the simple hell people give other people - without even thinking. Cry about the hell white people give colored folks, without even stopping to think that they're people too.

Harper Lee knew there were things children understand that adults don't. She knew children weep over injustice and lose this wisdom as they grow into adulthood. Adults excuse this loss, this forsaking of wisdom, by claiming it is a part of growing up, a part of the real world, never realizing that their real world is a world of their choosing and making, a world that has ever failed to attain unto wisdom, the wisdom they, in fact, had as children. And having forsaken such wisdom, contributing so much to this loss is the resulting failure of good people to confront injustice, to confront evil with absolute determination to win!

Every child recognizes and resents a bully. This is because children have the wisdom to believe in fairness and justice.

When the jury in the novel, because of ingrained, ignorant prejudice, finds Tom Robinson guilty of a crime he so very obviously did not commit, Dill and Jem cry. Scout would have cried if she had been just a little older. She was just old enough to realize a great injustice had been perpetrated, but still young enough to not understand and cry about it. She would learn to cry about such things later. And when Jem asks his father how the jury could have done such a thing, his father tells him, as Mr. Raymond told Dill: I don't know ... when they do it - seems only children weep.

It is, once more, the wisdom of the child that Harper Lee brings out so clearly, vividly, in her novel.

The point I want to emphasize from the above is how brutal it is to betray the innocent wisdom of a child. To betray in such a way that a child does, eventually, lose the wisdom and ability to weep over unfairness and injustice. And I could weep thinking of how little Scout will be forced when she grows up to deal with the difference between what happened to Boo Radley and what happened to Tom Robinson.

As a mere man, I have to confess that had I not had daughters, I would never have paid that much attention to the lessons of To Kill a Mockingbird, I wouldn't be nearly as sensitive to the lessons men need to learn from children and women.

But when it comes to trying to convince most women to take an active role in being examples of the lessons Harper Lee teaches in spite of the attempts of men to keep them in their place, in most cases I might as well be preaching forty acres and a mule!

The Equal Rights Amendment was a doomed effort, a failed experiment in equality because women had it wrong. Until children become the priority of America, nothing else is going to work; which only proves it isn't men alone who are the problem.

There is no royal path to knowledge; and most certainly not to wisdom. In spite of Brookings, SRI, etc., no think-tank has come up with the equation $k+w=p$. But the universities and think tanks are not given to solutions. They excel in stating the obvious and muddying the waters.

The reason for this failure of such vaunted institutions is, in fact, very obvious: They don't concentrate on women and children as of equal value to men. For such institutions, it is business as usual by not including women and children in The Great Conversation.

Is it reasonable for fourteen and fifteen year old girls to be unmarried and having babies? Is it reasonable for a society to be encouraging and approving of this? No. It is patently insane!

Recently, a flap in Bakersfield has occurred over parents removing their children from a class taught by a pervert. The parents do not want their children exposed to this pervert teacher.

But Caesar says parents do not have the right to remove their children from this pervert's class.

At the same time, some people are protesting their recent arrests by ABC agents in the Valley. They are carrying placards and protesting in front of the courthouse. But they seem blissfully unaware that Caesar has made them his slaves by the mechanism of taking away the rights of parents to remove their children from the influence of perverts. Once more, it is business as usual for Caesar who is totally dependent on his power that rests on whose ox is being gored, of good people refusing to accept the dictum that we will hang together or hang separately.

This calls to mind the point I made in the last TAP that good people are overwhelmed by the magnitude of the problems, the magnitude of Caesar's power, and feel helpless to change things.

What good people are consistently overlooking is the fact that Caesar must destroy the single most basic foundation of America, the family, in order to achieve his ultimate goal of enslavement of all Americans. He is already largely successful in this destruction of families. And it is Caesar's most powerful tool against parents and children, the schools, which he is using to destroy families. As I have mentioned, parents no longer have any real authority over their own children. And the schools, being such powerful instruments of Caesar, are teaching this to children at an earlier and earlier age.

I recently shared some of my views with our new California Governor Gray Davis. Governor Davis talked a lot in his campaign about his giving education reform the highest priority if elected Governor.

He replied thanking me for my input. But will anything change for the better? Not if I am the only one making any noise to the Governor. It will take a lot of people making the same noise.

The Amendment gives good people the chance to take back the power of government. But it is a daunting challenge to educate good people to see the connection, to see the connection between the power of Caesar through the schools, to arrest without cause on the basis of observation only, the power of Caesar to prevent good people from removing their children from the influence of perverts in the classroom, and the power of the Amendment to redress these abuses of Caesar.

Are Americans so spoiled and naive as to believe that they can save their cake and eat it too, that we can succeed as a society without moral restraint and without exercising personal responsibility? Yes. Insane!

Samuel D. G. Heath, Ph. D.

Within such an insane society, there is an obvious need for the Boo Radleys; there is an obvious need for the Amendment, the personification of Boo Radley, as a first step toward restoring sanity to America and to the human race.

But Caesar is depending on Americans giving themselves over totally to Bread and Circuses, to petty pleasures and entertainments, to anything but making children our priority, in order to succeed with his agenda of total enslavement!

We desperately need the skill of all the little Scouts of being girls. I believe in the power of the Amendment to give all little girls the chance to learn and develop this skill, to give all children the chance to develop all the skills of childhood. And I believe the Amendment gives all of humanity the chance to make that first major step toward finally achieving the wisdom that will make this possible for children.

For example, there is no more precious line in To Kill a Mockingbird than the one Harper gives to Jem during Scout's first day at school. It is his little sister's first recess and Jem is checking on her to see how she is doing. Harper has little Scout describe it this way "Jem cut me from the covey of first-graders in the schoolyard."

Only a woman could and would describe this action of Jem by such a precious phrase in such a precious way. Harper Lee had obviously acquired the skill of being a girl. And this is so very evident from this special line in the book, together with her sensitivity to all the things little Scout represents of the best of girlhood and its impact in bringing out the best of boyhood.

Every little girl needs to be cut from the covey by one who loves and cares for her and demonstrates it by doing so. Little girls are designed of God to bring out the best in boys and men, to cause them to cut little girls out of the covey when they need to be. It is a demonstrative form of cherishing.

When a man chooses a wife, he is to cut her from the covey and cherish her. But the woman had better have learned the necessary skill of being a girl while she is a child or it isn't going to happen. I may only be a man but I have learned and know at least this much about women.

The Amendment, by protecting children from the most vicious evil of all, molestation, will enable children to be raised in protected innocence, the most fundamental and basic right of humanity.

Parents will be able to focus on teaching their little girls to be ladies, their little boys to be gentlemen. Beginning with the Amendment, Caesar will begin to lose his power and We the People will begin to take back our government, our America, by making children the priority they deserve to be and must be.

In my former life I was a well qualified, card-carrying, chauvinistic redneck religious and political conservative. I wielded the Bible (and the flag) like a club to beat everyone into submission to my brand of wisdom and truth. And I could quote chapter and verse with the very best. Those who knew me well back then will vouch for this.

It is nothing short of miraculous that I think and write as I do now; most especially about women and children and the need for them to be accepted as of equal value to men in order for the world to attain to wisdom and peace.

In the old days if anyone had suggested to me that Jesus not accepting women as Apostles may have been a mistake on his part, that in not doing so he was as guilty as any other man of his time in placing a lesser value on women, I would have condemned the person to the outer reaches beyond redemption! Then I would have followed through with the appropriate sermon denouncing such a thing from my pulpit warning women in the congregation that the flames of the pit awaited any woman who did not agree with me!

After all, if women were of equal value to men, well of course Jesus would have chosen some to be Apostles. But they aren't! Didn't Sarah win the approval of God by referring to her husband Abraham as Lord? Didn't Paul, speaking for Jesus, say women were to keep silent in the churches; that it was a shame for them to teach or speak, to learn in silence and if they had questions they should ask their husbands when they got home?

In short, keeping uppity females in their place was part of being a Christian and a pastor. And I could always count on the men in my congregations agreeing with this and supporting me.

There is another side to this; the women who do not want any responsibility in the decision-making process. It's a convenient way to make sure men always get the blame when things go wrong. This was the problem with the ERA. Women wanted to save their cake and to eat it too.

If I could believe the Amendment is God's fault, His idea not mine, it would at least make some sense to think, speak, and write as I do now. I could blame him for my madness. But I don't know.

But I can't deny the Amendment makes sense regardless the source. It seems the sane way out of the madness that grips, and has always gripped, the world, making the world a lynch mob.

Nor can I deny how very important little children have become to me over the last few years, how their very innocence has penetrated my own dark heart, how the fate of those two little girls in Belgium, Melissa and Julie, gave me the nightmares that drove me to the Amendment and the Memorial Wall with their names and so many others in front of my house for all to see.

Intellectually, it has its attraction. I can, with great interest, contrast my former beliefs and state of mind with my present and I spend a good deal of time doing so. It is far safer, and far more comfortable, to intellectualize this and hold my emotions in abeyance.

But there is always the message of To Kill a Mockingbird to confront. There is always my former life to confront no matter how I try to bury it. And I may get away from these during the day when the sun is shining, but when I lay my head on my pillow in the darkness, they are still there.

It is at such a time I think of what little Dill said when Scout asks him: Why do you reckon Boo Radley's never run off?

Dill replies: Maybe he doesn't have anywhere to run off to.

It isn't any fun to admit at my age how wrong I have been about so many things. I was always ready to credit myself with more intelligence than to be taken in by hypocrites, thieves and liars.

Now, having to admit to such things, especially being guilty of these things in the name of God, is no easy task as you can well imagine. To have to admit to having been expert in the art form of holy lying and begging, worshiping and using the Bible as the instrument of my own unrighteousness, is a hard thing. And, to repeat, it is nothing short of miraculous that I have been able to see this and admit to it in my case.

Somehow, the children became my focus of attention. As I intellectualize it, I could write a book of my educational progress and experiences of life of which I could say: These are some of the reasons.

I say only some of the reasons because in my heart and soul I know these things alone cannot account for my present honesty, an honesty that is misunderstood by many good people, even close friends, and has hurt me so badly in so many ways. It is a very lonely position that no man in his right mind would choose; hence my willingness to blame God or my own madness.

Recently there was a TV special hosted by Maury Povich about the tombs of Egypt. Anything about the ancient past of Egypt, especially the pyramids, has always held a fascination for people. Charlatans like Edgar Cayce were entranced (no pun intended) by the subject.

Theories abound concerning the ancient monuments and tombs, the kings and queens, curses, the various deities, the enormous amount of time, money and energy devoted to the afterlife.

From the first excavations of archaeologists, to Cayce, to Chariots of the Gods, to Indiana Jones, to Povich, the fascination grows. Books, theories and films proliferate. Especially popular are the theories of ancient space travelers coming to earth and being either the builders or teachers of many of the ancient wonders. Theories of connections to lost civilizations like Mu or Atlantis abound as well.

Curiously, it seems that ancient peoples or space travelers never got around to attaining wisdom. Natural disasters seem to have been unavoidable to these ancient cultures, regardless of their science and genius, as well.

I have had to ask myself, in confronting so much gullibility on the part of so many people, why these ancient cultures, whether of earth or the stars, were so given to war rather than peace?

Not only is there no record of any ancient culture which is not a record of war, there is no record of the kind of wisdom which would lead to peace. Whatever myths, legends, or actual records you resort to, war is there.

For the UFO and X-Files aficionados, no interplanetary influence has ever been proven, let alone to have been, the source of peace in the world.

Of course, the easy way around this fact for me in the past was my belief in blaming God for the whole mess and preaching that the Rapture, Second Coming, and the Great Assize would sort things out. Pie in the sky by and by was an easy and comfortable out; a lot easier and simpler than accepting personal responsibility for the mess.

There is a point to all this. The record of humankind is one of blaming God, regardless of the religion or beliefs, for our own lack of wisdom, to blame God rather than taking personal responsibility for the evil in the world.

The Amendment, I believe, confronts this lack of responsible wisdom on our part. It puts to the test theories of ancient cultures being so far advanced. They didn't survive for one simple and basic reason: They never attained wisdom. And $k+w=p$ is the proof of this.

The world has never had the wisdom to overcome the case of Tom Robinson. As I said, Scout could accept the wisdom of not telling about Boo Radley being the mad guardian angel of the children. It would, indeed, have been sorta like shootin' a mockingbird.

But the case of Tom Robinson remained. And still remains. It always has. What Scout could never be asked to understand was the real difference between Boo Radley and Tom Robinson?

We can credit everyone connected to the case of Tom Robinson with sanity or we must charge the entire society with insanity. You don't try to explain this to a child whose own wisdom cannot possibly credit sanity to those responsible for the death of Tom Robinson. To a child, such a thing is obviously insane!

I have said that the Amendment is the personification of Boo Radley; the madman who acted with sanity. But he certainly appeared to be insane. He had committed an insane act against his own father. But his kind of insanity made children his priority.

The insanity of the Amendment is in making children, for the first time in history, the priority of a nation. And until this is done, the case of Tom

Robinson remains unresolved and insane. Not just for Scout and Jem, not just for 1935 in Maycomb, Alabama, but throughout the entire world throughout all of history, and throughout the world today.

There seems no end to the list of insanities we face today. For example, I just got a letter from Mrs. Mattie Jane Futrell asking my help for her son, John Futrell. He was one of the police officers involved in the shoot-out at a North Hollywood bank in 1997. He is being sued by family members of one of the robbers who murdered an innocent bystander in cold blood. The officer is being sued because he had the innocent victims given ambulance priority over the robber/murderer.

Well, it takes a special form of vermin, like the robber/murderer and his attorney, to bring out the best examples of the kind of insanity we confront as a society.

But it is the kind of insanity the Amendment confronts. If Americans are more concerned and interested in Egyptian tombs and flying saucers than children, if Americans continue to believe it is God's job and not theirs to protect children, if they continue to stomp ants while the elephants rampage through the village, so long will the case of Tom Robinson remain unresolved, so long will the little Scouts be unable to make sense of it all. And so long will the Ewells be the cause of injustice for the Tom Robinsons and be the stalkers, molesters and murderers of children.

Children need responsible action by adults on their behalf. Children need a guardian angel like Boo Radley in the form of the Amendment. But as long as Americans think themselves sane and the Amendment madness, so long will children and the Tom Robinsons suffer and so long will humankind fail to attain wisdom.

It is no small matter to offer people hope, hope that things can be done to save our children and our world. The Amendment offers such hope. But as long as men love darkness rather than light, so long will all of humanity remain at risk from the power of such darkness.

My closest friends remain those like Henry Thoreau and Harper Lee. They see through the darkness and offer me light and hope in a very dark and dangerous world.

If, in my sharing this light and hope with others, I am seen as the madman for confronting my own sins and those of others, I confess this leaves very little hope of things changing for the better; because I know it will take an army of people who share my dream (my madness?) of changing things. It will take an army who shares my belief that if good people know better, they will do better, to accomplish the purpose of the Amendment.

But if good people will let the children make their voices heard, this can happen. In the meantime, I will continue to read Walden and To Kill a Mockingbird, I will continue to try to hear little Scout and listen to what she has to say and try to shut out the sanity all about me that confronts my madness.

It's a hard thing, this thing of being all grown up. I can't help wishing I could join Scout and Jem and Dill at play. I want my business to be the business of a child, to play.

But there is the rub. I know it can't be a better world for my children until it is a better world for all children. And there is no getting around the fact that I am all grown up, and that we adults are the ones who have the responsibility of making that better world.

Years after the filming of To Kill a Mockingbird, several of the makers of it as well as those who played in it were interviewed. It was agreed that there were two truly magical moments in the film. The first is at the very beginning: the title sequences with the little girl humming and singing to herself, the use of the box with its contents like the rolling marble, together with the little girl drawing and then ripping the crayon picture of the mockingbird accompanied by her little girl's lyrically musical, giggling laughter.

The whole scene draws you into the magical world of a happy child, the happiest of all worlds imaginable.

The second occurred early in the film. It is bedtime and Scout is in bed and Atticus is listening to her read. As she is getting ready to be tucked in to go to sleep, she asks to see Atticus' watch.

The whole scene, the mystical, magical bonding between an innocent little girl and her father, little Scout's stretching and yawning, the way she holds her father's watch in her small hands and reads the inscription, cuddling her teddy bear while being tucked in and the sleepy questions to Jem about their mother is not only magical, it is the most touching scene of the film. It is the reason Mary Badham was nominated for an Oscar for virtually no one with a good conscience and a genuine love of children can help being touched by the captivating and precious tenderness of such a thing. It appeals to the very best in all of us as human beings.

But as Mary said years later, she wasn't acting; she was just being a little girl. And that is always magic. But it isn't the kind of magic to which the world awards its plaudits of recognition and praise. We adults don't reward the natural gift of the art and wisdom of childhood; we reward the adult who has to work hard at even pretending they still have this magical and natural art and wisdom.

The producers of the film in this interview that occurred so many years after the making of it were right. There has never been another film like To Kill a Mockingbird. There is no other film like it. And while all the superlatives have been used in attempting to describe it, I especially like what one person, I believe it was director Robert Mulligan, said of it in eloquently classic and elegant understatement: It is a very particular film.

But most of the major film studios wouldn't touch the book in spite of it being a Pulitzer Prize winner and so popular with the reading public because they couldn't see any real story in it that would appeal to moviegoers. The consensus of the studios, and to quote one executive, was: There's no story; there's no action, no romance, no obvious sex or violence.

This, of course, was an early indication that To Kill a Mockingbird was a book of far greater depth than anyone really knew notwithstanding its Pulitzer status. But it would take time for this to be discovered.

In its film form, it took the genius of people like Horton Foote (who won the best screenplay Oscar for his work), Elmer Bernstein, Robert Mulligan, and Alan Pakula to make the story, and it took the talented genius of those like the children and Gregory Peck to make it come alive on-screen.

It took real artistic genius for the makers of the film to accomplish so very successfully the transporting of an audience back to the time during which the events of the film take place, wonderfully enhanced by Bernstein's superb musical score and the exquisitely distinctive and natural Southern charm of Kim Stanley's voice as narrator.

But while Gregory Peck was an undisputed natural for the role of Atticus (and won an Oscar for his performance) the most difficult task confronting the producers was to find the right children for the roles of Scout and Jem. Hundreds of children all through the South were tried before Mary Badham and Phillip Alford were selected, only to discover they lived within four blocks of each other in Birmingham but had never met.

If miracles ever occur in film making, this was one. The two children were not only perfectly suited for the roles of Scout and Jem, even having the necessary family resemblance; anyone watching the film cannot fail to appreciate how naturally the two children interact as though they are, in fact, brother and sister.

Another miracle was in the totally innocent and naturally unaffected talent of little Mary Badham, this really setting the film apart from all others and making it what it is: a truly great film.

I certainly agree with those who say that there has never been a film like To Kill a Mockingbird. It stands alone and has a peculiar and distinctive place all by itself in the whole of the history of filmmaking. The film and its history are a worthy study in and of themselves.

But if there is a single most important aspect to the film, it is this: While Peck was given the Oscar; it should have gone to Mary Badham. It wasn't Peck who made the film what it is, it was Mary.

What makes this so very significant is the fact that adults still lack the wisdom of childhood. And adults made the film claiming to try to capture things through the eyes of children. They didn't. And the Oscar went to Peck.

But as I mentioned in the last issue of TAP, the film while a work of art in its own right, couldn't tell the real story of the novel, the real story Harper Lee captures so vividly through the eyes of the children, especially little Scout.

The film comes close during the title sequences and in that early scene between Atticus and Scout. And it shows, but without telling the why, little Scout walking Boo to his house with her hand in his arm rather than leading him by the hand. But as I also said, it would have taken a film of epic length to explain things like this and the filmmakers knew the film would only succeed on the basis of adult issues and behaviors, not those of children.

Further, it can be argued that in 1962 no filmmaker would dare touch the real issues of the book in the way Harper does in the novel itself. I would argue it isn't even possible now. And I am certain Harper had to hold herself in check at times, which is clearly evidenced by some of her hints and allusions of things and issues that people even today don't want to recognize or speak of.

However, I give the film makers and those who played in it a lot of credit, and most especially little Mary Badham, for creating a work of art that stands alone among films in its artistic greatness.

But to repeat, it didn't, nor do I believe it could, tell the real story of Harper Lee's novel. And it is that real story, or rather, I believe, the story behind the story, told the way Harper tells it, that makes her book stand alone as a work of genius which I compare with the best of Tolstoy or Dostoevsky; and even exceeding these in the very genius of the simplicity of its greatness. But, then, I maintain greatness is a simple thing, almost ingenuous if you will.

For example, the real test of greatness is time. The novel came out in 1960. I have had all these years of reading it and am still learning things from it. The story, the way Harper wrote it, is a treasure hunt, one I can compare with Thoreau's Walden. You may go over the same ground many times and miss a gem. Then, at some point in your life, simply due to the experiences of life, while you are going over such familiar ground your eye suddenly catches the glint of some exquisite jewel you missed so many times before.

I have only to look at the notations that I have made over the years in my copy of the book, the pages now fragile and yellowed by time just like my copy of Walden, to realize this. And, as with my copy of Walden, I am still making new notations every time I read it.

The thrill and excitement of discovery is often enhanced by the realization that in some cases Thoreau and Harper Lee missed the whole import of these things as well, that they wrote better than they knew. But as I have learned, one of the characteristics of genius is to often be unaware of its own genius.

This is why I believe Harper Lee, especially, wrote better than she knew. As she has Dill say (probably due to the influence of her childhood friend, Truman Capote, who was a kind of model for Dill) after the trial in spite of his weeping earlier: I think I'll be a clown when I get grown...There ain't one thing in this world I can do about folks except laugh.

Little Dill is already beginning to learn the wisdom of adulthood and lose the wisdom of a child; and much more quickly than Mr. Raymond had prophesied. Adult wisdom is already beginning its dirty work of destroying the child's wisdom of fairness and justice and replacing it with the adult wisdom of the cynicism: There's nothing you can really do about overcoming evil. And so it is that the history of humankind has been one of unremitting hatreds, prejudices, and warfare, by forsaking the wisdom of childhood.

Adult wisdom amounts to this: There's no use being a child unless you know the world is going to eventually break your heart! To which I reply: What's wrong with this picture?

But even as I say the words, I know it takes wisdom to figure this out, wisdom the world has yet to attain.

I have said I am normal enough to want the flowers and the praise of my good works before I die. Emerson's eulogy of Thoreau was too late. It would have served both Emerson and Thoreau far better to have had Emerson recognize the preciousness and special gifts of his friend before he died.

But too often the flowers and praise come too late, too late for the living, that is, that don't realize what they had in someone before they are gone. And the realization of this comes back as a specter to haunt in the midnight hours.

Or it can come when the sun is shining brightly and some familiar thing causes the loss of that loved one to assault us in an instant and explode full force upon our senses.

And so it is with so many things and people in our lives, which we fail to appreciate in their season. But as we live and grow, both as individuals and as a species, it does seem humanity would learn some of the lessons of such wisdom.

Harper Lee wrote at the end of her novel: Neighbors bring food with death flowers with sickness and little things in between.

And this is all part of life, and it is as it should be. Family, friends and good neighbors, these make up the most precious part of life. And it often seems so very unfair when parents have to bury a child, when the good die young, when the wicked prosper and perverted laws and leaders rule over good people.

I find it passing strange that I am the kind of man that loves books and films like Terms of Endearment and Steel Magnolias and still am the kind of tough-minded, hard-edged man I am in so many other ways. I believe it was my children who saved me from becoming callous, cynical, and bitter. And though I failed them in innumerable ways, it was my children who brought out the best part of me as a man.

After little Scout's miraculously ingenuous dispersal of the lynch mob, Atticus makes this observation to Jem and Scout:

So it took an eight-year-old child to bring 'em to their senses, didn't it? That proves something - that a gang of wild animals can be stopped, simply because they're still human. Maybe we need a police force of children....

An intriguing thought, isn't it, a police force of children. But that is exactly what the Amendment represents personified as Boo Radley, a mad man whose whole essence of being, his only focus of life, is concentrated on the children. The Amendment is further personified as Atticus, Jem, Dill, and little Scout together confronting the lynch mob of the world.

What will not be done for the sake of civilized and sane conscience, the law must do. Just law is for the uncivilized lawbreaker, the lawless who act without conscience, not the law-abiding who have no fear of just laws. On the contrary, the law-abiding, the good and civilized people of good conscience, applaud and support such laws; which made it all the more impossible for Scout, Jem and Dill to understand how that jury could have found Tom Robinson guilty. Such a verdict was so very obviously totally unfair, unjust, without conscience, and in fact, insane to them!

But a mob is often made up of one's friends and neighbors as Atticus points out to the children. Whenever I confront friends and good people with their own sin of hypocrisy by their agreeing that children must be the closest thing to the heart of God Himself and then live their lives as though there were something of greater importance, I am not thanked for the service I do them.

If I point out that the world itself behaves as a lynch mob because the greatest minds throughout history have lacked the wisdom to cherish children, that the greatest civilizations have warred and met destruction repeatedly because the greatest leaders of history have lacked such wisdom, that the particular cases of Boo Radley and Tom Robinson are evidence of things having never changed for the better for children, I certainly don't do so for the applause of the world. But if not, for what? Because I am compelled to try to speak for the children. Now before anyone resorts to trying to tell me or anyone else how easy it is to be on the side of the angels, you try it. Try it in this manner, as I do: Try making converts to the Amendment.

You won't find any children who in their wisdom wouldn't agree with the Amendment. You find the enemies of the Amendment among good adults, even fine, upstanding, church-going, flag-waving American citizens. Don't even try to tell me that children don't need someone to give them a voice or how easy it is to be on the side of the angels when you attempt to do so. These are lies. As are the lies preached from the pulpits of politics and churches of how truly concerned good people are for the children but live as though there were something of greater importance.

The mob that wanted to lynch Tom Robinson was composed of friends and neighbors of Atticus, many of them calling themselves, and undoubtedly even believing themselves, God-fearing people, Jesus-and-Bible-believing and loving people. And had not the children intervened, these good friends and neighbors, these God-fearing, Jesus-and-Bible-believing and loving people would have hurt Atticus to get to Tom Robinson and kill him.

But these very same people comprised the jury that found Tom Robinson guilty, it was composed of good people, God-fearing people, Jesus-and-Bible-believing and loving people, the same friends and neighbors who would have hurt Atticus and lynched Tom Robinson had not the children intervened.

The most difficult part of the message of the Amendment I have to teach and preach is that it confronts good people, good people who as a mob or unjust jury will condemn the innocent. But if good people will allow little Scout to confront them individually, the wisdom of a good and pure conscience will prevail.

It is on an individual basis that good people prove their ability to respond to the need to protect that wise innocence of children which is the single most precious thing that is the responsibility of adults to protect! Once that lynch mob was confronted by this fact in little Scout, they came to their senses. The challenge is to direct these good individuals to come together in concert for the good of children, all children. The Amendment gives good people the opportunity to do just exactly this; but not in the name of their peculiar institutions or religious beliefs, not in the name of Democrats or Republicans or any other. But simply because it is their duty and responsibility as adult human beings, simply because it is the right and wise thing to do!

This is one of the things that militate against people supporting the Amendment; they cannot hang any of their bigotries, religious or political prejudices on it. It carries no baggage beyond it being simply the right and wise thing for people, all people, to do.

But the lynch mob, the unjust jury, the comfortable congregation, is led of a pack mentality, a pack mentality that includes the insanity of groupthink.

Or, in such cases, the group insanity led of the prejudices that make good people so utterly lacking in wisdom agree together to commit evil in the hypocritical corruption of the very names of God, justice, and fairness.

Scout points out how Atticus needed her, how he couldn't get along a day without her helping and advising him. Atticus had done a marvelous job as a father raising his little girl to think in such a way. He had made her feel important and needed.

Of course Scout couldn't know as a child of the things that really made her so important and needed to her father, the things he responded to in his little girl that led her to believe he relied on her help and advice. She couldn't know how important and needed it was to Atticus for her to climb up on his lap and hug him, how important and needed it was to her father for him to be able to tuck her into bed and kiss her good night, and how important and needed she was in making her father a real man, a fair and just man, a real gentleman, who didn't dare betray his little one's love and trust.

We men need our boys. We want to be able to teach our boys to be men. But we need the cherishing of our little girls to make us men soft in the right places so that the melding of the hard and soft results in the right alloy of toughness to both be able to love as well as be able to confront, fight, and overcome evil.

There is absolutely no greater influence for good in the life of any man than to have his child climb onto his lap seeking the warmth of his love and protection. No king on any throne can possibly possess such wealth and power as a man with his arms about that trusting little one he is holding. And no man with such memories can straightaway go out and go about doing evil. God meant children to be this influence for good in men's lives, to bring out the best in the best of men.

And knowing this how is it possible that the world has never attained to the wisdom of such a thing? How is it possible that humanity still behaves as a lynch mob? How is it possible that humankind still looks to God or some messiah to deliver it from its own seeming helplessness and inability to confront evil and overcome?

But it is a self-imposed tyranny of evil through blind, ignorant, and hateful prejudices that makes good people seemingly impotent in the face of evil that has prevented enough good men and women in coming together in common cause for the common good of all humanity. Through this self-imposed tyranny of evil good people have failed to make that common good of all humanity, children, their priority.

Then, rather than accept personal responsibility for ridding themselves of this tyranny of evil, good people will turn to blaming others, institutions, and even God, for the evil!

And then good people will tell themselves that had they sat on Tom Robinson's jury they would not have caved in to such an injustice, that they would have stood up and been counted. And these same good people will say their prayers at night and go to sleep with an easy conscience while the children continue to be molested and murdered without hope of either protection or justice.

After the trial, Jem and Scout are asking their father how such an injustice such as that committed against Tom Robinson was possible in the face of his obvious innocence.

In the course of trying to explain, Atticus tells the children: It's all adding up and one of these days we're going to pay the bill for it. I hope it's not in you children's time.

My greatest fear for my own children is that humanity is running out of time, that the bill is due.

But if in fact the only two choices are k+w=p or #92 of the periodic table, shouldn't good people be getting the message that concerted action by them is required if we are to survive and progress, if we are to insure a future for humanity, our children?

Jem and Scout retire to Jem's room to discuss some of the things their father has told them. At this point in the novel, Jem is entering puberty and the change is confusing to Scout. He has become moody and their relationship is changing, and not to Scout's liking.

For example, Jem tells Scout to try to get along with their aunt Alexandra; that she is only trying to help Scout become a lady, something Scout heartily resents; in fact, when Jem says to Scout "Can't you take up sewin' or somethin'?" Scout's immediate and direct reply is "Hell, no."

Scout is only eight and has no real command or understanding of invective. She innocently uses the profanity because she thinks this is how she has to react to a big brother who is trying to push her around, insisting she become a lady, a traumatic change from Jem accusing her of acting like a girl such a short time ago, and this is the only device she knows to stick up for herself without mother or sister, or even a close girl playmate, in her male-dominated environment.

But things settle down between them and the children begin discussing what makes people different. Their aunt has told them they come from good people of good breeding, that some others like the Cunninghams are trash, and fine people like themselves, the Finches, should not associate with them.

Scout particularly resented this; in fact it infuriates her, causing her to lose her temper. This helps to account for her using the word hell; she was angry with her aunt and she became angry with Jem when he seemed to be trying to boss her. She likes little Walter Cunningham and would like to have him visit. But this brought on the comment by her aunt concerning what she considered suitable friends for the children. And Scout's resulting furious resentment.

Scout's resentment and anger is also borne of another source, one she simply cannot understand. Her father would never call anyone trash; he treated everyone alike, often going out of his way to be polite to people whom his sister, aunt Alexandra, obviously thought and spoke of as trash. How could her aunt be so different from Atticus? It didn't make sense. And all this fuss about background and ancestors, why should such things make a difference between people, why should such things be so obviously important to aunt Alexandra and not to Atticus?

Aunt Alexandra and Atticus were brother and sister. How could they be so close and think so differently? Scout and Jem sometimes wondered about stories of changlings.

As Scout and Jem calm down and begin reflecting on what their aunt has said and trying to work through the differences between people, Jem says in evaluating their aunt's remarks: The thing about it is, our kind of folks don't like the Cunninghams, the Cunninghams don't like the Ewells, and the Ewells hate and despise the colored folks.

Neither of the children can really understand why this is true. They just know it's the way things are. But they also know as only children do that there is something plainly wrong with this and are trying to make sense of it.

Scout says she thinks folks are just folks and that's the way it ought to be.

Jem's face grows cloudy and he says to Scout: That's what I thought too ... If there's just one kind of folks, why can't they get along with each other? If they're all alike, why do they go out of their way to despise each other? Scout, I'm beginning to understand why Boo Radley's stayed shut up in the house all this time ... it's because he wants to stay inside.

What normal adult can't understand the confusion of Jem and Scout? And who of us can't relate to Jem's conclusion concerning Boo Radley? How many of you, like myself, haven't wanted to stay in the house, pull the blankets over our head, and tell the world to just go away?

I'm as normal a human being as any in this way. Which makes it all the more inexplicable that I would be doing as I am in regard to the Amendment.

But as a reasonably honest and responsible man, I can't get away from little Dill's cynical conclusion: I think I'll be a clown when I get grown...There ain't one thing in this world I can do about folks except laugh.

This hurts too much. Children should never have to become so cynical or have the wisdom of childhood destroyed by adults who have given up the fight, thrown in the towel, and give countless and very practiced excuses for their forsaking their own personal responsibility to confront evil.

I repeatedly hear of this or that person doing good for children. But when I pursue these stories, too many times I discover such people often don't even know the name of their State or U.S. Senator, they don't even know the name of their Representative in Congress, they have never written a letter to an editor of their local paper or their legislator; local, state or federal. Some, God help us, aren't even registered to vote! And many who are registered don't bother!

Is it that such good people think they are really making a difference when they are not involved in the political process? But so many of these good people are the first to complain against unjust laws and corrupt legislators; this is hypocrisy which good people fail to recognize as such!

No matter how many good works people think they are accomplishing by teaching in a public or Sunday school or working with children in any capacity, they are doing nothing of any lasting value unless such people are actively involved with the political process at all levels: local, state, and federal.

I grow weary of the stories of this or that one, of how much of an effect they are having for the good of children when such people haven't so much as written their local supervisor or editor.

Don't delude yourself that real change for the better for children can ever be accomplished without good people being politically active. It isn't going to happen. The Devil and his wicked servants seem to know this even if good people don't!

But it is far easier to delude yourself that you are making a real difference by teaching a class of some kind. There you are, actually working with children and thinking all the while you are making a difference. It's a lie. You aren't. Making a real difference is being a responsible part of the power of We the People to change government so that you are a part of the solution for all the children, not the few you are working with. I spent many years working with thousands of children and suffering the same delusion that I was making a real difference before I realized the truth of this.

Go ahead and become an Albert Schweitzer or Mother Teresa, go ahead and build an orphanage, go ahead and become a teacher, be a foster parent, a Big Brother or Sister, a mentor, a Scout leader. These things are good, noble, and worthy works for children, for humanity. But they won't change anything! They never have and they never will!

As good and noble, as needed as such things are, in and of themselves they will never accomplish the goal of the Amendment in changing things for the better for all the children. The magnitude of evil, the size of the Beast, if you will, is too great for any single effort, or combination of efforts now existing because they are so fragmented and most often working at cross purposes, to overcome.

I wish I could get good people, We The People, to understand that unless we have good government, good leaders, and good laws, nothing is going to change for the better no matter how much time and energy they expend on all their other good works, no matter how many children they think they are saving. I wish I could get good people involved in the political process, that good people would recognize the Amendment is the way to accomplish something of substantive and lasting value for all children. As I came to realize, I could never make things really better for my own children until things became better for all the children.

Good people throughout history have allowed the insanity of their own prejudices to overcome the wise sanity of prioritizing and cherishing children, all children, and the result has been a history of the insanity of hatreds based on prejudices and always leading to the insanity of every description of lynch mob and war rather than the wise sanity of peace.

Looks simple enough on the face of it, doesn't it. Then what's the problem? The problem is the prejudices of good people who consistently fail to recognize or admit of such prejudices, good people who refuse to admit of their prejudices or face them for the evil things they are and consistently confuse what they believe with what they know. The problem is the same one throughout history that has always led to the need of the vigilante and Boo Radley, and to good people who will become a lynch mob or a jury condemning the innocent like Tom Robinson to death, to good people who will kill one another in the name of God, race, or political ideologies.

But when little Scout climbs up on her father's lap, when that little one knows she is protected, needed, and loved, ah, what a difference that makes in a man. No man with that memory, no man with such power and wealth in his arms, no man who loves as Atticus loved his children, is going to let any prejudice rule his passions. Such a man's passions, and his mind, already have a monarch, and one who rules with the wisdom of love, God Himself, through His most precious little agents of love and wisdom: Children.

Simple enough? Just try preaching this sermon. Watch good men, for example, nod their heads in the affirmative of the need of the civilizing influence of women and children to contravene war. Then watch good people, most especially men, in their hypocrisy go on about business as usual.

It is so very easy to accept the fact that there is no belief or fear of God in people like Mr. Ewell or his daughter, people who put their hands on a Bible and swear before God and all humanity to tell the truth, and then lie in order to put an innocent man to death. It is easy to accept the fact that a man who will swear with his hand on a Bible, a Bible he says he holds to be the very Word of God, who swears to be truthful and uphold the Constitution and the laws of America, and then betrays that oath, has no belief in or fear of God. But it is not easy to accept the fact that obviously good people may have no belief or fear of God in themselves.

But logic would seem to demand this to be the case. If good people are going to agree that children are the closest thing to the heart of God Himself and then live as though there were something of greater importance, the very least such good people are guilty of is the stench of hypocrisy!

I have said that most people would say it is easy to be on the side of the angels. I have also pointed out the fact that while this is easy to say, it is very difficult to practice; particularly when you attempt to be on the side of the angels in trying to speak for the children in confronting the prejudices of good people.

I find it an intellectual puzzle that I would be attempting this work of trying to be the voice of children. I have often pointed out the fact that I have no inordinate love of children beyond that of most parents for their own.

For those who believe I am on some holy quest, that the idea and the work for the Amendment somehow requires some kind of saint, I must appear at the very least an enigma, if not a downright embarrassment to such thinking because while I have done a lot of swimming I have yet to walk on water.

I wonder every day why I am doing this? I not only do not have any really satisfactory answer, the enormity of the task is so overwhelming that, viewed as a whole, and it makes me want to give up. It would be nice to believe that God needed an amanuensis and I got tapped for the job. As I've said several times, it's always a nice convenience to blame God for many things that are the fault of people. And it doesn't always take a mad man to use this device; good, normal people do it all the time.

I have tried to answer this question of "why" to others and myself many times because unless I can make sense of it in my own life, how can I expect others to make sense of it in their own? I owe people an explanation.

The best way I can describe it so far is that it seems to be just a job. I never think of it as some noble undertaking, it is just a job that has to be done simply because it is the right and wise thing to do. I don't think I could do the work if it were anything but just simply a job that needs to be done.

I sometimes wish I had some heavenly visitation, some epiphany or theophany that would make clear and declare from God Himself: This is your holy calling!

But nothing of the sort ever happened. And I don't suppose it will.

I think it comes down to this. The Amendment is the right and wise thing to do. And once it formed itself in my mind and I finally accepted it, it became just a job that needed to be done.

No one, I believe, has a healthier ego than me. I love it when people think and speak well of me. I am a perfectly normal man in virtually all respects.

I often speak and write of the two little girls in Belgium, Melissa and Julie. The horrible, monstrous deaths of these two little girls gave me nightmares. And still does. Something is horribly wrong with a species that could allow such a monstrous thing to be done to children! How is it that we allow such monsters to roam and prey on children in any society thinking and claiming itself to be civilized?

I hate bullies of any description. I have years of experience working with children and I have always had a natural hatred of those who would abuse children. But these things alone do not separate me from any other normal man.

When the Amendment suggested itself as a job that needed to be done, I believe that at the time I responded as any normal man would by rejecting the idea.

But the idea kept insisting itself to me. And perhaps if there is anything abnormal about me as a man, I finally began to realize how appropriate the Amendment was, how important it was that humanity make children the priority of all nations.

Normal men, as I have had to finally accept, do not respond as I finally did. But as I began to dig deeply into my own motives, those which caused me to first reject the idea, then those that made me finally accept it, I began to learn many things I would never have learned otherwise; most especially things about myself as a man.

And as I learned, I began to get a perception of what has been wrong with humanity throughout history, a perception of the very things within myself that prevent good people from overcoming evil.

One of the first things I learned was that I had reacted to the Amendment as a normal man would. I rejected the idea.

But if the Amendment was the right and wise thing to do, there had to be something wrong with what I considered normal! This was logical thinking. But not the kind of logical thinking I was anxious to pursue. Still, as an intelligent and reasonably honest and educated man and one who liked to think of himself as responsible, I seemed to have no choice but to pursue it.

As a writer, it was natural for me to express in print my thoughts and the things I was learning. I began to share these things with the readers of TAP, and lost many friends and readers in the process.

But from the very beginning, I knew I was only a man, a very normal man, notwithstanding my new insights as to what this really meant, without any heavenly vision or Holy Grail to pursue. The Amendment made sense. And it was my job to make it make sense to others.

And that is the only way I can pursue the work. I can't make my job anything else than just that: A job.

Most certainly the expression: It's a dirty job but someone has to do it! Often comes to mind. In fact, I face that expression every day in my own thinking. Sometimes I feel it was the luck of the draw and I'm just playing the hand I was dealt, wishing it were someone else's, that the job itself were someone else's. I can at least say this much: I never asked for the job.

Years after the making of Harper's novel into the film, Gregory Peck was interviewed and said that the role of Atticus was the one he counted the favorite of his career; that he felt he had to do it and that being asked to play the role was one of the luckiest things to ever happen to him.

I wish I could say this of the Amendment in my own life. But I can't.

I am an intelligent man. For this, like the natural skill of Atticus with a gun, I can take no credit; only a fool tries to take credit for the fortunate accidents of birth. It was an early lesson in my life, but one well learned, that it isn't so much what you've got, but what you do with what you've got that counts. I am also a very well educated man. For this, I can and will take the appropriate credit. This is taking what you have been given by birth and trying to make the most of it.

Because I am an intelligent and educated man, though I first rejected the idea of the Amendment, I was compelled to analyze why I opposed it.

Little by little I became aware that the Amendment required I take a hard and honest look at myself as a man. Little by little it made me aware of so many errors and evils within myself as a man; I began to understand why I had been so set against it to begin with. It made me ask questions of myself that no man wants asked him. Let alone have to answer.

There were also the responsibility and accountability factors the Amendment addressed. I wanted nothing to do with these either. And yet, I had always considered myself a very responsible and accountable man. What was wrong with this picture that I had of myself that seemed to be confronted by the Amendment in such a fashion that I rejected it?

Now I had had a lot of years in getting to know myself. But I had never known myself in the way the Amendment made me come to know myself. I was amazed, and at certain points, horrified! as I came to recognize so many hurtful errors and prejudices of thinking and acting in my own life, of how many of my own beliefs I had confused with knowledge.

If there is anything simple about the Amendment, it is this: It forces people, men especially, to look at themselves in such a critical and honest fashion that it also forces them to reject it at first. Just as I did. It exposed the errors of what I had considered normal. It exposed the errors of the historical definitions of normal.

I would never minimize the difficulty any person has in confronting the things I had to confront about myself in order to accept the Amendment as the right and wise thing it is. And I came to realize that there probably wasn't a human being alive who wants to examine themselves, and an entire society of which they are a part, as closely and honestly as the Amendment requires them to do.

It came down to a compulsion for me. I have no idea why I was forced to start examining my innermost ideas and feelings about the issue of children in light of the requirements of the Amendment. But it became just that: a compulsion.

Was I to commend myself for wanting to be that honest with myself? No. How do you commend yourself for a compulsion? You don't.

Neither did I want to deal with the issues of such deeply held, but erroneous, beliefs of a lifetime, beliefs that I finally had to admit were nothing but prejudices, things I had been taught as a child to believe, things I wanted and chose to believe.

Then what? Why? Nothing was left to me but the explanation of compulsion; which was no answer at all. But it was all I had by way of explanation.

I was driven by compulsion to accept the Amendment, to submit it to every Governor and U.S. Senator, to the President and influential figures of national and international reputation including Oprah and The Pope, to organizations like The Christian Coalition and even the United Nations.

Madness! That was the other explanation.

Was it madness or compulsion, perhaps a compulsion of madness, that forced me to decorate the front of my house with a Memorial Wall of Shame with the names of murdered children for all the world to see, for every passer-by to believe I am some kind of kook who should probably be put away and not to be trusted with sharp instruments? To post web pages on the Internet in support of the Amendment offering further support to those who consider me mad?

But I know the wisdom of the Amendment. I know this now. I didn't when I first started examining it. It came to me little by little. Early on I could accept the intellectual and logical necessity of it. But it took a woman, Harper Lee, to help me understand the wisdom of it.

Granting it took intelligence and an enormous amount of educated research to come to the realization that humanity had always lacked wisdom by excluding women and children as of equal value to men and this exclusion had doomed all efforts for a peaceful world, this was knowledge, not wisdom.

It took this knowledge together with my children; my years of working with children, and insights such as those of Henry Thoreau and Harper Lee for me to understand that it took factual knowledge plus wisdom to equal peace. I further had to come to an understanding that wisdom derived from love and compassion with an instinctive hatred of evil.

While Thoreau taught me many things about the evils of government, the wisdom of living simply, and so many other things, there was something missing. I always realized my friend Henry was deficient to a certain extent by his missing a large dimension of life through his never marrying and having children.

I also came to realize the world had always been lacking in wisdom by excluding women and children as equal in value to men. This is the reason the equation k+w=p could never be found in any of the works of men, including the Bible which, like all of these other writings of men, determinedly excludes women by treating them as of lesser value to men.

It would take the melding of both Henry Thoreau and Harper Lee to make it work for me. The two are representative of great genius, that of a man and a woman. It took such a melding of the genius of both halves of humanity for it to all come together and make sense of the Amendment. Neither, separately, could do this.

In a very definite way, it takes something of the combination of both Tom Sawyer/Huckleberry Finn and little Scout to make it work.

For example, at the same time that Harper can cause little Scout to think humorously of reasons why women are not allowed to serve on a jury, she can have Atticus say: Serving on a jury forces a man to make up his mind and declare himself about something. Men don't like to do that. Sometimes it's unpleasant.

It takes the wisdom of a woman to make this kind of observation through a man the way Harper does. And nothing brings this into focus the way the Amendment does.

But while the logical necessity of the Amendment is there, while it epitomizes wisdom, there is no way around the fact that every person must confront himself or herself as I did when confronted by the requirements of the Amendment. And every person will have to struggle with these requirements just as I did. And there is no minimizing the enormity of such a thing! History is against us as a species being able to do such a thing!

When little Scout reads Mr. Underwood's editorial about the shooting and killing of Tom Robinson, she thinks to herself about the due process of law that led to his conviction, his defense by Atticus and the jury finding Tom guilty in spite of his obvious innocence and tries to make sense of it all.

Then it comes to her: Atticus had used every tool available to free men to save Tom Robinson, but in the secret courts of men's hearts Atticus had no case. Tom was a dead man the minute Mayella Ewell opened her mouth and screamed.

And this has been the insane history of humanity. And it is in the secret courts of men's hearts that the Amendment will be tried. And it is in the secret courts of men's hearts that the Amendment will try them. Facts are often ugly, stubborn things. But all the wishing in the world won't change them. And the ugliest facts the hearts of men have to deal with are that they have never cherished children and they have never considered women and children to be of equal value to them.

But we can either submit to the fatalistic truth of little Scout's assessment and Dill's idea of becoming helpless clowns, we can continue to destroy the wisdom of childhood and refuse to declare ourselves thereby assuring our destruction, or we can face ourselves with the facts, accept them, and do those things necessary for finally attaining wisdom. And I submit that the Amendment is a first step in doing so.

For those good people whose hearts and minds the Amendment reaches, I would urge you to do as I have done. Get involved politically. Write those letters to the editor, your Governor and legislators. If you are on the net, chat and post your own messages or web pages.

I get many requests for support in the form of donations from individuals, organizations, and politicians. As a matter of course, I always reply by sending their material back with a flyer for the Amendment. I make a note to them: When I get your response to the enclosed, I will consider supporting you.

This always accomplishes at least one of three things: They will ignore me, take me off their mailing list, or respond.

A small thing? Sure. But it is just one of many small things that can add up to a major influence.

Some of you have a favorite columnist or TV newsperson or personality. Many of you have favorite actors and actresses, sports figures; many of you belong to churches or other organizations you support. Send or give them a flyer for the Amendment and ask their opinion. Don't ask for their support for the Amendment; ask them for an opinion. The support will follow if you can reach such people favorably. But first you have to get their interest; you have to make them knowledgeable that such a thing as the Amendment exists.

Equal rights for all, special privileges for none! is an ideal that has never happened; and isn't going to happen without wisdom. And until children are cherished, until women and children become of equal value to men, the wisdom of equality and denial of special privilege will remain unattainable.

Prejudice and bigotry don't make sense to children. As Scout, Jem and Dill struggle with the insanity of such things, Scout notices something strange.

Her third grade teacher is a Miss Gates. During a class discussion, the persecution of the Jews by Hitler comes up. Miss Gates, a Jew herself, waxes eloquent on Hitler's mistreatment of the Jews and uses his abuse of authority to compare it to the democratic government, the freedom and equality of America and American citizens.

But after Tom Robinson's trial, Scout overhears Miss Gates making very derogatory comments about Negroes. It doesn't make sense to Scout. How can Miss Gates talk about Hitler's mistreatment of the Jews square with her obvious dislike of Negroes as though colored people were the inferiors of Miss Gates?

Children are keen observers of adults. But it isn't possible for them to understand the prejudices and bigotry of adults. Scout couldn't possibly understand the hatred engendered in those like Miss Gates, most particularly Miss Gates, because of a Negro feeling sorry for a white woman. Such a thing was not only incomprehensible to those like Miss Gates and to those on the jury, it was inexcusable effrontery! Why, it was almost as much as those people saying they're as good as us! I underline those people because you surely realize that those people could be anybody to anybody. Such has been the entire history of the human race.

I mention this ugly incident because it so clearly underscores why Scout finally realized Tom Robinson was a dead man as soon as Mayella Ewell screamed. That's a pretty tough thing to hand a small child. And when in history has it ever been any different? It hasn't. Is it any different now? No. Children throughout history have been handed this very same tough thing and it is just as rampant today as it has ever been.

But you cannot possibly fight successfully against prejudice and bigotry while at the same time condoning other kinds of perversion such as homosexuality, infidelity in marriage, abortion and pornography. Children are wise enough to know this.

But if we, as adults, will confront, do battle and overcome these evils, showing children we do care about them, that we cherish them through guarding and protecting their innocence as it is our obligation to do, we will finally acquire wisdom.

And it will be the kind of wisdom that will save humanity, it will be the kind of wisdom that led little Scout to insist on Boo Radley offering his arm rather than her leading him home by the hand like a child.

When Boo pleaded so pitifully to Scout: Will you take me home? she knew he was a frightened child. The man, this mad man, who had just killed an evil man in order to save her and Jem, was now only a frightened child pleading for her to take him home.

Scout had already shown the depth of her wisdom, that great part of wisdom which only a child understands fully in its depth of love, compassion, and instinctive hatred of evil, in agreeing with Sheriff Tate that to tell the truth about Boo would be in Scout's words and thinking sorta like shootin' a mockingbird.

But now as her wisdom has increased, she faces the plea of this grown man: Will you take me home? the words said almost in a whisper in the voice of a child afraid of the dark, as Scout describes them.

She would lead him by the hand through the house and out onto the porch where the Sheriff and Atticus are discussing what to do. But she will not lead him home by the hand like a child. No!

Let Scout describe it in her own words:

I put my foot on the top step and stopped. I would lead him through our house, but I would never lead him home.

Mr. Arthur, bend your arm down here, like that. That's right sir.

I slipped my hand into the crook of his arm.

He had to stoop a little to accommodate me, but if Miss Stephanie Crawford was watching from her upstairs window, she would see Arthur Radley escorting me down the sidewalk, as any gentleman would do.

I can feel the sting of tears and a lump in my throat as I write of this. And I'm not ashamed to admit it. For your sake I have to admit it because I don't believe any one of any sensitivity can avoid feeling as I do when this whole scene unfolds. For those who do not feel as I do about this, I have to wonder....

A mad man, a mad guardian angel, their childhood bogeyman, has saved these children's lives. And now, little Scout is walking him home, her hand in his arm, a little lady and her gentleman friend. Let the neighbors stare and wonder! They would see Arthur Radley escorting me down the sidewalk, as any gentleman would do.

Folks, that is the epitome of wisdom on the part of a little eight year old girl, it is the wisdom adults pound out of children by bowing to the wicked dictum: When they get a little older, they won't cry about it anymore, they will understand they can't do anything about the evil in the world.

And so it is that good people have always excused themselves for not confronting and overcoming evil. To tell a child: You have to take what life deals you, and then to hypocritically refuse to do your part in doing all that is in your power to make that life all you can by being a responsible adult and doing your duty is damnable!

But this has been the history of the human race. And it cannot, must not, continue! Good people are going to have to confront their prejudices, their sins, and do better! If it is sin to kill a mockingbird, for example, isn't it a greater sin to allow the predators of children to roam our world or to murder an unborn child? Where, any thinking person must ask him- or herself, are our priorities?

We must ask ourselves, sensibly, are the present priorities leading to the advancement of civilized peace or Armageddon? And I believe any sensible person knows the fearful and horrifying answer to this question!

It wouldn't have occurred to Harper because of her being a woman, because of her being such a lady. She left it to me as a man to point it out and make something of it: Scout would be the only lady, a little eight year old lady, to ever grace the arm of Boo: Mr. Arthur Radley. And for me as a man, that is one of the deepest of the tragedies in the whole book. And yet...

Scout would not realize this of course. After all, she is only eight years old and should not realize it. It is one of the great benefits of childhood to not have to realize or even be aware of such things.

Scout never saw Boo again. But I like to believe he died peacefully and content. He had been the guardian angel of the children. In what had to have been the sanest moment of his life, he was there for them.

But, then, the children had been his guardian angels in turn. And at no time more than when a little lady graced his arm as she walked with him and he was no longer Boo, but the gentleman Mr. Arthur Radley escorting the little lady Miss Jean Louise Finch.

I believe I could die content with such a treasured memory alone.

It was only fitting that Scout should be sad thinking that in spite of all Boo's gifts to them, even saving their lives; she and her brother had never given Boo anything in return.

But Harper did point out the benefit to Boo in watching the children through the close-shuttered windows of his dark tomb of a house. The joy it must have brought to him in watching them and placing those small gifts in the hole of that tree for them to discover. Even taking part in a kind of game they devised about him that he surely watched through those shuttered windows, and even enjoying the attempts by the children to get a glimpse of him. Boo shared in the children's lives and they, unknowingly, gave that degree of reason and happiness to a mad man. They became his children.

And in the end, they became one another's guardian angels and Boo became Mr. Arthur Radley and Scout became Miss Jean Louise Finch. As I said, I like to believe Boo died content with that memory to sustain him to the end; would that all adults throughout the world, believing themselves sane, were as insane as Boo Radley.

But, then, it has taken the putting of many years behind me to take the first step and begin the long and torturous journey to such insanity myself. And that first step would never have been taken if it were not for my own children and grandchildren together with the screams of pain, and finally the lonely whispered prayers for the kindness of death, to deliver two little girls in a black, cold dungeon in Belgium which finally penetrated my own hard heart and made me hear and listen to those screams, and finally, the whispered pleadings for death of those two little ones.

I believe God has spared me the kind of nightmares that have to afflict any parent who has had a child tortured and murdered, as were little Melissa and Julie and so many others. I cannot perceive of any such parent retaining their sanity under such circumstance. I believe I wouldn't have the courage to continue living with such a nightmare.

I suppose such parents who do go on living become insane. It would take such a kind and humane mechanism to enable such parents to function as though they were alive though a portion of their mind would have to be disabled. As a behavioral scientist I can accept this.

The monsters that prey on children can usually be identified very early in their lives. But the laws protecting juveniles often prohibit taking preventive action. Agencies like the schools and Child Protective Services are so paranoid and jealous of their own empires, you will find virtually no cooperation from these institutions or agencies.

This is why so many agencies and institutions like the schools and CPS, intended for the good of families and children, are often at cross purposes.

Another factor in a failure of early identification is the threat of lawsuits. We are such a litigious society; there is virtually no area of our lives that does not invite suit at one time or another.

But as long as insanity rules a society, we can hardly expect things to get better. And it is insanity that rules.

The genius of Harper Lee was in using a mad man to balance the scales of justice. Civilized law, civilized people, could not protect the children against determined evil.

But it was the patently insane prejudice of civilized good people who loosed this evil against the children by condemning an innocent man. It is the children who always pay the price for such prejudice on the part of adults.

Our society is determined to make conditions ever worse for children by insanely continuing to let the monsters loose to roam and prey on them. And nothing will get any better until society puts these monsters away, permanently, at the very earliest.

And once these monsters are identified, the most charitable term I can use for a society that will continue to loose them to prey on children is the word insane. And if not insanity, what? A society that simply does not give a damn about children, a society that steadfastly refuses to identify these monsters at the earliest time, a society that acts like it hates children! You try to tell me what lies between these two choices!

I recently received a couple of mailings that accentuate what I am talking about, one very conservative from HUMAN EVENTS (read: Heritage Foundation) touting Robert Zelnick's expose of Al Gore, the other from the ACLU. I could hardly ask for better examples of two extremes.

Neither will touch the Amendment. And here is the reason:

Notwithstanding Emerson's failure to appreciate Thoreau, as he should have, nothing can detract from his contribution to transcendentalism. Emerson, as Thoreau, had the courage to face the errors of his childhood, the errors of his age, and lend his voice to addressing those errors.

In his essay Compensation, Emerson points out the kind of insanity on the part of good people that led to the jury convicting Tom Robinson and allowing the evil Ewell to be loose to prey on the children. It is the very kind of insanity the Amendment forced me to face and overcome in my own life.

In the era of Emerson and Thoreau, the ministry was an occupation for gentlemen. The universities were given largely to the training of promising young men for this occupation. Both Emerson and Thoreau received this university training. And both saw the inherent evils in orthodox religions and repudiated them after earnestly attempting to accommodate themselves to such teachings.

In his essay, Emerson points out a fatal flaw in the religious beliefs of most people. He had just come from a church service where the minister had delivered the traditional sermon that included the traditional promise of the Last Judgment:

But the assumption of traditional religion is that judgment is not to be expected or executed in this world, but in that which is to come. The wicked are expected to be successful and happy in this world and the righteous are expected to be unsuccessful and miserable.

Yet what import, Emerson asks, is to be expected from such orthodox teaching by the churches? Was it that houses and lands, offices, wine, horses, luxury, are had by unprincipled men whilst the saints are poor and despised; and that a compensation is to be made to these last hereafter, by giving them the like gratifications another day, - bank-stock and doubloons, venison and champagne? This must be the compensation intended; for what else? Is it that they are to have leave to pray and praise? to love and serve men? Why, that they can do now. The legitimate inference the disciple would draw was, We are to have such a good time as the sinners have now - or, to push it to its extreme import, You sin now, we shall sin by-and-by; we would sin now, if we could; not being successful we expect our revenge tomorrow.

The fallacy lay in the immense concession that the bad are successful; that justice is not done now. The blindness of the preacher consisted in deferring to the base estimate of the market of what constitutes a manly success, instead of confronting and convicting the world from the truth ... and summoning the dead to its present tribunal.

The key to Emerson's remarks is that phrase: not being successful we expect our revenge tomorrow. This is the excuse good people use for not doing their duty to confront and overcome evil. This leads to his most rational conclusion that this further leads to the fallacy which lays in the immense concession of those supposing themselves to be good to the evil; that the bad are expected to be successful and justice is not expected to be done now.

The bottom line of all such thinking on the part of good people is to blame God and not take personal responsibility for confronting evil! The perfect excuse derived from religion of good people from time immemorial.

But this is knowledge, and any reasonable person is able to understand and accept Emerson's remarks in the light of knowledge. The application of such knowledge to wisdom is another matter. And it is at this point that good people fail to gain wisdom from such knowledge for even Emerson and Thoreau failed in wisdom by not realizing or accepting the fact that ultimate wisdom is unattainable unless that other half of humanity, women, is accepted as of equal value to men.

How is it, though, that even such obvious knowledge as Emerson exemplifies is rejected by good people? Because of the prejudices of good people who choose what they want to believe in flagrant disregard of factual knowledge!

Good people holding onto their prejudices by disputing and in the face of facts thus assure a self-fulfilling prophecy of Armageddon. That there is nothing new under the sun is the fault of the prejudices of good people who will not confront their prejudices for the ugly, destructive things they are!

Only when differences based on such prejudices are set aside will good people come together in common cause to confront and overcome evil; which is the job of good people, not God or angels. Only then will there be something new under the sun, the prioritizing of children that will lead to wisdom and peace.

285

There is most certainly nothing new in Emerson's remarks. People have expressed the same thoughts since the beginnings of human history. They continue to be expressed now and, in fact, I have just done so.

But I do so to call attention to the need of the Amendment as a first step in going beyond such knowledge that Emerson expresses so succinctly, a first step toward a New Thing under the sun.

The success of the Amendment depends on good people recognizing this and acting accordingly. The Amendment gives good people a chance to set aside all prejudices of beliefs and act according to factual knowledge.

It is the right and wise thing to do. But can only be done by the setting aside of personal prejudices and coming together on the sole basis of making children the priority they have never been. And by doing so, to take that first step toward the kind of wisdom humanity has always failed to acquire and which will lead to our accepting personal responsibility for the kind of world we want for our children.

If, as Emerson alludes, we were able to summon the dead to our own tribunal, what do you suppose they would have to say? More importantly, let us suppose we were able to summon the murdered children to such a tribunal, what do you suppose they would have to say?

Can you even suppose the children would accept our feeble excuses, those excuses based on personal beliefs in God, angels, and Last Judgments of the wicked whether you are a Christian, Jew, Moslem, Hindu or without any particular or no religious belief, in lieu of our failure to do all that was our responsibility and in our power to protect them? I think not.

A while back I wrote the following:

The challenge the message of the children presents is that of awakening the consciences of adults to the all-too-often silent cry of children who cannot be heard.

What happened to a little girl that produced a woman like Mayella as opposed to a little girl like Scout and her so very different prospects as a woman? I know the Amendment confronts this monster and exposes it.

But the message can only be truly effective once it is able to find expression in the voices and language of the children. And the truth of that fact is, at times, almost more than I can bear.

It is trying to give expression to those voices of the little ones and in their language that tries my own soul. It is the searching of my own heart and mind, the writing of such things, that makes me wish there was someone who would hold my hand, someone into whose lap I could crawl just like little Scout, an Atticus who would hug me and make me feel loved and needed.

To that extent, I am not a mad man; I am as normal as any of you. I didn't ask to be born, but here I am. I wish my childhood could have lasted longer, that I could have retained the best of childhood into adulthood. But it didn't and I couldn't.

The conclusion of this gray hair: It can't be a better world for my children until it is a better world for all the Scouts, Jems, Dills, and Mayellas as well. And this isn't going to be the case until there is no further need of the little Scouts to confront lynch mobs; there are no more juries who will convict Tom Robinson, until there is no further need of Boo Radley to do the job supposedly sane and civilized people fail to do.

Good people can make this happen. But only once they get past their excuses and prejudices, and come together in agreement and with determination to overcome the evils directed at children and for the sole purpose of bringing this to pass.

As long as good people hold on to their peculiar beliefs and prejudices, making these things the priority in their lives rather than children, it will never come to pass. And if not, whom will we have to blame but ourselves?

CHAPTER TEN

Enlightened Self-interest has a basis in fact. It is a fact that the ownership of property brings responsibility with it. Since it is obvious that the owner of a home is going to be far more responsible for its maintenance than a tenant, that property ownership encourages working and building for the future, that it encourages people to be involved in the political process in order to protect their interests and investments, it is to a society's benefit to encourage home ownership.

Since the facts in such a case are evident, wisdom would dictate the application of these facts to the best ends. That is, wisdom dictates the encouraging of the ownership of property thus encouraging personal responsibility for the benefit of a society.

Such a society is far more likely to produce statesmen, rather than politicians, since such a society itself is future oriented. But the politician looks only to the next election and how he or she can stay in office rather than working for the future good.

Many, including the Founding Fathers, have seen the connection between property ownership and responsible citizenship, between property ownership and freedom. A man or woman is far more attendant on things which impinge on their freedom when it is their own property at stake. Failing to recognize this is the fatal flaw of systems such as Communism in its various forms.

As America sinks ever more deeply into a system where the distance between the rich and the poor widens, we face the concomitant loss of freedom. As this widening gap evidences itself more and more, the lack of wisdom becomes ever more apparent as well.

It is not wise to promote either the acquisition of wealth through avarice or to encourage indolence. A requirement of good government, especially on the part of those who would govern themselves, is to ensure the personal responsibility of the private citizen through enlightened self-interest. That is, to encourage the private ownership of property while at the same time discouraging the kind of avarice; which would promote a wide division between the rich and the poor.

While the facts of this are painfully obvious, the application of these facts in wisdom is painfully missing. And since the history of the human race has been one of warfare, wisdom has quite obviously always been missing.

Personal ownership of property must be that: Property ownership. Not being in bondage to moneylenders through excessive mortgages.

But it would take wisdom to avoid such a system of mortgages, which is as old as civilization. And such a system rightly calls into question the whole matter of just how civilized are we, really?

As to America, slavery was introduced early on. And this system of slavery was not, in spite of the wise counsel of men like Franklin, abolished by our Constitution at the beginning. But the reason it was not has its roots in very complex matters.

While it is easy enough to damn those who supported slavery on the basis of economics, not to mention the sheer immorality of such a thing, it must also be kept in mind that it was such an economy that produced much of the wealth which promoted our beginnings as a nation. The question naturally arises, would we have been successful in our beginnings without such wealth? The further question must be asked whether we should have succeeded on such a basis?

But to take the high ground, one must go back even further to the very origins of slavery itself and trace it to its basis in America. If one take the trouble to do so, the lack of wisdom in human history becomes evident since wealth in the hands of a few has invariably required slavery in some form or another. Our own forms of wage and welfare slavery are acutely self-evident.

It is equally evident that it is impossible to be both ignorant and free. Thanks in the greater part to our universities our own form of government has degenerated into a system which promotes a widening division between the haves and the have-nots, and between those who are truly educated and those who are not. It has become a system which promotes ignorance and indolence. Or, to put it another way, it has become a system which promotes slavery.

One of the ugliest manifestations of this form of slavery is found in the multiplied millions who, in perverted definitions of freedom and democracy, are housed, fed and clothed by the efforts of others, and therefore brings the greater majority into bondage whether productive workers or drones. Wisdom would dictate that such a system is doomed since it increasingly steals initiative from those who do the work.

If wisdom does indeed consist of the application of knowledge to the best ends, it therefore falls to those in authority to make such application. But in our case, those in authority are politicians rather than statesmen. As a result, such leaders as I have said are not future oriented.

But to change this would require an enlightened and educated electorate. And how is this to be accomplished?

As to a Weltanschauung, a world-view, wisdom dictates that as long as religious and political hatreds exist and are even encouraged, the world can never know peace. Wisdom further dictates that sophistries and arguments based on a priori presumptive ignorance avail nothing.

Without argument, some machinery of government is necessary for the collective and individual good. But such a government must be the servant of the people. And it cannot be so without just leaders and just laws. And these require wisdom, which in turn requires an educated and enlightened electorate.

But I have long maintained wisdom is impossible without including women in philosophy on a basis of equal value with men, for it is philosophy, The Great Conversation, which guides the course of nations.

At present, we in California face the fact of a corrupt police department in Los Angeles, which is making international news. Without question, when a society degenerates into one where money, avarice, is the motivating factor, abuses of authority are inevitable. When a so-called justice system is so corrupt that it becomes, in fact, how much justice you can afford, the end of a society, which encourages this, is easily predictable.

If ignorance and prejudice are encouraged in any society or nation, the end of such is easily predictable. Thoreau said of his time: Shams and delusions are esteemed for soundest truths, while reality is fabulous.

Have things changed for the better in this respect in the 150 years since Henry penned those words? No, they have not. As the popularity of astrology, belief in UFOs, angels and demons of every description prove.

I have written much about the wisdom of childhood. Of children, Thoreau wrote: Children, who play life, discern its true law and relations more clearly than men, who fail to live it worthily, but who think that they are wiser by experience, that is, by failure ... I have always been regretting that I was not as wise as the day I was born.

While my friend Henry never married nor had children, he was brilliant enough to discern the truth of the wisdom of childhood, the truth brought out so brilliantly in Harper Lee's To Kill A Mockingbird.

But Henry and Harper Lee both wrote better than they knew in this respect. The real wisdom of childhood rests in the fact that children recognize injustice and weep over it.

And while both writers recognized this, neither realized the foundation of such wisdom, which derives from the ability of children to recognize and avoid evil with an instinctive hatred of it. But adults will place their hands on a book of myths and superstitions like the Bible and swear to tell the truth, and then lie on behalf of injustice. In part because many recognize the hypocrisy of swearing an oath with their hands placed on such a book and respond in kind.

This is only one example of many hypocrisies which are taught to children by adults whereby children, as they grow older, lose the wisdom of childhood.

***

By President Clinton copied from CNN:

"Good morning. This week I had the honor of lighting both the national Christmas tree and the national Menorah. Both are symbols of a time of year filled with joy, hope and expectation. A time, too, when we reflect on what we've done and what is left to do, a time to honor our obligations to family and community."

DECEMBER 23, 2000

This prompted the following letter from me to George W. Bush:
President Elect George W. Bush
Number 411
603 West 13th Street, Suite 1A
Austin, Texas 78701-1795

Dear Sir:

As a California State Advisor to the National Republican Senatorial Committee I have an obligation to inform you of a major concern of mine. More than this, I feel it a duty and responsibility as an American Citizen to make this concern known to you as my next President

It is my most sincere hope that as our President you will not lend yourself to the kind of religious propaganda that makes for such a dangerous and demon-haunted world as Carl Sagan warned of.

It was enough that William Clinton disgraced our nation and made us a laughingstock, but the lighting of a "National Menorah" I find thoroughly repugnant to me as an American.

Make no mistake, I would find the lighting of a "National Cross" equally repugnant. And all the religious propaganda aside, the Menorah is as distinctive to the Jewish religion as the Star of David and the world recognizes this.

A major concern of mine as an American is the message this sends to those Arab nations in particular that America has taken the side of Israel in spite of the killing of Palestinians and the refusal of Israel on religious grounds to be reasonable in the peace process.

While I fully recognize the religious hatreds and prejudices on both sides, America cannot hope to lead in the peace process by engaging in such through taking sides on the basis of a religion, whether Jewish, Christian, or Islamic.

I am taking the liberty of sending a copy of this letter to a number of other people, including my congressman and senators, as well as some of the leaders of other nations. As an American citizen, I do not want other nations to think that I give my approval as an American to any religious superstition or prejudice.

The myths, superstitions, and prejudices of religion continue to make the world a dangerous and demon-haunted place. But the very idea of America approving a "National Menorah" is not only an affront to me as an American, it has to be an affront to other nations as well and just one more reason for the distrust of America on the part of other nations. Further, this has to be a "Line in the sand" that those like Saddam Hussein and Osama bin Laden will use to their propaganda advantage against America.

In all fairness and justice, America cannot be represented as a nation that favors one religion over another. And the separation between Church and State, as our Founding Fathers clearly and wisely perceived, must be rigidly enforced. As a nation, and for the sake of world peace, we cannot engage in the kind of national prejudice and hypocrisy that a "National Menorah" signifies.

Respectfully;
Samuel D. G. Heath, Ph. D.

***

Very few people outside the systems of entertainment and the universities know of the inordinate power of homosexuals within these. But when you wonder at the violent cartoon shows on TV, these are the product of the power of homosexuals who have taken over so much of children's programming.

The agenda of homosexuals is to promote their perversion and their target audience is children. The TV show Park Place is a perfect example of this.

You may well wonder at the part violence plays in this since the perception of so-called Gays, who are anything but gay in the correct use of the term, is one of non-violence. Thanks to Tom Hanks and Leonardo DiCaprio et al, every pervert is a sensitive artist.

Nothing could be further from the truth. Yet Hollywood and the universities promote this Big Lie. And since perversion has infected so much of our state and federal legislatures, it explains why so many in these institutions support the homosexual agenda.

As a deist, I believe in God but I despise systems of religion as superstition and no better than things like astrology, and having done far more harm than good throughout history. So I can hardly have a personal religious bias myself in regard to perversion.

But I do have a logical basis, one not dependant on whether one believes in God or not, upon which to confront homosexuals for the bullying tactics they employ. For example, how is it that a perfectly logical and normal revulsion to perversion is now called homophobic? Who made this a politically correct term? And for what purpose? One only has to look to the universities and the propaganda tactics of Hitler and Goebbels to understand this.

Thanks to the universities, the judiciary and Hollywood, it is politically correct to support perversion and incorrect to support family and family values. It is correct to attack white racism and incorrect to attack minority racism.

While racism on the part of whites against those of color is rightly denounced, where are the mobs of protesting marchers denouncing the racism of blacks against whites? A little white boy is dragged to death by a black man, a black man goes on a killing spree shooting white people loudly proclaiming his intentions of seeking out white people to murder, and a black boy murders a white girl at school. But there is no outrage on the part of black leaders against these criminal acts. Why is it that Jesse Jackson, Al Sharpton, Louis Farrakhan, and Alan Keyes are not denouncing these criminal acts of blacks against whites and asking for demonstrations against such racism on the part of black people?

It should be patently obvious that this is a rhetorical question. It is politically correct to denounce and demonstrate against white racism, but not black or Hispanic racism. And all the evidence, which is quite substantial, of racism on the part of white people does not excuse its parallel on the part of non-whites.

As I have pointed out to these black leaders, they do their own people a great disservice and cause grave harm to their own cause by not denouncing and demonstrating against such things in their own ranks. There is a monumental loss of credibility as a result. You simply do not denounce unfairness and injustice on the part of one group without attacking these things with equal fervor among your own and rightly expect to be taken seriously.

Religion, Race, and Politics are the predominant causes of an increasingly dangerous and demon-haunted world. Even as I write, the tensions between China and Taiwan, between India and Pakistan grow increasingly dangerous. North Korea seems determined on a nuclear arsenal. The conflicts in

Ireland and Africa show no signs of abating. And in each of these cases, the propaganda of political correctness holds sway, and is often rooted in religious prejudices such as those of India and Pakistan. And in Israel, moderate politics is threatened by religious fanaticism, which finds its match in the abominably cruel and totally uncivilized fanaticism of the Moslem Taliban.

Just recently Bill Bradley in his concession speech quoted Vince Lombardi: Winning isn't everything, it is the only thing! And for fanatics, this is absolutely true! And whether the fanaticism of race, religion or politics, winning is the only thing! But far too many people supposing themselves to be good people don't get the message. And that message is very direct and eminently logical: Evil can only be overcome by the good when the good confronts the evil with equal determination to win!

It is politically correct to attack gun owners and incorrect to support the rights of law-abiding citizens to protect themselves against criminals who abuse the use of guns. It is politically correct to attack legitimate, law-abiding gun owners instead of making the criminal abuse of guns the legitimate goal of prosecution.

It is politically correct to make the use of marijuana a crime and continue to leave tobacco and alcohol legal drugs. And in all reason we must ask why alcohol has not been attacked with the same fervor as tobacco? We need only look to the drunks in Congress to answer that one. Why is the drug war one that the leadership continues to pursue yet knows cannot be won? Here, as usual, follow the money is part of the answer. I say part because the rest has to do with power over the people and influence in the major drug-supplying countries like Mexico and Colombia.

Why is it politically incorrect to address the extreme abuse of law and taxpayer expense of illegal aliens when it is patently obvious that no other nation in the world puts up with this insanity, when logic dictates that no nation that cannot control its borders can survive? Follow the money; and the building of political agendas and empires. And how did it become politically correct to refer to these criminals as <u>immigrants</u> instead of what they are in fact: criminal illegal aliens? As with the bullying propaganda tactics used by perverts to advance their cause, call all those racists who oppose illegal, and by definition criminal, aliens entering America.

Why is making English the national language politically incorrect? Again: Money and political power.

It continues to be politically correct to arrest and prosecute women as prostitutes but not the men who hire them. But what makes people like J.F. Kennedy and W.J. Clinton exempt from treating women like prostitutes and jail women for prostitution? What kind of message does this send everyone, children as well as adults? No, I'm not that naïve, but I know it still isn't right.

Anymore than it makes me naïve to know we have a justice system that is one of how much justice you can afford.

Why isn't the murder of a child of equal gravity to that of a politician or policeman? Why is molestation not treated as a crime of the very gravest consequences to the whole of society? And why is it that the black leadership never addresses this issue which is pandemic in black communities and leads to the early puberty of black children? Talk about politically incorrect!

With over a quarter-million accidents a year caused by those who run red lights, who disagrees that cameras which record these drivers and enables a system which sends them a ticket is not a good idea? It won't be those whose cars, even lives, are destroyed by these law-breakers. Too many of whom are not even licensed or insured! Will anyone disagree who has had to bury a child killed by these law-breakers?

As politicians wring their hands and posture with endless rhetoric over the murder of a child by another child, where are their concerns properly directed at an entire society of their making which has exhibited little but indifference toward children? The history of lip-service by politicians which is only given for the reasons of an election or staying in office, not out of true concern for children, is evident to all.

I would be the last to say that addressing the real evils in society is an easy task. But I would also be the last to say that we have an elected leadership capable of addressing these evils.

But I won't let average citizens off the hook either. If you are not politically knowledgeable and active, you are a part of the problem as well. We get the kind of leadership we actively support!

Reform in education is impossible when the very people who created the problems are asked for solutions. But these people who created the problems in education are the very same who will say a six year old boy does not know what he is doing when he shoots another child to death. I would ask the reasonable question of these people: At what age does a child become aware that shooting another child to death is wrong? The so-called experts have no answer to this. But they are very quick to say it isn't six years old.

I totally disagree. I have known children this age that are fully aware of their actions. But such things are generally seen in their cruelty to animals and later acted out toward people. In such cases, where are the responsible adults who should be held accountable for their children?

But the experts in the schools, law, psychology will make every excuse to keep from being held accountable when the cruelty and bullying behavior of some children results in the murder of another child. Why do we not hold these experts accountable for their developing a system that creates victims in our schools and never holds the victimizer accountable; or their parents?

Then we come back to the origins of an evil that has done so much to destroy families, then denies any culpability for the consequences. It is truly an insane system, which continues to create victims, and does nothing to effectively remove the bullying predators of whatever age or for whatever reason they are so.

But there is one inescapable fact that the great majority of thinking people accept: No child, regardless of environment, genetics, or whatever, who bullies and threatens other children should be allowed to put other children at risk. The family and the schools should be held responsible for not allowing these kinds of children to put other children at risk!

***

AMERICANS FOR CONSTITUTIONAL PROTECTION OF CHILDREN

NO NATION THAT FAILS TO CHERISH ITS YOUNG HAS ANY FUTURE AS A NATION.

NOR DOES IT DESERVE ONE!

DEDICATED TO ZERO TOLERANCE OF CHILD MOLESTERS!

IT SHOULDN'T HURT TO BE A CHILD!

PROPOSED AMENDMENT TO THE U.S. CONSTITUTION

An adult convicted of the molestation of a child will be sentenced to prison for a term of not less than ten years.

If the child dies as a result of the molestation the person(s) convicted of the crime will be sentenced to life in prison without the possibility of parole.

A child as defined by this article shall be one who has not attained their sixteenth birthday.

The Congress shall have power to enforce this article by appropriate legislation.

HEATH'S EQUATION

Given that correct knowledge consists of facts as opposed to beliefs and that wisdom consists of love and compassion together with a love of truth and an instinctive hatred of evil:

KNOWLEDGE + WISDOM = PEACE

(K+W=P)

If this equation is correct, it logically follows that the world has never attained to wisdom since the world has never known peace.

It is my contention that the world can never attain wisdom as long as a full half of humanity, women, is excluded from having an equal voice with men in the decision-making processes guiding national and world affairs.

It is my further contention that men and women are of equal value on the basis of the compatibility of differences.

It logically follows that until children become the priority of nations and until women are accepted and included by men as of equal value that wisdom, and by extension peace, will continue to be unattainable.

If it can be agreed that parents, regardless of differences of circumstances and political or religious ideologies, essentially want the same things for their children, the same hope of a future for their children, the emphasis should be on the best way of attaining such a future.

Quite obviously it has been the exclusion of women from the philosophies of men, the exclusion of women as of equal value to men, the lack of proper emphasis placed on the future of our species, our children, the insistence on emphasizing political and religious differences rather than what is best for all children, that has kept the world in conflict these past thousands of years.

This must change. And the only way it can change for the better is for people to agree on a course of action that will lead to such a change on the basis of wisdom. I submit that the proposed amendment is a logical and wise first step in such a change for the better.

But we have reached a point of decision where the world has become far too dangerous and violent to any longer ignore the fact that until the proper emphasis is placed on the future of the human race, our children, Armageddon looms ominously.

The question that confronts all of humanity is whether the differences of religion and politics will continue to predominate or whether people of the world will come together and agree on a course of action that will insure a future for all children regardless of the historic hatreds and prejudices based on religion and politics.

The proposed amendment to the Constitution is a logical first step toward solving the historic problems of religious and political hatreds. The amendment addresses a problem about which all good people agree and proposes a solution completely devoid of any religious or political ideologies. It is simply the right and wise thing to do for the sake of our posterity.

No nation in history has ever made children a priority by virtue of its foundational charter of government. America, I strongly believe, has the obligation to be the first nation in history to do so. And, I further believe, with America leading the way, other nations will follow.

Samuel D.G. Heath, Ph. D.

***

Just how harmful is it to swear an oath on the Bible? The question has a lot of merit. Since my doctorate is in human behavior, such questions pique my curiosity. Just how has swearing an oath on a Bible affected history? And how does it still do so?

In my critique of To Kill A Mockingbird, I point out how neither Mayella nor her father had any reluctance to swearing to tell the truth in court, with their hands on a Bible, and then lied knowing their false testimony would send another human being to his death. Apart from Harper Lee's Pulitzer-winning novel, history is replete with actual cases of this nature, and the practice continues to this day.

We still hold to the hoary tradition of swearing in leaders to elected office with the oath of office taken by such leaders placing their hands on a Bible. William Clinton took such an oath, as have many others.

That many such people place no credence in such oaths and do not feel bound by them may have something to do with their knowing the Bible is a book of myths and fables, and therefore not to be taken seriously. And under such circumstances, neither is their oath of office or such an oath in a court of law.

There are millions such as the Ewells of TKM who will tell you they believe the Bible to be the very word of God. And then lie with their hands on the book. We may reasonably ask whether such people do, in fact, believe the book to be the very word of God. Which gave rise to the expression: I wouldn't believe him with his hand on a stack of Bibles!

While this use, and abuse, of the Bible has had a grave import in history, I do wonder if such a historical superstition and mythology continues to have an impact on our present day systems of judicial and government affairs?

That people like President Clinton, and the Ewells of TKM, do not feel bound to tell the truth under an oath in such circumstances, one should not discount the fact, and should consider it, that such people will defend the Bible as being the word of God, a holy book, the Holy Scriptures.

Then how to account for the discrepancy in fact by such people failing to practice what they say they believe? We are keenly aware of the parental admonition, if not always spoken at least believed: Do as I say, not as I do. It would be a mistake to take swearing an oath with hand on the Bible as simple hypocrisy, or even cynicism. It is far more than that. And it is far more than the formality of ceremonial tradition.

Many people believe, or would like to believe, that God has provided an instruction manual for humanity in the form of the Bible. Some believe the Koran to be such a manual.

There is a strong element of the need to believe which is implicit in such things. It is a most seductive thought, that God has literally given instructions to humanity, has actually spoken to men and women, and that these instructions and words of His are to be found in a book.

But underlying this need to believe, there is a strong element of doubt about such things, even among those who profess to believe. And there is also a large element of superstition, which treats of such writings much as a talisman, a charm or rabbit's foot. Believing in things like luck and various mechanisms to enhance chance, belief in astrology, all such things are in the same category as belief in books like the Bible and Koran.

With this exception: Charms, etc. are not usually treated with the fervor of religious fanaticism, as so closely related to divinity and deity.

When a person declares: God said! God told me! God says in his word! The Bible says! These declarations by people are much different than superstitions such as beliefs in lucky charms and amulets.

But a superstition of thousands of year's duration which has been proven to be without any foundation in fact and is still found relevant to a nation's leadership cannot be discounted as being detrimental to that nation's functioning.

It is, therefore, a legitimate source of inquiry as to the extent of the Bible's influence for evil in our system of law and leadership.

To a rational mind, the very idea that the Bible is, in fact, the word of God is repugnant. Still, the rational mind has to deal with the fact that multiplied millions in our society still hold the book to be, if not holy or sacred, venerated in some fashion.

Taken as simply a book, albeit one of antiquity in some respects, but keeping in mind there are other writings far more ancient, the Bible has no more to offer in wisdom or philosophy than many others. And the claims of supernatural origins are not only patently ridiculous, but are in fact injurious as per the wars fought and millions killed on this basis.

***

Special Education

The following is an excerpt from a larger work intended for governors Gray Davis and George Bush along with legislators like Dianne Feinstein and Barbara Boxer.

It was in another life it seems that I sat with California State Senator Ed Davis in his office in Sacramento. We had established a warm correspondence when he was LAPD Chief of Police and I was a fledgling freshman teacher at David Starr Jordan in the Watts district of South Central Los Angeles.

By the time of this meeting, I was no longer the naive young man who thought the problems in education would be relatively easy to fix. The travesty of the sixties in education such as Innovative Designs in Learning which cast out the things that had worked and instituted the things that made no sense whatsoever had done their dirty work. Children were going to pay the price of the adult abrogation of responsibility for their education.

The sacred cows remain the same, the universities which were untouchable then are equally untouchable today in spite of the damning indictment of them through research and writing like that of Professor Reginald G. Damerell and so many others including me.

I focused on Accountability in Education in my own Ph.D. dissertation only to discover it was such a hot button no publisher would touch it. Only one ed. publisher at the time was honest enough to tell me that the material in my dissertation was such an indictment of the schools he didn't dare publish it!

I discovered that the school systems from the universities on down are so rife with corruption and such cronyism and nepotism as to be inbred to the point of impotence. Then I discovered that legislators were dedicated to asking the very people who created the problems in education for answers to the very problems they had created! Insane on the face of it!

And while I would never accuse the educational hierarchy of the purposeful destruction of public education, I do say they could not have better designed a system for failure had they done so intentionally!

I found that schools are not held fiscally accountable because of such creative bookkeeping it is impossible to audit them and the money is embezzled at will in the amount of countless hundreds of millions of dollars every year throughout California alone. The fox that guards the henhouse, the State Department of Education, has its reasons for not wanting this publicized, not the least of these being the public outcry it would cause together with the potential loss of so much federal funding.

I discovered first hand how tenure was abused to the point that the worst teachers who wouldn't have been allowed to continue to work a week in the private sector were guaranteed jobs for life in education, especially in the universities, and children and college students paid the price for such incompetence and lack of accountability throughout the entire system of public education.

I was at ground zero when Special Education began to be the cash cow for schools, a blank check no one questioned as empire building at its very worst became the norm in the public schools. Had I not personally witnessed what I have in this system alone, I don't think anyone could fictionalize the enormous boondoggle of this single education bureaucracy!

I began to try to tell parents and legislators like Ed Davis and Gary Hart, governors like Pete Wilson, that the problems for children in education were not as bad as they thought, they were far, far worse!

I saw our classrooms being filled with teachers, products of the universities, who could not spell or do arithmetic and no one dared say anything about it! Why not? Because virtually every leader throughout society is a university graduate and would never criticize the institutions on which their own academic credibility and future success were based!

And teachers such as me with industry backgrounds knew the Ivory Tower mind-set was incapable of preparing children for real life. And most teachers who witnessed the terrible destruction of education would not speak out for fear of losing their jobs or becoming pariahs.

It has become the stock in trade of politicians to talk about educational reform. But politics being the trade of generalities does not deal with specifics and politicians always evade answering in specifics because they do not have any specifics when it comes to educational reform (or a host of other problems)!

No one knows better than I the enormity of the problems in education and the enormity of what will be required to fix them.

But as long as our children are defrauded of an education because politicians refuse to deal with the specifics, or even worse, have no idea of what the specifics are, I will continue to be a voice raised against the tragedy of ignorance that has invaded America and become the legacy of so-called educators and their crony political quislings passed on to our children.

Governor Gray Davis saw fit to pass my critique of To Kill A Mockingbird on to State Senator Gary Hart, the head of California's Education Committee. Senator Hart sent me a kind Thank you note.

Politicians have always been very gracious in thanking me for my concerns about our children and their education. But not a single one has ever followed through by doing the hard things my own research and experience proves need to be done. One school board president who tried to institute just a couple of the needed reforms I had suggested lost in the next election because of this.

In spite of my cautionary words, he didn't believe the furor this would cause among teachers who actively campaigned (illegally of course) against him in their very classrooms, even sending flyers produced in the school audio/visual department home with their pupils and taking out ads in the local paper against this man for re-election.

Of course, things were made pretty hot for me as well. I was betraying my kind and biting the hand that fed me.

It is easy to do the trend-forecast of where the present concerns about the latest enormously expensive and tragic boondoggle of education, that of Special Education, will lead. Nowhere. Once the noise dies down, it will be back to business as usual. The educational hierarchy from the universities on down depend on this.

Oh yes, audits there will be. A few arrests may even be made for blatant offenses and thefts that cannot be hidden no matter the creative book- and record-keeping.

But like the I.R.S. and California's Social Services, particularly Child Protective Services, the enormity of the task will make any meaningful audits virtually impossible. The educational hierarchy knows and depends on this to, as one principal told me, do their own dirty laundry and not expose it to the public.

His refreshing candor reminded me of that of a Downey Chief of Police who told me in an interview: We're not here to help people; we're here to slam the door on them!

Like expressed concern about child abuse, the problems in the Evil Empire of Special Education will sell papers and make for News at Eleven and political rhetoric for a while. And then, quietly fade away until someone sees a way of making headlines and political hay of it once more.

Harper Lee addressed the failure of the schools in Thirties' Alabama. I witnessed it as a teacher in Sixties' California. And not just during my tenure in the war zones of the ghetto of Watts and the barrio of East San Jose, but places like lily-white Castro Valley and throughout Stanislaus County; and, of course, my home county of Kern, the target of Edward Humes' Pulitzer-winning book.

It was in my home County of Kern that I had a group of high school seniors applaud me for telling them: Any real education you get here will be because you earnestly desire and work for it, not because this school is really prepared and dedicated to giving you an education.

These seniors knew the truth of what I was telling them. Their applause was for my being the only adult school authority that had made such a bald and honest confession to them of the failure of the school system to provide them the opportunity for an education, had in fact defrauded them of an education.

The applause caught the attention of teachers and administrators. When they discovered the reason for it, I was not invited back. But I knew that would be the result. I've always been known as a high-roller on behalf of the kids against the system. It is one reason I have worked in so many different school systems in spite of reaching tenure in two of them.

Tragically for our children and young people, my words to that group of seniors would apply with equal truth in schools across America. And while young people like the class of seniors mentioned know the truth and will applaud me for telling it like it is, it doesn't win me any friends among those adult authorities who should be my friends for telling it like it is.

***

CONVENTION ON THE RIGHTS OF THE CHILD

I received a letter from President Clinton in reply to my question why the U.S. has not ratified the Convention on the Rights of the Child? Since this is the second, direct and personal letter to me from the President I guess you could say we have become regular pen pals. I have to wonder if that phrase won't take on a different connotation at some future date?

He told me that before he sends the Convention to the Senate, he wants to insure there is nothing in it that would cause litigation in U.S. courts.

My reply to the President was that I shared his concern but would appreciate, as would UNICEF, the matter being given a high priority. It makes little sense for the U.S. to have played a major role in the writing of the Convention and then drag its feet on ratification.

By all means, tell others of the amendment and the Convention and try to make presentations to your church or any organization to which you belong. Encourage discussion but please, and this cannot be emphasized too strongly, know what you are talking about! Study the literature of the amendment and Convention before you speak to groups especially. If you make yourself look foolish, you make the cause you espouse look foolish as well.

For example, people will ask about false accusations of molestation leading to imprisonment. This is not a legitimate question since the constitutional guarantee of Due Process applies to all criminal trials equally of whatever nature. But you must be prepared to answer people who are concerned about such things in good faith.

For those with the computer capability, use a web site and the various chat rooms to advertise the amendment. The following are some important web addresses you should know:

UNICEF
http://www.unicef.org/pon96/cotransl.htm
Everyone working for the amendment should write UNICEF and request the material from the World Congress against Commercial Sexual Exploitation of Children and a copy of the Convention on the Rights of the Child. Please enclose a donation to UNICEF of a minimum of $5.00 to cover costs.

Address your request to:
UNICEF
333 East 38th Street
New York, NY 10016
Phone (212) 686-5522
Fax (212) 779-1679

National Committee to Prevent Child Abuse (NCPCA):
http://www.childabuse.org/5096sum.html
332 S. Michigan Avenue, Suite 1600
Chicago, IL 60604
Phone (312) 663-3520
Fax (312) 939-8962

National Center for Missing and Exploited Children:
http://www.missingkids.org/childsafety.html
2101 Wilson Blvd., Suite 550
Arlington, VA 22201
Phone (703) 235-3900

http://www.childabuse.com

Centers for Disease Control and Prevention (CDC):
http://www.cdc.gov/epo/mmwr/preview/mm4621.htm#article2

Part of the game unscrupulous people play is to use their organization to call someone world renowned for the sake of publicity, the old scholars-quoting-scholars ploy. By plugging each other, they build a circle of usually spurious wannabes.

That is the mechanism of propaganda. Tell a lie often enough and people begin to believe it. Call a pretender and charlatan an expert often enough and uninformed, intellectually lazy and ignorant people begin to believe it.

Universities are notorious for lying propaganda. For example, it was recently noted that college textbooks are actually pessimistic, even inaccurate, about marriage and marriage statistics. That's right. By trying to make perversion an acceptable lifestyle, since there are so many homosexuals in the schools, the universities have gone out of their way to denigrate marriage.

One researcher on the subject, Norval Glenn, says many such texts make marriage more of a problem than a solution to personal relationships and place the emphasis on divorce, problems of child-rearing, domestic violence, etc. This is the way of propaganda.

I'm a well-trained academic and researcher. I have the degrees, credentials and experience to support these positions. And my qualifications are open for all to inspect.

So when some person or representative of another organization wants to attach himself or herself to ACPC or wants to make it appear that ACPC is supportive of them, you better ask me if this is true.

Some very unscrupulous people are already trying to make it appear that I approve their organizations and movements in the name of ACPC. They lie!

While I often applaud the efforts of others in the battle against things like pornography, abortion, perversion and violence in the entertainment and print media, the abuses in government and the schools, ACPC has only one single purpose and focus: The U.S. Constitutional Amendment directed toward ZERO TOLERANCE OF CHILD MOLESTERS! This, I repeat, and this alone, is the single purpose and focus of ACPC!

But I do my best to make it clear to these others that the battle for, and the passage of, the amendment will have a monumental impact, a domino effect, in these other areas. Much of my writing is directed to educating people to the far-reaching and profoundly complex implications of the amendment legally and sociologically.

Another favorite mechanism of the unscrupulous is name-dropping. For example, it is the most difficult of tasks to get a politician to commit him or herself in writing.

Because of the very seriousness of the amendment, I have had phenomenal success in getting responses from the president, governors and others. But I'm used to not getting any response or say-nothing, non-answer responses as well. That comes with the territory.

But a person can get a response, a say-nothing response, and claim to others, Why, yes, senator so-and-so dropped me a line the other day in regard to my proposition, my organization, etc. Such people often take a paragraph, a sentence, a phrase or even a single term out of context in order to make it appear that the senator supports the person or organization.

I recently received material from an organization making great claims for itself to the benefit of children. Among the copies of claimed support by well-known personalities was one from Dan Quayle. His letter didn't even acknowledge the organization or direct a single comment toward its support.

But those in the organization could say, and even had the stupidity to print, the letter and claim Dan Quayle supported them. It is surprising how stupid such people in these organizations think others are. But they fool enough often enough to get the money. And for such organizations, that is the bottom line.

There are just too many scam artists out there for anyone to be so naive as to take any organization's word for anything. Learn to ask for facts, documentation, before sending any of them your money or take their word that they have the recommendation of influential people.

Small wonder that politicians become extraordinarily cautious in written communications; I have to exercise the same degree of caution in my own responses to inquiries that I receive.

A famous scientist, Karen Wetterhahn, died from a single, small drop of dimethylmercury that inadvertently fell on her latex gloves. She had worked with many extremely toxic materials for years and assumed the gloves protected her.

But neither she nor any others knew this form of mercury was actually promoted into the bloodstream through latex. That one, small drop killed her.

It only takes that one small lie, couched in the bulk of truth; to promote a personal agenda built on that lie.

For example, we all know of the lie that Madelyn Murray O'Hare was getting the FCC to ban all religious broadcasting. Millions of mailings were made to the gullible promoting this story. The FCC spent enormous amounts of money refuting this lie.

But a few unscrupulous people profited by getting the gullible to send them money to counter this attack of Satan.

And we all know of the myth, the lie perpetrated against Procter and Gamble and its logo of the moon and stars as a satanic symbol. Again, a few unscrupulous people profited by this scheme.

So when I recently received a mailing that railed against The Convention on the Rights of the Child (I've received many, by the way), it was immediately apparent that it fell into the same category as the myths of O'Hare and Procter and Gamble.

Reading this material and comparing it with the actual Convention, you have to wonder: Have these people even read the Convention for themselves? Or do they, as so many do, simply parrot the preaching of the ignorant and misinformed, the propagandists, without doing their own homework?

And in too many cases, the answer is a dismal Yes.

For those who are really concerned about this, simply write UNICEF, as I mentioned previously, and request a copy of The Convention.

For those who have been lied to, especially about the supposed loss of parental authority and control of children, you are in for a very big surprise when you read The Convention for yourself.

Those of us who have been through WWII and the Cold War know the threat Communism once posed. But a few of us were aware that it was a doomed system.

There is no question that America is the leader of nations. It remains a question of how that leadership is to be exercised. If patriots like myself can come to the logical conclusion that such leadership requires setting an example of morality above all else, that means an end to the lying politics that has so infected our leadership.

Other nations, the UN, are not stupid. Pressure has been brought to bear for the UN to reorganize and cut costs. This is good and necessary. But if America is to lead in this area, it must cooperate as well with other nations.

The key to this cooperation and leaving off lying, of not being the hypocrite in preaching human rights, is the passage of the amendment. If America proves it is willing through a Constitutional Amendment to make such a commitment to making children the priority they must become in order to achieve cooperation and peace among nations, this will have a domino effect.

The UN, UNICEF, and the Convention on the Rights of the Child are key elements to achieving this goal of world peace. If well-meaning individuals who exercise their prejudices in lieu of really doing their homework, that is read and talk to others besides those who only reinforce their prejudices, will approach this problem fairly, they will be amazed at the lies and false propaganda they have been subjected to.

I have many good friends who consider themselves good Americans and good patriots who damn the UN, UNICEF and the Convention and know nothing about these things first hand. Instead, they have been willing to blindly follow leaders who have an agenda of America First, My country right or wrong and only add to the problem rather than doing the hard work of going to primary sources. This, of course, is not only intellectually lazy but can be deadly to anyone who considers themselves knowledgeable about the subjects.

Bottom line as I tell people who want to work for the amendment, know your subject. In the words of Scripture: Study to show yourselves approved. It was with good reason that my soul brother, Thoreau, who was our best example of civil disobedience, said: God spare me from well-intentioned people. He was, of course, referring to those who thought they knew the subject but were, in fact, only the apostles of ignorance and prejudice.

I receive reams of material from organizations and individuals filled with glittering generalities and meaningless platitudes. What does it mean, for example, that Children are our most precious resource; they must be given a national priority? Not a damned thing unless accompanied by specific courses of action!

But the organizations, leaders and politicians who mouth such meaningless phrases, I remind myself, are of the category of those who decided you could put men and women together in the military and not have sex. So I am convinced that it is better by far that We The People should take the matter of children and family in our own hands when it comes to doing something of really substantive value for them.

And I have to continually remind myself that there are those people who want war, not peace. Much of the so-called patriot literature is directed toward fomenting conflict rather than reasoned and reasonable resolutions to the problems. Many are making big bucks off the gullible by beating this drum, not unlike unscrupulous TV evangelists.

Too much such preaching falls into the category of *My way or the highway!*

I'm getting used to being roundly condemned by those who think that America has such a message and it needs preaching. But I will maintain with all my heart that unless such people, themselves, start putting children first, and I mean the children of the world, they are preaching a false gospel and are no better than gospel-peddlers.

As long as I'm on the subject of liars, holy or otherwise, do you know that the medical profession has been guilty of covering up countless cases of child abuse and infanticide over the years by listing such deaths as Sudden Infant Death Syndrome?

An article in Pediatrics comes clean about this monumental cover-up. Some outrageous things have been discovered such as the videotaping of some mothers, suspected of abusing their children, actually trying to strangle and choking them! Many such deaths, the Pediatrics journal stated, have been written off as SIDS.

A book about this, The Death of Innocents by Richard Firstman and Jamie Talan is in most bookstores now. And I have to ask myself: If it weren't for the courage of Firstman and Talan, would Pediatrics have admitted to this?

I got a real kick out of one patriotic, anti-U.N. and UNICEF book I was sent recently. You'd never believe where this good, American book was published: Colombia! The title is Parent Police by Ingrid J. Guzman.

If these good patriots would take the trouble to read for themselves (and think for themselves) things like the Convention on the Rights of the Child, rather than being led by charlatans, they would soon know they are being propagandized and lied to.

Just recently I received a good (horrible) example of what I'm talking about from a right-wing publication entitled Awesome News. It was obvious the writer had an agenda of taking advantage of those already disposed to damning the UN and UNICEF. The writer counted on his readers never checking primary source material and being too prejudiced or intellectually lazy and gullible to read the Convention for themselves so he told outright lies; must have taken a page from Televangelists.

Well-meaning people, and some not so well-meaning, then believe these lies and pass them on to others (including me) as gospel.

Believe it or not, as I recently wrote one woman, the UN and Congress are comprised of well-educated and intelligent people, other not so commendatory realities about politician's aside. These people can rightly afford to laugh at the gullibility of those who swallow the ignorant, even intentionally lying, propaganda of so-called patriots of the ilk I have referred to.

At that point, what is the real difference between liberal and conservative when the doctrine of The End Justifies the Means is their basic creed?

The most painful, and hurtful, thing of all is that many good publications, which are excellent watchdogs of corruption in government, are made suspect because of the actions of the unscrupulous who prey on those who are too lazy or prejudiced to do the necessary homework.

Far too many so-called patriots fall into the category of Walt Kelly's statement: We have met the enemy and he is us!

But like the fondness for stupidly apocryphal, apocalyptic literature of the nature of Revelation (the Apocalypse if you're a Catholic) in the Bible, people are real suckers for things like 666 and Armageddon. Can you believe people still listen to and give money to charlatans like Hal Lindsay (The Late, Great Planet Earth)?

The resulting paranoia has always made for self-righteous disciples of Us vs. Them! It is small wonder world peace is not on the agenda of such professional haters!

Such people will consign me to the outer reaches for having friends like Andrej because he was born and raised under a Communist, atheistic regime. They will never understand how friendly, civilized manners and mutual respect for the views of others can overcome bigoted prejudice and contribute to world peace. Of course, world peace is not the agenda of these professional haters.

And guess where two such politically and religiously diverse men as Andrej and I find common ground? Children! I hope all of you get that message.

I know and love many people who call themselves patriots. But when I have to write things like the above I'm reminded of a statement in Absence of Malice when an editor tells a reporter:

I can choose not to hurt someone or I can tell the truth. I can't do both at the same time.

And this is all too often the case; especially when it comes to religion and politics.

As the amendment gains more and more attention, the battle will begin to heat up considerably. The enemies of children are numerous. Many recognize the enormous implications of the amendment and want nothing to do with such a revolution that sets such a standard for humanity. It is a standard of behavior that gets much lip service but in the black hearts of many, especially men, they want nothing to do with such a standard and will fight against it.

Philosophers and artists have long known that the truth doesn't pay; especially materially. In fact, the lesson of Socrates, Melville, Thoreau and Clemens is plain. There are very few people who even want to know the truth, especially the truth about themselves.

A truth of such magnitude as the amendment brings before society a mirror that betrays the actual ugliness of every line and wrinkle of hypocrisy. The hardest battle of my life was to face the truth about myself, to face the prejudices and hypocrisy in my own life. I don't expect it to be any easier for anyone else, let alone an entire nation or, eventually, the whole world.

The song in South Pacific, Carefully Taught, comes immediately to mind in this context. Children are not born hating those who are different. They have to be taught to hate.

I'm about the only friend Junkie Jerry has. Why? Because of his loud mouth and ignorant opinions; loudly expressed. I'm one of the very few people who will tolerate him; and that in small doses.

But I do so because, at heart, he's a good man. He just, shall we say, is somewhat lacking in formal education and the social graces.

As to ignorant opinion, Jerry keeps reminding me of the battle I fight as a teacher, and always have, against ignorance.

For example, Jerry will wax eloquent about his hatred of computers, of how they are taking over the world, of how the Internet is so evil, etc.

But Jerry wouldn't know a computer if it bit him on the nose. As I pointed out to him, he wouldn't even know how to turn one on, let alone use it.

This doesn't deter Jerry from being an expert on the evils of computers. No sir. Just ask him. He'll tell you, loudly, how expert he really is about such a thing in spite of the fact he knows virtually nothing about computers.

How many so-called patriots really know anything about the UN or UNICEF apart from what they read in The New American and the hate literature to which they subscribe the so very selective conservative talk shows to which they are addicted? Junkie Jerry's abound.

And they abound equally in the so-called liberal camp as well. Just look at what passes itself off in the name of People for the American Way, an organization rife with perverts!

As to my friends who consider themselves patriots and good Americans, I say this: You better start studying the UN objectively and rid yourselves of the preposterous notion that the U.S. will ever get out of this world organization. It shouldn't and it won't!

Instead, study it in order to help America, as the leader of nations, to make it a better organization. Your time, money and effort will reap far greater benefits in this manner rather than the utterly counterproductive, self-righteous, wasted methods of ignorant hatred and prejudice.

Samuel D. G. Heath, Ph.D.
Americans for Constitutional Protection of Children

***

It is very difficult to take a dispassionate view of some subjects, particularly when the subject is that of religion or politics. But a real love of the truth, the foundation of wisdom, demands such dispassionate objectivity.

Few would accept the criticism of their not being objective. Most people like to consider themselves objective rather than prejudiced to a point of view. For the fanatic, whether of religion or politics, the person actually believes he or she possesses the truth and therefore is objective. But when a fanatical point of view is subjected to reason and facts, the prejudice is obvious.

The Jesus believer, for example, will cry quite loudly that their belief in Jesus is not religion, but the truth; as with the devout Jew or Moslem. But such religious prejudices remain just that, religious prejudices.

A dispassionate and objective view of things strongly believed is virtually impossible for the individual who is persuaded of such things and has chosen to believe in spite of reason and facts to the contrary.

To speak of Albert Schweitzer or Mother Teresa is to speak of people who exemplify the goodness of self-sacrifice for the benefit of humanity.

But to view the goodness of these two people in the light of the fact that their sacrificial goodness has not made the world better or safer, has not made the world less dangerous, is difficult to accept. But it is the truth.

The dispassionate facts of truth and wisdom do not allow of the sentiment of the emotions to rule. While the goodness of some serve well as models to emulate, such models do not change the world or make it less dangerous.

How often it is said that to touch just one life is a matter of great significance. And true as this may be, to touch just one life will not save the world or change the course of history for the better. To do this requires an idea which will touch and change multiplied millions of lives, not just a few.

History is replete with examples of ideas touching millions of lives which have resulted in hatred and bloodshed. Stalin and Hitler were idea men of this nature. The ideas of Jesus and Mohammad, though espousing peace, resulted in the slaughter of millions. And continue to generate hatreds and prejudices.

But no matter how the original intent of ideas may be distorted and twisted to evil ends, the fact that an idea which can persuade millions remains.

Such an idea which would be embraced by multiplied millions must be, by its very character, revolutionary. Emerson and Thoreau dreamed of a revolution without cannon or musket. But by denying women an equal voice in philosophy on the basis of equal value, such a revolution which would lead to world peace is impossible.

Opinion is our natural state of mind. Problems arise when opinion, too often uninformed, willingly or unwillingly, degenerates into prejudice or bigotry. We do in many instances decide what to think. The choices of what to think in a given instance about any subject or person are the product of our circumstances of family, education, those we choose as authority sources, personal experiences, and society.

The religion or political ideology into which a person is born, for example, often plays a vital role in that person's deciding what to think as he or she grows into adulthood. The person's choices concerning the many issues of life, unless that person becomes well-educated, will likely be prejudiced in harmful ways.

But as is abundantly clear, even a good education is no guarantee of overcoming prejudices.

One must have an appetite, if you will, for a certain subject in order for that person to study and master that subject. Without the appetite, the compelling desire to learn of the subject and pursue it to the length of mastery, it is a distasteful thing to be avoided.

Addiction is the result of unwise choices. The person, for any number of reasons, many quite complex, decides to think wrongly. Of the various problems with an addiction is that it can become so powerful that the person literally lives for it, their lives become totally devoted to satisfying the addiction. In this way, the person becomes utterly selfish with no consideration for anyone or anything that gets in the way of satisfying the addiction. The religious or political fanatic is an addict of passions which overrule logic and reason; and, in many instances, any vestige of true conscience or compassion. The addiction to a belief can become so powerful it literally overrules what we would call civilized behavior. In this way the fanatic is no different from a person addicted to drugs.

The decisions one makes as to what to think are complex in the extreme when analyzed concerning their roots. Using Roman Catholicism as an example, particularly if the person is born and raised into it, has many conveniences such as the Confessional to expiate what the system considers sin. If, because of the choice of what to believe, what to think, results in an easing of what we call conscience, the reason for choosing to think in this fashion is obvious.

But when such a choice, a decision to think in a particular way, is used as a mechanism to excuse what would be considered criminal behavior such as molestation or murder, the rational mind finds the use of such a mechanism as the Confessional as a means of easing conscience repugnant.

No less is the mechanism of the Protestant version of the Confessional subject to such a use for selfish ends. To say a sin, a criminal act such as molestation or murder is forgiven and washed away by the blood of Jesus is no less repugnant to a rational and civilized mind. Particularly when no demand is made on the conscience for real contrition and restitution for the sin, the crime, committed.

When a person makes the decision to think in a certain way, and that way is colored or distorted by choosing a belief over rational facts, the result is a prejudice. As many tried to justify slavery in this nation by choosing to believe it was morally correct to own other human beings as chattel, the choice to believe in such a thing is no less repugnant to what is rightly called the rational and civilized mind.

If someone tries to justify the deification of a human being such as Jesus or Mohammad, if they say books like the Bible or Koran are the very word of God, such a choice to decide to believe in such things repugnant to reason are as much the result of addiction as anything else. Whether the prejudice is one of religion or politics, the results of such addiction to belief over reason is harmful to humanity as a whole.

While examples of such addictions can be multiplied, suffice it to say that the rational mind always finds addiction repugnant and harmful.

***

On January 1, 1831 William Lloyd Garrison began publishing the "Liberator," dedicated to renouncing slavery, in a small room on the third floor of Merchant's Hall in Boston. This was shortly after he was released from jail, having been imprisoned as a result of his outspokenness on the issue of slavery.

It would be twenty-one years later (1852) that "Uncle Tom's Cabin" would appear in book form. This was the book that galvanized anti-slavery sentiment and provided the emotional foundation for the Civil War.

On the basis of having spent a night in jail for not paying his taxes, Thoreau later delivered to the Concord Lyceum an address entitled "The Relation of the Individual to the State." In 1849 Elizabeth Peabody published the lecture in the single issue of her periodical "Aesthetic Papers" under the title "Resistance to Civil Government." Later reprints carried the title "On the Duty of Civil Disobedience." It is now best known simply as "Civil Disobedience."

Thoreau's friend and mentor, Ralph Waldo Emerson, in his address "The American Scholar" made the statement: The sluggish mind of the masses; slow to the incursion of reason."

And so it would seem to be, proven by the absence of wisdom throughout history, wisdom defined as the application of knowledge to the best end, a lack of which that has been the basis of unremitting warfare.

It would be thirty years after beginning publication of the Liberator before Garrison would see the war to end slavery. He had early made the statement: A few white victims must be sacrificed to open the eyes of this nation. I expect and am willing to be persecuted, imprisoned and bound for advocating African rights.

At the time he made this statement, he had no idea such a thing would eventually cost the lives of hundreds of thousands. Nor did Harriet Stowe have any idea of the enormous role her book would play in causing the Civil

War. Nor did Thoreau, nor could he, have any idea of the enormous impact his little discourse on Civil Disobedience would have in cases like that of Gandhi and Martin Luther King, Jr.

In 1852 John Henry Cardinal Newman stated in his "Idea of a University" that virtue and decency were in the minority. The history of humankind being a history of unremitting war would seem to prove his dismal assessment. On this date of my writing, November 6, 2000, the day before our presidential election, the statements of Emerson, Thoreau, Garrison, Newman, et al have an inescapable timeliness.

We would hardly credit our presidential candidates as exemplary of virtue and decency, for example. But we would credit them with "relative" virtue and decency. Neither is guilty of murder or molesting children.

But "moral relativism" has a high price. The price throughout history has been paid by the lives of countless millions killed and maimed that had no idea why they were being killed and maimed. But the price is inevitable due to the lack of wisdom, the lack of enough of the good, the virtuous and decent, willing to confront determined evil with equal determination to win!

It took the decades-long efforts of those like Garrison for this nation to see an end to slavery. That he was a willing, living martyr to this cause may not be to his credit on the basis of self-sacrifice since he seemed to be compelled to do what he did, as did John Brown. And one can hardly give or claim credit on the basis of a compulsion.

In this sense, there is no credit of nobility of cause or purpose to be given. That what he did was the right thing to do makes no claim to nobleness of purpose.

But the battle against slavery was a long one. We might say that lesser men than Garrison would have given up. But I think Garrison himself would disagree that he was any whit a better man for not having done so. The cause was right, and once given to that cause, he simply followed through. And this kind of perseverance, I believe, distinguishes the good from pretenders.

Having said that, it is equally apparent that the evil is quite able to persevere as well; proving Thoreau's statement that there is never an instants truce between vice and virtue.

The problems in the Middle East for example, hatreds, prejudices of such antiquity, certainly give one pause whether wisdom will ever overcome such dark evil. We do know that something believed "Holy" or "Sacred" is not amenable to any intrusion of reason. The very idea that a city can be thought "Holy" and be the cause of such misery and evil, even war and murder in the name of God, is a contradiction to reason, let alone wisdom.

Garrison, Whittier, Thoreau, Emerson, Stowe, Lincoln, could not know the minds of Negro slaves. But they had enough humanity to know that slavery was evil. More than that, they knew slavery was a reproach to any calling themselves "good" that did not oppose such an evil.

Yet Robert E. Lee, being morally opposed to slavery and most considering him a good man, led the armies of the Confederacy. His allegiance was to Virginia and the South; his morality misguided to the point of rather than determined opposition to slavery, prosecuting a war in its favor.

Virtually no one would attempt to discredit Lee's avowed Christianity and morality. Still, in spite of such Christian morality, he prosecuted a war that, if won, would sunder the Union and retain slavery.

We are asked to excuse Lee on a number of points: His integrity and virtue, his sincerity in his beliefs. But, to quote Lincoln: If slavery is not wrong, nothing is wrong!

If Robert E. Lee is to exemplify anything, it is the fact that even the best of good people may be sincerely wrong, that this great man and general of the Confederacy is proof of my equation k+w=p. For the one thing lacking in the beliefs and thinking of people like Lee is wisdom.

Would any disavow the Christian morality and sincerity of Cotton Mather? But how many would approve the Salem Witch trials?

In 1886 Henry Grady in his address *The New South* accused the leaders in the South of committing Southerners ...to a cause that reason could not defend or the sword maintain in the light of advancing civilization.

But those Southern leaders paid no heed to reason; there was nothing of reason or wisdom in their defense of an evil institution such as slavery. But there was a good deal of religion used in the defense of this evil cause, not just a corruption of State's Rights.

And if the evil of hatreds and prejudices continue to prevail and oppose advancing civilization as they do in the Middle East, such evil can only prevail on the basis of Cardinal Newman's observation that virtue and decency remain in the minority.

I have paraphrased Lincoln's statement *If slavery is not wrong, nothing is wrong* to say: *If perversion is not wrong, nothing is wrong*. For as long as children suffer at the hands of perverts, they remain ever bit as much in bondage as the Negro did under his slavery. As long as children continue to suffer without the protection of the proposed amendment, so long do they do so in opposition to advancing civilization.

No greater accolade has been given Lincoln as that of William Grady's assessment of the Great Emancipator as ...the first typical American, the first who comprehended within himself all the strength and gentleness, all the majesty and grace of this republic – He was the sum of Puritan and Cavalier for in his ardent nature were fused the virtues of both, and in his great soul the faults of both were lost.

Shortly after his second inaugural address, and only about five weeks before his assassination, Lincoln said: Men are not flattered by being shown that there has been a difference of purpose between the Almighty and them. To deny it, however, in this case (slavery) is to deny that there is a God governing the world. It is a truth that I thought needed to be told; and as whatever of humiliation there is in it, falls most directly on myself, I thought others might afford for me to tell it.

To arouse social conscience to the point of action is very difficult. And as Garrison and others found out, there was no polite or easy way of doing so ... It was not enough to discern evil, action was required. And while no civilized mind would applaud the course of John Brown, neither can the scholarly mind fail to recognize the circumstances that resulted in his course of action, including that of religious fanaticism.

The civilized mind will not accept the dictum of "The end justifies the means." So it is that we call upon wisdom and reason, we hearken to Socrates and Thoreau's "Civil Disobedience" in the hope that the continued questioning of amoral, evil authority and passive but questioning resistance to such will multiply into the millions required to take a stand against the evil and overcome it. But it will require these millions who go contrary to the historical fact of virtue and decency being in the minority to change things for the better.

It takes only a handful of evil martyrs, fanatics, to wreak havoc on the innocent. The threat of a nuclear suitcase bomb going off in America is very real. And what makes America the target of such evil fanaticism? It is the lack of wisdom and virtue in America.

The Russian poets long ago described America as a nation without a soul. They were right. America has no identifiable national purpose, no identifiable major group of millions dedicated to the betterment of all humanity. We are no longer claimants of scholarship or literary greatness ... We are seen by religiously fanatic nations and leaders as "Godless," given to hedonistic materialism. As for wisdom, where does America exemplify this most necessary and essential virtue?

Make no mistake, religiously fanatical nations and leaders do believe themselves possessed of virtue and godliness. To many in such nations to be the enemies of America is to be the friends of God.

The citizens of these nations have only to look at what America produces on TV to be confirmed in their minds as to the lack of virtue and decency, let alone godliness or wisdom, in America. And the choices the citizens of America produce for political leadership speaks for itself.

Like the abolitionists of over one hundred and fifty years ago, I have one cause: The abolition of molestation. I am a fanatic dedicated to the freeing of children from the slavery of molestation… a fanatic dedicated to giving children the legal right to an innocent childhood by our foundational charter of government, our Constitution. And I believe that had our Founding Fathers been able to foresee present conditions in regard to their posterity, the children, they would have included the proposed amendment in that venerable Bill of Rights, for what is more basic and fundamental to all the rights of humanity than that of a child to a protected and innocent childhood?

There had been "Holy men of God" quoting their "Holy Book" in favor of slavery for centuries. Such men persisted throughout our Civil War, claiming God's approval of an unholy and "peculiar" institution. There are those now in Israel and Arab nations that believe they are justified in murdering the innocent on the basis of beliefs as erroneous as those that died in America defending the evil of slavery.

There are those now who decry my stand for children in much the same way, claiming such a thing as the proposed amendment is contrary to "freedom" and "tolerance," that it is "bigoted" and "prejudiced" - The same people, most in the universities and Hollywood using these as their unholy pulpits, that use the propaganda techniques so successful for Hitler to make heaven into hell and black into white, that manufacture terms like "homophobic" while the truth is "heterophobic," the same people who sold America on the use of the term "gay" instead of the truth of "pervert."

It is without doubt or controversy an increasingly dangerous and demon-haunted world. But until America and the rest of the nations of the world make children the priority they must become, there is no hope of peace; there is no hope of wisdom and reason ever prevailing over religious and political hatreds and prejudices.

The proposed amendment brought many things into focus for me that caused Benjamin Franklin and Samuel Clemens to despair of humankind; that led them to wonder if the species were worth preserving? Such common frailties as greed and avarice are an indictment that deserves consideration. Those things that result in political corruption and religious chicanery being commonplaces are certainly an indictment of our species.

But the most troubling of all are those things that led Cardinal Newman to the conclusion that virtue and decency are in the minority.

I asked myself, is this because the bad people outnumber the good? No, I do not believe this to be the case. But I do believe that far too many good people do not involve themselves, do not trouble themselves, to do their fair part in confronting and overcoming the bad.

For example, over the past ten years I have had many articles and letters published in our local paper. In the great majority of cases, I have had people call me or come by and thank me for these articles. But they had never troubled themselves to write the paper to express their views in my support. But those that opposed me did write.

The same can be said for my correspondence with legislators. Such people can depend on good people doing nothing, on virtually never writing. But those that support bad legislation, legislation to curry favor or some selfish interest, these will write ... and in far greater numbers than good people.

Are homosexuals proper role models in the classroom teaching our children? I say no! But when it came to a vote in California when Reagan was governor, he vetoed a bill that would have excluded homosexuals as teachers in our classrooms. And people like John Wayne supported him in this view. Why? Because of the Hollywood interest and connection; and as with the case of Anita Bryant in Florida, Reagan knew good people would be conspicuous by their absence. Those few good people that did speak up were called "intolerant, homophobic, bigoted" and "prejudiced."

This was an instance where millions of good people who should have spoken remained silent. As a result, the will of a few thousand prevailed over those millions. And the real victims would be the children who would be taught that perversion was perfectly acceptable, that to oppose perversion was to be "intolerant, homophobic, bigoted," and "prejudiced."

The tail will always wag the dog when good people fail to do their part in opposing evil. But throughout history the case has been a failure of good people to actively oppose the evil ... hence the assessment of those such as Franklin, Clemens, and Newman.

Nobel-winning Physicist Michio Kaku has pointed out the very real danger the world faces because of nuclear proliferation. There is no denying the substantive evidence of such a threat. But it will take leaders of great knowledge and conviction to confront and overcome the obstacles to peace.

I call your attention to the fact that women are conspicuous by their absence in the UN. I ask you, can wisdom ever be achieved by the exclusion of a full half of humanity in the decision-making processes and leadership of nations?

Yet I have pointed out to women, and I believe most would concur, that their historical exclusion from the King of Disciplines, Philosophy, the discipline that guides the course of history and nations, must be overcome in order for them to have such a voice.

During all the turmoil of the years preceding our Civil War, a few women like Elizabeth Cady Stanton and Lucretia Mott were active abolitionists. But because they were women, they were refused admittance to the Antislavery Convention in London held in 1840. The commentaries of Sir William Blackstone held sway and continued to enslave women to their historical status as legal and political nonentities.

But Mrs. Stanton and some other determined women were resolute in changing their "slave" status. So it was that in 1848 the Seneca Falls Declaration of Sentiments and Resolutions came into being. Patterned after the Declaration of Independence, these women cited their grievances and asked for justice, especially in respect to the franchise.

But it would be another seventy years, 1920, before women won the right to vote. And only one woman, Charlotte Woodward Pierce, of that original meeting in Seneca Falls would live to cast a vote for President.

It is to America's credit that our nation would fight such a horrendous war on behalf of freeing slaves, though other major factors such as state's rights as well as the accidents of history, avarice and egos, are to be considered also.

It is to America's credit that such a meeting as that of Seneca Falls could be held and widely publicized (though most certainly unfavorably many times) ... This in spite of the fact that it would take seventy years to accomplish the purpose of that original meeting in 1848.

I find it a curiosity of history that the two, abolition of slavery and woman suffrage, should be so intertwined in time; but perhaps, given the similarity of the causes, not so curious. And I would point out that the battles of Civil Rights and Women's Rights would boil over and still be fought in the recent history of the sixties.

But in spite of the passage of time, even to this date, it cannot be said that women have achieved equal status with men, either in America or any place else in the world. For this to be accomplished requires wisdom, the kind of wisdom that denies prejudice and bigotry and leads to equal value, something not to be confused with equal rights and something not considered during the Seneca Falls meeting for women or by Martin Luther King, Jr. on behalf of minorities.

It will take the kind of perseverance evidenced by those like William Garrison and Elizabeth Stanton to accomplish the task of equal value. More, it will take exceptional women like Stanton and Mott, as diverse, educated and intelligent as Susan Anthony and Elizabeth Cochrane (Nellie Bly) and others, to develop a philosophy distinctive of women that will meld with that of men and, through the compatibility of differences correcting the errors in the philosophies of men, thereby making for a complete philosophy on the basis of equal value.

I give America credit for being a nation that considers fairness and justice of such great importance, a nation that fought a war to end slavery, a nation that would advance the cause of justice and fairness toward women. And we are a nation that has a history of being charitable beyond that of any other nation towards other nations, especially following WWII and in many other instances. We are a nation that in spite of many failures such as our treatment of Native Americans has a generally proud heritage of fairness and justice.

But my overriding concern is the fact that no nation in history can survive that does not cherish its children. I ask further: Can a world survive that does not make its priority its children?

Children, their future as the future of our species, should provide the basis of dialogue between nations. But we have never seen this happen.

It is my conviction that America, given its historical character and as the freest nation in history, has the obligation to lead the way in this dialogue, to open it by way of the proposed amendment through being the first nation in history to make such a commitment to children by its foundational charter of government, our Constitution.

And while it doubtless requires the kind of perseverance evidenced by those already mentioned as examples, like the abolition of slavery and women's suffrage the amendment will prove to be the right and wise thing to do.

I cannot think of anything of greater import or impetus that would restore the soul of America; that would create such a noble national identity and national purpose as a people than the proposed amendment.

AMERICANS for CONSTITUTIONAL PROTECTION of CHILDREN

Dedicated to Zero Tolerance of child molesters

No nation that fails to cherish its young has any future as a nation

Proposed amendment to the U.S. Constitution

An adult convicted of the molestation of a child will be sentenced to prison for a term of not less than ten years.

If the child dies as a result of the molestation the person(s) convicted of the crime will be sentenced to life in prison without the possibility of parole.

A child as defined by this article shall be one who has not attained their sixteenth birthday.

The Congress shall have power to enforce this article by appropriate legislation.

This amendment will reduce prison and welfare populations by breaking the chain of molestation. In the shorter term, it is well substantiated that children having babies is an enormous burden on taxpayers. These babies of girls as young as eleven years old are invariably doomed to substandard care which increases medical costs. As such children grow, they are far more likely to be anti-social, under-educated and begin early criminal activities loading our juvenile justice systems, and, eventually, our courts, jails and prisons.

If adult molesters of such girls faced life in prison, there would be an immediate impact on this problem that is contributing to so much heartache and fiscal difficulty in our nation. In the longer term, there will be fewer such children growing up to a life of crime, thereby reducing prison populations. Fewer such children being born will have a dramatic effect on our economy by reducing the problems they create for the schools, medical care and other financial burdens to taxpayers.

A major factor is what this amendment will do for a lower divorce rate and the strengthening of family in this nation. Men and women will have to seriously consider the dramatically increased risk of molestation of children due to divorce.

Fully one-half of our little girls are molested in one way or another and the trauma carries into their adult relationships, especially marriage. By radically reducing such molestations, we have taken a huge step toward establishing healthy marriages, and, by extension, a healthier society.

Consider the boys that are molested and the enormous cost, mentally, socially and fiscally to America. Such boys are far more likely than others to become molesters and involved in crime and sociopathic anti-social behavior.

This amendment will virtually eliminate the inhumanity and national disgrace of child prostitution and the tragedy of children infected by AIDS. By force of law, it will encourage sexual restraint, self-discipline and responsibility and will greatly reduce the number of child pregnancies thus reducing the number of abortions.

It will also dramatically impact Child Protective Services, forcing that agency to act in a far more humane, responsible and professional manner. With the power and authority of this amendment, CPS will have to do a better job of identifying, establishing factual case evidence, and removing the predators of children from society.

Why should children any longer be denied the Constitutional rights adults take for granted? Yet nothing in the Constitution is specifically addressed to the needs of children. It thus leaves vulnerable the most helpless of America's citizens and denies them the most basic and fundamental of all human rights, the right to a lawfully protected and innocent childhood.

Knowing how critically related employment is to stable homes, the amendment will force the political leadership to address the issue of jobs realistically. Virtually no one argues the fact that a vital component of encouraging responsibility and minimizing child abuse in general is employment!

This amendment is clearly one of empowering We The People to take action against an evil about which all good people agree, action we can take for the sake of the future of our nation: Our Children!

Samuel D. G. Heath, Ph. D.
http://solo.abac.com/sdghacpc

About the Author

Samuel D. G. Heath, Ph. D.

Other books in print by the author:

BIRDS WITH BROKEN WINGS
DONNIE AND JEAN, an angel's story
TO KILL A MOCKINGBIRD, a critique on behalf of children
HEY, GOD! What went wrong and when are You going to fix it?
THE AMERICAN POET WEEDPATCH GAZETTE for 2008
THE AMERICAN POET WEEDPATCH GAZETTE for 2007
THE AMERICAN POET WEEDPATCH GAZETTE for 2006
THE AMERICAN POET WEEDPATCH GAZETTE for 2005
THE AMERICAN POET WEEDPATCH GAZETTE for 2004
THE AMERICAN POET WEEDPATCH GAZETTE for 2003
THE AMERICAN POET WEEDPATCH GAZETTE for 2002
THE AMERICAN POET WEEDPATCH GAZETTE for 2001

Presently out of print:
IT SHOULDN'T HURT TO BE A CHILD!
WOMEN, BACHELORS, IGUANA RANCHING, AND RELIGION
THE MISSING HALF OF HUMANKIND: WOMEN!
THE MISSING HALF OF PHILOSOPHY: WOMEN!
THE LORD AND THE WEEDPATCHER
CONFESSIONS AND REFLECTIONS OF AN OKIE INTELLECTUAL
or Where the heck is Weedpatch?
MORE CONFESSIONS AND REFLECTIONS OF AN OKIE
INTELLECTUAL

Dr. Heath was born in Weedpatch, California. He has worked as a manual laborer, mechanic, machinist, peace officer, engineer, pastor, builder and developer, educator, social services practitioner (CPS), professional musician and singer. He is also a private pilot and a columnist.
Awarded American Legion Scholarship and is an award winning author.
He has two surviving children: Daniel and Michael. His daughters Diana and Karen have passed away.

Samuel D. G. Heath, Ph. D.

Academic Degrees:
Ph. D. – U.S.I.U., San Diego, CA.
M. A. – Chapman University, Orange, CA.
M. S. (Eqv.) — U.C. Extension at UCLA. Los Angeles, CA.
B. V. E. – C.S. University. Long Beach, CA.
A. A. – Cerritos College. Cerritos, CA.

Other Colleges and Universities attended:
Santa Monica Technical College, Biola University, and C.S. University, Northridge.

Dr. Heath holds life credentials in the following areas:
Psychology, Professional Education, Library Science, English, German, History, Administration (K-12), Administration and Supervision of Vocational Education and Vocational Education-Trade and Industry.

In addition to his work in public education, Dr. Heath started three private schools, K-12, two in California and one in Colorado. His teaching and administrative experience covers every grade level and graduate school.

Your writing is very important. You are having an impact on lives! Never lose your precious gift of humor. V. T.

You raise a number of issues in your material ... The Church has languished at times under leaders whose theology was more historically systematic than Biblical ... (But) The questions you raise serve as very dangerous doctrines. John MacArthur, a contemporary of the author at Biola/Talbot and pastor of Grace Community Church in Sun Valley.

You have my eternal gratitude for relieving me from the tyranny of religion. D. R.

Before reading your wonderful writings, I had given up hope. Now I believe and anticipate that just maybe things can change for the better. J. D.

I started reading your book, The Lord and the Weedpatcher, and found I couldn't put it down. Uproariously funny, I laughed the whole way through. Thank you so much for lighting up my life! M.G.

Doctor Heath, every man with daughters owes you a debt of gratitude! I have had all three of my girls read your Birds With Broken Wings book. D. W.

I am truly moved by your art! While reading your writing I found a true treasure: Clarity! I felt as if I was truly on fire with the inspiration you invoked! L. B.

You really love women! Thank you for the most precious gift of all, the gift of love. Keep on being you! D. B.

Your writing complements coffee-cup-and-music. I've gotten a sense of your values, as well as a provocativeness that suggests a man both distinguished and truly sensual. Do keep up such vibrant work! E. R.

Some men are merely handsome. You are a beautiful man! One of these days some wise, discerning, smart woman is going to snag you. Make sure she is truly worthy of you. Desirable men like you (very rare indeed) who write so sensitively, compellingly and beautifully are sitting ducks for every designing woman! M. G.

Now, poet, musician, teacher, philosopher, friend, counselor and whatever else you have done in your life, I am finally realizing all the things you say people don't understand about a poet. They see, feel, write and talk differently than the rest of the world. Their glasses seem to be rose colored at times and other times they are blue. There seems to be no black or white in the things they see only soft pastel hues. Others see things as darker colors, but these are not the romantic poets you speak of. C. M.

You are the only man I have ever met who truly understands women! B. J.

Dr. Heath;
You are one of the best writers I've had the privilege to run across. You have been specially gifted for putting your thoughts, ideas, and inspirations to paper (or keyboard), no matter the topic.
Even when in dire straits, your words are strong and true. I look forward to reading many more of your unique writings. T. S.